THE LOST CANADIANS

THE LOST

DON CHAPMAN

CANADIANS

A STRUGGLE FOR CITIZENSHIP RIGHTS, EQUALITY, AND IDENTITY

Pugwash Publishing

Vancouver/Phoenix

To everyone who ever gave of themselves on behalf of their fellow man, from the really famous to the small child who on his or her own accord did something beneficial, and not just for themselves. After all, we are our brother's keeper.

Pugwash Publishing
Vancouver BC / Phoenix AZ

ISBN 978-0-9940554-2-2 (hardcover)
ISBN 978-0-9940554-0-8 (paperback)
ISBN 978-0-9940554-1-5 (ebook)

Names and identifying details have been changed to
protect the privacy of some individuals.

Library and Archives Canada Cataloguing in Publication

Chapman, Donald L., 1954—, author The lost Canadians :
a struggle for citizenship rights, equality, and identity /
Donald L. Chapman.

1. Chapman, Donald L., 1954—. 2. Citizenship, Loss of—
Canada. 3. Stateless persons—Canada—Biography. I. Title.

JL187.C53 2015   323.6'3   C2015-900949-99
C2015-900950-2

Cover design by Peter Cocking
Cover photograph by Daniel Grill/Tetra Images/Corbis
Printed and bound in Canada by Marquis

15 16 17 18 19   5 4 3 2 1

CONTENTS

Foreword: Lost Canadians:
Resolving the Contrails of Corruption   *vii*

Introduction: Raining Ashes   *xi*

Prologue: Against All Odds: The Story of Flight 811   *xiv*

PART 1 **LOST CANADIANS UNDER THE LIBERALS**

1   **The Long and Winding Road**   *3*

2   **I'm Not Alone in This Universe**   *16*

3   **Is There Political or Bureaucratic
Intelligence in the Universe?**   *27*

4   **The Politics of Politics**   *43*

5   **In This Corner, the Prime Minister;
in That Corner, the Lost Canadians**   *59*

6   **Ottawa's Nitty-Gritty, Down-and-Dirty Shenanigans**   *77*

PART 2 **TO STAND ON GUARD FOR THEE**

7   **"Thee" Is You and Me**   *102*

8   **Lest We Forget ... Lest We Ignore**   *119*

PART 3 **LOST CANADIANS UNDER THE CONSERVATIVES**

9   **Changing of the Guard**   *133*

10   **On the Scales of Justice**   *151*

11   **Dog Poop, Farts, Toads, and Britney Spears**   *170*

12   **And the Winner in the Stupid Category Is...**   *191*

13   **Tora! Tora! Tora!**   *205*

14   **Mr. Smith Goes to Washington;**
     Mr. Chapman Goes to Ottawa   *221*

15   **The Right Thing to Do for the Right Reasons**   *245*

16   **Lucy in the Sky**   *266*

17   **The Gold Medal Olympic Gamble**   *288*

18   **Please, Put Me Out of Business**   *304*

19   **Teaching Old Dogs New Tricks**   *321*

PART 4 **WRAP UP AND ANALYSIS**

20   **That's a Wrap**   *347*

21   **Analysis and Recommendations**   *350*

Appendix 1 **Lost Canadians on Citizenship**   *366*
Charles Bosdet on Citizenship and Nationality   *366*
Marion Vermeersch on Her Status (post–Bill C-24)   *367*
Paul Diekelmann on His Status (post–Bill C-24)   *368*
Fred Colbourne on Citizenship:
What Parliamentarians Need to Know   *368*
Esther Harris on Her 5.4 Status   *371*

Appendix 2 **The Revised History of
Canadian Citizenship**   *372*

Acknowledgements   *380*

Notes   *381*

Text Credits   *403*

LOST CANADIANS: RESOLVING THE CONTRAILS OF CORRUPTION

IT WAS THE quirky American television commentator Sam Donaldson, during the turbulent Senate hearings into President Clinton's sexual escapades, who inadvertently demonstrated why Canadian governments so mishandled the act of granting citizenship. "The trouble with Bill," Donaldson explained on air, "is that when he's in the witness box and swears to tell 'the truth, the whole truth and nothing but the truth,' he then tells three different stories."

The connection is vague at best, but that's exactly what's gone wrong with the system of issuing citizenship to Canadians caught in special circumstances. Courts, boards of appeal, legal circuses of various levels of incompetence—all have their say and all issue their often brutal sanctions. But the theme never changes. There is no standard procedure on how the bureaucrats' self-contradictory regulations are enforced. Phone the Department of Citizenship and Immigration's call centres, ask a Canadian consular attaché, and talk to any MP about how best to retrieve your citizenship—and you'll get three different answers.

As this unusual book amply demonstrates, no one really knows the stone-cold hard truths that govern our citizenship rules. The answers may be blowing in the wind, waiting to catch the attention of the beholders; but decades of amendments, and amendments to amendments, have led to so much confusion that if murderers were treated in the same loosey-goosey way, convicts could never be sure whether they would spend the rest of their lives munching saltpetre in the hoosegow or be nominated for Kiwanis scholarships.

At the moment, the best anyone can advise the many individuals whose Canadian citizenship is being questioned is that they will be treated in one of two ways: by being told either, "Sure, Charlie, finish your Molson. Of course you're the very model of a good citizen ... we think," or, more likely, "No damn way, Joanna, you gave up your citizenship when you danced the night away on your twenty-fourth birthday while on March break in Orlando ... we think." The difference seems to depend on a combination of whim, ignorance, news of counter-coups in Syria, and the prevailing mood of the inquisitors. They know nothing about disrupting narrative arcs. If the process was in any way clearer, the courts wouldn't be so busy with citizenship actions.

Gaining citizenship should be a natural act for Canadians. As the pages that follow clearly demonstrate, obtaining Canadian citizenship has become something of a fixed lottery, a game of mischance. Some sunny Friday, following the equinox, the lively green paint on the bureaucrats' office walls will signal spring and the voluntary handing over of the proper documents, followed by a high-five. But the identical documentation request, issued on a rainy Wednesday in the same green office, might end in tears.

It is, as the King of Siam tried to explain a long time ago, a puzzlement. When this book is published, I fully expect the ministry that operates the lottery of granting citizenship will accuse me of misinterpreting its regulations. Damn right. I don't understand them either. I hate to think that I have misinterpreted them as frequently as they do, but, yes—that is quite possible. Even likely.

Which brings us to the unlikely hero of this unlikely volume: Don Chapman—part United Airlines jetliner pilot boasting captain's flying duds with the four gold stripes; part seldom-humbled missionary looking for new positions; and part Eagle Scout who deserves a great deal more credit than he has harvested.

I met Don Chapman through a chance introduction by Daniel Veniez, a mutual friend, successful political columnist, and would-be BC Liberal MP whom I admire a great deal. Chapman resides on British Columbia's misnamed Sunshine Coast, one of my former stomping grounds, where I missed becoming named Mr. Hopkins Landing by only 500 votes in a community of barely 100.

This is how this book started: Don being the storyteller. Actually, it's more a cri de cœur. It is a call to arms for a fresh approach to the most fundamental rite of passage—from birth to citizenship—that ought to be easily claimable instead of being tied up in the brutal "dynamics of delay"—a phrase that ought to be reproduced in petit point on every bureaucrat's hope chest. The system has improved, at least in part because of Chapman's radical advocacy.

The word "radical" possesses damaging characteristics in Stephen Harper's government lexicon, but its dictionary definition has nothing to do with occupying bankers' offices. The process of radicalization simply means getting to the root of things, which Chapman does effortlessly (and twice on Sunday) without even working himself into a sweat—and he ain't no radical.

What has united his army of Lost Canadians is the simple credo that being hung out to dry is not a legitimate or desirable posture.

The functionaries of Switzerland's administration, who thrive on it, coined the best phrase to describe how governments hibernate: its meticulously inactive burgher-bureaucrats boast about exercising "the dynamics of delay" as an admissible tactic. It is certainly effective but it solves nothing. Indeed, worse than nothing because its practitioners and victims alike reap no benefits, only anger.

The upside for Don Chapman is that he has met a band of brothers and sisters whom he counts among the most admirable, if damaged, Canadians. Their bravery and stubbornness almost equal his own. In the face of injustice, his victories on behalf of victimized Canadians have been his reward.

Chapman, his family, and his remarkable retinue of Lost Canadians believe they have found a way to beat down each challenge to existing regulations. Sadly, their crusade has gone no further afield. Ottawa has retreated to its bad old ways and, despite some favourable fallout from the C-37 legislation, that useful bill also served as the evidence of its system's remaining inadequacies. Case in point: no one, including Citizenship and Immigration Canada, is consistent when telling people if they definitively are, or definitely are not, Canadian citizens. That's the real nut: How can you run a major G-8 country that isn't certain who among its 35 million people are or are not citizens?

Our thumb-sucking savants like me spend their cloistered lives attempting to define the boundaries of the Canadian identity. It turns out that this is easy, compared with divining who is or isn't entitled to it. Most of the inhabitants of this magnificent hunk of geography north of the forty-ninth parallel are Canadians not by persuasion but by convenience, or worse, by inadvertence. "I am trying to change that," Chapman declares.

Having worked with Don and met many of the Lost Canadians, I believe in his cause. I am also convinced there is only one solution to Canada's citizenship dilemma: the priority of tabling a brand-new citizenship act— meticulously conceived, non-political, but redrafted so that its mint-fresh approach sheds light instead of creating even more shadows.

It's that simple. And that difficult. But it must be done.

PETER C. NEWMAN

RAINING ASHES

I'M AN AIRLINE pilot currently on leave of absence from United Airlines. Pilots are analytical people, always striving to understand the truth. Plane crashes are investigated to discover what went wrong. The objective is to learn the cause of the crash, be it mechanical, electrical, or human error. We never want to repeat the same mistakes.

To get into the pilot's seat of a Boeing 747-400, as I have many times, one must have a high degree of training and years of experience. Pilots are constantly taking written and oral examinations, practising on simulators, and watching training videos. Poked and prodded, we are examined for physical or mental problems, and even then we have federal inspectors showing up unannounced, often at the last minute before a flight, to spot-check our performance. If the feds aren't satisfied with what they see, we can incur penalties, including fines, and even have our licences pulled. The point is that, despite our rigorous training and there always being more than one pilot at the controls, mistakes happen, albeit rarely. In contrast, some career fields seem prone to constant gaffes and blunders—like politics. And so it behooves us all to remain vigilant, knowing that, as humans, no matter how accomplished, we are not impervious to error.

For me, the statement "I've been to hell and back" is synonymous with "I've been to Ottawa and back." I'm the person behind seven parliamentary bills, all dealing with Canadian citizenship law. This book is written through my pilot lens in the hope of exposing what went wrong, and of making Canada a better country. The wrongs made and perpetuated against

Lost Canadians should never have happened, let alone be repeated, and there's a lot of blame to go around.

In an accident, pilots are frequently the first to die. Hence, we share a common goal with our passengers: to arrive safely at our destination. In politics—in governments around the world—there exists a disconnect between the people and their respective leaders: politicians often don't suffer the consequences of the legislation they pass into law. Something has gone terribly wrong.

This book isn't just an historical account of the Lost Canadians but an "accident investigation" of what went wrong and is still wrong in Ottawa. The deficiencies are not unique to Canada—everywhere one finds a politician, there seems to be a corresponding problem.

Most Lost Canadians were completely unaware of their precarious situation. For years, the government denied knowing how many were out there, indicating to the media that the numbers were relatively small. In 2007, Citizenship Minister Diane Finley suggested 450. Today, Citizenship and Immigration Canada (CIC) admits to there being at least 750,000, though we believe the figure is closer to 1 million. Either way, that's substantial in a country of about 35 million. It means that somewhere between 2 percent and 3 percent of all Canadians were or still are Lost Canadians. And if you're not one of them, then odds are that a family member or friend was or is. Without question, the legislation that came about because of our advocacy, in one way or another, touched every Canadian on the planet.

I lost my citizenship as a six-and-a-half-year-old child because I was born in wedlock, in Canada, and wasn't adopted. Had any of these factors been different, I would have remained Canadian.

Confused? No wonder. Canadian citizenship law is outdated, mystifying, and unfair, and what you don't know can hurt you. No use trying to make any sense out of this, because you won't be able to.

Roméo Dallaire discovered, quite by accident, in the early 1970s that he wasn't considered Canadian.

During the summer of 2010, eighty-seven-year-old Canadian war bride Priscilla Corrie was denied a passport—her previous one had expired—when CIC abruptly stated that, as a non-citizen, she wasn't entitled to one.

Quan Louie, born in Vancouver in 1922, died in 1945 when his bomber was hit by enemy flak over Magdeburg, Germany, and exploded. The federal government now claims that not only was he never a citizen but neither were the other 111,000 Canadian war dead from World Wars I and II.[1]

Guy Valliere was born in Montreal in 1926. He grew up, married, had a family, voted, paid taxes, and was a soldier for Canada in World War II. He went to his grave disenfranchised simply because he was born in wedlock.

Jackie Scott came to Canada with her British war-bride mother and Canadian-soldier father in 1948. She was turned away for being born out of wedlock.[2]

For marrying a non-British subject before 1947, Velma Demerson was a woman without a country for the next half century. Apparently, this sort of thing happened with some regularity: Canada was particularly adept at rendering children stateless.

Sarah Currie and her husband, Mike, were both Canadian citizens at birth. Both were military brats. CIC would not recognize their adopted son on the grounds that the couple hadn't demonstrated a "substantial connection" to Canada. It didn't matter that Mike had served three tours of duty in Afghanistan as a Canadian soldier.

Heather Harnois is a Canadian First Nations woman; her roots in North America go back thousands of years. Her child was born in Canada, yet the government says Heather isn't Canadian.

It's hard to imagine all this going on in a post–Charter rights Canada. But it was, and is. The laws have still not been fully corrected. These real-life stories of fellow Canadians will touch your heart—they're gut-wrenching, tearful, maddening, and joyous. And the stories are many, as are the government's reasons for rejecting its own people.

I'm the leader of the Lost Canadians, which consists of a hodgepodge, really, of individuals from across Canada and around the world. Among our ranks are Nobel Prize winners; Hollywood actors; NHL players; members of Parliament; everyday folks; and everything in between. We fought a long battle with Ottawa, and we won.

In these pages you'll discover a chronicle of Canada, from its beginnings to where we're going as individuals and as a country—from discrimination to acceptance. Like that of David and Goliath, this is a story in which a handful of average people take on the fed, and win. It's the narrative of navigating across the treacherous waters of Ottawa, in and around the hallowed hallways of Parliament. It's the story of the little guy being victorious, and of how those actions changed a country, its history, and its people. It's about an ongoing battle, which probably began the nanosecond two people stood together on planet earth, to achieve that which we all deserve: justice, dignity, and equal rights.

AGAINST ALL ODDS:
THE STORY OF FLIGHT 811

When you are going through hell, keep on going.
Never, never, never give up.
WINSTON CHURCHILL

Fall seven times, stand up eight.
JAPANESE PROVERB

DURING THE WEE hours of February 25, 1989, in Wellington, New Zealand, Susan Campbell sat straight up in bed with a clear vision of her son. Sensing her anxiety, husband Kevin put his arm around her for reassurance. After a few minutes they both fell back to sleep. Little did they know how much that moment would forever change lives; not just their own but also thousands of others around the world. If there was any peace to their sleep, it would be the last for many years. In just a few short hours they would learn of their son Lee's passing.

Earlier, on the other side of the international dateline, in Honolulu, Hawaii, Brian Kitaoka, a United Airlines ramp serviceman, prepared to do something he'd done countless times before: close the main cargo door of Flight 811. It was a simple procedure, holding down the toggle switch located in a small recess of the forward, right-side fuselage near the lower corner of the doorway of the huge Boeing 747. It took all of maybe twenty seconds for the main cargo door to close. Kitaoka's final action was to reach up and push in a palm-sized handle, which mechanically closed two pres-sure-relief valves while simultaneously swinging eight J-shaped aluminum bars into place. The door was now sealed and the plane ready for flight.

Taking off from Runway 8 in Honolulu requires an immediate right turn. It's what those in aviation call a "noise abatement procedure." Almost straight ahead of the runway lie the Waikiki hotels full of tourists, who would be less than thrilled if, every few minutes, they were forced to endure the roaring of jumbo-jet engines at takeoff power not far above their heads. So immediately after liftoff, Captain David Cronin, First Officer Al Slater, and Flight Engineer Mark Thomas put the plane into a 30-degree right turn to a more southerly direction, almost in parallel to the beaches of Waikiki and just a few miles offshore.

At 10,000 feet above sea level, pilots transition from a sterile cockpit—that of talking only about matters that pertain directly to the flying or safety of the aircraft—to a more relaxed one. At 18,000 feet, the landing lights are turned off on the climb to cruising altitude. For Flight 811, while the pilots casually checked their gauges, talked to air traffic control, and flew the plane, the fifteen flight attendants were preparing the meal service. On board were 337 passengers, many getting ready to nod off for their long flight to New Zealand. It was all routine.

As the plane neared 23,000 feet above the black nighttime ocean, at exactly nine minutes and nine seconds past 2 a.m., a loud thump was heard. Captain Cronin shouted, "What the hell was that?" It was followed, 1.8 seconds later, by a mammoth boom. *Had a bomb gone off?*

Curt Christensen, one of the flight attendants, was assigned to the rear of the plane. Immediately after the explosion he felt the cold of the outside air. Debris flew through the cabin amid swirling grey smoke. Ceiling panels fell, as did door and side panels—often right on passengers' heads. Thanks to his years of airline safety training, Christensen went into emergency mode. Noticing a dim light toward the front of the airplane, he made his way forward through the jungle of oxygen masks and rubble. He paused to help passengers, clearing debris off them. As he reached business class, he saw a glow from the numbers three and four engines on the plane's right side. But, to his horror, something was missing. Where the passengers and seats are normally located there was nothing but a void—a gaping hole in the airplane. The entire section was missing. Sparks and flames shot back from the engines as far as the eye could see. Below, nothing but the cold, uncaring Pacific Ocean. For a split second he wondered if the plane would be ditched but then realized the water would immediately gush in through the massive opening. Either that or, worse, the plane would break apart upon contact with the sea. And then, even if a few people were lucky enough to survive the crash landing, what about the sharks? His fate, and that of everyone else, was now in the hands of three people: the pilots.

Aviators know that, in an explosive decompression, many things can happen. Immediately we don our oxygen masks—depending on altitude, a human has only so much time of useful consciousness. We then ascertain we're able to communicate with each other and with air traffic control—it's imperative that everyone is on the same page, so to speak. The first job is getting the plane safely down to an altitude where passengers can breathe on their own, usually 10,000 feet. There's much to consider in precious little time. The wrong move could mean disaster. A direct lesson from Eastern Air Lines Flight 401, which went down in the Florida Everglades on December 29, 1972, is that a pilot must at all times never forget to fly the plane, otherwise, the results can be disastrous. With Flight 401, the pilots' attention was focused entirely on a mechanical problem. The result? They flew a perfectly good airplane into the ground. So just imagine a bomb going off in your airplane—you're responsible for the safety and lives of perhaps hundreds of people, but your mind must be focused on something else: flying the plane. Easier said than done. And the pilots of Flight 811 knew this.

Yet fly the plane they did—not necessarily by the book, because what had just happened was never contemplated. After donning their oxygen masks and communicating with each other and air traffic control, they assessed their situation, making sure the plane was still airworthy. Then they began a slow descent to heavier, more breathable air. The airplane was turned back toward Hawaii, and Thomas went downstairs to the lower deck to see for himself exactly what had happened. He must have had a sickening feeling, looking at the gaping hole and out at the glowing engines. He had no idea if or how many passengers had been sucked out and into the engines.

Given the debris and carnage, he too surmised that a bomb had gone off. On returning to the cockpit, he gave his assessment to the captain and first officer, reporting a wide-open hole from the right side, forward emergency exit back maybe ten feet. Considering the damage to the plane, he recommended a top flying speed of 250 knots—half of what it was doing just before the explosion. It required precision flying, as the plane still had full fuel tanks and so was far heavier than desirable for low-level manoeuvring. It was also at half power, since the numbers three and four engines had failed. The structural damage was even more extensive than Thomas realized: the nine passengers sucked from the cabin, seats and all, had become projectiles. Some were ingested into the engines, others hit the leading edge of the wing and rear stabilizer, causing tremendous destruction, even to the flight controls. Flaps and leading-edge devices, when deployed, allow an airplane to fly at greatly reduced speeds without stalling; but on Flight 811, Captain Cronin lost the ability to use full flaps. With a stall speed of around 240 knots, there could be no mistakes. Flying the plane required every bit of skill and precision the three pilots had amassed over the years.

Around 4,000 feet above the sea, the plane finally levelled off. In front of it were the flickering lights of Honolulu. There would be no consideration for noise abatement or the tourists in Waikiki this time.

The landing speed for a 747 is normally 135 to 150 knots. With only partial flaps being extended, Captain Cronin would have to nurse Flight 811 in closer to 200. Would the brakes hold? Would the brakes even work? Would the landing gear buckle? Was there enough runway for the plane to stop at 200 knots?

The noise was so deafening that no one in the cabin could hear the captain's order to assume brace positions. Curt Christensen and his fellow flight attendants knew what to do and prepared the cabin and passengers as best they could. For the last few minutes, all that was left for them to do was to wait, and hope. Some probably prayed.

Captain Cronin made a wide, circling approach back to Runway 8. All three pilots knew they had one chance only to get it right. Everything had to be precise: the rate of descent, the landing speed, the touchdown point. There was no room for error or misjudgment. In the end, it was a perfect touchdown. The pilots did their job, and they did it to the highest degree possible. Later they were given the Award for Heroism by the US Secretary for Transportation, with accolades read aloud in the US House of Representatives.

But the story of United Flight 811 was far from over. In fact, the investigation was just beginning.

AFTER EVERY aircraft accident or incident, hearings are held to determine the cause. The objective is not to place blame on individuals but to understand exactly what went wrong. If the cause was mechanical or electrical, all airplanes of the same design are usually grounded until the defect is corrected. If the cause is attributable to the crew, procedures and training changes are made. With Flight 811, the investigation in turn needed to be investigated, but that story is for later.

For Kevin and Susan Campbell in New Zealand, the news came several hours after Susan's sudden awakening. How does one describe the devastation parents feel when confronted with a phone call telling them their child is missing and presumed dead? What should have been a banner day, with welcome-home hugs, became the worst day of their lives. Lee, their son, was one of the nine people sucked out of the airplane and flung to their deaths.

At about the same time that the Campbells heard the news, on the opposite side of the world, the top investigators of the US National Transportation Safety Board (NTSB), representatives of the Federal Aviation Administration (FAA), and the best of the best Boeing engineers were in the process of being dispatched to Honolulu to determine why the accident happened and how a similar situation could be prevented from happening in the future.

Accident investigation is an exacting science. Together, investigators piece together like a jigsaw puzzle everything from parts of the airplane to people's lives. Nothing gets taken for granted. Many years back it was the Canadians who discovered that the hairlike filament in a light bulb the size of a pebble could, under close inspection, reveal whether the plane had electrical power before crashing, and also its speed at impact. Black boxes aren't the only thing examined—everything is scrutinized.

Investigators take a close look at the pilots: How much sleep did they have? Did they have any family problems? Was there something, anything, no matter how trivial, that could in some way be a contributing factor? Fatigue, interpersonal communications, training, you name it, everything gets dissected. The investigators talk to the dispatchers, look into the company procedures, Boeing procedures, aircraft history and maintenance, weather, aircraft controllers, other airlines, and similar incidents or accidents. No stone is left unturned.

Often, years pass before a final accident report is released. For United Flight 811, it was just under fourteen months. On April 10, 1990, the NTSB stated that the cause of the accident was either a stray electrical signal or, most likely, the sloppy operation on the part of United Airlines ramp serviceman Brian Kitaoka when he closed the cargo door. The findings were merely speculation, nothing definitive. The NTSB released its final report without ascertaining the cause of the accident, despite that being its mission.

Now consider, for a moment, that you are Brian Kitaoka. How do you feel, knowing that two powerful government agencies—the National Transportation Safety Board and the Federal Aviation Administration (both supposed to be neutral when striving for the truth), as well as Boeing, the world's leading manufacturer of airliners—are pointing their collective finger directly at you, telling the world that because of your sloppy work nine people died violent, horrible deaths. You'd have to live with it for the rest of your life. Pretty devastating, and not just for Brian and the victims' families. I imagine everyone around Mr. Kitaoka—spouse, children, parents, cousins, friends—felt some sort of shame. How could they not?

But that wasn't the end of this story. Nor was it the end of the investigation. Kevin Campbell—Lee's father—was a retired auto dealer and expert mechanic with a background in mechanical engineering. From the moment the formal government hearings began, he and Susan immersed themselves in the investigation. On their own, they combed through thousands of documents on the cargo door of the 747, from service manuals to service bulletins, from FAA orders to United maintenance records. Like the pilots of Flight 811, Kevin could not accept mediocrity. In the ensuing months, Kevin and Susan set up their home as a forensic laboratory of sorts. Meanwhile, Boeing was working with the NTSB and the FAA on its own investigation, and while there was no denying the 747 cargo door had experienced previous deficiencies, Boeing's top aeronautical engineers believed Flight 811's incident was most likely due to human error, and not just by Brian Kitaoka but by other ramp servicemen too, who, over the years, had manually closed the door. Words like "believed" and "most likely" aren't reassuring in an investigation report—pilots and the public alike want more definitive answers. But speculation about what might have caused the door to blow out was all their combined research produced. Of importance, Boeing's findings neatly swept aside the NTSB's conclusion that the accident could just as well have been caused by a stray electrical signal. The latter possibility, of course, was potentially embarrassing and costly to Boeing.

Airplanes are noted for their backup systems, meant to ensure that a failure of one component is not catastrophic. In the case of the electrically operated cargo door, mechanics could, with a wrench, manually crank it shut if the electric system failed. The Boeing 747 is one of the world's most popular planes, in service since the 1960s. Several times over the years, airline crew have had to manually close the door. The mechanical inner workings operate identically whether closed automatically with the electrical switch or manually with a wrench. But if closed with a wrench improperly, it's possible to damage the locking mechanism.

Almost without exception, aircraft accidents are a result of a chain of events. It's rare to have one single thing take down a plane. Pilots study various mishaps and crashes to learn what went wrong, so as not to repeat the same mistakes with the same possibly fatal consequences. The idea is that, if you break the chain, the accident never happens. In my studies, I've noticed a commonality among pilots: often they utter shortly before a crash, "I'm uncomfortable with this" or "This doesn't look right." Kevin and Susan Campbell had the same feeling about the government's investigation.

Boeing maintained that workers who manually closed and latched the cargo door with a wrench damaged, over time, the locking mechanism, setting in motion the chain of events leading to Flight 811's cargo door failure. According to Boeing, ramp servicemen, when manually closing the door, first set the locks in place by depressing the lock handle, then wound the latch actuator in reverse—toward the open position—to confirm that the latches bumped against the locks. This is called "backwinding." Ramp workers have always denied doing this, and no hard evidence has surfaced that this highly unusual procedure was ever widely practised.[1] In a 110-page deposition, Brian Kitaoka denied he closed Flight 811's cargo door manually.

Independently of the Campbells, another private citizen got interested in the investigation: retired Boeing pressurization expert Elliott Maylor, self-described as a casual observer. He too had a difficult time accepting Boeing's backwinding theory. As Seattle Times writer Byron Acohido put it, "Neither Maylor nor the Campbells seemed likely candidates to tilt lances at the all-powerful closed fraternity of industry executives and government regulators that is the U.S. aviation-safety system."[2]

Meanwhile, the NTSB examined other airlines specifically to see the history of not just the 747 cargo door but also of any other Boeing planes with similar operating systems. What became clear was that Boeing knew problems existed with the cargo door as far back as 1975—fourteen years before that fateful Flight 811. A number of airlines reported trouble with the locking system, made out of lightweight aluminum that could bend when the door was closed manually. Boeing issued advisory bulletins, suggesting the airlines reinforce each of the door's locking arms with an additional aluminum plate. Twelve years went by. Then, in March 1987, a Pan Am 747 lost all pressurization shortly after takeoff from London, England. The cause was later determined to be the failure of the cargo door's locking system. The only thing that kept the door from blowing off were two pull-in hooks. The investigation concluded by saying that several times in the past the door had been improperly closed by backwinding. The Pan Am incident was one of the links in the chain, a precursor to Flight 811.

A weakness in the chain was the FAA. With the dual purpose of being an overseer of safety and a promoter of aviation, the administration has sometimes been accused of giving in to the huge airline lobby, of putting a price tag on safety. In the investigation of Flight 811, Boeing had a powerful influence over the FAA and the NTSB. Although possibilities of the door experiencing some sort of electrical malfunction, such as an intermittent power surge, were on the table, Boeing kept the focus on backwinding. And disturbingly, the FAA went along with it.

Kevin Campbell was meticulous in his investigation; he even built prototypes of the locking system. He pored over technical documents—more than 2,000 pages of them—and with the help of a nearby New Zealand university even devised computer simulations. Together they tracked down survivors, interviewing them about any recollections they had, no matter how inconsequential. Two things stood out: something on the cockpit voice recorder, and a statement by a fellow passenger. The first was Captain Cronin yelling, "What the hell was that?" just before the door ripped from the plane. The second was Roland Wilhelmy, a passenger, saying he heard a buzzing noise about two seconds before the explosion. Kevin surmised that the electrical power for the door actuating switch was coming alive.

Could it be that the problem wasn't at all as Boeing suggested, but a design flaw? If so, Boeing would be forced, at considerable expense, to redesign all of its 747 cargo doors, as well as face liability for damages. The Campbells, as private citizens, were up against some big guns with lots of money, and they became cannon fodder—Kevin was discredited and dismissed as a backyard garage mechanic who had no business competing against Boeing's specialized, high-tech aeronautical engineer PhDs, with their supercomputers. What kept the Campbells going was their desire for the truth. For their son, for everyone on that and future flights, they had to know why Flight 811's cargo door had failed.

Examining photographs taken by investigators, Kevin and Susan discovered tiny scorch marks and loose wiring in the switch that activated the cargo door locking mechanism. To them, it was evidence that "the switch had arced—that is, an electrical charge had leapt from one wire to another in midflight, starting up the motor that opens the door." [3] Independently, Elliott Maylor in Seattle reached the same conclusion.

Records from past cargo door malfunctions noted malfunctioning switches. That ramp servicemen had to at times close the door manually was proof the switch could fail. After all, why would anyone want to manually close the door when a perfectly good automatic electrical system was available? Furthermore, despite a history of 747 cargo door electrical problems, despite United's maintenance records for the very same cargo door that malfunctioned on Flight 811 indicating it had experienced electrical problems in the ten weeks leading up to the accident, despite all kinds of other supporting evidence, and despite NTSB investigator Ron Schleede's acknowledgement of the Campbell's remarkable efforts, he ultimately dismissed the stray electrical signal scenario put forward by the Campbells as "highly improbable."

Now, more than ever, it was clear to the Campbells that the accident investigation also needed to be investigated. Why was so much obvious evidence overlooked? In the issued formal report, it seemed that the NTSB had relied heavily on Boeing's analysis, saying the cause was the "sudden opening of an improperly latched cargo door."[4]

The official investigation may have been over, but the problem hadn't been solved. Why not? Because the NTSB, the FAA, and Boeing were wrong. Or worse, could it be that they were in denial about the truth?

Thousands of people remained in harm's way.

The smoking gun came in 1991 on a different United 747, this one out of New York's John F. Kennedy International Airport, bound for Tokyo. As the cargo door was closed its associated circuit breaker popped open. When reset, it popped again, suggesting an electrical short circuit. The door was then closed manually, the breaker reset, then tested several times to make certain that it was working properly. The door was then closed and latched but not yet locked when suddenly, without anyone touching the open-close toggle switch, the latch actuator came to life and rotated the latches open. The door hooks pushed the door open and the lift actuator extended the door to its fully opened position. Twenty-eight months after Flight 811, the Campbells' theory of stray electricity was proven. The NTSB was forced to reopen its investigation into Flight 811.

Kevin and Susan Campbell, along with Elliott Maylor, were vindicated. So too was Brian Kitaoka. Imagine how he and his family felt when told that his actions did not in fact contribute to the deaths of nine people, that he had not done "sloppy" work. The Campbells proved not only what had caused the terrible tragedy on Flight 811 but also that the little guy, if doggedly persistent, can overcome the federal government and corporate America. Above all, they saved a lot of lives. Most people who have flown on an airplane with an outward-lifting cargo door similar to that on Flight 811 would have no idea that their being alive today might be a direct result of the Campbells' efforts. It mattered not that Kevin and Susan were discredited by the powers that be, it didn't matter that the FAA, the NTSB, and Boeing all said they were wrong; the Campbells knew they were onto something—and that revealing the truth meant many lives could be saved. They pressed forward as laypeople with no expert knowledge of a 747, let alone the complex workings of its cargo door. From the moment they received a horrifying, early-morning phone call about their son Lee to the day they were able to teach the world's leading experts, including the plane's manufacturer, a thing or two about that airplane, they were obsessed with getting to the truth. Theirs was a mission with unbelievable passion. Their motivation came from deep inside: they knew they could make a difference, and that the truth must be told. They did it for the same reason I took on the Canadian government in citizenship law, enduring personal hardships, a dismissive government, a mostly uncaring media, indignant bureaucrats, uneducated and uninterested politicians, and a completely indifferent Canadian public—all because it was the right thing to do.

For Flight 811, as with all mishaps in aviation, there's a venue for investigating causes. The US has its congressional hearings, whose objective is to seek the truth, to learn. The hearings on Hurricane Katrina and the BP oil spill in the Gulf of Mexico are but two examples. But with the Lost Canadians, despite knowing citizenship problems have existed for more than half a century, Parliament has largely ignored the issue; any sort of accident investigation, an avenue to seek the truth, is virtually non-existent. If a forensic account of what transpired on Flight 811 and of the follow-on investigation, and then of the investigation into the investigation, were written by the Campbells, it would have much in common with this book. Except, in the story of the Lost Canadians, not all the Brian Kitaokas have been vindicated and, worse, cargo doors continue to malfunction. In the end, the Campbells made an extraordinary difference to aviation. Sadly, the malfunctioning of Parliament on the issue of Lost Canadians has yet to be fixed.

As you read this book, you'll see that I approach the issue as a pilot, seeing things through the lens of an aviator. From hour one on the first day of pilot training, it's drilled into us pilots that accidents are the outcome, the consequence, of a chain of events. Break the chain and the accident never happens. In Canada—in citizenship law—the chain has not been broken. By the tens of thousands, unsuspecting Canadians remain at risk. And you might be one of them.

PART 1

LOST CANADIANS UNDER THE LIBERALS

CHAPTER 1

THE LONG AND WINDING ROAD

A journey of a thousand miles must begin with a single step.
LAO TZU, FOUNDER OF TAOISM

VISITING CANADA WAS always an adventure for me. As a kid, it was fun getting out of the car at the border crossing, then running into the country through the Peace Arch. There were so many neat things about returning to Vancouver, the place where I had come from. The drive from Seattle was about 225 kilometres, which meant that in less than four hours—years ago, there were no multi-hour border wait times—I'd be out playing with my cousins. They lived near our maternal grandmother, whom we visited every few months. As a special treat, she'd give me a couple of dollars—a real $2 bill—to spend as I wished. My other grandmother did the same, so it was fun teasing my cousins Barbara and Scott, since I had something of an abundance, which they didn't. The elation lasted but a short time. When we got to a neighbourhood store, almost always run by a Chinese family, I'd end up buying candy for everyone: Mackintosh's toffee, snack bars, sesame seed candy, and sticky red licorice. It was a child's dream. I loved Canada.

One morning in 1962, when I was in second grade, my mother put out my Mariners' blue blazer, pressed and ready to wear. My brother, sister, and I were about to become US citizens, and my parents wanted us to look our best. The ceremony would take place just after lunchtime at a courtroom in downtown Seattle (we lived in the pleasant suburb of Bellevue), so we'd still attend school in the morning. At around 10:30 a.m., I stood outside the principal's office, waiting to be picked up. I didn't like the idea of becoming

3

American.* It's not that I had anything against the country—I loved the States—it's just that I was Canadian. Everyone in my family was from Canada. I loved listening to my maternal grandmother's stories of growing up in Antigonish, a town occupying a coastal nook in northeastern Nova Scotia that became known as the province's "Highland Heart." My grandmother was born in 1885, and her father and her father's father were both physicians. In his day, her dad was one of only two surgeons in all of Nova Scotia. She'd explain what life was like at a time when transportation was strictly by horse and sleigh.

My great-great-uncle William Alexander Henry was a Father of Confederation and, later, mayor of Halifax, as well as a judge on Canada's newly formed Supreme Court. Henry embodied our family's political bent, spending equal time as a member of the province's Liberal and Conservative parties, eventually rising to become solicitor general in both administrations. My maternal great-great-grandfather Alexander Wentworth Macdonald was the first president of the Antigonish Highland Games, the oldest continuous highland games outside Scotland. His arrival in Canada was rather unusual. He'd been the ship's doctor when sailing from Scotland to Canada. According to my grandmother, the captain was cruel, often beating crewmembers who didn't perform to his brutally demanding standards. There was a mutiny, and Dr. Macdonald joined the mutineers. That sealed his fate: he couldn't return to Scotland. In my family, it seems there is some sort of genetic code of rebellion, one passed down through the generations.

That was my Scottish ancestry in Canada. On the French side, it went back even further. My other maternal great-great-grandfather, Henry Gesner Pineo from Pugwash, Nova Scotia, was born in 1798 to a mother who had also been born in Canada. It was in his house that the famous Pugwash Conferences were held, earning Cyrus Eaton a Nobel Peace prize. Then there were the Chapmans, Scotts, Oldridges, Harringtons, Seamans, Strachans, and probably at minimum fifty-seven more instances of family ties. After several centuries, the white pages tend to be filled with names of relatives. I believe myself to be an eighth- or ninth-generation Canadian,

---

* I dislike using the word "American" because everyone from the far north of Canada to the bottom tip of Chile and Argentina is American. The reality is that there are North Americans, Central Americans, and South Americans. Somehow, the people of the US have adopted the term "American" in describing themselves as if no one else had claim to the name, and the Canadians (and others) have gone along with it. Hence, I acquiesce throughout this book in describing our southern neighbours as Americans.

maybe more. Over the years, some ancestors attained notoriety. One of my great-grandfathers was the only casualty of the great flood in London, Ontario, in 1937. The story passed down was that he'd been rather inebriated and couldn't find the way out of his own basement. He was English. (On the Scottish side of my family, you'd find a few overindulgent relatives who also loved the drink.) My paternal great-grandmother was Irish.

We're a family of all kinds of people from many countries. Over the centuries there have been labourers, small-business owners, CEOs (Empire Brass Manufacturing—EMCO—in London, Ontario), politicians, doctors, dentists, orthodontists, and one lone airline pilot: *moi*. In times of war, we took pride in defending our country, probably with no more or no less enthusiasm than any other long-standing Canadian family, and with similar results: scars, injuries, and death. Nova Scotia was one of the final destinations of the Underground Railroad. Family lore has it that my maternal great-grandmother's people had taken part in the network, helping slaves from the States get into Canada.

My maternal grandmother was a women's rights advocate and, when given the chance, typically voted for a woman over a man. She also encouraged young women, including my mother, to seek professions outside traditional female occupations. My Vancouver-born mother graduated from the University of British Columbia in 1937, earning the first BA granted in its School of Sociology. My parents emphasized that we should strive to leave the world a better place, that individuals can and do make a difference, and that we should always stand up for what is right. I've tried hard to follow these principles.

My dad's best friend, Jack Rose, lived across the alleyway from him in Vancouver. Dad was on Fifteenth Street just west of Arbutus; Jack's house faced Fourteenth Street. My mother was on Maple, not far away, in Kitsilano. She remembered when a neighbour, Mrs. Johnson, crossed the street in front of a streetcar and didn't quite make it. She was scooped up by the cow-catcher. They freed her at the next stop a block away—her only wound being to her self-image. Today, it's hard to imagine there ever being cows wandering near downtown Vancouver. Mum walked across the Burrard Bridge the day it opened on Dominion Day 1932. So many memories—the Nine-O'Clock Gun, the fiery sunsets over English Bay.

In World War II, Jack was taken prisoner by the Japanese in Hong Kong and, on his repatriation to Canada, became a spokesman for the Japanese Canadians interned on the west coast. My dad was stationed in Port Alberni, far from the horrors of war.

To put himself through school, Dad had worked as a waiter on the CPR trains, earning all of ten cents per hour plus tips. He was up by 4 a.m. and got to bed when the last passenger called it quits, usually around midnight. Working on the trains was also the only way he could afford to go back and forth between Vancouver, where he visited his family on holidays, and Toronto, where he was studying. He graduated from the University of Toronto's Faculty of Dentistry in 1943, just in time to be commissioned into the Canadian Armed Forces' Canadian Dental Corps. At the graduating ceremony, when officers saluted with swords, Dad used a toilet plunger. He didn't have the money to buy the real thing and, besides, why spend money on a weapon when, he figured, there'd be little need for a sword as a dentist. At least he hoped not.

I grew up playing hockey as a centre on the PeeWee, Bantam, and Midget teams from the Seattle area. Fifty cents bought a Seattle Totems hockey ticket. Seattle often squared off against the Vancouver Canucks in the Western Hockey League. In the winters, my team would travel to Vancouver for tournaments and, in the summers, I'd return there for hockey camps. In 1967, to get to practice, I'd board the bus in Kerrisdale, on Vancouver's west side, and make my way through downtown, then across the Lions Gate Bridge to the North Shore. Lining the streets were flags and ornaments commemorating Canada's 100th birthday. The return bus drove past the corner of Fourth and Arbutus, where many of Canada's West Coast hippies hung out. One time the *Vancouver Sun* published a photo of me standing on the ice with Max McNab, then coach of the Vancouver Canucks and former Stanley Cup champion with the Detroit Red Wings. For a kid, it didn't get any better than that.

The pride of being Canadian was simply a part of me. There was never a time I didn't have it. Growing up in Seattle, I hung an image of BC's shield by my bed. I felt as one with the land. Now, as an adult, I understand the First Nations peoples when they say they feel as part of the soil on which they walk. Everyone has ties to their beginnings. Like salmon fighting upstream, we share the instincts of wanting to return.

That's why it was so difficult that morning in 1962, waiting for my parents to pick me up. I wanted to be Canadian, not American. At the citizenship ceremony, when it came time to take the oath and pledge allegiance to the US flag, I remained seated and silent. It helped being only seven years old and surrounded by tall adults—no one seemed to notice. What I didn't know at the time was that I had lost my Canadian citizenship almost a year earlier.

Apparently, my mother had a hard time conceiving, so my parents decided to adopt. My adopted sister and brother are, respectively, five and six years older than me. Mum and Dad thought that was it as far as having kids were concerned until, quite unexpectedly, I appeared on the scene. In citizenship law, that made all the difference, in both countries. When my father became a US citizen on April 10, 1961, I too was recognized as American, since I was my parents' natural offspring. But because the US didn't easily recognize foreign-adopted children, processing my brother and sister took an extra year. My parents, not wanting to expose this differential treatment to us siblings, kept our citizenship status secret. Only years later did we realize the truth of it.

Because I got US citizenship on the same calendar day as my father, Canada cancelled my citizenship. If it sounds confusing, that's because it is. The idea was that if the "responsible parent" was Canadian on the same calendar day that the child got his or her citizenship, the parent could sign away the Canadian child's status (the child being chattel). If the parent became a US citizen on a different calendar day than did the child, in the eyes of CIC (Citizenship and Immigration Canada), the parent was a foreigner and, as a non-Canadian, wasn't allowed to participate in the revocation of the rights of their Canadian child, whether adopted or natural offspring. That's how it was supposed to work, but often didn't. My brother and sister, because they became US citizens a year after our father (or more specifically, on a different calendar day), were supposed to retain their Canadian status. It wasn't for another four decades, when I was well into my battle with it, did CIC at long last recognize my brother and sister—but not me. For close to half a century, CIC had been wrong and now, going forward, while my siblings got their citizenship recognized after only forty-two years, CIC continued to deny me mine. If there was one CIC consistency, it's that it was inconsistent, constantly doling out wrong and misleading information to the detriment of the individual.

Both my mother and father were Depression-era kids, and both were incredibly happy living a modest life. The 1970s had been financially challenging, whereas the '80s ended up being good years for stock investors. By 1989, my dad had a net worth of several million dollars and, with his lifestyle, there was no way he was going to outlive his assets. At age seventy-one, he took a quarter of his money and started a charitable foundation with my mother. He then donated over $2 million to UBC and $1.4 million to the University of Toronto. As my dad's health deteriorated, I became the sole manager of my parents' portfolio, as well as being the head of the family foundation. We also helped fund the UBC Learning Exchange to the tune of $1 million and established the Chapman Chair in Clinical Sciences at the University of Toronto, and the Lloyd and Kay Chapman Chair for Oral Health at the University of Washington. Today, ten years after my father's passing, the charitable foundation lives on, its sole purpose to help make for a better world. To CIC, none of this mattered—as an immigrant, I remained undesirable.

In Gibsons, BC, my wife and I became donors to, or created bursaries for, many organizations—for battered women, the high school, parks, the local playhouse, museums. You name it, we tried to do our part. We started a summertime family music concert series called Music in the Landing. Over the years we also became significant donors to the SickKids Hospital in Toronto, UVIC, SFU, and UBC's Trek Program. The program, as its website explains, allows students to "explore real-world issues through community service learning," which is a fancy way of saying that students go out into their community and volunteer. In Vancouver alone, tens of thousands of man-hours were donated—all sponsored by my family. At UBC, there's the Chapman Learning Commons, which quotes my mother on its website: "We chose to fund the Learning Commons because we've always believed that people learn best when they are engaged in discussion, sharing ideas and insights with one another."[1] Quite true; my family believes strongly that a better world is made from collective thought and discussion. That's why we set up the Chapman Discussions, with the mandate of inviting academic leaders, professors, graduate students, upper-year undergraduates, and the general public "to share their constructive perspectives on issues of significance."

As a family, we gave back to our communities, doing everything in our power to be good citizens. Yet, in CIC terms, I didn't have enough points to qualify as an immigrant, nor would my parents have, if they had applied.* My parents had left Canada for medical reasons. Dad had arthritis in his hands, and he knew this would result in an early retirement. Hoping to prolong his working days as an orthodontist, he moved us to Hawaii but soon discovered the state's protectionist ways: "foreign" doctors weren't wanted. This is a common problem in Canada today. Medically trained, experienced physicians are driving cabs, their foreign credentials not recognized by the provincial governments. In the mid-1950s, that's what my

---

* In a letter dated November 28, 2001, CIC stated I had "obtained insufficient units of assessment to qualify for immigration." And I paid CIC a fee of $1,950 for that.

dad was up against, and not just in Hawaii. Only two states would allow a Canadian orthodontist to practise without US credentials: Washington and West Virginia. He decided on the former, which is how I ended up spending my childhood in Seattle. Today my heart really is in both places: Canada and the US Pacific Northwest.

Coming of age in the '60s and, especially, spending my formative years in the States was anything but boring. The Vietnam War was escalating; there were the Kent State shootings; the civil rights movement, with its attendant protests and civil disobedience, Dr. Martin Luther King Jr., and the Watts Riots; both Kennedys (Jack and Bobby), the Cuban Missile Crisis, Richard Nixon; the Seattle World's Fair; the Beatles and rock 'n' roll music, Woodstock, Haight-Ashbury, the first landing on the moon, the maiden flight of the Boeing 747, the Cold War, the Smothers Brothers, Sonny and Cher, Eric Clapton, Jimi Hendrix, hippies and psychedelics—it was a kaleidoscope of characters and events that became historical game changers. These events also changed me: I began to realize that one person really can make a difference.

The arthritis eventually got the better of my dad's hands, so in June 1970 he retired and we headed south to Venice, Florida. As an almost-sixteen-year-old avid hockey player, I wasn't pleased. The only saving grace was my perception of Florida as a place where there were lots of girls running around in bikinis. As politics shows us, perception and reality don't always go hand in hand. When we got to our new home in Venice, the people closest to my age in the sixty-two-unit condominium were my parents. Most of the folks were in their seventies and fortunately for all concerned the grandmothers had forsaken their skimpy two-piece bathing suits close to half a century earlier.

The 1970s were challenging for everyone, including US president Richard Nixon. During that first summer of the new decade, the Vietnam War continued, with no end in sight. I graduated from high school in '72 and, as a young American, was required to register for the draft, just as my brother had done years earlier. It was well known that Canada was a haven for draft dodgers, but becoming one had never crossed my mind. In the fall of '72, I began my studies at the University of Washington. Each weekend I'd drive to Vancouver to help care for my grandmothers. I was eighteen and, for the first time, I could vote in the upcoming November presidential election. I so wanted to cast my vote against Nixon—it would be just one vote, not much in a country of a quarter of a billion people, but it mattered. One burning question remained—not regarding which way to cast the vote, but whether

I should cast it at all. On the one hand, how could anyone possibly remain silent when a war, and in my opinion an unjust war, raged on? But would voting seal my fate as an American? Would Canada allow me back? Because the stakes were so high, I thoroughly investigated the potential ramifications. I went to the CIC Vancouver offices and asked the questions. I wanted to know if there was any way I could be Canadian. I wanted my citizenship.

The answer was a resounding no. In the eyes of Canada, I had lost my connection to the country eleven years earlier and didn't qualify. To Canada, I was American. It was terribly disappointing.

It wasn't easy for me to vote. At the polling station, I kept thinking it really did mean my ties to Canada were being severed. Nevertheless, I headed into the voting booth, pulled the curtain closed, and marked my ballot in favour of George McGovern. The day would prove doubly disappointing: Nixon won and I lost. My ties to Canadian citizenship had, I felt, been cut.

Years later, I discovered CIC had been wrong. In cases like mine, where the parent of a Canadian-born minor child got status in another country, there was a provision for the child to recover his or her Canadian citizenship; the law said that such a child, "within one year of attaining the age of twenty-one years or under special circumstances with the consent of the Minister within any longer period than one year, make a declaration that he wished to resume Canadian citizenship and he shall thereupon again become a Canadian citizen."[2] Thus, the citizenship minister was obligated to give me back my citizenship—something CIC nevertheless steadfastly refused to do. Today, I know of only one Lost Canadian who got it back this way.

While the mistake was my loss, it was Canada's as well. Tens of thousands of now-grown kids like me might have come back—PhDs, business people, physicians, NASA scientists, aeronautical engineers (when Canada cancelled the Avro Arrow, many top engineers found work in the US, becoming leaders in their fields but losing their Canadian citizenship). Or put another way, the Lost Canadians were exactly what Canada was looking for—they were the perfect fit: fluent in at least one of the two official languages, often still with relatives in Canada, and familiar with the culture. And many of them wanted nothing more than to return to their homeland as productive citizens. Little did I know that when it came to immigrating, I was from the one country in the world CIC didn't embrace—the hardest country in the world to get into Canada from: Canada.

I also had no idea then of the sheer number of layers to the problem; I did not yet know there were at least twelve ways in which a once-Canadian could have lost citizenship unwillingly or even unknowingly. Nor did I know that hundreds of thousands of others were snarled in the same bureaucratic and political nets. By the time I discovered the many anomalies in the law that negatively impacted all manner of Lost Canadians, the country had fully opened its arms to welcome refugees and immigrants with abandon; Canada wanted everyone, it seemed, but former Canadians.

In February 1974, on my first day of a new job as a driver for a local mini-bus line in Venice, I met my British-born American wife. I was nineteen, she was seventeen, and with hot pants being her fashionable attire, my initial attraction had nothing to do with her brains.* Soon I asked the question: What do you think of Nixon? Neither one of us could stand him. I had found a soulmate. On our first date, I confessed to being Canadian, though in spirit only. We were married three years later. Our only regret was that we weren't living in Canada.

While my wife and I were attending Expo '86, in Vancouver, we talked about moving to Canada, but it wasn't to be—I had no legal right to stay. Three weeks after Expo closed, our first daughter, Katie, was born. What Canada had done to me by cancelling my status, it had also done to her. It was a disappointment not being able to raise our children in Vancouver—my wife and I thought it would be a great place for the kids, especially with all sorts of relatives nearby. Thanks to both extended vacations and quick trips, over the years we ended up spending a fair amount of time in BC. My kids studied in Canada during the summers, attended sports camps, and were involved in local community arts and activities. We purchased a house in Gibsons, on the Sunshine Coast but, unfortunately, it was to be a summer home and not our permanent residence because of my lack of status.

Today, I can view Canada as both an insider and an outsider. Canada is my soul in its entirety, but my heart and personality have two facets. My more amiable, far more polite Canadian side has been nurtured since birth, influenced by my Canadian parents, extended family, and experiences. I have a deep loyalty to this country.[3] Yet, although I think of myself as Canadian and certainly appear to be so in speech and disposition, that pleasant Canadian-ness has been tempered, after many years of living in the States, by a stubborn inability to just sit back and be accepting: in a very real sense, as a Lost Canadian, I discovered my American side, the side that is far more likely to push back at perceived injustice, to loudly speak up against

---

* My wife thinks the "hot pants" reference should be taken out.

personal discrimination and, most of all, to be confident that a single person can indeed fight city hall and win.

Although I'd made several attempts to regain my citizenship, my long and frustrating quest to return home as a Canadian citizen really began to expand exponentially with the advent of the Internet in the 1990s. It was then that I discovered my citizenship had been stripped and kept from me only because of archaic British-based laws dating from a period that allowed all manner of blatant discrimination. I began to fight the law, privately at first, then publicly. Citizenship bureaucrats and Canadian politicians soon discovered they were battling with someone shaped by both countries, and that I wouldn't just politely go away when told to. I'm not a bit afraid to react with courage against injustice and discrimination. And I bluntly call it as I see it. These traits have not endeared me to many in Ottawa.

The Citizenship and Immigration Department and I have been locked in close battle for going on two decades now. I've clashed with eight different ministers of citizenship and immigration and outlasted seven of them... so far. It has not been a one-party issue: I've been an equal-opportunity pain in Ottawa. Holding no preference for any one side, I've tangled with elected officials from all major parties in the House of Commons, including non-elected senators, trying to enlist them in the cause, passionately explaining the discriminatory and archaic rules that took the birthright away from hundreds of thousands of Canadians. I've tried to get the support of elected politicians at every level, from those at the smallest local offices all across the country to those in the halls of Parliament. Although affiliations and political party do not matter to me when it comes to citizenship issues, these politicians do have one thing in common: they've discovered that, when pushed, I'll stand my ground, get right in their faces, and will never quit. And quite a few in Ottawa also share something in common: they don't really like me.[4]

Happily, over the years, I've also picked up many amazing and politically connected allies: a few very helpful, informative insiders at CIC, assorted hard-working MPs who came to deeply believe in this cause, and even a member or two of the various Privy Councils.

Most surprising, though, I've also had to continually beg, chase, and debate the Canadian media, trying to get the stories found here in this book publicized and to bring the issue to the forefront. One of the biggest problems for Lost Canadians is that members of the Canadian public are, for the most part, blissfully unaware of the issue; even sadder, upon hearing about it from one of us who has been directly affected, they tend to sigh and agree that it's an awful situation. And then nothing. End of involvement.

The general lack of enthusiasm and dismissive attitude of the media about this issue, and the fact that journalists and broadcast executives have generally ignored it, is not the most shocking part of their reticence. The most heinous action of the Canadian media was fleeing from the Lost Canadian story in response to governmental pressure and threats of funding cuts. Thankfully, I've also slowly gathered a few allies among the media, and over a number of years, the stories of the Lost Canadians have occasionally been told, sparsely scattered in print, on television, and on radio.

During the first decade of the twenty-first century, I was, as I mentioned, the force behind seven bills in Parliament on the subject of Lost Canadians. Thanks to the publicity from the few courageous members of the media who stepped up and spoke out, and to the support of our ally politicians, who influenced their committees and encouraged their colleagues to vote with us, two of the bills finally passed unanimously, while a third went straight down party lines. As a direct result, citizenship was restored to hundreds of thousands of former Canadians in 2009. The change in law also brought long-delayed equal rights for women from that point forward. (The denial of these rights in the past remains another matter: according to the 1947 Citizenship Act, Canadian women were not afforded the same rights as Canadian men to pass citizenship on to their children.) In 2009, I too regained my citizenship, but it was accomplished through the immigration process. It had taken forty-seven years.

Sadly, the fight continues for a few hundred should-be Canadian individuals who remain "lost."* Their cases do not fit under the provisions of the laws that were corrected. As I write this, pending lawsuits could prove to be an enormous slippery slope for the federal government. Not only do many legal experts think these final cases will open up a veritable Pandora's box in the broadest sense, but they steadfastly believe the government is on the wrong side of the moral equation. It won't win. It can't win. The stakes are too high: our coveted Charter of Rights and Freedoms is at risk, as the government would need to argue against equal rights. Further, its victory would mean that all 111,000 Canadian soldiers who fought and died for Canada in World Wars I and II were never actually Canadian citizens. It raises a question for the common Canadian: Just who's in charge of common sense in the House of Commons?

---

* I'm not alone. Today we have a small but dedicated group of "freedom fighters."

So why am I doing all this? Why did I not just stop fighting when my own citizenship loss was resolved in my favour? There are a lot of answers to those two questions: top among them has to do with my many years of professional training. It's drummed into us airline pilots (and I do mean drummed in, over and over) that the purpose of an accident investigation is not to place blame on an individual; rather, as I've said, we need to discover the cause of the accident, the chain of events leading up to it, and thus learn how not to repeat the same mistakes. I've written this book in the fashion of an accident investigation. Something in Canada went terribly wrong. Canadians, like pilots, need to know how and why such a massive error could have happened in the first place, and never allow our politicians and bureaucrats to repeat the mistakes of the past.

If I ditched an airplane in the Hudson River, I would either rescue all of my passengers or die trying. I couldn't, in good conscience, leave 5 percent of the folks behind. But that's what the Canadian government is now doing to the remaining Lost Canadians. Being silent and accepting when injustices are happening around me is not my nature. Besides, what kind of person—more specifically, what kind of Canadian—am I when fellow compatriots are being unjustly targeted and my response is silence? Dr. Martin Luther King said it best: "History will have to record that the greatest tragedy of this period of social transition was not the strident clamor of the bad people, but the appalling silence of the good."

There can be no question that, as Canadians, we're incredibly lucky. We happened to win the birth lottery. Life is very good for most of us. Going forward, passing our country, with all of its rights and freedoms, onto our children and grandchildren will take effort from everyone. The status quo won't cut it. Unfortunately, Canadians are much too complacent and much too willing to accept mediocrity. Allowing this to continue—if we do not demand more of our politicians, if we do not insist they take control of the vast bureaucracy only they can reign in and demand open and transparent courts and government—we risk handing our children a country much in despair.

In the beginning, my citizenship quest was just about me. I didn't set out to change the laws. Nor was I thinking of others. I had no idea it would morph into something so immense in size and scope. But I soon found out, again chiefly through the Internet, that I was far from alone in this injustice. Late in the 1990s, a techie friend created a website for me, so that I could make my case online. Almost immediately, people in the same boat began contacting me. Other former Canadians and should-be Canadians emailed as well; although they had very different stories, the outcome was the same: we'd all been stripped of our citizenship, usually in circumstances beyond our control.

My personal battle turned into quite a crusade. The fight for justice, delayed and obstructed, became a focus of my life. Along the way, I've become the personal contact for thousands of other Lost Canadians. But that's a tiny percentage of the numbers affected. I still get emails nearly every day, some from people hoping to benefit from the new law, others from those who, after learning the change does not apply to them, are distraught. I continue pressing forward, trying in every way I know how to fight for the remaining Lost Canadians. I've become the public face for this group—all of us believing to our core that we are truly Canadians.

So are or were *you* a Lost Canadian? Are you actually Canadian right now? Don't be too sure about your answer and, no matter what, don't take your status for granted. Despite what you've always believed yourself to be, and no matter how crazy this sounds, getting too cozy by sporting moose and beaver mementoes around the house could prove too much a leap of Canadian faith. As many of our parliamentarians (including MPs and senators) and Canadian icons—scientists, Hollywood actors, musicians, Nobel Prize and Order of Canada recipients—but mostly average, everyday people have discovered first-hand, you just might be surprised.

CHAPTER 2

I'M NOT ALONE IN THIS UNIVERSE

All truths are easy to understand once they are discovered;
the point is to discover them.
GALILEO, 1564-1642

PILOTS HAVE INTERESTING personalities. We're used to taking command, being in charge during life-and-death situations, but also to working together as a crew. It matters not whether the pilot sitting next to you is a woman or a man, and of a different religion, political persuasion, sexual orientation, or race. All that matters is the ability to work together in getting the aircraft, with its sometimes hundreds of occupants, safely from point A to point B. Your life depends on your crewmates, and their lives depend on you. It's about as far as one can get from the political corridors of Ottawa and Washington, or wherever politicians gather.

Years ago, pilots were sent to special classes to study interpersonal behaviour, or more specifically, how we interact with one another in the cockpit. Although the captain is always in charge, the old way of having one person in total control was now considered deficient: more accidents were occurring because of this vertical hierarchy. So we were taught that, despite one's rank, every pilot on the airplane had a voice—that, in fact, it was every pilot's duty to speak out. We were to use "all available resources" when solving problems. The idea of synergy—everyone working together for a common cause—produced results that far exceeded expectations. In brain power, one plus one suddenly added up to three.

Wouldn't it be nice if it worked that way in politics? But the political world often does not see its inadequacies, inherited from hundreds of years of doubtful precedent, continuing to stumble along old, ineffective ways time and time again, to the considerable detriment of its citizens.

Pilots bid their flight schedules on a monthly basis. The domestic routes generally go to the more junior pilots, while the more senior crewmembers fly internationally. In terms of bidding, United regarded Canada as domestic flying. Without tons of seniority, for years I bid the Canadian routes. My favourite, of course, was to Vancouver. On the layovers, I made a point to go downtown, back to the CIC offices, hoping the department would finally recognize my citizenship. The negative answer that always came was terribly disappointing. The only consolation, something it couldn't take away, was my right to return to my Canadian roots as a visitor, sharing with my children all that had mattered to me as a kid. On summer holidays in 1997, we travelled to Gibsons, and from then on it was our summer getaway. It was a great life, disappointing only in that we wanted to stay in Canada for good but couldn't. Before the school year started, we'd close up the house and head south.

Throughout the summer of 1998, I stepped up my efforts to regain my citizenship, writing letter after letter, contacting CIC, and doing everything I could think of to acquire what should have been mine in the first place. The best CIC could suggest was that I apply as an immigrant. Once again, CIC's response was upsetting. Why should I have to apply to get back a right that had been taken away from me as a kid, especially when I had had no say regarding my own destiny? I held out not only because the suggestion was insulting but because I really believed that eventually common sense would kick in somewhere within the bureaucracy, and if not, that I could appeal to the citizenship minister herself. But no matter whom I contacted or what I said, it felt as though I was hitting a triple-brick wall.

That fall and winter, back in Phoenix, I refused to let up. I contacted MPs, the media, and anyone else whom I could think of. Being told by the bureaucrats to pound sand when I'd been born in Canada to two Canadian parents—well, it just didn't sit right having to first become an immigrant, especially when Canada seemed to be accepting almost all newcomers, from all corners of the world, so long as they weren't Canadian.

By the following summer, 1999, my wife and I had come to know many people in Gibsons, and our kids had their own sets of friends. We'd fallen in love with the place, and our desire, which was slowly turning into an obsession, was to be more than summertime residents. We wanted Gibsons to be our permanent home; we wanted to be full-time members of the town, schools, and rec centre, to establish bonds as productive members of our community. Easier said than done, because if there was any simple way to return, we had yet to find it. Several events would soon alter our fate, and not just ours but that of many thousands of others as well.

The first was meeting Keith Thirkell, a local reporter and photographer on the Sunshine Coast. One evening, with our wives, we met for dinner at a restaurant. As the evening progressed, Keith, who was also a local historian, and his First Nations wife told fascinating stories about BC, many about the Natives. I could have listened to them for days. The essence of my being emanated from those same shores. By the time dessert had arrived, I'd spilled my guts about my desire to return to Canada but how, in the eyes of the government, I was a foreigner. Keith offered a couple of suggestions. The first was that he write a short human-interest story about my plight for the local newspaper. The other was that I contact Joe Clark, the Progressive Conservative leader.

Being brought up in the States, I was a novice in Canadian politics. Clark was clearly a big shot and, despite my rebellious nature, I had no idea that a peon like me could call an MP in Alberta, and not just any MP but a former prime minister. The next day when his legislative assistant in Ottawa, Lori Dawe, answered her phone, I was the petitioner on the other end. I began by saying how unusual my story must be, my losing Canadian status as a young kid when my father took out US citizenship and that now CIC wasn't allowing me to get it back.

There was silence. Finally, Dawe said, "I was expecting your call."

"Excuse me? You were expecting me?"

"Well, not you exactly. It was only a matter of time before excluded children like you would start showing up. You're the first."

Lori was referring to the 1977 Citizenship Act, by then some twenty-two years old. Although I wasn't the first person wanting to regain citizenship, I was the first to contact Clark. I would later learn that a heated discussion had taken place shortly before the '77 act came into effect, with the MPs and bureaucrats well aware that children had been stripped of their Canadian status without ever having a say-so. The bureaucrats were adamantly against our return, whereas the MPs were in favour. Later, through different channels, I was told that the bureaucracy threatened to delay the '77 act if these children were included. The MPs' compromise was to pass the act, then go back afterward to address the issue. Talking with Lori that day, two decades after the legislation went into effect, it was apparent that the promise to take up our cause had long been forgotten.

Lori spilled the beans, telling me I wasn't alone in my predicament—a sitting Conservative MP was in the same situation. However, unlike mine, his was under the radar, and not just as far as CIC was concerned but with the media and his colleagues as well. And Lori wasn't about to reveal who this legislator was. Over time, she became my ally, which gave me a feeling of security, believing Joe Clark was out there doing everything in his power to help. How could one not feel good about having a former prime minister on board? And, as a bonus, Joe's wife was known as a supporter of women's rights and equality (and those rights—or denial of—figure largely in the denial of citizenship, as we shall see). It was like having one of Ottawa's own gods on my side.

Not long after, on the 1999 Canada Day long weekend, Gibsons hosted a wooden tugboat festival at the lower end of the town's wharf, made famous in the CBC show *The Beachcombers*. Despite it being July, the weather was typical of a mid-March coastal-town morning: overcast and damp. It had been advertised that the MP for the riding would be there, so I arrived early. Knowing that through the lens of CIC I wasn't Canadian, my presumption about citizenship rights was that I had none, including representation. Yet the pilot in me told me that I had to at least try to make contact. And I'm glad I did, as it was this meeting that began the process of, eventually, seven parliamentary bills going forward.

It didn't take long to spot John Reynolds. There was no mistaking him: he's a big man with a commanding presence—"Gravitas" is his middle name. I waited patiently behind several people already lined up for his attention. My three daughters accompanied me for support, all of us eager for the opportunity to introduce ourselves. John had been the citizenship critic for the old Reform Party for an entire year, so it was hard to imagine he wouldn't know the laws. When it was my turn, I pulled out a small laminated birth certificate from my wallet—I'd been carrying it around for nineteen years—and explained to him how CIC told me I wasn't Canadian. With his powerful voice, and pulling no punches, he stated it wasn't true, that indeed I was Canadian. Identity-wise, for the first time since I was seven years old, I felt whole. My wife took a few pictures of me and the girls with John and, after assurances that he'd call Ottawa to set things straight, we returned home. Once there, however, I got to thinking. *What if John was wrong?*

That week, John contacted his people in Ottawa, as promised, asking them to confirm my citizenship. To his complete surprise, they verified that I wasn't Canadian, as he had assumed, and that I was far from being the only such one.

Together, John and I over the years made several attempts to get the citizenship and immigration minister, Elinor Caplan, to recognize my status. Thinking it might help, I amassed letters of support and documented my employment history—in short, I did everything possible to make a solid case for recognition. Caplan's letters of rejection, which John would forward to me, always had some comment like "While I sympathize with Mr. Chapman . . . " No matter, she never once backed down from her insistence that I first had to become an immigrant Canadian. Looking back, I surmise that she was either ignorant of the law that took away my citizenship in the first place, the 1947 Citizenship Act, or didn't care enough about it. What I didn't know at the time is that, years earlier, her own cousin, the architect Frank Gehry, became an American citizen. And that more recently, Jean Chrétien, the then prime minister, offered to reinstate Gehry's citizenship. Caplan got involved and immediately the ball was rolling. It seemed like she had no problem extending the welcome mat to one of her own family members while denying citizenship to the rest of us. Definitely, for those in power, some people were more equal than others.

So I finally acquiesced to Keith Thirkell, agreeing to let him tell my story in the local paper. It was difficult going public for two reasons. First, as a pilot, when you go to work, you leave town. That meant my wife, along with our three daughters, was left alone at home. To broadcast my profession was like an advertisement to someone who preys on women. That's why pilots tend not to talk about their work schedules. Second, I was a US citizen, and while I loved the US, my political views and psyche were now out of sync with what was becoming more and more mainstream America as the nation continued to gravitate to the far right. My fight to regain Canadian status had nothing to do with the States, yet most Americans I had spoken to felt I was abandoning the country that had given me shelter. I didn't want them to view me as ungrateful. To broadcast my plight publicly meant that everyone on both sides of the border would be privy to my life story, which could put my family at risk. But I also realized that the only way to gain traction on the issue was through the media.

Within a few weeks of Keith's article being published, three people contacted me. I didn't yet have a website and my phone numbers in Arizona were unlisted, which meant they had made a concerted effort to contact me. That alone made it interesting—that others would be so moved. Their stories were unique. I couldn't help but feel empathy. My parents' teachings—that we need to make a difference in this world—coupled with my 1960s mildly radical background began to emerge. Leaving behind others while I became Canadian just didn't seem right. That set the wheels in motion—there could be no turning back. As I mentioned earlier, I didn't set out to make citizenship a political crusade; I just wanted my own. But now there were others to think about. I was acquiring a new and broader view of things. Little did I know how all-consuming this would become.

The first three of my new-found compatriots in trouble were Ron Nixon, George Kyle, and Keith Menzie. Ron Nixon was on a Sunshine Coast holiday a week after Thirkell's article appeared. A typical trait of someone in my position is a desire to explain their situation to other Canadians. After Ron told a few locals his story of rejection, one of them suggested he get a copy of last week's newspaper to read the article about me. He did just that, then contacted me with his story:

> I was born in October 1946 in the US to two Canadian parents. During World War II, my mother was a secretary for the RCMP and my father served in the Royal Canadian Navy. My Uncle George was with the Royal Canadian Air Force. He died as a result of being shot down during a bombing run over Germany. After the war my parents moved from Ontario to Lansing, Michigan, so that my father could get a degree in hotel and restaurant management from Michigan State University. In 1957, my mother and father acquired American citizenship. I was eleven years old, and as it happened, because Canada considered my brother and me to be property of our father, we lost our Canadian citizenship as well. The decision was never mine to make. [Upon my] turning legal age, at the very least, Canada should have asked what my preference was—US or Canadian. Today, due to age discrimination, my younger brother qualifies for Canadian citizenship, since he was born after 1946. Because I was born just prior to 1947—ten weeks [prior] to be exact—I'm being rejected.

Then there's George Kyle's story (both George and Keith found me through an article that appeared in the *Vancouver Province*):

> I was born in Vancouver, BC, in 1927. I emigrated to the US in 1950, as no jobs existed in my chosen profession west of Winnipeg, and I found work in Seattle, 140 miles from home. I took out US citizenship in 1954, and

it was only in the early 1980s that I learned I had lost my Canadian citizenship as a consequence. I was shocked, as I never formally renounced my Canadian citizenship. In 1994, I was told by CIC that I could not get landed immigrant status because I was over 65 and retired, and was therefore unable to come up with enough points according to the rating system in use. That put me in the situation whereby I couldn't even get residence in the country in which I was born, which effectively put landed immigrant status out of reach.

How could this be possible? In a Western democracy? In Canada?

While I was living in Europe in the late '80s [and] early '90s, I was often asked in France, Switzerland, Italy, Austria, etc., where I'm from or where I was born. I would say Vancouver, BC. They would respond, "Oh, you're a Canadian." And I would say "No, I'm not a Canadian." Then they would say, "But you must be, you were born there." And I would just respond, "You don't know how things work in Canada." They would insist I got it wrong. They couldn't believe Canada would do something like that.

The discrimination created by the lack of retroactivity of the 1977 Act is Canada's shame.

And Keith Menzie's:

My mother has always felt strongly Canadian. She's told the story many times about how, in the spring of 1956 when she was nearing my birth date, [she'd refused] to go across the border to visit my father's parents in Bellingham, Washington. Her fear was that I might accidentally be born in the US, and she wanted her baby born in Canada. Later that same year, I was born in Vancouver.

In 1964, Dad had an opportunity to work in Brazil on a USAID project. To go, he first had to be a US citizen. My sister was born in Arizona and was a US citizen, but I was naturalized with Mom and Dad at eight years of age. Mom and Dad were assured when they took this action that it would in no way jeopardize my birthright Canadian citizenship.

Today, had I actually been born in the States rather than in Canada, I'd still be a citizen. But because I was born in Canada, I remain a US citizen only.

Apparently, I wasn't the only one in the universe—there were others caught in the same CIC vacuum. I spent the better part of the following year calling everybody and anybody who might be able to help. There was hardly a newspaper, magazine, or television station in Canada I didn't contact. John Reynolds arranged for me to make a brief appearance on CTV's *Canada AM*, with Valerie Pringle. It meant having to commute from Gibsons to Vancouver the night before, pay for a hotel room, and be ready to go at around 5:30 a.m.—which I did. At the studio, the crew powdered my nose for the lights, hooked me up for sound, and then put me in a room to talk with a dummy. Not a live dummy, of course: the host was in Toronto, so the studio technicians placed a mannequin by the camera—that way, when you looked at it, viewers got the impression you were talking directly with the host. After a short interview, the lights dimmed, the techs unhooked my mic, and I was ushered to the exit. To be on the show as its guest, helping with its news story, cost me about $150. It became the way of Canadian media, money being so tight that many staff barely had the budget to report the news.

Shortly after the *Canada AM* interview, I got a call from producer Karen Burgess at Vancouver's talk-radio station CKNW. She invited me to the studio for a thirty-minute taped interview. One pressing question, whether from the news media or MPs, was how many people in the same position as me were out there. At the time, I was aware of only a handful but, logically, there had to be more. Nevertheless, even though they viewed me as an authority on the topic, I had to qualify my answer as being nothing more than guesswork. What eventually happened with Karen's interview remains a mystery to me—although she might have used it, more likely it wound up in the station's file 13. I never did hear the broadcast, nor did any Canadian I know of ever make reference to it—there was no set air date, and no one at the station could answer my question of whether it did ever air.

Just maybe, news shows like CBC's *Fifth Estate* and CTV's *W5* would be interested. They weren't. Indeed, they seemed to mirror the Canadian suspicion of Americans trying to get into the country for benefits such as health care. As a pilot, I had private health care coverage, which was superior to anything in the Canadian medical system. My desire to regain citizenship had nothing to do with the social safety net. Rather, it was born the nanosecond I thought I had lost it, at age seven, which isn't exactly a time when medical insurance and health care benefits are high on one's priority list. If there was such a thing for a kid, it probably would come in way, way below toy fire trucks, a dog, or even the neighbour's goldfish. Another impression was that Canadians seemed to resent my being American. In time, I discovered that most every Lost Canadian experienced this.

PILOTS, ON the front line, constantly get security briefings. In 1997 and again in 1999, two events really grabbed my attention. Looking back, it was part of the chain leading to 9/11. The first incident, an apartment fire, took place in Manila. After extinguishing the flames, the firefighters entered the adjoining apartments to be certain that the fire hadn't penetrated the walls. In one of the suites, sitting right there in the open, were the plans and bombs to blow up twelve United 747s. Six flights went in and out of San Francisco, six from Los Angeles. If successful, a dozen planes would have simultaneously disappeared over the Pacific Ocean with hardly a trace. With 408 passengers, 18 flight attendants, and 4 pilots per plane, that's over 5,000 casualties—significantly more than in 9/11. And these were the exact routes and planes I flew. And yet, it seemed, Canada was allowing terrorists into the country.

On December 13, 1999, Canadian Ahmed Ressam and his accomplice Abdelmajid Dahoumane were arrested in Port Angeles, Washington. In the trunk of their rented car were enough explosives to wreak massive carnage at the Los Angeles International Airport, their intended destination. It turned out that Ressam had been working with Canadian Mokhtar Haouari, whose specialty was forging documents. Not only was my airplane a target but now too was the airport where I was based. In aviation, it was a whole new ballgame. I couldn't help but wonder how these men got into Canada when I couldn't. With the exception of Lost Canadians, the bar had been set to a very low standard.

And if that were not enough, while this was going on, the Liberals were actively recruiting newcomers. They boasted about wanting upward of 300,000 people—representing a full 1 percent of the country's population— to immigrate to Canada each year. So why, then, were they giving people like me such a hard time?

On one of my trips to India, I discovered *The Hindu*, a newspaper with a daily circulation of over 1.4 million. Right there on the front page was a large full-colour ad offering seminars to help people get into Canada.[1] According to John Reynolds, my MP, the Canadian government was well aware of the ads. Apparently, they ran for quite some time—simply because they worked at getting people to sign up to come to Canada. I'd obviously been born in the wrong country. Years later, a headline of the Vancouver-based *Asian Pacific Post* stated, "Canada Helps Malaysians Break Citizenship Laws." The article read, in part: "Canadian diplomats in Kuala Lumpur are helping Malaysians residing overseas secretly maintain dual citizenship."[2] Malaysian law may not have allowed dual citizenship, but Canadian law did, and

Canadian consular officials were helping Canadian citizens of Malaysian origin get facilitation visas, despite breaking Malaysian citizenship laws in doing so. Yet Lost Canadians were being told an unequivocal no.

IN 2000, I attended the Summer Olympics in Sydney. Not only did I have tickets to the whitewater rafting and field-hockey competitions, I had an appointment at the Canadian Consulate. When I showed up for it, I felt as though I were at a bank's drive-through teller—at the counter, I had to pass my documents to the attendant in a sliding drawer beneath a thick glass window. After a while, a woman came out to talk with me, leading me into a small room. I was hoping she'd be able to help, maybe with a suggestion or two as to how I might regain my Canadian citizenship. But nothing. As I turned to leave I asked, "Where in Canada are you from?"

Her reply: "I'm not from Canada."

"Yes, but where did you live in Canada?"

"I've never been there."

I could hardly believe it; the consular officer talking to me about how to get into Canada was not even from Canada herself. In fact, she was from India, and she was contract labour. Hiring foreign nationals over Canadians—it was crazy, almost surreal, but that's how the government did it.

The system was ripe for abuse. Somebody from India, living in Australia, made decisions regarding my citizenship, and I was from Canada.

During the spring of 2001, on one of my stopovers in Hong Kong, the proprietor of a gift shop asked, "Where you from?" I replied, "Vancouver." Her response: "We Canadians from Vancouver." It turned out that she and her husband had bought a house in Vancouver, got their citizenship, then immediately moved back to Hong Kong. She readily admitted that their status was merely for convenience.

Then, at the airport before my return flight, I spoke with a United dispatcher named Raymond, who noticed the Canadian flag decal on my flight bag. He inquired, "Are you Canadian?" Raymond had taken out Canadian citizenship and, like the gift-shop proprietors, had no intention of actually moving to Canada. I sensed his citizenship was also just for convenience. For me, it was anything but.

On September 9, 2001, I arrived home from a seven-day trip to India. It was my first time in Phoenix in three months. On the tenth, I called Citizenship and Immigration Minister Elinor Caplan's office and, admittedly, my mood wasn't chipper. Disgusted that my family wasn't good enough to get into Canada, sad that my kids weren't able to grow up and go to school in Gibsons, my tone would never have won a congeniality contest, not by a long shot. I got one of Caplan's people on the phone, then began to tell him exactly what was on my mind.

"Pilots are always on the lookout for terrorists. Do you have any idea of the number of shady people who are in Canada right now? I can't get the Canadian media interested in my story, so I'm going to go tell the US media—they'll be interested in just who gets into Canada and who doesn't."

"Are you threatening us?"

"Of course I am. You're letting in all sorts of undesirables while keeping Canadian families out. What you're doing is wrong."

At that point, I felt I had nothing to lose. Little did I know that in less than sixteen hours, the world would change.

CHAPTER 3

IS THERE POLITICAL OR BUREAUCRATIC
INTELLIGENCE IN THE UNIVERSE?

It's no wonder that truth is stranger than fiction.
Fiction has to make sense.

MARK TWAIN

MOMENTS AFTER I walked into my computer room the morning of September 11, 2001, the phone rang. It was unusual to get a call this early in the morning, so I rushed to answer, hoping the ringing wouldn't wake anyone. The familiar voice was that of Dave Ducell, a United Airlines dispatcher. It's his job to help plan and monitor a flight's progress and advise the flight crew of possible perils—like, for example, a tsunami in Sendai. Dispatchers have the power to delay, divert, or cancel any flight. Dave is an enjoyable chap; this time, though, his tone was sombre. "Don, we just had a plane hit the World Trade Center—go turn on your television. And, by the way, we have another plane missing."

Immediately I turned on the television, then logged onto my computer to try to access United's internal computer system; as a pilot, I had access to much of the dispatch information. The company had already taken quite a bit of it off the system—I'm sure it had anticipated that every pilot would be doing the same thing. I then went to wake up my wife and kids. As we gathered in front of the television, well before the collapse of the first tower, my kids realized that it could have been me flying that plane. I'd flown every one of United's Boeing 757s, so, regardless of which 757 crashed, at one time or another I'd have been its pilot. The only difference between the four United airmen who died on that day and me was one of timing, and my kids knew it.

My wife and I kept the kids home from school that day. It was a traumatic day for everyone, and my kids were more than aware how close up and personal this was—and how, going forward, it still could be. The names of the victims, including the crewmembers, had yet to be released, and the phone rang several times, family and friends wanting to make sure I hadn't been on any of the crashed planes. Being acquainted with many United pilots and flight attendants, I too was anxious to know who'd been on board.

It was a terrible week. The night of September 17, my birthday, instead of being one of celebration, was unsettling. All three of my daughters cried—my wife and I too shed tears—as they pleaded with me not to go to work the next day. I was to commute from our home in Phoenix to Los Angeles, then fly to Hong Kong. In the morning, saying goodbye, I hoped it wouldn't be the last time I hugged my family. Soon, the lives and welfare of hundreds of others would be in my hands.

To say the mood was tense at the airports would be a gross understatement. No one trusted anyone—even pilots were suspect. After I arrived in LA, Terminal 7 was blocked off because of a bomb threat. It was eerie. Here I was, about to embark on a fifteen-and-a-half-hour journey over the ocean, and I kept thinking, *Did a terrorist plant a bomb on my plane?* When Flight 811 from Honolulu had its cargo door blown off just minutes after takeoff, the plane barely made it back to safety. What if something happened to us a thousand kilometres from land? Would my life, and my passengers', end up being a statistic? Why hadn't the government listened to our union's safety people years earlier when they advised to have cockpit doors reinforced? As it was, the doors gave about the same resistance as they would if made of cardboard—in fact, they were designed to be easily kicked open. Would some whack-job on board the plane attempt to do just that?

We lined up our 747-400 on Runway 25 right waiting for takeoff clearance. I silently thought about Jimmy Doolittle, contemplating what had gone through his mind the moment he advanced the throttles of his B-25B Mitchell bomber for the first air raid over Tokyo during the Second World War. At precisely 13:20, the tower called, "United 1, Runway 25 right, cleared for takeoff." One minute later, the wheels came off the ground. Inside the cockpit it was business as usual: "Positive climb, gear up." We were on our way.

Passing over the beach below, I felt relief that no one had fired a hand-held rocket. My thoughts then turned to my crewmembers, particularly the flight attendants, knowing they'd be the first in the line of fire if there was a terrorist in the cabin. Even the thought of how much fuel was on board had become a concern. Upon takeoff, our fuel weighed more than twice as much as the entire plane that hit either of the Trade Center towers. Just think of the size of that ball of fire. 9/11 was without a doubt my day of infamy.

Arriving in Hong Kong was a tremendous relief. Finally, I could relax. For now, at least until the next flight, our passengers, the other crewmembers, and we the pilots were alive and safe. We'd done our job, and we had done it well.

That last sentence—We'd done our job, and we had done it well—was but a pipedream when it came my expectations of the elected politicians and the bureaucrats of Ottawa and Washington. Jr. Bush proceeded to make a senior mess out of things to come. I watched his "Either you are with us or you are with the terrorists" speech from my Hong Kong hotel room, cringing at his every word. In times of war, wide-body crews become a part of a country's Civil Reserve Air Fleet, which meant, if Bush did take the US into war, the next time I went to work, I just might be heading to a combat zone with 400 troops on board.

From my window I had a view of the harbour, and of Hong Kong's old Kai Tak Airport. That's where Jack Rose, my dad's best friend, was first taken as a Japanese POW. I thought of his suffering during World War II, and of how Canada was denying citizenship to some of the children of the very soldiers who sacrificed everything for their country. Jean Chrétien and CIC were treating these vets and their families with complete disregard, telling them how they weren't deserving of citizenship. My resolve grew stronger; I became a man on a mission. I had to stand up for what was right.

The phone in my hotel room rang. It was Kathy Tomlinson of CBC, a veteran reporter I had been courting to cover the Lost Canadian story. Knowing I was a United pilot, knowing it was my company that lost two airplanes just a week earlier, she wanted an inside scoop. For anything to do with the citizenship issue I was more than happy to talk, but I kept quiet about anything having to do with the attacks—it simply wasn't my place to say anything. Nor, with national security at stake, did I think it would be proper to. Kathy took her ball from the playground and went home. Never once in the more than ten years since contacting her did she show any sympathy for the Lost Canadians, despite my many attempts to get her involved. Although, in fairness to her media instincts, I have no doubt that if we had been blown up out over the Pacific on my return flight, Kathy would have been the first newscaster in Canada to suggest "a former Canadian died today while at the controls of a Boeing 747." For her and the rest of the Canadian media, it would have made a great story.

Upon returning home from Hong Kong, I contacted Liberal citizenship and immigration minister Elinor Caplan's office, this time with a sense of greater urgency. Once again, I asked for my citizenship. I explained how I flew all around the world, how terrorists were known to ask for the passports of their hostages, and, if mine said "United States of America," I would be in far greater danger than those people in possession of a Canadian passport. Leon Klinghoffer's murder on the cruise ship *Achille Lauro* in 1985 proved my point. I pleaded for citizenship on compassionate grounds. No dice.

I'd hoped there'd be more understanding. I had been Canadian—I was born in Canada and, until age six, was a legitimate citizen. I hadn't renounced my status, nor had I actually vowed citizenship to any other country. I just wanted to go home. Also, I really was at risk—hell, my company, my fellow pilots, my place of work, had all been targeted. Sixteen of my co-workers were dead. After 9/11, I never felt completely secure flying. Yet, after the terrorist attacks, CIC made it even more difficult to get in to Canada—not just for me but for all the Lost Canadians. Canada had a mean streak, and I came to realize that the country's reputation for human rights, fairness, and compassion was being threatened from within.

Around this time I met three people who would become integral to my quest to restore citizenship to those from whom it had been wrongly taken. Two were like me—born in Canada and stripped of their citizenship as kids. The third was a Canadian lawyer. The four of us teamed up and, over the next few years, became a force in Ottawa.

Knowledge surrounds us and it's free for the taking. For pilots, it's imperative to keep learning—if there's a better way to do something, we want to know. We've also been trained to contemplate possible situations or potential problems well in advance. We prepare for contingencies: What do we do if an engine quits, or if a passenger has a heart attack? I began planning my Ottawa offensive strategies using the same method as if I were planning a flight, always having a wide variety of backup plans should the primary strategy fail. And I was more than willing to seek help.

I had heard of a Supreme Court decision that had been a game-changer in citizenship law: *Benner v. Canada*. In 1962, Mark Benner was born in the US, in wedlock, to a Canadian mother and American father. He came to Canada in 1986 and later applied for citizenship. That's when his Canadian problems began. Because he'd been born in wedlock, he was chattel of his father according to the 1947 Citizenship Act (he would have been chattel of his mother if he'd been born out of wedlock). Because he was for-eign-born and because his father wasn't Canadian, CIC said he had no right of citizenship. Had it been reversed—his father Canadian and his mother American—he'd be Canadian, plain and simple. Gender, and only gender, of the parent was the deciding factor. Canadian women were not afforded the same rights as Canadian men to pass citizenship on to their children.

It's hard to imagine, but our government fought Benner tooth and nail all the way up the judicial chain to the Supreme Court of Canada. Why the government was so against equal rights for women is a fascinating question in and of itself, but let's take it further: add to the equation that the *Benner* case happened in a post-Charter Canada (fifteen years after implementation). The Liberals had been the party to bring about the Charter, and now the Liberals under Chrétien were arguing vigorously for the right to discriminate against Canadians based solely on gender. It was appalling. It mattered not that section 15 of the Charter expressly prohibited this unequal treatment. And the cherry on top? Canadian taxpayers' dollars were paying for the crazy foolishness of it all—as if there wasn't anything better to spend taxpayers' money on.

The gist of the high court's unanimous decision was that all in-wedlock, foreign-born children of a Canadian parent (regardless of whether the parent was the mother or father) had a right to citizenship. The government had been violating its own Charter.

Now another doozie: If I'd been born outside Canada, the *Benner* decision would have affected me—meaning I'd be Canadian. I was now being denied citizenship in Canada only because I was born there. It's enough to make just about anybody shake their head in bewilderment.

I contacted the firm representing Mark Benner in the hope of finding his sympathetic lawyer. It turned out to be Jeff Wan.* Eventually we hooked up, and Jeff became an incredibly valuable ally, doing all his work for the Lost Canadians pro bono. He too just wanted to do what was right. I asked him how he won the *Benner* case, especially when his expertise wasn't in citizenship law. (There'd been a team of government lawyers, all intent on fighting him.† The odds were far from being in his favour.)

---

* Jeff Wan is not his real name, but in the true fashion of a hero, he wishes to remain anonymous.

† Someone once told me there are 7,000 government lawyers in Ottawa. I don't know how accurate that number is, but I do know you can't swing a cat around Parliament without hitting a ton of them.

His reply? "For the entire month before going to court, I sat in the library and thought."

I understood his answer but, in time, its meaning became even more apparent. Jeff is one of the smartest people I've ever met—a very deep thinker. No matter what argument the government used against Benner, Jeff not only had thought of it but had a counter-argument ready.

Next there was Charles Bosdet. By now I had a website, www.LostCanadian.com, but it really didn't amount to much. I was still rather ignorant about the Internet, and a man in Arizona had offered his services, although for more than a year the site's contents hadn't been changed, nor did it include my contact information. One day as Charles's wife, Peg, was surfing the Internet, she discovered my website, on which I had made a reference to a Victoria realtor I had befriended, David Else. Peg immediately called David and asked him to pass on her and Charles's information to me. Straightaway David rang me at home in Phoenix, and seconds after that, I called the Bosdets. Connection made. As it turns out, I had found, as Anne of Green Gables would say, "a bosom friend."

Charles was a perfect fit, for both me and Jeff. He had a background in writing and had been the news and opinion editor of the largest daily legal newspaper in the US. Like me, Charles was a minor child when his Canadian father took out citizenship in another country, but unlike with me, the country wasn't the US. His dad became Mexican. Nine years after that, his father became a US citizen and, apparently, so too did Charles. Like my siblings, who got citizenship in the States on a different calendar day than our father (hence, they should have retained their Canadian status), Charles got his citizenship on a different calendar day than his dad. Legally, he too should have been Canadian. But CIC didn't take it upon itself to follow the law; it refused Charles. Both Charles and Jeff have incredibly keen legal minds, and they became an extraordinary combination. Dolly Levi, the matchmaker in the movie *Hello, Dolly!*, couldn't have done it better.

Before long, another Lost Canadian surfaced, rounding out the quartet. I met her through a family lawyer in Gibsons, Judith Wilson. Judith mentioned a colleague friend in Vancouver who dealt with immigration issues. After meeting George Kyle, one of the first Lost Canadians I met, I realized how much age can adversely affect one's chances of becoming an immigrant. I was approaching fifty and knew that time was not on my side. With Jr. Bush on the path of what could be an endless war and Dick Cheney wanting to conquer the world (or so I believed), my fatherly instinct of protection kicked in. Would my daughters be drafted when they were older? So many questions. And so, I gave in for the sake of my children, deciding to at least inquire about immigration, even though the idea of it went down as smoothly as a tall glass of cod liver oil.

I called Judith's lawyer friend in Vancouver to introduce myself. He explained what was going on with one of his clients (without divulging her name or contact information, of course). The story was just so incredibly atrocious. Without hesitation I asked him to give her my phone number. Shortly afterward, his client called. Enter Magali Castro-Gyr. She'd lost her citizenship at age sixteen when her Canadian father, and only her father, took out US citizenship. Magali, her mother, and her brother refused to become American. They remained Canadian—or so they thought. Over the years, Magali moved back to Canada, got passports, worked, voted, paid taxes, and lived as a Canadian. She even sponsored her Swiss husband to Canada, a sponsorship that had been accepted and approved by CIC. Magali genuinely believed she was Canadian—and why wouldn't she? Can you imagine her shock when, suddenly and years later, CIC reverses course, changing its mind about its previous decision and rendering her a woman without a country?

Now, it didn't matter that Magali was fluent in both English and French, that she was born in Quebec as a tenth-generation French Canadian, or that she was a schoolteacher in Kelowna and her husband was a school principal. Nor did it matter that they had two kids. Nor was it recognized that her parents had moved back to Canada, and that her father had regained his Canadian citizenship. Nor that Magali had a valid Canadian passport and driver's licence. All that CIC cared about was that her father had become a US citizen when she was a minor child and therefore Magali wasn't Canadian, period.

Hence, Magali was stateless. It was a blatant violation by Canada of UN conventions on human rights—the Convention on the Rights of the Child, and the Convention on the Reduction of Statelessness. As a signatory to those conventions, Canada was obligated to uphold them. That appeared to be of no concern to CIC as it forced Magali into court. And to add insult to injury, she was going to have to pay for it all. It was to cost her family their home. Over the next few years, her situation went from bad to worse.

By now, other Lost Canadians were beginning to show up on my email doorstep, so to speak, with some regularity, and I began passing their information over to John Reynolds's people. JoAnne, his legislative assistant on the Sunshine Coast, mentioned something about a private member's bill. I had no idea what that was: when it came to the parliamentary process, my knowledge was still in its primordial infancy—I had a big learning curve ahead of me. It turns out to be a backdoor way for parliamentarians to get legislation introduced. But since the chances of success, especially when its sponsor is not part of the governing majority party, are virtually nil, introducing one is more often about making it appear as if the parliamentarian is actually doing something. The submission process of a private member's bill involves first the drafting, then its introduction into the House.* But just because an MP wants his or her bill read in Parliament doesn't mean it will be. Names are drawn in lottery style to be put into a queue. Bills come forward in sequence, time permitting, so just it seeing the light of day can be a long shot. A saving grace is that MPs are allowed to trade their positions in the queue.

Being a complete parliamentary novice, I trusted John's judgment. It also helped having a Tory powerhouse as your MP, and one who was really out there advocating your position.

On February 4, 2002, Bill c-428, the first of what would become five Lost Canadian private member's bills, was introduced. At 3:05 p.m., on the first order of business after question period, John Reynolds stood at his front-row desk on the Opposition side in the House of Commons and said, "Mr. Speaker, my private member's bill would correct a long-standing injustice in the Citizenship Act which has disallowed Canadian citizenship to certain individuals who seek and deserve this privilege. My bill would be exclusive to those individuals who fall within the parameters of losing their citizenship through no fault of their own as a consequence of their parents taking out citizenship in another country."[1]

The motion passed, but not unanimously. The Liberals, the majority government, didn't want it. As written, the bill was fewer than sixty words—about as simple as it gets in legislation. But "simple" is far from the correct word to describe what was to happen over the next decade.

The year 2002 was to be a year of all-around frustration. In mid-January, Denis Coderre replaced Elinor Caplan as citizenship and immigration minister. I figured he had to be better. As a former insurance broker, public relations officer, and radio announcer, he lacked much by way of qualifications. But maybe he'd make up for it in compassion. As it turned out, Coderre made Caplan look good. In between flying, I lobbied the media and non-profit organizations that claimed to promote equal rights and human rights, hoping someone would take an interest in the story. The

---

* References in the text to "the House" refer to the House of Commons, the lower house of Parliament (the Senate being the upper house).

organizations were fabulous at asking for donations, and lousy at carrying out their mandates—that is, actually doing something. Often I'd get a sympathetic ear, followed by an explanation of how money was tight, time was stretched thin, or other issues—like endangered mosquitoes in Myanmar—were more important than Canadians and citizenship. Always there were convenient excuses justifying why they were unable to do anything. On the media side, I called the *National Post*, the *Globe and Mail*, and all the major networks and newscasts—CBC, CTV, *Global National*—eager to have someone take the story and run with it. Barbara Wickens, a reporter from *Maclean's*, was interested, but her magazine wasn't. Allan Thompson at the *Toronto Star* took a pass. And then, finally, a nibble. Christie Blatchford of the *National Post* in Toronto agreed to meet with me after the Salt Lake Olympics. Arizona and Utah being adjoining states, it wouldn't be too far for me to travel.

During the Games, two things of great significance to Canada happened. The first was Canada winning the gold in the men's hockey. The fifty-year drought of losing was over, and Canadians were ecstatic. Within minutes of it becoming official my phone rang. It was Charles Bosdet. Both of us had waited all our lives for this moment, and now it was real.

"Don, how do you feel?"

"Honestly, Charles, I've dreamt of this and, now that it happened, well, I'm happy but also indifferent."

"Yeah, me too."

Before the conversation ended, we had come up with an analogy: It was like watching your family open up their Christmas gifts, except, rather than being with them gathered around the tree, you were outside the house looking in through a side window, knowing you weren't welcome. It was quite the testimonial to how a country could so take the wind out of two of their biggest patriots' sails. It had become painfully obvious: Canada didn't want us. To me, it was the ultimate in identity theft.

The second thing of significance to the Canadian experience at the Olympics was the judging scandal involving figure skaters Jamie Salé and David Pelletier. When the Russians won the gold by a narrow margin, there was a public uproar. Eventually, the French judge said that she'd been pressured by the Russians, though she later recanted. Either way, Canadians were appalled. The scandal became the topic of conversation from coast to coast. How could such an injustice happen, two Canadians being denied a gold medal that seemed rightfully theirs? I agreed—everyone agreed—that what had happened was wrong and must be corrected. Of course, both Salé and Pelletier were legally entitled to return to Canada as Canadians, with all the benefits and privileges that go with citizenship. They had the right to represent their country as Canadians. And yet, some Lost Canadians, like Magali, had no country. And for all of us Lost Canadians, Remembrance Day, Canada Day, and the Olympic Games were painful times.

And then, to add insult to injury, Christie Blatchford of the *National Post* stood me up, never returning my calls. Her words about getting together after the Olympics were empty.

Stephen Smart, former producer for Vancouver's CKNW talk-radio host Rafe Mair, might be aptly named. However, I felt he missed the Lost Canadian story even when it was handed to him on a platter. I had met Smart while taping a segment for Karen Burgess, the very first media person to call me. He and I exchanged pleasantries, and he asked if I'd keep him in the loop. About every three months, I'd call to give him a quick update. We had two encounters that summer, both memorable. The first involved Magali: unbelievable as it was, Denis Coderre was pressing forward—Magali was going to court.

On June 27, I took the ferry to Horseshoe Bay, then rode the local bus into town. My first stop was the Toronto-Dominion Bank building, where I took the elevator up to the CKNW studios. As the doors opened, there stood Smart, along with another producer. Since they were heading down to the lobby, I stayed in the elevator, and proceeded to explain to them that, in two hours, almost directly across the street, Magali's federal court case would commence. I was certain Mr. Smart would have some journalistic smarts. After all, just weeks before, the radio station, along with the rest of the Vancouver news media, jumped all over the story of the Ross family.

Originally from South Africa, the Ross family had been in Canada legally for years. They had a business in Vancouver, with several employees. Their problems began when their visas needed renewing and their autistic son's application was denied on medical grounds. It seemed that the entire city responded to the numerous news stories highlighting the injustice of kicking a productive family out of Canada. CKNW alone dedicated hours and hours to discussion. Surely, upon hearing about a Canadian-born woman being put into judicial review, also being shown a one-way door out of Canada, wouldn't Vancouverites feel a similar obligation to speak out? I thought so, but they needed to hear about it. And that meant the media had to be involved. For the most part, the media refused, electing silence instead. Because no one in the media cared to report the story, the public didn't learn about it and so didn't speak out, which allowed the government to proceed against Magali unchecked. It was an appalling circle of indifference.

For the Ross family, thanks to the public outrage, CIC backed down. The Rosses' battle to remain in Canada lasted a few months—the real heat lasting for just a few weeks. For Magali, her issue dragged on for years. If the Ross family were forced to leave Canada, they had a country to go to. Magali was stateless.

When I arrived at the federal courthouse, Magali and her husband, Duff, were standing in the hallway just outside the courtroom. It was the first time we had met in person. I sensed Duff's frustration. As a youngster, he had lived with his family in Canada for a short time. Duff had had fabulous impressions of the country and its people, and he had fallen in love with both. Now here he was, paying out of his own pocket to help defend his wife's birthright citizenship, knowing the government was taking direct aim at her. The events unfolding shattered his mythical childhood dream of Canada.

During lunch, Magali and I spoke openly. We both agreed that we were, to use a metaphor, refusing to sit at the back of the bus. I had begun to view Magali as Canada's Rosa Parks, yet no one in the media was remotely interested. Smart was a no-show at the trial. That afternoon on CKNW's news, not a single word was uttered about Magali. I silently made the comparison between the lack of Canadian media coverage and that of Southern journalists during the Mississippi Burning. Both were shameful.

Four days later, on Canada Day, I was still furious about what had happened, so my mood was hardly celebratory. I wanted to fly my Canadian flag upside down, indicating to everyone my displeasure with the government, but I also realized that doing so would hardly make Canadians sympathetic to my cause. In a compromise, I put a six-inch flag upside down out on my porch; in order to see it, you had be within three feet of it. The day's protest was really just for me.

My kids had left to be in a parade in nearby Sechelt. (What kind of father wouldn't go see his own kids in a parade? That tells you what kind of mood I was in.) I turned on the radio, wondering, if Canadian citizenship wasn't worthy of being news, what was? My radio was set to CKNW, and there was talk-show host Rafe Mair, inviting listeners to call in. So I did.

I was placed on hold, waiting my turn as Mair told listeners about his growing up in Vancouver during the 1940s. Life was not always so wonderful in Canada, he said, and mentioned the restrictions for Jews, Asians, and Aboriginals. He even talked about there being a whites-only restaurant in Vancouver.

"Isn't it wonderful," he said, "that Canada no longer has discriminatory laws like that from the 1940s. Let's take caller number ten."[2]

That was me. "Well, I lost my citizenship because of an old 1940s discriminatory law where I was stripped of my citizenship only because I was property of my father," I began.

Click. The phone went dead.

Continuing to listen to the radio, I heard Mair take the next caller, who said, "Hey, I wanted to hear what that last guy was talking about."

Click. Mair moved on to the next caller.

Furious, I called back to the studio, this time on its "insider" line. Mair's producer, Stephen Smart, answered the phone. I ranted. Smart made it clear that he wanted me to get lost.

I fired off an email, accusing him of deliberately ignoring Magali. He wrote back, suggesting I was stalking him. That's the last time I ever made contact with him. I'd never stalked anyone in my life, nor would I. As a pilot, I'd been through numerous medical examinations, both physical and mental. Airlines have to know their pilots are fit and, particularly after 9/11, mentally balanced.

It was the worst Canada Day I'd ever had—a new high in low. Then it got worse.

The day before, at the grocery checkout, I saw on the front cover of a television guide CTV Vancouver news anchorwoman Pamela Martin. Evidently, Pamela, born and raised in Detroit, wasn't just any old American—she was a bit of a celebrity. In 1968, she toured the US and Japan as Miss Teen USA. Pamela was scheduled to take her Canadian oath of citizenship on Canada Day. Her fellow newscasters sensed a story and decided to make it a big one. Big enough that it made the front cover of the television guide. About thirty years earlier, she had accompanied her Canadian boyfriend to Canada. At the border, he encouraged her to take out landed immigrant status. But on that particular day, the border guards had run out of applications. She was advised to return the next day—back then it was relatively easy getting into Canada (unless, of course, you were a Lost Canadian. I too had shown up at the border decades earlier, but, being a former Canadian, was turned away).

Since then, Pamela has been living and working in Canada as an American. What I found interesting was that the press made Pamela the big Canada Day story in Vancouver. Rafe Mair and Stephen Smart had hung their phones up on me, and four days earlier, Magali was in court fighting to stay in Canada. Yet not one journalist was interested, and the media event was not that Lost Canadians were systematically being eliminated from the

Canadian "family," but that Pamela Martin, after almost thirty years, had finally decided to become a citizen. That evening, in a televised event, to the delight of many of her fellow newscasters, Pamela was sworn in as a new Canadian.

The following week I called CTV several times, asking to speak with Ms. Martin. After many attempts, I was finally put through to her. I explained my predicament as a United Airlines pilot and asked for help. As a new Canadian and an old-time journalist, she'd be, I figured, particularly moved to help someone in need. This is how she responded:

"Why do you want to be Canadian? You'll only have to pay higher taxes."[3]

I couldn't believe what I was hearing. For me, citizenship had nothing to do with paying taxes. It was who I was, no different from the Inuit, the Metis, or the First Nations people. I asked her, "Why did you become Canadian?"

Her answer was that, after 9/11, she felt it necessary for security reasons.

Okay, I can accept that, but I was an airline pilot flying for a company that had not one but two airplanes involved in the very disasters that inspired Pamela to take out Canadian citizenship. One has to wonder why, after twenty-plus years, nothing else had moved her into doing this. She never again took my calls. Nor did she do a story about Magali or the Lost Canadians. She was safe and sound knowing that, when travelling at least, she'd be more secure with her newly acquired Canadian passport.

Later I phoned Rex Murphy's producer at CBC, who told me he wanted only "water-cooler" items, meaning stories Canadians were already well familiar with and would talk about on coffee breaks. Then, after getting a handful of journalists to finally take notice, I called back to CBC, but this time to Theresa Burke at *The Fifth Estate,* to ask her why the program wouldn't do a story on the Lost Canadian children. Her reply: "We only like exclusives."

Either way, we were damned.

All was not lost, however. Here are stories that did make the news:

A-73, Springer the Whale was being returned to Canadian waters. This was big. So big, in fact, that the government of Canada got in on it. CIC, along with Citizenship and Immigration Minister Denis Coderre, decided that, because the whale had been born in Canadian waters, the whale should be formally recognized with citizenship. I kid you not. CTV's *W5* then dedicated an entire show to the whale. How fitting: the whale makes national news because it was supposedly born in Canada, yet Magali, a tenth-generation French Canadian, is on trial, and her story wasn't considered worthy of one minute of news coverage.

From my house in Gibsons, pacing back and forth in complete frustration while looking out over the waters of Howe Sound, I called Malcolm Fox, senior producer of w5 (who, incidentally, isn't originally from Canada) and asked him why he wouldn't do a show on the Lost Canadians. My conversation with him did not sway him to do a segment on the Lost Canadian children of Canada. And as time went on, we Lost Canadians were shunned while bears and cats and dogs, even birds, took centre stage.

Magali kept her sense of humour. She told me she had noticed the fundraising cans that often sit next to cash registers at restaurants and convenience stores, the kind you drop money into through a slot at the top. Usually two or three sit together—maybe one for the Happy Cat Haven, one for the SPCA, and one for schizophrenic kids. One day, in frustration, she made some statement about Canadians caring more for animals than people and, to prove it, she walked up to the cans and lifted each one. Giving them a shake, she could tell that the cans for the cats and the SPCA were about half full with coins. For the schizophrenic kids, she could hear just two quarters banging against the sides. After she called, telling me of her discovery, I too started lifting cans. Sure enough, the cans seemed to support her statement. To get into Canada, it seemed, we should have been cats or dogs or whales—or maybe whooping cranes.

In an article titled "Dead Whooping Crane Comes Home to Canadian Roost," the Canadian Press reported an international tussle over the carcass of a legendary whooping crane. In 1964, Canus (the bird) was found in Fort Smith, Northwest Territories, with a broken wing. One of only forty-two known whooping cranes then in existence, he was taken to Patuxent Wildlife Research Center, in Maryland. There, he became a virtual breeding machine, fathering 186 descendants. At age thirty-nine, Canus died, and the Center had him stuffed and exhibited at a museum. Canada balked, saying the bird had been born in Canada so deserved to be back in Canada. Battles ensued and, in the end, Canada won. Canus's final resting place is now a small museum in Fort Smith. Our government was insistent about the birthright issue: the bird was Canadian. If only Magali, Charles, and I had been animals. George Orwell's *Animal Farm* was alive and well in Canada— as some animals were indeed more equal than others.

Then there's the story of the Canadian Maher Arar. In September 2002, one year after 9/11, Arar was on his way back to Canada after a vacation in Tunisia, when, during a stopover at John F. Kennedy International Airport, in New York, US authorities arrested him on suspicion of being an al-Qaeda terrorist. After holding Arar in solitary confinement for several weeks, the US decided to deport him—not back to his home in Canada—but to his native Syria, a place known for its inhumane treatment of prisoners. Immediately upon arrival, Arar was interned and tortured. Some 373 days later he was released back to Canada. Eventually found to be innocent of terrorism, Arar received a large cash settlement and an apology from the Canadian government.

Years later, another huge flaw in the system emerged. Syrian general Bahjat Suleiman, the powerful chief of Syria's internal intelligence service, had family members who were pregnant and wanting to have their babies in Canada so that their babies would have Canadian citizenship. The Canadian Embassy in Damascus issued tourist visas for both the daughter and daughter-in-law of the very general who led the Syrian department involved in the torturing of an innocent Canadian citizen. Noted Vancouver immigration lawyer Richard Kurland had this to say: "Our Middle East foreign policy bureaucrats couldn't manage to get Arar out of a Syrian prison, but they sure could facilitate citizenship for the family of Syria's notorious intelligence director." One source noted that an aim of high-level Syrian officials is to secure a safe haven for their children, as well as inexpensive schooling. "It is common for the children of senior Syrian regime figures to travel to Canada to deliver their children," he said.[4]

Talk about babies and citizenship of convenience. Not to mention how their babies, as Canadian citizens, might one day sponsor other family members to come to Canada—aging parents and grandparents, including the really, really contemptible ones. How in the world could CIC and our politicians allow this atrocity to happen? Similarly, how could CIC have the audacity to keep us out? Here were Magali, Charles, and I, desperately trying to get into Canada, and being told we didn't have the required CIC points to qualify.

Remember how, at the Canadian Consulate in Sydney, the woman screening me for entry into Canada was contract labour from another country? Consider the same scenario playing out in Syria: General Suleiman's daughter goes to the Canadian Consulate, wanting the officer to facilitate her entry to Canada. Suppose the non-Canadian worker—a Syrian national, this time—denies her request; just what do you think could happen? Would the contract worker disappear into the secret rooms of the general's torture chambers? People have disappeared for lesser reasons. My point is that the odds are extremely slim that a Syrian put into this situation would deny or hold up the daughter's entry into Canada. There's an obvious conflict of interest. Yet, this scenario could very well happen, and as a result, a brand-new Canadian citizen of Syrian descent with an infamous grandfather comes into this world, born in Canada.

Pilots would have red-flagged this issue as a potential disaster long before it occurred. With Citizenship and Immigration Canada, strange things like this happen with odd regularity, and it's not always to the benefit of Canadians. And so I began to understand what the citizenship portfolio meant to the Liberals: votes, plain and simple. Immigration was the perfect avenue for campaigning, albeit through the backdoor. Some 300,000-plus potential new votes came in that door each and every year—immigrants tend to vote for the party that allowed them into Canada. It was enough to make any political party salivate over the potential. Liberals know how to keep their jobs: just keep the votes coming. Canadians, being complacent, had front-row seats to the unfolding saga. Yet no one spoke out and just about no one in the media deemed it worthy of much attention. The vote-getting ways of the Liberals were allowed to continue. My education level was now well past Politics 101: I had discovered that politics wasn't about you or me; it was about the politicians.

The rest of 2002 continued as it began—with frustration, anger, denial, and few in the media taking notice of the Lost Canadian story.

Shortly into the new year, 2003, just after I was a guest speaker at the University of Toronto (speaking to dental students about finances), my wife called. She had learned that the Standing Committee on Citizenship and Immigration was studying a bill, C-18, before the House.[5] It was to be a complete rewrite of the 1977 Citizenship Act, correcting the one Canadian law which to date remained non–Charter compliant. Yet, there was no mention in it of the Lost Canadians.[6] My wife had called the clerk of the committee, Bill Farrell, who said there was an upcoming meeting and, if I called, he could fit me in. In a New York second I was on the phone to him. Sight unseen, I scheduled Magali and myself to speak in Ottawa on January 28. Thirteen days later, the committee, on a cross-Canada tour, would be in Halifax. I called Charles in Cape Breton; before long, his testimony was scheduled for February 10.

Just maybe our fortunes were changing.

CHAPTER 4

THE POLITICS OF POLITICS

Two roads diverged in a wood, and I—
I took the one less travelled by,
And that has made all the difference.
ROBERT FROST, "THE ROAD NOT TAKEN"

DR. MALCOLM YASNY, a former orthodontic instructor, former director of alumni affairs, and former director of Continuing Education at the University of Toronto's Faculty of Dentistry, once said that I should have hired a lawyer to fight Ottawa. "In the end," he advised, "it would be less expensive." He was referring to the insatiable appetite politicians have for money and donations. "With a lawyer, when the issue is over, you pay their bill and you're done. Get a politician involved and they'll forever be coming back to the political donation trough wanting more." Malcolm is a wise man. By now, 2003, the Lost Canadian issue was more than a full-time job, and it would have required a bevy of lawyers working around the clock. Fighting a government doesn't come cheap. I related to black Americans who had fought for their country, then returned home, only to be shunned. Why did they do it? The same question applied to me: Why was I doing this? The country clearly didn't want me, and, overall, Canadians were okay with that. To the soldiers whose battles involve the harnessing of public conscience, you hoe a tough row. Making people feel guilty awakes their resentment.

But giving in wasn't my way. My Canada was worth fighting for. Plus, there were others out there not so fortunate as I was. Most would never be able to wage a protracted battle. Some Lost Canadians were old; many were veterans. All of them deserved to live their remaining years with security, knowing they belonged to the Canadian family. I'd been taught that, in my own way, I needed to make this a better world. I began this journey simply as a quest for my own citizenship. But, over the years, it had become apparent that the issue was a great deal larger. Magali, Charles, Jeff, and I pressed forward.

Magali and I arrived in Ottawa on Saturday, January 25, 2003. Our testimony before the Citizenship Committee was to take place in three days. My wife accompanied me and, coming from sunny Phoenix, found the bitter cold punishing. It was exciting, being in the nation's capital on a mission to change a law. Standing at the Commemorative Flame, looking up to see the flag waving in the wind over Centre Block—it was electrifying, especially knowing that we were now a part of the process. Every encounter was new, even the much needed break Magali and I took, skating on Rideau Canal. My problem with that, though, was clothing. I had enough layers to keep me warm running between buildings, but skating the entire canal? The hotel was nice enough to loan me a parka, and with that, Magali and I headed out. Bending over to lace my skates, something didn't seem right. Apparently the parka had been tailor-made for a woman and, for the first time in my life, I had breasts. Not wanting to trudge back to the hotel, I swallowed my pride and skated out into the crowds. Other than feeling self-conscious, hoping no one would make a pass at me—male or female—I had a wonderful time. On the way back, we walked through the area cordoned off for Winterlude, where ice carvers were busy doing their thing. I silently wondered if a nearby ice statue had been carved or was simply some unfortunate frozen soul from Phoenix who'd decided to exchange his wrong-gender jacket.

Back at the hotel, we practised our speeches. In a way, it was scary testifying before a bunch of parliamentarians. Early on the twenty-eighth, we headed to the West Block. After we had been wanded, scanned, and badged, the guards gave us the green light to go directly to the committee room. We made our way through the hallways, then, rounding a corner, saw a bunch of people standing by a door.

Wow, something big must be going on! I thought.

It turned out to be the Ottawa media and, wonder of wonders, they were waiting for us. I couldn't believe it. For years, no one showed much interest. And now we had a mini-scrum. Microphones were held out to capture our every word. Christina Lawand of CBC wanted to do a story for *The National* that evening. I had no doubt John Reynolds had set that up. As the official leader of the Opposition, he really was a powerful man.

Eventually, we entered the room, took our seats, laid out our paperwork, and began our testimony. Magali went first and, as I would witness over and over during the next few years, she was brilliant. She's a small woman, but her way of putting just the right words together is powerful. She told her story of how she and her husband had shelled out $20,000 for legal fees and court costs; the terrors of her being stateless; the pride that her son had just received a Canadian citizenship merit award in school. She held up her valid Canadian passport. It was almost surreal. The MPs could hardly believe what they were hearing. Hers was an incredibly hard act to follow. But now it was my turn. Always more outspoken, I used the word "exile," telling the MPs that, from my vantage point, that was exactly how it felt. Magali nodded in agreement. Going further, I compared the situation in Canada to the civil rights movement of the 1960s:

"The only analogy I can think of is Mississippi in the 1960s. At that time it was immoral, but legal, to have white-only and black-only drinking fountains. The US recognized the injustice; they corrected their laws. I applaud them for recognizing a mistake. I applaud them for correcting it. They changed their laws to say that anyone can drink out of any drinking fountain. But interestingly, if Canadians had written the civil rights laws of the 1960s the way they wrote the 1977 Citizenship Act, they would have said, if you're black and born from 1961 on, drink out of any drinking fountain; but if you're black and born prior to 1961, you will forever be stuck drinking out of the segregated black man's drinking fountain. The Lost Canadian children are forever stuck with the morality and the laws of 1947."

And then, as if that were not enough, I said, "If there was ever a lesson to be learned from Germany in the 1940s, it's that you never create a class of people and take away their rights. When you do that, bad things happen."

Admittedly, my words were blunt. But I was just calling it like it was. I mentioned how Elinor Caplan herself, as citizenship minister, had stated she could "process anybody in twenty-four hours." Those were her exact words in reference to giving someone citizenship, and if that was the case— and I presume she was telling the truth—why did Magali have to go to court? Why was Charles being denied? Why not just take twenty-four hours and fix the problem?

I then said, "I am asking for no more and no less than any other Canadian has. It's equality under the law, a novel idea. After fifty-six years, it's high time Canada joined pretty much all the other nations of the world. To end my presentation, let me quote from an actual history book being taught [from] in Canada in the 1940s. It's called *Building the Canadian Nation*, by

George W. Brown... 'The "civil liberties" they are called, and we can be sure that we shall enjoy them only so long as we value them enough to preserve them. They did not come easily.' Therefore, the responsibility of protecting civil liberties rests where it must always rest in a democracy, on the people themselves. You as committee members have the power to effect real change in Canada, just like they did in the civil rights [struggle] of the 1960s. In your actions you are writing Canadian history."[1]

For the most part, the MPs had no idea such inequities existed. The statement we found the most profound was that by Liberal MP Andrew Telegdi: "Thank you very much for your testimony. I found it quite shocking. As a member of Parliament, let me start by apologizing because this clearly should not be happening."[2] Over the next decade, Andrew would prove he was not the stereotypical politician. I could count on his every word, and he put people first, even if that meant bucking up against his own party. The two of us became partners going forward. Andrew was fully aware of my connection to John Reynolds, a Conservative, and John knew I had hooked up with Andrew, a Liberal. Both men were okay with each other. What mattered to all of us was correcting the tragically flawed legislation.

Up next was Charles Bosdet. He and his wife both testified before the committee when it was in Halifax thirteen days later. It was enlightening to look at his testimony in terms of not just his losing citizenship but also what he'd been forced to do to have it restored. For years, CIC had asked Charles to document details about his family and, despite complying with its every request and in doing so proving he was Canadian, CIC still refused him his citizenship. Now, we're not talking about the average person here. Charles is highly knowledgeable in law, government, and legislation.

Charles was born in Winnipeg, a fifth-generation Canadian with French and Scottish ancestry. His ancestors had settled in the Cape Breton area. His McGill University–educated grandfather was a mining engineer, who, unable to find employment in his field in rural Nova Scotia, left for work in Mexico. When World War I broke out, he paid his own way back to Canada, enlisted in the army, then went off to fight for his country. By war's end, he'd been in Arras, Amiens, the Somme, Vimy Ridge, and one other noted battlefield. With his own camera he took a picture of the red Flanders Fields poppies that symbolize Remembrance Day. The man witnessed it all—in a Canadian uniform, as a Canadian soldier, as a Canadian. Wounded, he spent more than six months recuperating in a Canadian hospital. Recovered, he made his way back to Mexico for work. When that dried up, the family moved to Victoria, where he lived out his remaining years. At the local church in Cape Breton are many grave markers, for the generations of the Bosdet family buried there. Charles Bosdet III could not be more Canadian. But CIC didn't see it that way.

Charles explained to committee members how CIC had wrongly interpreted Mexican law.[3] Goodness knows, bureaucrats were having a hard enough time figuring out Canadian citizenship law, never mind Mexican regulations. He testified: "The Government disputes that I am still a Canadian. What is important here is not merely that my Canadian citizenship has been denied and my birthright has been denied, but *how* that birthright was denied. I suppose in part I'm here because the how suggests to me implications for others—in fact for everybody in this room. I want to touch on two issues, birthright inequity and what appears to be an adversarial approach to citizenship proceedings."[4]

Charles was right: In Magali's situation, her father, who was from France, years earlier had given up his French status to become Canadian. Magali, like Charles, was born in Canada to a Canadian mother and Canadian father. Yet CIC had decided that she wasn't Canadian. This was, in part, because of the way it interpreted French law, which really didn't apply, since Magali wasn't French. Think of what it would be like having Russian bureaucrats deciding your fate as a Canadian citizen. Of course, it's absurd, but in essence this is what CIC was doing when attempting to decipher citizenship laws from other countries.

The way Charles ended his testimony was superb: "On the issue of the approach to citizenship, it appears to this witness that citizenship evaluators do not look for reasons that you are a citizen, they look only for the check-box reasons why you are not a citizen. It's an adversarial approach that seems to be much more in tune with immigration proceedings than with protecting the rights of one's citizens."[5]

That evening, CBC's *The National* featured us. Magali and I believed that the media pendulum had begun swinging toward us with some momentum, but our optimism proved to be short-lived. Over the years, I had tried to keep the issue in the news, but the media did only occasional stories. Never did anyone delve into the root cause—the way we do in aviation when investigating accidents or incidents. Most journalists' attention spans were limited to 600- to 900-word stories or, for television, a minute or two of narrative in which Canadians were given a chance to sympathize. Regrettably, the detailed background of the whys and hows of this citizenship fiasco were of no concern. It was a one-day story, old hat by dinnertime. Barbara Wickens of *Maclean's* wrote an article, but I sensed the interest was hers alone and not that of her editors. One of the three people featured in the article was Patrick Forbes.

Born in Ontario during the 1950s, Patrick by age ten had moved with his family to the US. He remembers as a youngster standing next to a warm radiator at the courthouse in Camden, New Jersey, where, unbeknownst to him, he became a US citizen. He had no idea that he was no longer Canadian till years later. In 1969, at the Saint Stephen crossing in New Brunswick, on his way to see family in Canada, he began chatting with a customs officer. The elderly man spontaneously spoke out: "I believe there's something in the act saying you can get your citizenship back."

This took Patrick by surprise. For years, he'd been writing letters, making calls, trying everything he could think of, only to be denied by CIC. The officer mentioned something about a paragraph in the 1947 act dealing with the issue of minors who had lost their citizenship. He went into a backroom, soon reappearing with the news. "You can be Canadian, just go into a citizenship office and refer their people to that paragraph." It reads:

A person who has ceased to be a Canadian citizen under subsection one of this section may, within one year after attaining the age of twenty-one years or in special circumstances with the consent of the Minister within any longer period than one year, make a declaration that he wishes to resume Canadian citizenship and he shall thereupon again become a Canadian citizen.[6]

It was that simple. In the '47 act was a provision for people like Magali and Charles and me. Yet, this particular CIC officer was the only one we ever encountered who actually seemed to know the law. Two months later, Patrick took the oath while he was in the Beaver Hall Hill area of Montreal and was immediately issued a Certificate of Canadian Citizenship. That was it. The end. No huge government expenditures, no court cases, and no parliamentary hearings—the entire cost a mere $2. What came later, however, was shocking.

In 1971, Patrick was living in Montreal. It was almost 11 p.m. and he was sound asleep. Suddenly, he was awoken by a knock on the door. Jumping out of bed, he made his way to the living room window to see what was going on. Outside was a police car. He opened the door to see two gendarmes.

"Are you Patrick Forbes?" asked one.

"Yes, why?"

"We have information that you're an American citizen."

"No, I'm Canadian, and I have a paper to prove it."

The gendarme was surprised, not expecting this answer.

"Yes, sir, I'll show you my citizenship certificate."

He retrieved it and handed it to the officer, who looked at it intensely, then turned it over, closely examining both sides before passing it to his partner, who did the same.

"Sorry to have disturbed you."

To Patrick, it seemed that the gendarmes couldn't leave the house fast enough. At the same time that Canada was welcoming US draft dodgers, it was rounding up Lost Canadian children for deportation to the States. There are 105 names on the North Wall, the Canadian Vietnam Veterans Memorial in Windsor, yet estimates of the actual number of Canadian casualties are between 500 and 1,000. What I'm alluding to is the more pressing question of how many Lost Canadians died fighting for a country they did not feel a part of. Ron Nixon is a Lost Canadian Vietnam vet. So are many others. It's not necessarily that these fine vets weren't willing to defend the US. Rather, the odds are good that others like Patrick Forbes were out there being rounded up by the Canadian government and sent to a country and a war that Canadians shouldn't have had to fight. It's appalling.

Our little band of Lost Canadians began growing, and as each newcomer shared his or her particular story, we discovered, as Charles Bosdet's testimony demonstrated, that in citizenship law, the government of Canada is not your friend. Unlike countries going out of their way to defend their populace, Canada had become a country that looked under every nook and cranny to find ways of eliminating its own people from the citizenship rosters. It was a perverted way of doing things. Governments should at all times advocate for the rights of their people. But here in Canada, the bureaucracy, supported by unqualified and unmotivated politicians voted in by unaware and apathetic Canadians, undetected by an indifferent media, weren't just free to go after their own people but encouraged to do so. In the years to come, the world witnessed uprising after uprising in countries that forgot their people had democratic rights. The Egyptian, Syrian, and Libyan upheavals are good examples. Sadly, Magali, Charles, Jeff, and I discovered, and Charles proved, that Canada had to be added to the list of offending countries—at least in citizenship law—regarding human rights violations. We witnessed first-hand CIC's almost limitless roadblocks and hurdles against Canadians, forcing them to substantiate over and over again why they should be citizens. The burden of proof was not on the government to substantiate that they didn't belong. Rather, it fell to the individuals to prove that they did. And when you did prove it, the government still turned you down.

But that's Canada, and in the years to come, we amassed evidence from court documents showing that CIC had been on a sixty-plus-year witch hunt—that what it was doing to us was nothing new.

Spoiled were Charles's and my idyllic boyhood visions of Canada. But then, truthfully, all countries have their shameful past. How Canada treated its Aboriginals, Asians, Chinese, blacks, and women, among others, is a history soiled with abuse. What became clear was that one more group needed to be added to the list of unwilling victims: Lost Canadians.

Validating this was something that happened just two weeks after Charles's testimony: on February 25 in Toronto, Henry Sieradzki, like Magali, was forced into federal court at his expense.

Henry was born in Thunder Bay in 1956; his family moved to the States in '62. Seven years later, when Henry was twelve, the family took out US citizenship. After returning to Canada in 1999, he applied for a passport. Penalizing him for being a Lost Canadian, the government took a year to issue it, and then it was valid for just twelve months. Typically, Canadians get five-year passports issued within weeks of application. Henry was a professional golfer, and he now represented Canada on the Malaysian PGA tour. Life was grand. With tremendous pride he wore the Maple Leaf on his attire. The elation proved short-lived. In Wall Street terms, the bubble was about to burst. In July 2001, the Canadian High Commission in Kuala Lumpur asked him to immediately surrender his passport, saying he wasn't Canadian. This meant Henry was in Malaysia illegally. Given less than twenty-four hours to leave the country, he had no choice but to leave many of his possessions behind. He had lost his sole source of income and was humiliated, but it only got worse. Both countries regarded him as if a con artist, fraudulently attempting to represent a country to which he didn't belong, and where he wasn't wanted. All this because his father took out US citizenship when he was a child.

Back in Canada, he was forced into a judicial review at his expense (taxpayers got to pay for the government's significant expenditures).[7] Having lost his source of income, Henry didn't have the means to obtain legal representation. For the government, it was easy pickings, like shooting a lone fish in a barrel. Not only did it deny his citizenship, it had him escorted to the US border. Devastated, dejected, demoralized—words cannot begin to describe his feelings.

Like Magali, Henry had a valid Canadian passport, and he believed he was Canadian. Had he or Magali or Charles or I, or the thousands of others like us, been born on or after February 15, 1977, or had we been foreign-born (recall the *Benner* decision), none of this would apply—we'd all be Canadians.

Apparently, Canada was incapable under the Liberals of correcting this injustice. Except for in our testimony and in seldom-opened backroom files at CIC, we didn't exist, it seemed.

Andrew Telegdi was with the Liberal Party which, at the time, led a majority government in both the House and the Senate. The Liberals could vote in anything they wanted or, the reverse, they could kill any bill not to their liking. For us to win, someone had to break ranks. As with any majority rule, a minority will never have rights unless someone in the majority has the courage, often moral courage, to speak out. For Lost Canadians, that person was Andrew. Because of him, our issue gained huge momentum, picking up even more steam when the NDP's Bill Siksay and Bloc Québécois's Meili Faille came on board a few months later. Putting it in pilot terms, I was using "all available resources"—I was more than happy to seek help from anyone who'd give it. John Reynolds and Andrew Telegdi became our lighted channel markers, guiding our way back into Canadian harbours.

On February 18, the Citizenship Committee heard testimony in Vancouver. Once again, Magali and I appeared before it. Worth noting are several statements by the committee chairman, Liberal MP Joe Fontana:

"It's a two-way street when you have legislation," he maintained. "It's not only at the convenience of the government, but more important, it ought to be for the rights of the citizen or the person . . . The problem is obviously between that 1947 and 1977 period . . . I would hope, because I'm not a cynic, that it probably was an administrative error that was never corrected, but two wrongs don't make a right. Was 1947 wrong or was 1977 wrong? . . . I think they're both wrong."[8]

NDP MP Libby Davies first called the government's actions against us ridiculous, then added, "The chair is saying maybe the Canadian government is worried about a precedent and they're going to [attend to the problem] case by case. They've created a precedent now in a negative way and we need to actually go back and redress it."[9]

Magali, with her ability to put words together so precisely, posed the question, "If Canada allows its laws to continuously discriminate against its natural-born citizens despite the 1977 Citizenship Act, despite the Charter of Rights and Freedoms, yet all the while forever amending legislation to protect foreign-born Canadians and immigrants, then we should all seriously address a very simple question: what are we doing here?"[10]

She told the MPs to always remember that, in the word "citizenship," the "c" for "citizen" came before the "i" for "immigration." Somehow Canada had got the two reversed, becoming almost obsessed with making sure immigrants were treated better than Canadian citizens. I'm not suggesting immigrants be treated badly—quite the opposite—but the objective should be to make immigrants good Canadian citizens, not the other way around. Lost Canadians were being told by CIC to become immigrants. Magali predicted that, one day, the people of Canada would look back to the solution of the Lost Canadian issue as being self-evident. Yet here we were being ridiculed, ignored, and harassed.

Given the lottery system, John Reynolds's Bill C-428 was going nowhere. So he approached a colleague who'd won the private member's lottery and asked him to sponsor a new Lost Canadian bill, C-343. And so began that bill's long journey from first reading to, we hoped, implementation. In effect, C-428 had been reincarnated, the only difference being the sponsor's name, Okanagan-Shuswap Conservative MP Darrel Stinson. This was our second legislative attempt.

On April 7, the bill was debated in the House.[11] The discussions went along almost straight party lines, with the Conservatives in favour, and the Liberals saying Lost Canadians first needed to become immigrants. Liberal MP Sarkis Assadourian, originally from Syria and now parliamentary secretary of citizenship to Minister Coderre, was adamant in saying we had to be immigrants. Even some Conservatives, including Layola Hearn, agreed. The Bloc took the stance that, instead of C-343, an amendment would suffice in the government's proposed new citizenship act, Bill C-18. The NDP's Libby Davies argued that the bill didn't go far enough, that C-18 did not include Lost Canadians. She said that, until Magali's and my testimony in Vancouver, she and her party had never heard of the citizenship anomalies, and that our situation was historically wrong and must be corrected. John Reynolds then took the floor to argue in our favour. Liberal MP Marlene Jennings had the last word, saying that, although her party sympathized, we first needed to prove our connection to Canada—which meant that we had to become immigrants. Although a vote would be forthcoming, it wouldn't happen until June.

I was so ticked off at the Liberals that I picked up my phone in Phoenix and called Jennings. I got her Ottawa legislative assistant and lit into him:

"Marlene would have made a great SS officer." There was silence at the other end. I continued. "Marlene's a lawyer, and she has no concept what the laws are. She simply took the party line—without any personal thought—and went with it." Canadians aren't used to being talked to that way and, admittedly, it wasn't typical of the way I talked either. Her assistant didn't know how to respond. Finally he spoke. "Marlene sympathizes with you—her father is an American."

That was all it took. I was a man on a mission, and Marlene became my target. I wanted to investigate if she was a Lost Canadian. After all, I was being denied citizenship because I had a US father. Why was she Canadian under the same circumstances? In the years ahead, I would get my answer.

A week later, Magali called. She'd discovered that in Winnipeg on April 17, on the twenty-first anniversary of the Canadian Charter of Rights and Freedoms, the celebrated, incredibly wealthy, media-empire Asper family would bring together hundreds of people—leading, influential Canadians—to announce the Aspers' vision for a several-hundred-million-dollar Canadian Museum for Human Rights. I called Moe Levy, executive director of the Asper Foundation and board member of the Friends of the Museum, and he extended a personal invitation to me for the event, saying we could talk more at length about Lost Canadians then.

Weather-wise, Winnipeg was a radical change from Phoenix, as Ottawa in the winter had been. Canada really was a cold country. Growing up in the Seattle-Vancouver area, I'd never really experienced *cold*. Now I had. The wind was strong and fierce. Caution had to be exercised when walking around a corner so that you didn't get blown off the sidewalk into oncoming traffic. I had taken a taxi from the airport into town. The driver, an immigrant Canadian, shared his story with me. He was originally from India (I was from Canada). He was Canadian (I wasn't). He had no problem immigrating (I didn't have enough points to satisfy CIC). With pride he stated how he'd personally sponsored 162 people into Canada, most of them now working as cabbies in Winnipeg. I contemplated asking him to sponsor me.

The next morning, I walked from the hotel to The Forks, the site of the future human rights museum, and the location for the day's celebration. I entered a room set up for some 500 people. Guests began to arrive. As a who's who of Canada, this was it. Ministers of Parliament, cabinet ministers, premiers, top business people, correspondents from every major news organization—and of course, one lone, rather insignificant, airline pilot.

Glancing toward the front of the room, I caught the eye of Sarkis Assadourian, the immigrant Canadian from Syria who, remember, happened to be not only one of the MPs on the Citizenship Committee but also the parliamentary secretary to the minister, Denis Coderre, who was at that very moment forcing Magali into court. He also helped defeat John Reynolds's Bill C-428. I approached him and asked why he had opposed the bill. All he could say was not to worry, that I'd have my citizenship within six months. (Not so: it took another five years.) Assadourian was polite but, from my perspective, the by-product of a totally dysfunctional political system who drank way, way too much Kool-Aid prepared by both his party and the bureaucrats. How ironic that after losing his riding in the election of 2004, his party appointed him to be a citizenship judge.

The ceremony began with a video in which Kevin Newman, the anchorman and executive editor for the Asper family's *Global National* evening news, gives the introduction, asking us, the viewers, to take a moment, and "imagine" the significance of a Canadian museum for human rights. The video then transitions to a voice-over proudly proclaiming April 17, 1982, to be one of the most significant days in the history of Canada, the day the Canadian Charter of Rights and Freedoms became law. It was the day, viewers are told, that "Canada officially came of age, as well as Prime Minister Pierre Elliott Trudeau's defining moment." [12] We're then told that the Charter bans *all* forms of discrimination and persecution: "Almost twenty years after the Charter, we realize that you can outlaw discrimination, but only education and enlightenment can change human nature. The museum will reflect Canada's reputation for enlightened leadership and human rights. The Canadian Museum for Human Rights will be a museum of personal engagement and personal responsibility actively involving people and challenging them to think."

The celebration wrapped up with Izzy Asper speaking. "It's time to create a centre for the renewed battle against intolerance and injustice," he said. "It's time to stand up and create a grand symbol and gesture of our tradition and enduring commitment to human rights. It's time for the Canadian Human Rights Museum. The message you come out of this with should be that we have to be vigilant. We cannot rest on the subject of human rights."

I was probably the only attendee actually living under discrimination, knowing first-hand what the museum was supposedly trying to eliminate. Looking at all the television news cameras, I thought, *If only you knew about the Lost Canadians.* At that point, Izzy said, "I wouldn't be here today if it were not for Prime Minister Jean Chrétien."

I came so, so close to standing up when Izzy said that. I wanted to shout out in a voice that all 500 attendees would hear, "I wouldn't be here either if it weren't for Mr. Chrétien." I felt my legs come to life and the words bounce on my tongue. Of course, Izzy Asper was talking about Chrétien being a supporter. To me, he was an obstacle. But, as difficult as it was, I stayed silent. After all, the day wasn't about me. It was about the museum and the concept of human rights. Hopefully, it would also become part of Canada's identity.

Back at the hotel that evening, quite unplanned, I rode the elevator twice with CBC's Peter Mansbridge. The first time, taking advantage of the moment, I threw out a teaser: "I was here today regarding the new human rights museum. If only everyone knew about the Lost Canadian children of Canada."

The elevator doors opened onto the lobby and Mansbridge got off. He showed no particular interest, and I really couldn't blame him. In all likelihood, the man is constantly encountering people wanting to tell him their "special" stories. I was probably just one of thousands. He went on his way, and I on mine. About an hour later, I came back to the elevators, to return to my room. There stood Mr. Mansbridge. Again we exchanged pleasantries. For him, that was the end of it. He got the story he had come to Winnipeg to get—the one featuring Canada as a champion of human rights.

Back in my room, I contacted Moe Levy. To my complete dismay, he told me he'd be too busy to see me. Our meeting was off. Once again, I'd spent scads of money for nothing. Other than aggravation, all I got was watching hundreds of prominent people talk about how wonderful Canada was when it came to human rights. My magnificent hope turned into disappointing reality. I phoned Magali and Charles, saying, "Same old, same old." Neither was surprised.

A few months later, Izzy died. He never saw his dream come true, which really, in the grander scheme of things, was my dream as well: the dream of equal rights for all. On the positive side, I began to understand more about Dr. Martin Luther King Jr., especially when he led thousands across the Edmund Pettus Bridge in Selma, Alabama. In life, most people watch. Few actually march. With this added wisdom, my trip had not been in vain.

In the spring, Magali and I called Brenda Carbonell, the government's lead lawyer waging the court battle against Magali.* The government was dickering, suggesting there might be a settlement. Brenda had no idea that I sat in my chair in Gibsons, listening in. Magali was on the phone in the

---

* In fairness, we considered Brenda more an ally than a foe. Our suspicion was that she was uncomfortable having a fellow Canadian being put through the judicial process. For the record, we liked Ms. Carbonell.

other room and wanted a witness to the conversation. Brenda admitted her intense dislike of forcing Magali into court—she was, in her own way, trying to facilitate Magali's citizenship—but then said that the government had no choice—the number of Lost Canadians out there was far too large. Up until then, we could only guess at the magnitude of the problem. And now we knew. It was huge. The conversation left us wondering just what the government would offer in the way of settlement. Soon we'd have the answer, and it too was a shocker.

In May 2003, Denis Coderre, minister of citizenship, agreed to recognize Magali and her two sons, but only on a condition. First, she would have to admit she wasn't Canadian. Then she'd have to leave Canada. Then she'd have to apply to be an immigrant, but only after paying thousands of dollars in fees. She'd have to get medical clearance and security clearance. Then she would have to reside in Canada for one year. And then she'd have to apply to resume her citizenship (after paying more fees). She'd have to stop her court case, and agree not to go public with her story. It was a gag order: Coderre and the Liberals agreed to give Magali citizenship only on the condition that she would shut up and not tell anyone, and especially not the media.

Magali declined, telling the minister, "You have taken away my rights as a woman, my rights as a child, and now you want my freedom of speech. Minister Coderre, I understand Canadian citizenship more than you do, so let me say, Canadians do not sign gag orders."[13]

In true Rosa Parks fashion, Magali Castro-Gyr told Jean Chrétien and Denis Coderre to stuff it.

In July 2003, Magali was forced to leave her "home and native land." What a sad day it was for Canada, and for Canadian journalism. How ironic that her Canadian parents were living in BC while she and her stateless brother were forced to live in other countries. So much for Canadian fairness and compassion. And so much for the Liberal Party's idea of family reunification.

CBC's Bonnie Allen and Gary Symons reported Magali's story, though Bonnie never did much by way of follow-up. Gary, on the other hand, became my main media contact, always willing to help. He did a fabulous story for the CBC radio news show *The Current*. As time went on, Gary featured many other Lost Canadians in his stories. One day, he shared with me one of his frustrations. "So many CBC people don't get it," he said. "They just don't think this is much of a story."

Of course, I had come to that conclusion years earlier. But there was an odd comfort in hearing it from an insider. Gary earned our respect. On the other hand, so many others at CBC, CTV, *Global National*, and those at most newspapers and magazines across Canada should be ashamed.

Noted US civil rights activist Rosa Parks was sent to jail. Magali was sent packing. And the government didn't pay a penny to offset her one-way ticket out of Canada. She had to leave the country before August, which she would do with her head held high. Like Henry Sieradzki, the situation was financially devastating for her. With her bank account dwindling, she and her husband had no choice but to sell their Kelowna home, just before the enormous upturn in the real estate market.

On June 11, the House of Commons voted on Bill C-343. The yeas totalled 99, the nays, 125.[14] In a free vote, the Lost Canadians had lost by 26 votes. The Liberal Party gets complete credit for killing our attempt to return to Canada. Another disappointment was Conservative leader Joe Clark. Until then, I thought he'd been on my side. But once the votes were tallied, his name would be forever etched into the roster of those in the "no" category, as well as etched into the minds of all Lost Canadians as a hypocrite.

It wasn't easy battling against a majority government. But then, other than money, I didn't have much to lose. Magali, Charles, Jeff, and I vowed to press forward. Besides, eventually all governments fall, and with the support of John Reynolds and Andrew Telegdi, I felt that, in fact, I couldn't lose: in time, common sense would prevail.

If anything, I was learning the politics of Ottawa. Many of the Lost Canadians were growing older, and it seemed apparent that CIC's method for handling us was through attrition. There's a line from the movie *Red Tails* that says it best: "Politics is the art of delay until the issue is no longer relevant."[15] And as the Cowardly Lion would say, "Ain't it the truth? Ain't it the truth?"

While all of this was happening, my wife had her own encounter with the bureaucrats. She was in charge of securing our family's landed immigrant status, coordinating this with a law firm in Toronto. After lots of fees, security background checks, and medical exams—from blood tests to providing stool samples, and being poked and prodded—news came that CIC had accepted our applications. We then had to document everything we owned; it took months. On November 8, the whole family flew from Phoenix to Vancouver, where we "landed." Immigration officials at the airport received and stamped our forms, and then, after about an hour, it was official: we were landed Canadian immigrants, all five of us—though my distinction was being a "born in Canada landed Canadian immigrant." Each one of our US passports got stamped "Landed Immigrant—Canada." We also got permanent resident cards. In other words, we still were not Canadian citizens. The next day, we flew back to Phoenix.

From Magali's escapade on, I began working closely with Gary Symons. He told me about a CBC colleague in Toronto, a Lost Canadian who refused to come forward. Over the years, I discovered many people like that, Lost Canadians who knew only too well what the government had done to Magali. Several Lost Canadians—both well known and not well known— were thrilled that I would make the sacrifice for them, just so long as they remained hidden. Like ostriches with their heads in the sand, some wanted no part of it, wrongly thinking that I would expose them. Rather than offering any assistance, they retreated into silence, reacting to me as though I carried a disease—a particularly virulent form of leprosy, judging from their reactions.

In December, Denis Coderre was replaced as minister by Judy Sgro, a career politician. I immediately called to introduce myself, feeling that anyone would be better than Coderre. Sgro was indeed surprising—to the Lost Canadians, to her fellow MPs, to the media, and to the Canadian public. Her moniker could have been "Calamity Judy." From ethics accusations to controversy over an alleged conflict of interest, scandals plagued her time as minister. Political bombshells abounded.

I didn't know what to expect from Judy Sgro. For whatever reason, the qualifications needed to be the minister of citizenship—the leading authority and guardian of the people's right to belong, of being Canadian—seemed to me were having just enough sense to fit into a thimble, and the compassion of a repressive dictator. They also had to be thrilled playing second fiddle while simultaneously being an enthusiastic supporter and defender of bureaucratic thuggery. To quote George and Ira Gershwin, "Who could ask for anything more?"

CHAPTER 5

IN THIS CORNER, THE PRIME MINISTER; IN THAT CORNER, THE LOST CANADIANS

Wherever there is a man who exercises authority,
there is a man who resists authority.
OSCAR WILDE

AN ARGUMENT COULD be made that the Canadian Parliament must be the most efficient place to do business in the country, and just possibly one of the most efficient on the planet. The 37th Parliament, 2nd session, came to an end on November 12, 2003, with the next session, the 37th Parliament, 3rd session, beginning on February 2, 2004. Translated, that means the MPs had eighty days off straight.

Now consider the typical five-day-per-week worker: he or she gets weekends off. For the parliamentarians, it was better than the opposite in that it equated, during a typical year, to working one day, then having six off. As the Bible tells us, God supposedly worked for six straight days and, on the seventh, rested. Being God, that's your schedule. Canadian parliamentarians had it reversed: they worked one day, then rested for six. Schedule-wise, they had it way better than the Almighty. That's why our MPs have to be so efficient—being able to work together, carrying out all of Canada's business, safeguarding their people, and doing it in the most part time of part-time jobs.

Granted, many parliamentarians work their tails off. What I'm suggesting is that 198 days off in a year seems overly excessive. But this is Ottawa, and that's how they do it.

In January 2004, parliamentarians took the entire month off—possibly exhausted from taking all of December off. For me, their recess made for a good time to lobby organizations and groups, hoping someone would lend a voice of support. Once again, I contacted organizations such as the Canadian Human Rights Commission and the BC Civil Liberties Association. Both refused to help. After receiving an urgent plea for money from Amnesty International, I contacted its offices in Canada, New York, and then London. I figured it was a sure thing; after all, the correspondence sent to my home came in a black envelope with broad, all-caps white lettering on the front stating, "The worst thing you can do is look away." After hearing our story, Amnesty International looked away.

In a sense, Lost Canadians were like desperate medical patients willing to try almost anything for a cure, possibly even going to a back-alley doctor in Mexico. When your rights have been trampled on, you have no pride—you're willing to seek assistance from anyone prepared to help.

Two and a half months earlier, I attended a function on the Sunshine Coast touting the Olympics. On July 2, 2003, Vancouver was awarded the 2010 Winter Games and, in October, John Furlong, president and chief executive officer of VANOC, the Vancouver Olympic organizing committee, gave a speech in Sechelt on the upcoming role of the Sunshine Coast. The list of big shots attending was impressive; it even included Gordon Campbell, then BC's premier. A friend, Klaus Fuerniss, was chairman of the Sunshine Coast Olympic committee and, with his encouragement, I flew in from Phoenix for the big event. Seated in the middle of the packed movie theatre, where the speech was to take place, I waited for Furlong to come to the podium. He did, talking at first about the meaning of the Olympics. I took copious notes. He said all the usual stuff about the pride of being Canadian, of being able to showcase Canada to the world. And then he made a statement that really stood out. The Olympics, he said, are about getting a country to admit its mistakes. Now, that's not at all what I picture the Olympics to be, but when the head guy says it, I'm not about to argue. Later, I contacted his office, asking him to support the Lost Canadians. I eventually got back the typical we-wish-you-well-in-your-endeavour letter. From that day forward, I looked at Mr. Furlong's words as empty—Furlong was actually an immigrant Canadian who had his citizenship while the rest of us were damned. Even after the Olympics and being awarded the Order of Canada, he maintained his distance from the Lost Canadians.

When Parliament resumed at the end of January 2004, John Reynolds wasted no time strategizing a plan of attack. His idea was to put two identical Lost Canadian bills forward simultaneously: one in the House and the other in the Senate. For that he needed a senator partner—not just any senator but a well-respected powerhouse like himself. Enter Nöel Kinsella, leader of the official opposition in the Senate of Canada.

On March 25, 2004, in both chambers, bills went forward. On the House side was John's private member's bill C-503.[1] In the Senate was Noel's private member's bill S-17.[2]

Getting the Senate involved was a stroke of genius. For me, it was learn as you go. Not understanding the parliamentary process, I didn't know that bills rejected in the House could be reincarnated with a new name in the Senate. Although winning seemed next to impossible, especially with a Liberal majority in place, we always had a feeling that, since C-343 had been defeated by just twenty-six votes, maybe on another working day the tally would change in our favour. The key was to step up the lobbying. I kept flying my regular routes with United—usually three round-trips to Australia per month—then, on days off, going to Ottawa. One problem was how to dress. While it was summertime in Sydney, with temperatures of plus 30 degrees Celsius, in Ottawa it was winter and typically minus 20 degrees. My fellow crewmembers thought I was nuts showing up in LA with a heavy wool overcoat and muffler (as a pilot, my luggage allowance was limited, hence, I had to carry or wear them). But it was either that or end up in Ottawa wearing shorts. If you have to choose, you dress for the cold. The intense travelling extracted quite a toll; it meant crossing eighteen time zones every week. But if you're David and taking on Goliath, you literally must go the extra mile to have any chance of victory.

On April 22, testimony began in the Senate on Bill S-17. Invited to speak was Patricia Birkett, then acting director general, Integration Branch, Citizenship and Immigration Canada. Before her testimony concluded, Senator Wilbert Keon described her this way: "To someone sitting opposite you who is trying to come in, you come across as a pretty tough lady." He continued, "I am not sure if I agree with your definition of fairness. At times we have suffocating bureaucracy and that is completely unfair, regardless of what the rules are."[3]

The good senator was alluding to Birkett's insistence that Lost Canadians first become landed immigrants by passing the required background checks. When asked about the Supreme Court's 1997 *Benner* decision, Birkett made a flippant remark about the court's judgment being transitional.

That in itself needs to be explained: The court's job is to interpret law, making certain that it conforms to the Charter. Often the court's decisions set precedent for future court cases. In *Benner*, the court unanimously declared that citizenship law, as then enforced, violated the Charter because it discriminated against some, but not all, foreign-born children (children born in wedlock outside Canada to Canadian women were afforded fewer rights than were children born in wedlock outside Canada to Canadian men). Because Benner had been born in the US in wedlock to a Canadian mother and American father, CIC denied him citizenship. Had it been reversed—his father being Canadian and his mother, American, or if he'd been born out of wedlock—he'd be a Canadian citizen. The bias was clearly against women. The court ruled that, despite his being charged with several offences, including murder (he later pleaded guilty to manslaughter)—Benner was a Canadian citizen. Granted, court rulings *are* transitional: legislators rewrite the law to make it Charter compliant, and when the new law comes into force, the court ruling becomes moot. But until the laws are rewritten, the court rulings are to remain in force.

Birkett argued vehemently against us, saying we had to first become immigrants. Going further, she quoted Citizenship Minister Denis Coderre, who said this about restoring citizenship for the Lost Canadians: "I have listened to the concerns of former Canadians... and I'm willing to apply more lenient rules to these cases... To this end, I have asked my officials to ensure that these cases are dealt with as quickly as possible under Canada's current immigration and citizenship legislation."[4]

The senators didn't buy it. They asked about Magali Castro-Gyr and why, if Coderre and CIC were so lenient, she was forced into court. Birkett's response? "You are aware that I cannot talk about the individual case and reveal any information." That was typical of how the politicians and bureaucrats justified not answering questions, and the media pretty much always let them get away with it.

This book opens with an account of United Flight 811. Can you imagine the safety investigators in the case asking particular questions about an accident, only to be told by the so-called experts, "We do not discuss individual accidents or incidents"? How would the truth ever be discovered? It wouldn't. Yet here were our senators asking specific questions about the operation of law and how it affected Canadians, and both the citizenship minister and his bureaucrats hid behind a shield of silence. How could the top legislators write proper law when they were denied the facts? They couldn't, and the bureaucrats knew it.

Birkett went on, justifying the continued discrimination by CIC, rationalizing her opposition to Bill S-17 by saying, "My notion of fair is that everyone is treated the same. In 2004, I am still answering people, saying[,] here are the rules about resuming. I would like to continue having the same answer and not suddenly change and say 'Now we decided that even if you did something back in 1952 we have changed the rules.' That is not fair. For me, 'fair' means we have consistent rules and apply them the same way to everyone. Fairness in the sense of what is nice or kind is a different issue."

Under that logic (or illogic), women would never achieve equality of rights. It would be like arguing that because mothers and grandmothers in 1952 had fewer rights than men, it wasn't fair to give young daughters equal rights in 2004.

And that was what we were up against. Who would have guessed that, twenty-two years after the passing of the Charter of Rights and Freedoms, Canada, of all countries, seemed to do everything possible to discriminate against Canadians? The next week, Charles and I went back to the West Block to tell our stories. We were ushered into a waiting room until it was our turn to testify. Having just arrived from Australia—it was my third round-trip that month—I was wiped out. Charles sat upright in a chair while I slumped in a stupor. When it came time for us to speak, Charles kicked at my extended feet, saying, "We're on." We made our way down the corridor to the committee room, where we sat at the end of a rectangular table, behind the microphones designated for witnesses.

Charles began by saying that Bill S-17 was designed to correct an inequity in existing law. He broke it down into four categories: children born before 1977, those born after, children born in Canada, and those born elsewhere. Of the four, only one group had difficulty getting citizenship: the Lost Canadian kids born in Canada before 1977. Basically, members of the other three groups simply had to inform the minister that they wished to be Canadian and that was it. For us, we were forced to become immigrants, prove our connection to the country, pay fees, and still often be denied. Let me explain it this way: You were Canadian if you were (a) born in Canada on or after February 15, 1977, or (b) born outside Canada to a Canadian parent on, before, or after February 15, 1977. Conversely, you could be denied citizenship if you were born in Canada before February 15, 1977, and, while you were a minor child, your "responsible parent" took out citizenship in another country.

Here are Charles's words:

> [Citizenship] ... is a different situation for those people who were born in Canada before 1977.
>
> The testimony received before the committee last week from the department is that these people—we will call them the lost Canadians— should be treated fairly. The definition of "fairness" is that they are treated the same as everyone else...
>
> There is no oath requirement for two of these [citizenship] categories but the lost Canadians are required to take an oath. There is a waiting period to be admitted for immigration. This does not affect the people in the first two columns on your chart, but it is applied against the lost Canadians. There is a one-year waiting period required after immigration for lost Canadians but for no one else. Permanent residency is required of the lost Canadians but not of the other two categories. Citizenship is automatic upon application for the first two categories but not for the lost Canadians. Lost Canadians have the distinction of being subject to the security and criminality checks, not once but twice, while neither of the other categories must undergo them.
>
> I guess I would liken this situation to this: You get to choose your friends but not your relatives. The Department of Citizenship and Immigration came before this committee last week and said clearly that what it wants to do with these lost Canadians is choose its relatives. I do not dispute for a moment there may be some people who might have come back to Canada under Bill S-17, if it were enacted, that I might not want to invite to dinner; but I do not get to choose my relatives and this is not an immigration matter.[5]

Then Charles brought up a point that CIC had ignored:

> I want to mention something that does not come up very often. There seems to be ... an emphasis on demonstrating one's attachment to Canada and whether these [people] are really Canadians. After all, you left at age 5 or age 10. What do you know? I would point out that the first five years or so of anyone's life are probably the most impressionable years and I think that any number of psychological studies would bear that out.

It is worth keeping that in mind when, let us say, a family moves to the United States, it can be likened to a bubble moving across the 49th parallel. They do not shed their Canadian ethics, values or ways by virtue of crossing the border—all of that moves with them, especially for someone like me, who was thoroughly familiar and in love with the icons of Canada and what they stood for, as I understood them at that tender age.

At this point, the red "on" light beneath Charles's microphone extinguished and mine illuminated, signalling that it was my turn to speak:

Canada seems to have an identity problem. The country does not really seem to know what being a Canadian citizen is, but when it comes to defining what is not a Canadian, clearly it is a lost Canadian child. This is really Canada's shame. What kinds of parents turn their backs on their own children?

CIC has been consistent in saying that we are not citizens. They are inconsistent on almost everything else . . .

We are guilty only of having a father who took out citizenship in another country when we were minor children. We are guilty of being in love with our homeland. Sometimes I ask myself why in the world I am doing this [trying to get back to Canada]. I have come to know some of the Tuskegee Airmen, a contingent of black pilots who flew in World War II . . . Last July, and again about one month ago, I was at one of their conventions. I keep asking them about after the war, when they were in France, where they were treated so well, and yet they returned to the United States of the 1940s, when being black was not the same as it is now. They said they did it. I related so well. They said they did it because they had to correct it [the injustice] for the next generation. There was something wrong in their country and they could not turn their backs on it.*

The question I asked merits consideration. What kind of parent would turn their back against their own children? What impression would you have of a parent who actively distanced themselves from their kids?

The senators wholeheartedly agreed with Charles and me. To them, the issue was a no-brainer, despite the majority in the Red Chamber being

---

* In my testimony in 2004, I talked about the Tuskegee Airmen being based in France. Today I stand corrected. The Tuskegee Airmen's 332nd squadron, composed of the 99th, 100th, 301st, and 302nd fighter groups, were all based in Italy, not France, and for the most part the Italians treated the men of the 332nd with respect and dignity.

Liberal. I had never seen cooperation like this in the House, where MPs constantly went for the jugular. In the Senate, although without question there's partisanship, the killer election instincts didn't dominate the senators' every thought. Instead of encountering the antagonistic attitude so prevalent at CIC and in the House, we worked in a spirit of cooperation. The senators were much more interested in common sense than in the hot-off-the-press Ekos polls. What a refreshing delight.

Our problem came the next day, when Patricia Birkett went back on her warpath, submitting a response to the committee, and in one moment changing everything:

> Witnesses mentioned a special provision of the current Act which gives access to citizenship to children born in wedlock outside Canada to Canadian mothers under the former Act (under the former Act, children born in wedlock could only derive citizenship only through their father.) This provision has been subject to Supreme Court rulings as it affects a provision that was seen to be discriminatory by virtue of the situation of a person's birth. This provision was included in the Act as a transitional clause and will expire on August 14, 2004.[6]

In those last eighteen words, she announced that CIC would not uphold the Supreme Court decision in *Benner v. Canada*. Giving a drop-dead date of August 14, the bureaucracy would, in just three and a half months, restore the previous policy of actively discriminating against women. A unanimous Supreme Court decision, the Charter, and human rights were of no concern to CIC, and not one senator or MP picked up on the ramifications of Birkett's announcement.

How can Canadian bureaucrats overrule the Supreme Court? They can't, but they did. How so? Because no one challenged their actions. Not the media, not even the Canadian Bar Association. Maybe the CBA was too busy doing other things, like calling for the repatriation of Omar Khadr—after all, he was a minor when he fought as a child soldier alongside the terrorists. To us Lost Canadians, it felt like a double standard, the CBA speaking out for Omar Khadr while saying nothing for Lost Canadian children who were also minors when they lost their rights. I can only surmise that either the CBA was asleep at the wheel, not knowing what CIC was up to, or it didn't care. For it to allow a bureaucrat to defy a Supreme Court ruling, effectively cancelling it, is a big deal in setting legal precedent. I believe that the CBA should have to explain its silence on that issue, and on that of the Lost Canadians. And I'm glad pilots don't fly airplanes with the same apparent complacency as the CBA or the Canadian media—there'd be a lot of dead bodies scattered around the smoking wreckage.

Despite the impending August deadline, Bill S-17 sailed through the Senate with unanimous support, arriving in the House for first reading on May 7.[7] Its counterpart, Bill C-503, sat idle, collecting dust in the House. What a stark difference in efficiency between the Senate and the House.

What happened next simultaneously killed three citizenship bills: C-503, S-17, and C-18.[8] An election was called. Jean Chrétien stepped down as prime minister in December 2003, replaced by Paul Martin Jr. How ironic that it was Martin's father, Paul Sr., who was the main mover behind the 1947 Citizenship Act. I would have thought the son would correct his dad's discriminatory mistakes, the '47 act obviously being a product of its time. Many Canadians fell victim to its inequalities. Sure it was wrong, but that was Canada in the 1940s. Sadly, it also turned out to be Canada of the 2000s, as Martin wasn't about to correct his father's mistake. At one point, a senator asked me if there was something I'd like to say to the parliamentarians and CIC. My response was quick and to the point: "I'd give them the same advice I'd give to my kids when they make a mistake: admit it, apologize, correct it, then go on." But that wasn't Paul Martin's style, nor his party's, nor CIC's.

Two things of significance occurred before the election. In March, Magali flew back from Switzerland—the government had capitulated and offered her citizenship through a section 5.4 grant, which allowed the "application for resumption of citizenship under section 8 by a person who is 18 years of age or older." By now, the financial damage was severe—she and her family had been decimated after being forced to sell their home to pay huge court costs and lawyers' fees and, adding insult to injury, moving costs from Canada to Switzerland, her husband's homeland. Nonetheless, Magali still wanted to be Canadian, again. The one consolation was that the government offered to pay her cab fare to the private swearing-in ceremony.

Together we flagged a taxi, paying the driver with a CIC-provided chit— all we had to do was fill in the amount and add a gratuity. We came really close to tipping the driver the same amount Magali spent on legal fees: $20,000. Arriving just minutes before the designated time, we saw several bigwigs already there. Some were from CIC, others were MPs. I stood next to Magali, and when she was finally pronounced a citizen, she broke down weeping. She turned toward me and we hugged for a long moment. I was the only one in the room who fully understood the unmitigated devastation of denial. With tears in her eyes also, knowing what the government had put Magali through, the citizenship judge told her that not only was it an honour to be the presiding judge but that restoring Magali's Canadian citizenship was without question the most significant moment of her judicial career. Even the CIC folks smiled in approval. Just days later, Magali returned to Switzerland, the family not having the money to move to Canada. Nor did they have jobs waiting in Canada—those were given up when they were forced to leave. Besides, her husband no longer held Canada in high esteem. Who could blame him?

On May 17, 2004, in *Augier v. Canada*, the Federal Court ruled that a section of the current Citizenship Act specifically dealing with born-out-of-wedlock children was unconstitutional.[9] It was quite a blow to CIC's temperament and legal standing. This was what happened.

Gideon McGuire Augier was born out of wedlock in St. Lucia in 1966. His father was allegedly a Canadian citizen and his mother, a permanent resident. In September 2002, Gideon applied for proof of Canadian citizenship, claiming to have derived status from his natural father. CIC determined that, since Gideon was born out of wedlock, outside Canada, pursuant to the legislation then in force, Canadian citizenship could be derived only from his mother, and because she wasn't Canadian at the time of his birth, the application for proof of citizenship was refused.

The court ruled that being born out of wedlock could not be a factor for denial of citizenship.[10] Augier won. He was deemed Canadian. Once again, CIC, just as with the *Benner* case, had been contravening the Charter. The bureaucracy despised both decisions. Truth be told, Birkett's drop-dead date of August 14, 2004, had the double effect of also undermining the *Augier* decision. To the informed, it appeared obvious that her recent declaration to the Senate was a calculated effort to ignore both court rulings. Sadly, the Canadian public didn't know about this. There were few checks and balances on the government. In Canada, the bureaucrats, not the politicians, seemed to rule the roost. It is akin to our ambassador in Libya dictating Canadian policy to the prime minister. The chain of command seemed completely backward. The bureaucrats could covertly do almost anything and get away with it.[11]

After months of media outreach, I got one broadcaster in all of Canada, CBC, to tell the story of CIC's spurning the *Benner* and *Augier* decisions, a story that ran just hours before the August deadline. It was August 13, three and a half months since Birkett's bombshell in the Senate committee meeting. The next day, August 14, CIC's self-imposed drop-dead date would take effect, allowing the government the freedom to once again discriminate against women, blatantly violating both the Charter and the Supreme Court decision.[12] In time, it provoked many lawsuits against CIC, at great taxpayers' expense. In the first case to be argued, Wayne Babcock challenged the government without benefit of counsel and won.[13] This sort of accomplishment by an individual is quite a feat: it meant that his arguments were rock solid. To the courts, the truth was obvious. After all, the real decision had already been rendered by the Supreme Court. Where else but Canada would a lower court be called upon to uphold a higher court's ruling? The illogic of it all was shocking, especially when the government was taking direct aim against its own people.

On October 4, Parliament reconvened and, just two days later, a new Lost Canadian bill, S-2, emerged in the Senate. The bill was an exact remake of S-17.[14] Two weeks after that, it had its second reading. Eight days later, it was discussed in committee. Then another five days and it went to third reading.[15] One of the sponsors, Senator Nöel Kinsella (Conservative), stated: "In 1977, parliamentarians recognized that there were deficiencies in the Citizenship Act of 1947... Bill S-2 will remedy the lacuna."[16]

Liberal senator Joan Cook continued, "Honourable senators, we have an extraordinary opportunity to right a wrong and to give meaningful consideration to those individuals who have been disadvantaged by the operation of the 1947 Citizenship Act."

In less than four weeks, the Senate unanimously passed the bill and in the process proved the impotence of the House of Commons, where John Reynolds and Andrew Telegdi anxiously awaited their turns.

It was a first for Parliament. I was told that never before had the House pre-studied a bill from the Senate. Andrew Telegdi, as chairman of the House Citizenship Committee, began discussions before S-2 made it to first reading. Andrew anticipated, and was correct in his assumption of, its lightning-speed passage through the Red Chamber. He had personally lobbied several Liberal senators on our behalf. On November 15, S-2 was first read in the House, then referred to committee.[17] It sure helps having allies, especially when the Conservatives were chomping at the bit to call another election, which would once again kill the bill, since any bills not passed into law would die on the order paper once legislature was dissolved. All our work would have been for naught. While Telegdi steered his committee on a direct course to our finish line, S-2 wouldn't get to second reading in the House for another three months.

The last quarter of 2004 proved to be jam-packed with news and events.

Because the US government has the right to charter civilian airliners for troop movement, in mid-October, as a commercial airline pilot, and particularly a wide-body 747-400 pilot, I was flying US troops to the war in Iraq. It was incredibly sobering taking young men and women to a war zone and then picking up others, sometimes in coffins, for the return trip home. I couldn't imagine the terror of being dropped off halfway around the world for combat.

It's almost impossible to imagine sixty-plus years from now the US government cancelling these soldiers' citizenship, telling them they weren't welcome. But that's exactly what Canada was doing to its World War II vets. By now, war-bride children had started calling me, reporting how CIC was denying them citizenship. Same thing with some of the military brats—children of Canadian soldiers who'd been born outside Canada.[18] One woman called, saying her husband had been Canada's most decorated pilot in World War II; indeed, Queen Elizabeth personally recognized his achievements. He died disenfranchised, despite being born in Canada. And now, by golly, CIC was telling her she wasn't Canadian either. She lived in Alberta. I vowed to keep up the fight—not for me but for them.

Citizenship Minister Judy Sgro announced the theme of Citizenship Week, to be held October 18 to 24: Celebrating Freedom, Respect, and Belonging.[19] Lost Canadians must have cringed. Without citizenship we weren't free to do anything in Canada. We didn't have the government's respect, nor did we belong. The theme was nothing but a lie. CIC got away with it because the media simply went with it, yet on the issue of Lost Canadians, they remained largely silent. Sgro refused to meet with me. Her chief of staff, Ihor Wons, made it clear it was because I had gone to the media.

Soon after, George W. Bush won his 2004 re-election bid. Two days later, I was in Ottawa at D'Arcy McGee's pub with Charles Bosdet and Kevin Bosch. Kevin worked for the Liberal Party in the Office of the Prime Minister. Our conversation centred on the Lost Canadians, but with Bush back for another four years, the election results entered into our conversation, which went something like this:

Bosch: "Yesterday, more than 200,000 Americans went onto CIC's website, asking what it would take to get into Canada."

Bosdet: "What are you going to do?"

Bosch: "We don't want them."

Me: "Why not?"

Bosch: "Because they're the smart ones. If we take them, what's left? We need those people to stay in the States to stand up against Bush."

Put that way, all we could do was laugh. It seems Bush's "resistance" would not be coming to Canada. Nor, apparently, were the Lost Canadians. For sure Prime Minister Paul Martin was not our ally. A few weeks later, he was in Kelowna, home territory for CBC's Gary Symons. Gary cornered the prime minister and asked him about our issue. Martin hemmed and hawed, saying he wasn't certain if he'd support the Lost Canadians with Bill S-2. He admitted we'd lost our citizenship unfairly through an obscure section of a past Citizenship Act but then stated, "There are very important issues of fairness here. Obviously, equity is something that all of us support, but, at the same time, there are a number of questions that have to be answered, that have to be reviewed, and that's what the minister [Judy Sgro] said that she wants to do."[20] I found his comments dumbfounding considering that his citizenship minister refused to discuss the issue with us. Martin was busy drafting equal rights legislation for same-sex couples, and his own Liberal senators had unanimously voted in our favour. I felt he was ignoring his own Senate.

Imagine air traffic control warning a captain that if he doesn't immediately climb or turn, the aircraft will impact the mountain in forty seconds. Captain Martin responds: "What did the flight attendant say was for dinner?"

Co-pilot: "Steak or chicken."

Captain Martin: "I'll have the steak."

Aircraft impacts mountain. There are no survivors. From that day forward, I called Paul Martin "Captain Steak or Chicken."

In aviation, we work as a team, and everyone trusts each other. In the matter of Lost Canadians, while the Senate made its understanding of the issue "unanimously" clear, there was little to no teamwork within the government of Canada. The House, supposedly representatives of the people, ignored the Senate, implying it believed the Canadian people just didn't care.

On the afternoon of November 30, Bill S-2 was discussed in Parliament. Although the debates had their moments, the real festivities were going on just outside Centre Block, where George W. Bush was stopping in for a state visit. Crowds stood at the entrance. Something like 13,000-plus protesters objected to Bush's visit.[21] Security was so tight, you couldn't get a rubber band past the guards. No one was allowed into Parliament except those on official business. Andrew Telegdi escorted me through underground tunnels and, when I got to the spectator section to watch the MPs debate the merits of S-2, I was the only one there: the visitors' gallery was empty.

All of us, even the MPs, were abundantly aware of the masses outside the walls of Parliament chanting and carrying signs, all in unison against the US president. I couldn't help but recall the remarks of Jean Chrétien's communications staffer Françoise Ducros when she called Bush a moron.[22] It made worldwide news, with many in Canada, including Harper, calling for her resignation. Yet I kept thinking, *But he is a moron*. At precisely 1 p.m., the acting Speaker announced the House would proceed to its private members' business. John Reynolds took the floor and began to speak:

> This is also a story of a federal department, citizenship and immigration, that has run amok and roughshod over the wishes of Parliament, its political masters, and over the rights of the Canadian-born individuals we call the lost Canadians.
>
> It is there in the Department of Citizenship and Immigration where the real resistance is to recognizing and returning the lost Canadian children to their birthright.
>
> In that department, decisions are made to allow known war criminals and fugitives from justice and those accused of genocide to land and claim the protection of the charter of rights.
>
> It is in that department where we can find the fiercest resistance to allowing the lost Canadian children to reclaim their birthright and their Canadian citizenship.
>
> It is that department that the citizenship and immigration committee of this House should be closely investigating to determine why there is such willingness to thwart the will of Parliament...
>
> ... It is time to bring these lost Canadians home. It is time to tell the world we no longer believe that married women and children are mere chattels of the husband and the father. It is time to tell the world that Canada no longer believes that married women, children, lunatics and idiots are all categorized as somehow being lesser human beings.
>
> It is time for this Parliament to welcome the lost Canadian children home...
>
> Canadians are also mystified as to how a foreign-born stripper can be fast-tracked by the immigration minister after working on the minister's election campaign, while a Canadian-born, outstanding individual like Don Chapman, like so many others, gets the cold shoulder.
>
> Should Mr. Chapman have flown to Toronto to work on the campaign of the minister? Would that have endeared him to her sufficiently enough for her to order her bureaucrats to give him back his Canadian citizenship?[23]

Citizenship Minister Sgro at around this time was being hammered in Parliament about the Romanian stripper scandal. At the end of November, allegations surfaced against Sgro that she had accepted campaign donations for the Liberal party from an owner of a strip club and, in turn, was in a position to fast-track Romanian strippers wanting to work in Canada.[24] One woman who worked for Sgro during her re-election campaign was granted a special residence permit to stay in Canada. Sgro defended this, saying she offered it on humanitarian grounds.

I'm not taking a position regarding the merits of allowing or denying strippers into Canada; nor am I attacking Ms. Sgro personally. But to me, a Lost Canadian, it was outrageous giving higher consideration to foreign strippers over Canadian-born children. I even contemplated asking a restaurant proprietor friend in Gibsons to have a Lost Canadian stripper night. Maybe then we'd get Sgro's attention. In the House, the MPs were blasting the minister and questioning the ethics and possible conflict of interest violations. It would not be the only time Minister Sgro would find herself under fire. On January 13, 2005, she resigned as citizenship minister. Five months later, federal ethics commissioner Bernard Shapiro concluded that there had been an apparent conflict of interest for two members of her staff.[25] In a sense, Sgro reminded me of the line from the movie *Field of Dreams*, "If you build it, he will come." Just change the verbiage to "If there's a scandal, she'll be in it." She was.

Next to speak was Liberal Don Boudria:

The hon[ourable] member [John Reynolds] raised a very good point as regards children born of a Canadian father and a foreign mother. It seems extremely unfair to me that, currently, the child of a Canadian father and a foreign mother is a Canadian—we are talking about pre-1977 cases—while the child of a Canadian mother and a foreign father is not. From a biological point of view, it is easy to see that this is ridiculous. If anything, it should at least be the contrary. There would then be some semblance of fairness. In fact, some religious denominations—such as the Jewish religion—are based on the principle that the only parent who can always be recognized is, by definition, the mother. It seems to me that there is an element of unfairness in the existing legislation. I mentioned it on several occasions and it should be corrected.[26]

Before it was over, Meili Faille (Bloc Québécois), Bill Siksay (NDP), and Andrew Telegdi (Liberal) stood in our defence, with the only opposition coming from Liberal Hedy Fry. Fry was then parliamentary secretary to Sgro, which meant that Fry simply echoed Paul Martin's official stance against us. The Liberal Party wanted us to be immigrants, over and out—no more discussion. Fry was the only member of the Citizenship Committee to oppose us. How ironic that Trinidad and Tobago, the country she was from, corrected its own convoluted citizenship law similar to the law that I was fighting in Canada, our common British ancestry being responsible for it.[27] In 2000, that country brought back all their Lost Trinidadians, which means Fry was eligible to regain her citizenship in Trinidad and Tobago. What was fair for her was not fair for us.

When Parliament recessed for the evening, I left along with the others. Not by the way I arrived, through the tunnels, but directly out the front door of Centre Block. When it opened, the 13,000-plus protesters fell silent. They knew Parliament was off-limits because of the Jr. Bush visit, so, logically, whoever emerged had to be a huge VIP. For a moment, the protesters looked at me and I stared back. They were on their side of the police barrier and I was on mine. After a brief pause I walked up to the barricade, jumped over it, and joined the Bush protest. The crowd went wild with delight. The next day, *Vancouver Sun* columnist Daphne Bramham wrote about the incident, saying my dislike of Bush alone proved how Canadian I was.

For the Christmas holidays, from December 16 through to January 30—forty-six straight days—parliamentarians went home. For the entire year of 2004, our MPs graced their Ottawa offices just 101 times, taking 265 days off. In their defence, it *was* a leap year.

On January 31, 2005, they were back and raring to go. Unfortunately, in my estimation, the new citizenship minister, Joe Volpe, wasn't just as bad as Judy Sgro—he was far worse. Things can get done quickly if the government wants them to. The Liberals' same-sex marriage bill, C-38, got introduced for first reading on February 2 and put into law on July 20. Bill S-2, on the other hand, was my fifth legislative attempt, and now, out there at the same time as C-38, it put Paul Martin between a rock and a hard place. First, how could he argue equal rights for one group and not for the other? Second, his own Liberal senators had made wonderful supporting speeches for S-2, then voted unanimously for its passage in the Red Chamber. Yet, in the House, Martin stood staunchly opposed. If he defied his senators, he risked degrading the institution of the Senate. But by capitulating he went against his own convictions. Captain Steak or Chicken responded by doing something he was noted for. He waffled.

To be successful, Martin had to be the political equivalent of a master

juggler, smiling with one corner of his mouth while frowning with the other.
His lips had to move in opposite directions. Exactly two weeks after its introduction, C-38 was debated on the floor. Paul Martin was the first to speak.
To the legions of Lost Canadians who heard the speech, his words about
equality and Charter rights rang hollow:

> I rise in support of a Canada in which liberties are safeguarded, rights are
> protected and the people of this land are treated as equals under the law.
>
> This is an important day. The attention of our nation is focused on
> this chamber in which John Diefenbaker introduced the Bill of Rights
> and in which Pierre Trudeau fought to establish the Charter of Rights and
> Freedoms.
>
> Our deliberations will not be merely about a piece of legislation or sec-
> tions of legal text. More deeply they will be about the kind of nation we are
> today and the nation we want to be...
>
> ... I stand before members here today and before the people of our
> country to say that I believe in and I will fight for the Charter of Rights. I
> believe in and I will fight for a Canada that respects the foresight and the
> vision of those who created and entrenched the charter. I believe in and I
> will fight for a future in which generations of Canadians to come, Canadi-
> ans born here and abroad, have the opportunity to value the charter as we
> do today, as an essential pillar of our democratic freedom...
>
> ... All of us have been elected to serve here as parliamentarians. And,
> as public legislators, we are responsible for serving all Canadians and pro-
> tecting the rights of all Canadians...
>
> The charter was enshrined to ensure that the rights of minorities are
> not subjected—are never subjected—to the will of the majority. The rights
> of Canadians who belong to a minority group must always be protected
> by virtue of their status as citizens, regardless of their numbers, and these
> rights must never be left vulnerable to the impulses of the majority.
>
> We embrace freedom and equality in theory. We must also embrace
> them in fact...
>
> The charter is the living document. It is the heartbeat of our Constitution.
>
> It is also a proclamation. It declares that as Canadians we live under a
> progressive and inclusive set of fundamental beliefs about the value of the
> individual. It declares that we are all lessened when any one of us is denied
> a fundamental right...
>
> For those who value the charter yet oppose the protection of rights...
> I ask them: if the Prime Minister and a national government are willing to

take away the rights of one group, what is there to say that they will stop at that? If the charter is not there today to protect the rights of one minority, then how can we as a nation of minorities ever hope, ever believe, and ever trust that it will be there to protect us tomorrow?

My responsibility as Prime Minister, my duty to Canada and to Canadians, is to defend the charter in its entirety, not to pick and choose the rights that our laws will protect and those that are to be ignored, not to declare those who shall be equal and those who shall not be equal. My duty is to protect the charter as some in this House will not . . .

Why is the charter so important? We have only to look at our own history. Unfortunately, Canada's story is one in which not everyone's rights were protected under the law. We have not been free from discrimination. We have not been free from bias or unfairness. There have been blatant inequalities. Remember that it was once thought perfectly acceptable to deny women personhood and the right to vote. There was a time not so long ago when if one wore a turban one could not serve in the RCMP. The examples are many, but what is important now is that they are part of our past, not our present.

Over time, perspectives changed. We evolved and we grew and our laws evolved and grew with us. That is as it should be. Our laws must reflect equality, not as we understood it a century or even a decade ago, but as we understand it today . . .

The people of Canada have worked hard to build a country that opens its doors to include all, regardless of their differences; a country that respects all, regardless of their differences; and a country that demands equality for all, regardless of their differences.

If we do not step forward, then we will step back. If we do not protect a right, then we deny it. Together as a nation, together as Canadians, let us step forward.[28]

All of the above suggested only one thing to me: that, in regard to S-2, Paul Martin could speak with a forked tongue. Behind the scenes he was allowing some of his cabinet ministers to actively fight against the Lost Canadians, which meant, for me to win with S-2, all I had to do was overcome the prime minister of Canada.

CHAPTER 6

OTTAWA'S NITTY-GRITTY, DOWN-AND-DIRTY SHENANIGANS

I am convinced that the truest act of courage, the strongest act of manliness, is to sacrifice ourselves for others in a totally non-violent struggle for justice.

CAESAR CHAVEZ

FROM WINTER TO early spring 2005, developments in Ottawa were happening fast and furious. Keeping pace were Magali Castro-Gyr, Charles Bosdet, Jeff Wan, and me—the Four Musketeers, if you will—operating in overdrive like a fine-tuned racing car bearing down on the checkered flag.*
We needed parliamentarians to stay put in Ottawa, which wasn't the forte of cynical politicians. To be successful, we'd have to outmanoeuvre both Prime Minister Paul Martin and his new citizenship minister, Joe Volpe.

We also needed luck on our side, as we weren't the only ones bearing down on the Liberals. Similar to lions in the Serengeti, the Conservatives were anxious to pounce, ready to use any opportunity whatsoever.

Two bills sat before Parliament—C-38 (same-sex marriage) and S-2 (Lost Canadians). Martin fully supported one while opposing the other. Picture two horses racing next to each other, one given steroids to make it run faster, the other, a tranquilizer to make it sleepy. Which is more likely to win? Without the prime minister's support, S-2 was the legislative equivalent of the

---

* This chapter is dedicated to Magali Castro-Gyr, Charles Bosdet, and Jeff Wan.

77

latter. We headed into the last remaining parliamentary stretch. *Would the bills survive to the finish?* Both would die if an election was called.

Earlier, I mentioned that Hedy Fry, a native Trinidadian and parliamentary secretary to the citizenship minister, had benefited from Trinidad and Tobago correcting its citizenship legislation in 2000, removing from its books the same archaic laws that I was fighting in Canada. Following that country's lead, Australia was getting ready to welcome back its Lost Australians. By now, almost every former British colony had either already done so or was about to change its similar-worded, nonsensical, leftover British laws of identity. Canada was one of the last holdouts. As an airline pilot, I've noticed that the mood of a crew seems inexorably tied to the personality of the captain. Competent and personable leaders radiate mellowness to the crew. It works the same way in politics and in business. CEOs tend to surround themselves with like-minded people. So, if the CEO is personable and competent, I'd expect he or she would hire people who shared similar values. To me, the appointment of Joe Volpe as the new citizenship minister reflected the ethics of Paul Martin. In time, I found both men to be tremendous disappointments. Volpe's mother was Canadian, but because she married an Italian prior to 1947, and since the Canadian laws at the time treated married women as chattels of their husbands, she had lost her Canadian status upon marriage.[1] Afterward, the couple lived in Italy, where young Giuseppe Joseph "Joe" Volpe was born, on September 21, 1947, in the hill town of Monteleone di Puglia. His having a former Canadian mother was not relevant to CIC, so, for Joe to get Canadian citizenship, he first had to become an immigrant. I couldn't help but wonder whether this led him to make sure all Lost Canadians would be forced to do the same. It mattered not that most of us were born in Canada to Canadian parents, and our fathers had fought for Canada in World War II. One time, on camera, Volpe looked directly at me and said, "If I had to become an immigrant, then so do you." It seemed that Mr. Volpe had a mean streak. And with boss Paul Martin not embracing Lost Canadians, it came as no surprise that he'd appoint a less-than-enthusiastic citizenship minister.

On February 10, S-2 was debated, with the NDP, Liberals, and Conservatives all weighing in. In the House, Joe Comartin of the NDP got things started with a profound statement: "Mr. Speaker, this private member's bill should not be here because it is such a ridiculous set of circumstances that has brought the bill before the House. The issue should have been taken care of by the government quite a long time ago. I will set the scene. I have no doubt that the bill will pass because we are in a minority government situation and all of the opposition parties are in support of the bill. It is going to pass at some stage in the process."[2] Next came Massimo Pacetti, a Liberal MP who spoke against us. How ironic that five years later he would introduce Bill C-302, the Italian-Canadian Recognition and Restitution Act that promulgated itself "an act to recognize the injustice that was done to persons of Italian origin through their 'enemy alien' designation and internment during the Second World War, and to provide for restitution and promote education on Italian-Canadian history."[3] Pacetti was hot-to-trot to acknowledge and correct past injustices against Italian-Canadians, but when it came to Lost Canadians, he was okay with keeping those past mistakes alive. The big concern motivating the Liberals was that if Lost Canadians were not first vetted through the immigration process, criminals would be allowed into Canada. While the argument sounds reasonable, past criminal activity was a huge part of the Supreme Court decision in *Benner*, where the court ruled it could not be a factor in denying Benner citizenship. It was also one of Charles Bosdet's points—that people can't pick their family. We were born Canadian citizens, and now, if the Liberals had their way, we'd be the only Canadian-born citizens in the world having to first pass a type of litmus test before being accepted.

Less than a week later, on February 16, the Liberal Party opposed S-2 as introduced. John Reynolds responded:

> Last week the member for Saint-Léonard–Saint-Michel [Massimo Pacetti] said that Bill S-2... could allow serious criminals to reacquire Canadian citizenship and return to Canada. This week the Conservative Party has learned that a convicted repeat sexual predator will soon be living again in Canada.
>
> A 33-year-old refugee was convicted of two separate sexual assaults on young girls, the second while on probation for the first. We know that following those sexual attacks he returned to Afghanistan from where he had originally fled. Now he is back and the Liberals have granted him refugee status again on compassionate and humanitarian grounds.[4]

Exactly an hour and fifteen minutes later, Paul Martin took the floor to talk about C-38 and same-sex marriage. Let me reiterate:

> I rise in support of a Canada in which liberties are safeguarded, rights are protected and the people of this land are treated as equals under the law... as public legislators, we are responsible for serving all Canadians

and protecting the rights of all Canadians... We embrace freedom and
equality in theory. We must also embrace them in fact ... My responsibility
as Prime Minister, my duty to Canada and to Canadians, is to defend the
charter in its entirety, not to pick and choose the rights that our laws will
protect and those that are to be ignored, not to declare those who shall be
equal and those who shall not be equal. My duty is to protect the charter."

As I watched, from the gallery above, the parliamentarians comparing
C-38 to S-2, the prime minister seemed hypocritical. How could he support equal rights for one group but not the other? I felt it was nothing but
double-talk. Incredibly, no MP challenged him, asking why he opposed
equal rights for Lost Canadians yet favoured them for everyone else. Two
hours later, S-2 was read a second time, then immediately voted on. Our
multi-year efforts were on the line. A no vote meant that everything we'd
accomplished to date would disappear, whereas a yes vote kept the bill, and
its chances of eventual passage, alive.

Fortunately, it passed—not due to Liberal support, but rather because all
three opposition parties were now solidly behind us. Exactly as the NDP had
predicted, the Liberals as a minority government couldn't muster enough
votes for denial. It also helped that Liberal Andrew Telegdi had converted
several of his party colleagues to vote in our favour, which meant that Paul
Martin was now boxed in from all directions. Not giving in to defeat, Martin
and Volpe would soon be attacking S-2 from a different direction.

As this was happening, four other war-bride children contacted me, but
only after discovering that they too had just been designated as being not
Canadian. Their issue hinged on the question, just when did Canadian
citizenship begin? CIC was drawing an unyielding line in the sand, insisting Canadian citizenship didn't exist prior to January 1, 1947, which, if
true, ignored several Canadian federal government statutes and Orders
in Council issued under statutory authority and decisions of the federal
courts, including the Supreme Court of Canada. Furthermore, CIC has
made such an assertion despite the fact that the attorney general of Canada in 2007 claimed before the Manitoba Court of Queen's Bench that all
inhabitants of Manitoba, except treaty Indians, became full Canadian citizens on accession of Manitoba to Canada in 1870.[5] The decision of the
Manitoba courts was upheld by the Supreme Court of Canada. In legislation and in bureaucratic handouts, there were thousands upon thousands
of references to "Canadian citizenship" before 1947, including a definitive
definition of "Canadian citizen" in the 1910 Immigration Act.[6] In addition,

for CIC to ignore previous legal stances, it also had to disregard Prime Minister Mackenzie King's comments in August 1946 when he welcomed the war brides as "Canada's newest citizens." Further, CIC was paying no attention to its own predecessors who, before the war brides disembarked at Pier 21 in 1946, handed them a pamphlet stating, "As soon as the ship docks Canadian Immigration officials will come aboard. These men will complete the formalities for your entry into Canada which automatically make you a Canadian citizen."[7] It was as though the Big Bang of CIC's Canadian citizenship universe happened on January 1, 1947, and, as with those opposed to the teaching of Darwin's theory of evolution in Tennessee schools, which led to the Scopes Monkey Trial, there would be no further discussion. Case closed. To me, it seemed the bureaucrats were leading Martin and Volpe like dogs on a leash, not the other way around. In aviation, it would be no different from a skycap telling me how to fly my airplane.

Away from the House, Andrew Telegdi set up a three-person meeting between him, Stephen Heckbert (Joe Volpe's deputy chief of staff/director of communications), and me. What came out of the meeting was a letter written by Volpe saying that the war brides were indeed Canadian on January 1, 1947. He made no mention of what they might have been before. In later years, his letter had significant ramifications in the courts.

On February 24, the Citizenship Committee met to discuss two issues: Vietnamese family reunification and Lost Canadians. The minister and top CIC officials wanted to welcome thousands of Vietnamese who'd been separated as refugees after the war, yet for Lost Canadians like us, they remained staunchly opposed. It was fascinating. Canadian kids having to be immigrants while Vietnamese families were viewed as people in need of resettlement. Like a skipping record, Hedy Fry went on the offensive, putting forth an amendment to S-2, again stipulating that we must first be immigrants.

Let me dissect just one of several deficiencies of her amendment. To apply for permanent residence in Canada en route to later applying for citizenship, most every applicant had to fit into one of three categories: (1) be a skilled worker, (2) be a student accepted by a Canadian institution of learning, or (3) bring in a lot of money, with the commitment to use it to start a new Canadian business. Obviously, these rules would exclude most (probably many thousands) who couldn't meet this criteria—like the war-bride children who'd been living in Canada for almost sixty years. It was, simply, discrimination of a different colour. Certainly, Hedy must have been aware (as parliamentary secretary, it was her job to know), and worse, she was willing to forever bar a large portion of Lost Canadians from ever regaining citizenship by invoking the requirement that they first become an immigrant. With absolutely no kind of "Canadian compassion" or acceptance whatsoever, CIC, the government, the prime minister, the citizenship minister, they all went after us in the worst way. It was brutal.

At this point, Conservative Diane Ablonczy made several telling comments about the amendment:

> This amendment would completely destroy the principle of Bill S-2. The principle is that when you are born in Canada you're a Canadian unless you choose to give up your citizenship... That means we [the politicians and bureaucrats] don't get to pick and choose—either you're a Canadian because you were born here or you're not...
>
> That brings me to my second point. Under the amendment, the federal cabinet could deny citizenship... this behind-closed-doors, without-due-process anti-democratic provision of the current Citizenship Act... says you can be stripped of citizenship or denied citizenship without any legal recourse...
>
> The third objection I have is that this is incredibly hypocritical. This is a government and a department that without any urging on the part of the U.S. wrote into the safe third country agreement huge exemptions for people who want to come to Canada to claim refugee status on the basis that they have a relative here. These people can come in without any criminal checks or medical checks at all. They just come and are in the country claiming refugee status. But get this. This is the real kicker. If the person has committed a capital crime, that in itself is a basis to admit the person into Canada to claim refugee status.[8]

What an insult. Murderers could get into Canada with no checks or balances; all they had to do was claim refugee status. Meanwhile, honest, outstanding Lost Canadians—people born in Canada as Canadian citizens— were being rejected. As Ablonczy noted, "You can't have it both ways... I see no reason to have different standards in Bill S-2 than we have in the safe third country agreement."*

Fortunately, Hedy Fry's motion was voted down, since all three opposition parties disagreed with her, as did all the other Liberals on the

---

* At one point (at the committee hearings of February 8, 2005), Ms. Ablonczy actually equated stripping citizenship from an individual to capital punishment.

committee. Had her amendment made it into s-2, the bill would have been just one more in a long line of flawed immigration laws.

The next day, the committee report on s-2 was presented to Parliament with no amendments. Hedy Fry had lost.[9] In the meantime, c-38 raced toward the parliamentary finish line while disenfranchised Vietnamese families were preparing to move to their new homes in Canada. The welcome mat had not yet been extended to the Lost Canadians.

The entire parliamentary process was difficult. Governments, like parents, are supposed to protect their offspring. Yet it was as though my siblings were favoured with special treatment while I sat listening to my parents argue about why they didn't want me. Worse, my parents wished for more kids and were adopting everyone—even murderers—yet had absolutely no desire to nurture me. How could anyone not feel the pain and agony of rejection?

Afterward, I headed to the airport for my return flight to Phoenix. Right behind me in the security queue stood Liberal cabinet minister John McCallum. I turned around and asked him how he planned to vote on s-2. After a brief pause, he asked, "How does the prime minister feel about the bill?"

I swear, if I'd been carrying a funnel like the one on the Tin Man in the *Wizard of Oz*, I'd have held it above McCallum's head and sung "If I only had a brain." Seriously, why bother having more than 300 MPs if all they're trained to do is vote as instructed by the prime minister or their party leader? It defeats the purpose of the democratic process, and it inflicts enormous cost on the taxpayers, who have to pay for hundreds and hundreds of deadheads. If MPs are going to be strict followers, voting exactly as they're told, we might just as well elect a leader from each of the major parties and give them representational votes. It would produce the same "McCallumized" results and be far cheaper in the long run.

Once back in Phoenix, I received an email from Andrew, who suggested that the beginning of May—providing the government didn't fall—would be the target date for third reading. Having experienced so many letdowns over the years, I didn't know if we should be getting ready to cry or celebrate. Feeling optimistic, I made plans to return to Ottawa, this time with my entire family.

On May 3, two of my daughters flew in from Vancouver, while my wife, my third daughter, my mother, and I arrived from Phoenix. Coming from the States, we would have to go through customs. On the plane, the flight attendants handed out declaration cards. We needed two, since my mother had her own residence. I filled out both.

After landing, we made our way to the customs hall, and then to a customs booth. My mother, with her own declaration card, waited her turn. There was never a time I didn't find it difficult filling out those damn forms. Usually, one box tripped me up, but today there were two. My problem was the question regarding nationality. Sometimes I'd write "Former Canadian." Or I'd write "Cancelled," "Revoked," "Stripped of it," or whatever came to mind. Admittedly, my answers were cheesy, but I didn't care. I wrote from the heart, and that was exactly how I felt. Almost without exception, after hearing my story, the customs officials apologized, often with raised eyebrows and a statement like "You should see the people we have to let in every day." (On rare occasions, I'd be sent to the next level, where a supervisor would key my passport number into the system, at which point a photograph of me and accompanying information would pop up on a computer screen. Then the expression on the officer's face would transform from that of "we've got a problem" to a less serious one with an ever-so-slight smile. Maybe he or she had just read warnings by former prime ministers—and the current one—as well as by the various citizenship ministers, of my capacity for shenanigans. Invariably, the officer would take a red felt pen and cross out "Revoked," replacing it with "US.") On this particular day, for "Citizenship" I had written "To be determined." For "Purpose of Trip" I wrote "To do battle with the prime minister and citizenship minister of Canada." I got waved through with no problem. Next came my eighty-nine-year-old mother. The officer took a look at her card, paused, gave her a stern glance, then called over a colleague, who asked my mother, "Ma'am, did you fill out this form?"

"No, my son did."

I was standing with my wife and daughter a few feet away on the "Welcome to Canada" side of the customs hall.

"Ma'am, could you please read this?" He pointed at the "Purpose of Trip" section, where I had written "To accompany my son, who will be doing battle with the prime minister and citizenship minister of Canada."

About all my mother could say was "Oh my. It sounds like something my son would write."

We must have made the customs officer's day. Several officers gathered after our being cleared, and we could sense their amusement. Fortunately for us, arresting an under-five-foot-tall, unsuspecting eighty-nine-year-old grandmother was not their shtick.

Now it was off to the parliamentary battlefields. Magali had flown in from Switzerland, so head to head it would be: Martin/Volpe versus Castro-Gyr/Chapman. The boxers' bell was about to ring.

The first punch came from deep inside the Liberal trenches—I imagine the MP was simply following Paul Martin's orders. Her name was Susan Kadis, a junior MP and Elinor Caplan's successor in the Ontario riding of Thornhill. Just days before s-2 was going to the final vote, Andrew Telegdi got word that his fellow party member would introduce a resolution on the House floor, in essence blocking s-2. The outcome, quite possibly, would be its demise, relegating it to the heaps of old dead bills. Knowing that time was of the essence, I called Kadis's office and asked to speak to her. Later that day, word came that she was not willing to talk to me. I ended the conversation by saying, "Okay, but she's about to make a fool out of herself. Have her call me if she'd like to know why." The call never came.

If someone said that I, as a pilot, was about to make a huge error, I'd want to know what that error was. Imagine a surgeon being warned by a nurse, "Doctor, you're about to take out the wrong lung," to which the doctor replies, "I have no time to listen to you."

But this was Ottawa, where politicians and bureaucrats are forced to listen just enough to get re-elected. Not only was Kadis about to learn a hard lesson, but she also didn't seem to have a clue what the ramifications were to Canadians if her amendment had actually been successful. Because the old laws were so discriminatory, and because they so favoured men over women, the Liberals would have created a self-induced CIC monster. Since I was born in wedlock, I lost my Canadian citizenship as a child because my Canadian father had taken out US citizenship. It had nothing to do with my mother. She didn't count. Now factor in the Kadis amendment, a security clearance amendment aimed only at Lost Canadians like me. All of a sudden, children of Canadian mothers who took out citizenship in other countries would find themselves at risk, which meant that, for thousands of current Canadian citizens, the possibility would exist that to keep their status (or to get it back if the government cancelled it), they'd first have to prove their worth and, like other Lost Canadians, go through the entire immigration process—but only if they were first deemed as being desirable. I'm sure Hedy Fry was pleased. In *Benner*, the Supreme Court had two choices: give foreign-born children of Canadian women citizenship, or cancel the citizenship to foreign-born children of Canadian fathers. Either way would produce equality. Of course, the court went with the former, granting a right rather than retroactively removing one. Martin, Volpe, and Kadis were attempting to do it the latter way.

Fortunately, behind the scenes on that day, we had two saviours. Andrew got together privately with the Speaker of the House, Peter Milliken, to explain what was happening. In law, the answer was clear, but nonetheless it helped that Milliken had been forewarned.

On the evening of May 4, my family, along with Magali, sat in the upper-level gallery looking down on the proceedings. At 6:56 p.m., following six full roll-call votes, Speaker Peter Milliken announced: "The House will now proceed to the consideration of private members' business as listed on today's order paper."[10] Not understanding the nuances of parliamentary procedure, we watched from above with bated breath.

Immediately put forward was the Kadis amendment. Now in round twelve of the boxing match, within seconds, the victor would either be the Paul Martin Liberals together with CIC or the four individuals representing tens of thousands of Lost Canadians. One side was about to take the brunt of a knockout punch.

Just a little more than a month earlier, the Globe and Mail's Ottawa correspondent John Ibbitson wrote a column about the Liberals' budget implementation bill, which was going into second reading: "The Tories could support the bill on second reading, then try to get the Kyoto clauses deleted when it goes to committee, but that would be backing down; to approve a bill on second reading is to approve it in principle."[11] Ibbitson's article was about the House of Commons Procedures and Practices, arguing that it was wrong for a party to support a bill in second reading, then try to kill it in committee. But that was exactly what the Liberals were doing with S-2.[12] Our bill passed in second reading, then passed again in committee, and now, in third reading, the Liberals were trying to attach an amendment identical to what had already been voted down in committee.* In so many words, the Paul Martin Liberals were outside the limits of

---

* With new legislation, politicians begin with a concept, which then gets written into a bill, but only after making its way through all kinds of channels—CIC, CSIS, Justice, and so on—with each giving input, if only to justify its existence. Usually a bill originates in the House (although that's not always the case), where it then goes to first reading, then to second reading, after which, if it passes the vote, it's studied in committee, with committee members free to add or subtract parts, or even kill the bill altogether. If it survives, it goes back to the House, in what's known as the report stage, for further debate (during which last-minute amendments are sometimes made), third reading, and a final vote—this time by all MPs. Then it heads to the other house (e.g., the Senate), where the process is virtually identical. The Senate conducts three full readings, interspersed with its own committee hearings. It too can add amendments (in which case, it goes back to the House of Commons). Only when debated and passed in both the House of Commons and Senate can the bill be signed into law, called royal assent. At least, that's how it's supposed to work. With all the Lost Canadian bills, pretty much everything was not done through the ordinary channels. Not only did S-2 originate in the Senate (not the House of Commons), but the House studied the bill before it even made it to first reading. That is, Bill S-2 was being studied by the House Citizenship Committee before the bill had been officially presented to them. We made all kinds of firsts in Parliament.

parliamentary protocol, and Peter Milliken knew it. The steady-as-you-go Speaker of the House delivered the knockout punch: "There is one motion in amendment standing on the Notice Paper for the report stage of Bill s-2. Motion No. 1 will not be selected as it is identical to an amendment proposed and defeated in committee. The House therefore will now proceed to the motion for concurrence at report stage."[13]

Straightaway, the bill was headed to a full vote. The Liberals were well aware of the public relations nightmare that would ensue if they didn't immediately switch sides: that of being the party that brought Canada the Charter of Rights and Freedoms yet also the party that refused to defend it. John Reynolds stood up and moved that the bill be passed in third reading. Milliken asked if the House agreed to adopt the motion. It agreed. He declared it passed unanimously. The House adjourned. The whole thing took maybe two minutes. In a rare showing of unanimity between the parties, Conservative John Reynolds and Liberal Andrew Telegdi met halfway between their seats and shook hands. Magali and I hugged, then I turned to my family. My wife, children, and mother too had given their all. We fought as a family and now it was over.

And what a feeling—Martin, Volpe, and Kadis going down in defeat. How ironic that Susan Kadis was the Liberal chairwoman of the Standing Committee on the Status of Women. To me, it was like putting Colonel Sanders in charge of the chickens.

That night, my family hosted a celebratory dinner at the parliamentary dining room. Joining us was a brand-new person who quickly became an integral part of my inner circle of Lost Canadian freedom fighters: Melynda Jarratt, one of Canada's leading historians on the World War II war brides. For the next ten years, we were comrades-in-arms in the continuing battle to right Canada's outstanding citizenship wrongs. We knew that Martin's government was in a precarious position. The Conservatives were chomping at the bit to take him down. The Ottawa rumour mill suggested it could happen at any time, and, until s-2 received royal assent, it wasn't law. Martin, of course, had one more trick up his sleeve. Would he use it? Our fear was that Martin would delay sending the bill to Governor General Adrienne Clarkson for her signature. Then, if his government fell, so too would our bill. That would be his last punch. And it wouldn't just kill s-2 but subvert the apparently unanimous will of Parliament.

Fortunately, our fears were short-lived. The next day, the bill's sponsor, Senator Nöel Kinsella, helped move mountains in getting s-2 over to Rideau Hall. After years and years of relentless effort, Magali's and my biggest concern now was getting to the Charles-Lynch Press Conference Room for our late-afternoon news conference.

Like the Bush protest where 13,000-plus people filled the Hill, that day, on May 5, probably 10,000 people showed up outside Centre Block. The opening statement in the House by Anita Neville explained why: "This House solemnly commemorates the 60th anniversary of the liberation of the Nazi concentration and death camps."[14]

Liberal human rights minister Irwin Cotler stood to give his thoughts on the lessons of the Holocaust, one of them being "the danger of silence, the consequences of indifference." Magali and I found him so hypocritical in that he never once spoke out for the Lost Canadians, and he was not only the former chairman of the House's Subcommittee on International Human Rights but also, at the time of s-2, the minister of justice and attorney general of Canada. The laws we just changed were the very laws he'd been enforcing to keep us out. For the next nine years, Cotler never once called me regarding other remaining Lost Canadian issues, retreating instead into, to use his words, "silence, [and] the consequences of indifference."[15] Outside among the massive crowds, while Prime Minister Martin and the opposition party leaders Stephen Harper, Jack Layton, and Gilles Duceppe sat together talking about the lessons of the Holocaust, Magali and I stood watching. In fifteen minutes we were to meet Senator Kinsella for our press conference.

Just inside the senators' entrance on the east side of Centre Block, we met up with Janelle Feldstein, Kinsella's chief of staff, who escorted us downstairs to the press room. There we joined the senator, and MPs Lynne Yelich and Diane Ablonczy. We stood on an elevated platform with a centre podium, behind us the flags of Canada and each province and territory. Kinsella stepped up to the microphone. The news conference, like any held there, would be piped into newsrooms across Canada.

After Kinsella spoke, Magali and I both got to say a few words. But it was Magali who stole the show. She stepped up to the podium, adjusted the microphone down to her level, looked out to the cameras and journalists, and, unscripted, said:

> Fifteen minutes ago I was listening to the prime minister and others speaking about the lessons of the Holocaust. They said that never again should a country be allowed to take away a person's identity, reducing them to being nothing more than a number. My grandfather was put to death in

Auschwitz two weeks before it was liberated sixty years ago. He was a Jewish French freedom fighter who first had his identity taken away, then [was] reduced to a number, then to ashes. Well I'm a Canadian freedom fighter. I too had my identity taken away, then [was] reduced to a number by Citizenship and Immigration Canada. Today we won the right to have our Canadian identity restored.[16]

Magali had said it all. Her words were jewels. Too bad CIC and the politicians weren't listening, because in the coming years, we'd be experiencing more CIC-induced problems. Yes, we had won. But having a right and turning that right into a reality were two entirely different things. It didn't take long for us to discover that because of a lack of will from politicians, a complacent media, and a mean-spirited bureaucracy, the potholes in our road were still there and numerous.

At the hotel late that evening, unaware that CIC was erecting another Lost Canadian roadblock, I sent an email message out to hundreds of people: "We won! A unanimous vote in favour of S-2. You are now all Canadians."

Was I ever wrong.

The next day, CBC News put out a story titled "B.C. Man Wins Citizenship Crusade." The article stated that we'd "soon be welcomed back as official Canadians," and "the new law also returns citizenship to the war brides of Canadian veterans who went overseas between 1939 and 1945—and [also to] their children."[17] Even some parliamentarians were making statements to the media, saying we were now all Canadians. They too were wrong.

A month after royal assent, CIC sent to the Canadian Press a survey the government had done on the Lost Canadians—my contact inside CIC said the person behind it was none other than Hedy Fry. The title of the Canadian Press piece about Lost Canadians was "Parliament's Move to Assist 'Lost Canadians' Out of Step with Opinion: Poll."[18] By a huge majority, those polled said no, we don't want them. It wasn't exactly a warm welcome back to the family.

But to really comprehend this answer, you first have to know the questions. Here are the survey questions, as sent to me by my insider friend:*

---

* Emphasis mine.

Individuals who **are considered a risk to national security** should **not** be able to resume their Canadian citizenship.
Yes
No

Individuals who **pose a threat to public health** should **not** be able to resume their Canadian citizenship.
Yes
No

Even if **an individual is ill** and may place a significant demand on the health care system, I still think they **should** be allowed to resume their Canadian citizenship.
Yes
No

Even if they have **criminal convictions** inside or outside Canada, these individuals **should** still be able to resume their Canadian citizenship.
Yes
No

This, obviously, is what I might have asked:

Do you believe that **men should own their women and their children**?
Yes
No

Do you believe that a country has the right to **unilaterally cancel citizenship** against women and children?
Yes
No

Do you believe the **standard for human rights** and the way Canada treats its people today should be the same as in the 1940s?
Yes
No

Do you believe that Canada should **be a leader in the world for human rights?**
Yes
No

Do you believe that the politicians and bureaucrats and media **could have done a better job** in their handling of the Lost Canadians, the war brides, and their children?
Yes
No

Think of this the next time the phone rings and you're asked to respond to a survey. Depending on how the questions are asked, the survey results can be predetermined. The government holds all the cards and, in our situation, CIC was the equivalent of a mean schoolyard bully armed with baseball bats.

Although the survey didn't come as a complete surprise, what happened next did. CIC delayed putting out the forms we Lost Canadians needed in order to apply for reinstatement. Without the ability to apply, we essentially remained locked out. Then, in a one-two punch, it said that, although I could move to Canada—after the appropriate forms were processed and approved, my fees were paid, and I'd taken the oath of citizenship—my minor-age children had to be left behind. They weren't welcome. It was the Liberal "family reunification" program in reverse.

The discrimination becomes clearer when one compares the typical Lost Canadian with another young Canadian lad who was unquestionably Canadian. I was not without sympathy for Majid Yourdkhani; his wife, Masomeh Alibegi; and their Canadian-born son, Kevin.[19] The Iranian couple claimed refugee status upon their arrival in Canada in 1995; in 1997, Kevin was born. In 2005, the parents' claim for Canadian status was denied, and the family was deported back to Iran in December of that year. The news made headlines in Canada. Even Amnesty International got involved. The point was that young Kevin was born in Canada and, as a Canadian citizen, he had rights. It wasn't that the government said Kevin couldn't live in Canada. It's just that his parents weren't welcome. And separating parents from their minor-aged child was understandably a huge human rights no-no.

At the heart of the matter was the 1990 UN Convention on the Rights of the Child, which, as a signatory, Canada was supposed to uphold. Article 7 states that a child has "the right to know and be cared for by his or her parents," while Article 9 says, "States Parties shall ensure that a child shall not be separated from his or her parents against their will."[20] In the end, because of intense media pressure, the government caved, meaning Kevin and his family were welcomed back. Not so for Lost Canadian families who remained split apart. Legally, the argument, whether it was for the Iranian family or the Lost Canadians, was identical. I was learning some hard lessons about politics at its worst.

Doing things because they are the right things to do didn't seem to be the politicians' priority. What was important to them, the reason for their being, was to preserve and secure their jobs. It mattered not which part of the government they belonged to. Bureaucrats and politicians alike were anxious to remain employed, supposedly representing the best interests of Canadians.

In *Iron Jawed Angels*, a movie about the women's suffrage movement in the US in the 1910s, Hilary Swank plays noted civil rights leader Alice Paul. In one particular scene, she's soliciting other women, mainly common labourers, to join the cause for equality of rights and voting privileges. Ms. Paul's response to a woman who shrugs her off goes to the heart of the matter: "The ruling class is the one with a voice that's heard. To be heard, you must vote. No one cares about you." How true that statement is. Far too many politicians care about their jobs, which translate into them wanting you, the voter, to cast your ballot in their favour. Period. As Lost Canadians, our group had no rights of citizenship. Hence, one of the most basic civil liberties associated with citizenship, the right to have a say in the way your country is run, had become an unattainable dream. Without the power of the ballot box, our collective voice was not heard. In the delicate mix of Ottawa politics, few people cared. Not the press, nor the bureaucrats, and certainly not the politicians.

In Kevin's case, the media were fervently chasing any and all tidbits of detail about his family. The public was enthralled with the story. Voices were raised, particularly by the powerful Canadian-Iranian community, demanding that justice be served. Everyone had their own particular self-interests: Kevin's family wanted to be in Canada. Amnesty International wanted to increase the money it takes in. The media wanted to sell advertising. And the politicians wanted to keep their jobs. As far as I could tell, nobody thought of doing something just because it was the right thing to do, or, put into Canadian lingo, "to stand on guard for thee."

I watched the story unfold with mixed emotions. Why was the Iranian family worthy of being in Canada when Canadian-born people were not? I sensed that the issue was about two things and only two things: votes and money. The Iranian community not only represented potential votes but also stirred the media's interest, which in turn kept the politicians engaged. For Amnesty International, the issue was synonymous with raising money, potentially huge donations, and not just from Canadian-Iranians. The resulting publicity for it was like a twenty-four-hour, around-the-world, neon advertisement that the fight for justice and civil rights is never-ending, and not only in human-rights hot spots like the Congo but also in Western countries like Canada. The motto for the politicians could have been "Keep the votes and money coming."

Alice Paul would have said, "Because Lost Canadians don't vote, no one cares." And she'd be right.

My other huge Ottawa lesson was this: just because a bill becomes law doesn't mean that it will accomplish what the parliamentarians intended. Here's a grade-school example. Remember the sentence game in which one person makes up a sentence, then whispers it into the ear of the person next to him or her, and that person, in turn, whispers it to the next person? After passing through the chain of people, the sentence comes back to the first person, radically different. The first time I played this was in around fourth grade. I didn't know it but, it was also my first lesson in politics.

Think of Ottawa or Washington or Canberra or London or anywhere politicians and bureaucrats gather in an attempt to come together over an issue. Although the objective of the grade-school game is to keep the sentence intact, it proves to be a near impossibility. Now throw in layers and layers of dimensions, maybe a House committee or two, such as Citizenship and Immigration, Status of Women, Human Rights, or Heritage. Add to that several departments, such as CSIS, Justice, and Finance, which now work in concert with their counterparts in other countries, for instance, Homeland Security in the US. Make certain to include the bureaucrats in each department, throw in politicians from opposing political parties, then run everything by the government bean counters, who will examine the equation in terms of budgets and costs—human variables are of no concern to them. Then run it by the government lawyers (remember, in Ottawa alone, they number in the thousands). Guaranteed, the result will not be what you expected. And that's just the House; there are more committees in the Senate. It's like cracking a couple of eggs into a frying pan and then, five minutes later, coming back, lifting the lid, and finding meatballs. You're thinking, *How the hell did I get that from two eggs? Who laid the meatballs?* Being creative, you throw in some noodles and you've got spaghetti. There's no resemblance whatsoever to what initially went into the pan. But being hungry, that's what you eat. Same principle with the sentence game except, in politics, the distortions are often exponential.

When S-2, or any bill for that matter, becomes law, the legislators pretty much wash their hands of it. So guess who gets the responsibility of administering the new legislation? You got it: the bureaucrats. And in our situation, we were back to the same mean-spirited bureaucracy of CIC. Hence, it wasn't putting out the forms for our repatriation, and our kids weren't welcome. Now guess who the recess hall monitors were while all this was going on? Paul Martin, Joe Volpe, and Hedy Fry.

In July, two things of significance happened. The first was that C-38 received royal assent. In just five and a half months, the same-sex marriage bill known as the Civil Marriage Act sailed through the parliamentary process from conception to implementation and Canada never looked back. Amazing how quickly things can happen when the government and bureaucrats want them to.

Second, I visited with a friend, David Choi, who'd been a judge for Vancouver's Honda Celebration of Light, a four-night fireworks festival. Typically, three countries are represented, each one trying to outdo the other. Spectators can easily number half a million each night. David was allowed to bring one guest to the special preshow dinner beforehand, and that turned out to be me. Some folks were instantly recognizable; others, like me, were not. People were inquisitive, perhaps hoping I was the nephew of Warren Buffett or maybe a Hollywood producer or some other big shot. If the others at my table were disappointed, they didn't show it.

Always the question gets asked, "What do you do?" That's a tough one for me to answer because I do many things. The *Vancouver Observer* one time referred to me as "Canada's leading irritant." I work with investments, I'm a pilot and a union rep, I'm an active father, and now, in one fashion or another, I'm in a perpetual human rights struggle with Ottawa.*

CKNW radio broadcaster Jon McComb sat at our table, and I really wanted him to hear the Lost Canadian story. Not that I was expecting he'd embrace the issue—CKNW had been so rude to me in the past—but it was always interesting trying to get the media involved, even those who'd earlier turned a deaf ear. Just as I finished explaining the situation, the mayor

---

* I've also written a monthly column in the union rag, and was involved with aviation safety. In high school, I washed dishes and bused tables at a local restaurant, I worked at a gas station, and I had my own business washing and waxing cars and airplanes. In college, I worked driving a cab, then went on to be a radio station announcer.

of Vancouver, Larry Campbell, walked up to the bar not far from us. In an October 2004 letter to his office, I'd asked for a brief meeting with the mayor. A reply came back from his personal assistant: "Mayor Campbell is aware of the Lost Canadian issue and has sympathy for your fight. However, he does not believe that it is a civic issue and so will not be meeting with you."

Campbell's response was most disappointing. My family had done much for the city he served. That letter was the tipping point after being denied and ignored in Canada for decades. I wrote him back with a Martin Luther King Jr. analogy, pretending Dr. King had written a letter to the mayor of Birmingham asking for a meeting, only to get the same sort of brush-off:

"Dr. King, I am aware of the fact that you can't drink out of the white man's fountain, and I do have sympathy. However, as mayor of Birmingham, I do not believe this is a civic issue and thus will not meet with you."

I continued, "Mr. Campbell, there is nothing more civic than citizenship."

The mayor might not have made the connection, but in May he issued a proclamation on behalf of the city on the documentary film *Continuous Journey*, which debuted in the Vancouver DOXA Film Festival. The proclamation acknowledged the racist policies that prevented the mostly Sikh passengers of the *Komagata Maru* from disembarking. Vancouver city councillor Jim Green had read the proclamation on behalf of Mayor Campbell, naming May 23 "Komagata Maru Commemoration Day."[21] No question, what happened more than ninety years earlier was wrong, and the victims deserve recognition. But that said, what was happening in the here and now to Lost Canadians was also wrong. It would have been most helpful to my continuing fight with Ottawa, and healing for all of us, if the City recognized our struggle. After all, so many of the government's court hearings against us had taken place in Vancouver, which, for Lost Canadians, was starting to feel like the Nuremberg of the West.

After being so coldly rejected by Campbell's assistant, I appealed for the mayor to reconsider. He didn't. It was as though we didn't exist. The Great Wall of Vancouver had been built, standing directly between city hall and the Lost Canadians, with a shiny brass plaque reading, "Erected in 2004 by the City of Vancouver, Mayor Larry Campbell presiding."[22]

With Larry Campbell just a few feet away, I turned to the people at my table, who were agreeing with me that the solution to our issue was a no-brainer, then said, "Watch this." I went up to the mayor, someone I had never met or directly communicated with before, and introduced myself. "I'm Don Chapman and I'm a Lost Canadian."

That was all it took. Mr. Campbell threw his right arm up toward my face, turned his back, then briskly walked away, grumbling that he wanted nothing to do with me. I turned to the people at my table and posed a rhetorical question. "Would it have made any difference if I said I lost my citizenship because I was black, because I was a woman, or gay, or maybe if my grandfather had been aboard the *Komagata Maru*?"

To be the top representative of Vancouver, a person in a position to help correct historic wrongs, to be an elected official vowing to uphold basic human rights, and to so blatantly disregard the idea of equality for all Canadians was, to me, disgusting. And even though I had anticipated his reaction, I also still felt humiliated being treated so poorly in public by the mayor, the official spokesperson for the city. I could only hope he didn't represent the views of his constituents. Straight away, with Larry Campbell at the city's helm, I began thinking of Vancouver as the Birmingham of the North. But it didn't last long. Two days later, Captain Steak or Chicken appointed him Canada's next senator, which meant that for me to get further legislation passed, I'd be forced to work with or around Larry Campbell. Even in victory I was shunned.

Like the NHL season, Parliament resumed in the fall, but Senator Kinsella's words about revisiting the matter after S-2, of taking the Lost Canadian issue a step further, was not to be. It was as though he'd checked out along with his colleague Senator Donald Oliver, who over the years refused on several occasions to help me champion the issue.[23] A few months earlier, the Martin Liberals narrowly averted an election, but now the Conservatives smelled blood, and the members of their caucus were much more obsessed with becoming the ruling party than they were interested in helping a bunch of old women and their aging kids with citizenship. Anything and everything cooking in Ottawa had been highly seasoned with partisanship. Every political party out there had relegated the war brides and their children to the back of its bus.

Joe Taylor, one of the Lost Canadians I was helping, after being denied citizenship by Joe Volpe, was forced like Magali into filing for a judicial review (once again, in Vancouver). How ironic that Volpe, who'd been born in Italy to a father who chose to live in a country that was at war against Canada in World War II, was now telling the son of a Canadian soldier that he wasn't welcome. It made the theme of Citizenship Week 2005 all the more insulting: Canada, We All Belong.[24] The day after Citizenship Week ended, Volpe announced its enormous success in a news release, saying that nearly

1,800 newcomers had taken the oath of citizenship at forty-three special ceremonies in communities across the country, with almost 200 municipal proclamations and the presentation of eighteen Citation for Citizenship awards.[25] Five and a half months after s-2's passage, not one of the 1,800 new Canadians were Lost Canadians or, better stated, Found Canadians.*

One of the municipalities taking part in Citizenship Week was my own town of Gibsons, and, unlike Mayor Larry Campbell, our mayor and the town councillors had no problem issuing a proclamation that pretty much reflected exactly CIC's verbiage: "Canada's Citizenship Week provides an opportunity to reflect on the value of citizenship... and to focus on the privileges, rights, responsibilities and obligations of citizenship."[26] It was a moving experience for all, yet I couldn't help thinking about CKNW's Jon McComb, whom I'd met at the fireworks celebration. Before flying to Vancouver from Phoenix, I contacted McComb's producer, asking to be a guest on his talk show. It wasn't surprising that the show turned me down, but what happened next was comical. With limited airtime, radio stations must carefully allocate the time slots to subjects of particular interest and importance to their audiences. Instead of hearing me out on the Lost Canadians, McComb did a show on the new Ken and Barbie dolls. It seemed that Mattel, the toy manufacturer, had recently put out a new line of fashion design for the dolls, complete with plastic pink underwear. That's what trumped us. It didn't matter that s-2 had passed, that thousands of people were legally entitled to citizenship and couldn't get it, nor that CIC had erected multiple roadblocks against our return. McComb and his producer chose dolls' pink underwear.

With the Liberals at the helm and Joe Volpe their top guy in citizenship issues, our navigation through the bureaucratic maze was akin to trying to figure out the mathematical square of infinity. Nowhere was there a "welcome to Canada, glad to have you back" attitude.

I wrongly figured that with the passage of s-2 our battle would be mostly over and my political foes would be jumping aboard. It was quite the opposite. Having never been through a divorce, I could only imagine that it was like a vindictive ex forever attempting to make your life difficult—the stuff of Hollywood movies. That's how CIC treated us before s-2, and worse after. John Reynolds pointed out a light at the end of our tunnel, saying that if

---

* Of the many, many people who had dedicated years of their lives helping Lost Canadians, none that I know of ever got recognized by CIC with any sort of citizenship award.

there was an election, Harper would correct the Lost Canadian issue "with the stroke of a pen." The mood was definitely thick with impending ballot fever.

By November, the Ottawa players had reverted to back-to-the-voting-booth mode. Their self-interests seemed to be paramount. The politicians were concerned with keeping their jobs and feared what an election might bring; the media went back to ignoring our issue (except for Gary Symons at CBC, though CBC pretty much ignored Gary, so what's the difference?). The Conservatives were like a pack of wild dogs about to pounce on their prey, the bureaucrats were erecting fences to keep Lost Canadians out of their country, and Amnesty International was back to chasing the next big fundraising story.

I comforted myself with the words of Winston Churchill during a particularly difficult situation shortly after the outbreak of World War II. "This is not the end," he stated. "It is not even the beginning of the end. But it is, perhaps, the end of the beginning."[27]

PART 2

TO STAND ON GUARD FOR THEE

THE MOVIE It's A Wonderful Life *is told through flashbacks. The movie adaptation of H.G. Wells's* The Time Machine *is chiefly narrated through the lens of the future. In the pages that follow, as far as the saga of the Lost Canadians is concerned, I'm going to do a bit of both.*

I'm taking some liberty here in that I'm getting a bit ahead of myself by sharing with you next the story of an event that transpired just around the time of the January 2006 election. (And, by now, who won that election is old news—I won't be letting the genie out of the bottle by saying Stephen Harper became Canada's twenty-second prime minister.) But I want to relate more fully what it was like for me, living this nightmare on a day-to-day basis. There was no pause button as the politicians moved out and onto their campaign trails. Daily, I had real people to contend with, and since many were elderly and just discovering their citizenship quagmire, my normal high-speed life was forced further into overdrive, this time away from Ottawa.

An important lesson I was learning through all this was just how Canadians got to where they are as a country. The average Canadian is not fully aware of the country's history. If not for the Lost Canadians, I too probably wouldn't know much about our past. Izzy Asper, the late media mogul, echoing others before him, once posed an incredibly appropriate rhetorical question: How do we know where we're going if we don't know where we've been?

CHAPTER 7

"THEE" IS YOU AND ME

We are not makers of history, we are made by history. Almost always the dedicated creative minority has made the world better.
DR. MARTIN LUTHER KING JR.

ON THE LAST day of 2005, I found myself with three other people—Garth Pritchard, cameraman Daron Donahue, and my daughter Katie—filming a Lost Canadian documentary. We gathered at the train station in Geneva for a three-and-a-half-hour ride to Paris, where we rented a van and then drove for another three hours to Dieppe. I didn't know quite what to expect there, nor how I'd react. This was the place where so many Canadians (916, to be exact) gave their all in the first Allied invasion of World War II. Back then, Canada essentially adopted British military protocol when burying its fallen warriors. In World Wars I and II, Canadian soldiers, just as those of Britain, were buried pretty much where they fell. Hence, Canadian graveyards are spread all over the world, particularly in Europe and especially in France. When a US soldier dies on foreign soil, the country does everything in its power to return the body for burial in the homeland, as Canada did for its fallen soldiers in Afghanistan.

I've heard it said that a Canadian's rite of passage is a cross-country train journey. Let me suggest one other: a trip to Dieppe. Despite my extensive knowledge of Canadian citizenship, I discovered a part of myself in Dieppe. As we drove into the town, there was no question that a Canadian aura enveloped the land and its people. It was there on the road maps and on the signs next to the highway, some leading to the 19th August 1942 Memorial Museum, others to the Dieppe Canadian War Cemetery and to any number of other significant Canadian landmarks. There was a presence, a feeling that in some way my being alive and enjoying life as I know it came about partly because of the sacrifices of my fellow countrymen buried somewhere in Dieppe. We rounded the corner past the last buildings before the English Channel and, suddenly, we were there. Before us lay the very beaches, the very cliffs, where almost a thousand young men had taken their final breaths. Against howling winds, one could hear the waves crashing on the rocky shoreline. Rain poured down from the sky. I got out of the van and made my way toward the water, coloured a very light green. My mind's eye visualized this spot as it had been so graphically depicted in the 1993 Canadian miniseries *Dieppe*, the water dark red from the blood of our soldiers. Knowing that Garth wanted to film my initial reaction to what I saw, my daughter urged me back to the van so that he could capture the moments on film the next day when the camera was rolling.

We decided to relax after our travels, and to celebrate New Year's at a local restaurant. We drove to our hotel, the Aguado, and right there in the lobby, everywhere you looked, were signs and mementoes of Canada. At the front desk sat two books. Thumbing through the pages of one, I saw that people from all over the world, but mostly from France, England, and Canada, had signed their names, along with some sort of expression of gratitude to both the Canadian soldiers and the country they represented. The clerk proudly showed off her Canadian flag, proclaiming it to be more than thirty years old. In the planter next to the counter stood three flags, one British and two Canadian. The proprietors, with warm, charming smiles and incredible pride, welcomed us as "Canadians." It was the last day of the year, only about seven hours before 2006; everyone was preparing for their New Year's celebrations, yet the hotel staff made time to phone the head of the local Canadian museum, as well as several elderly citizens—custodians of knowledge—and all readily agreed to open the normally closed-for-the-winter museum just for us. They very much wanted to give something back, to personally give us a tour and express their gratitude for what our country had done for them. We set a time, 2:30 in the afternoon on January 2. We then went to our rooms to wash up and ready ourselves for the wonderful French cuisine that awaited us.

Walking to the restaurant, we again noticed the Canadian influence— Canadian flags hung in many of the shop windows. And in the restaurant, on every table, were several gold-coloured maple leaves, the owner proudly explaining that his wife hand-painted every one of them. There could be no question: the people of Dieppe loved Canada.

After a marvellous cod dinner, complete with French wine and a dessert of profiteroles, we headed back to the hotel. Garth and Daron retired for the evening while my daughter and I went walking. We made our way to the beach, which in this case was nothing but rounded small rocks. It was dark and I didn't notice the Canadian monument, beds of poppies lining its base, at the edge of the shore. About twenty feet from where the waves were breaking, I stopped, reminded of Waimea, on the northern side of Oahu, in the Hawaiian Islands, where the waves are so strong that over time they've carved a steep ravine into the beach. The difference was that in Waimea there is sand, and in Dieppe there are rocks. I couldn't imagine carrying full military gear—rifle, backpack, ammunition, you name it—and trying to run on these rocks, all the while having thousands of soldiers taking dead aim at me, shooting to kill. For many of the Canadian soldiers there, this had meant certain death. My daughter could tell that my thoughts were going back to World War II so she hustled me off to continue our stroll about town. Everywhere I looked I saw Canadian markers. The residents of Dieppe do not need the reminder "Lest we forget." They haven't.

After ringing in the new year back at the hotel, we went to sleep. We had a busy day ahead of us.

The next morning, the four of us gathered for breakfast. Garth and Daron wanted to scout the area and set up the gear, which meant that my daughter and I were free for the next three hours. Katie, not being as used to international travel as I am, went back to sleep. I went walking. Knowing that Garth wanted to catch my initial reactions on film, I found it difficult making my way around town: every time I came across some tribute to the Canadians, I had to quickly look away, as I wasn't supposed to see it yet.

After spending years flying to and from Paris, and having only Paris as my experience of France, I can now say with conviction that dog poop on the sidewalks is not just a Parisian thing but a French thing. All over, everywhere, there it was, and with so many Canadian markers up at eye level, I spent the next several hours looking down where little dogs, bigger dogs, and absolutely monstrous dogs had been allowed to do their business. That's why, despite having a wonderful walk, it came almost as a relief when Garth arrived back at the hotel, telling us that he was ready to film.

The first stop was le cimetière militaire Canadien—the Dieppe Canadian War Cemetery—just a few kilometres away. Turning west off the main road leading out of town, we immediately found ourselves in the countryside—a few houses, some with thatched roofs, scattered here and there, and farm-land. A kilometre more down the road and there it was, off to our left. Katie and I climbed out of the van and walked out to it. The first headstone we came upon was for a man who died at age fifty-one. My age. Believing that I still had lots of life left in me, and hoping one day to play with my grandchildren who'd yet to be born, I could feel the loss of this man's life; it hit close to home. Even more horrifying, next to his grave sat the marker of another soldier who fell at just age nineteen. My God, that was Katie's age. I couldn't conceive how his parents felt as they stood over their child's grave. I learned that all the soldiers' families were allowed just one sentence to be carved onto their loved one's marker. Common were the words "Will always be loved and missed by mother, father, brothers, and sisters." I looked at Katie and contemplated the horror of losing her.

My father, my uncles, everyone in my family was in some way a part of World War II, yet today, the citizens of Canada hardly know about the Lost Canadians, the war brides, and the war-bride children. For those who are familiar with the dilemma of the Lost Canadians, why do they remain silent? Nothing at that moment seemed rational to me. Of course, the average Canadian, probably like the average German, didn't know the whole story; governments are good at spinning history. I began to think of the Canadian media, wondering why they hadn't come to our rescue. For them there was no excuse; they had deliberately ignored us. Seeing the sheer number of graves, I realized that many of the relatives of these fallen soldiers were Lost Canadians and war-bride children. Surely these fine men didn't give their all so that their families could be denied Canadian citizenship and rights. I thought of two Joes, one of them the current immigration minister, Joe Volpe, and the other, Joe Taylor, the son of one of the Canadian soldiers who had fought against the Germans in France. In the next month or so, the latter would be forced into court by the former. How poignant that the same convoluted CIC logic that zapped Volpe's family when his own mother had been stripped of her Canadian status upon marrying her Italian husband was now zapping Joe Taylor. Now add a twist: Mr. Volpe's family lived in Italy during World War II while Joe Taylor's father fought as a Canadian, landing ashore in northern France, somewhere just like Dieppe, maybe not far from where Katie and I were now standing. So the son of a father who, by choice, lived in a country at war with Canada was now aiming his Canadian bureaucratic artillery at the son of a Canadian war hero. It made no sense.

Just two weeks earlier, two of my daughters had finished their final exams, one at the University of British Columbia and the other at Simon

Fraser University, then returned to Phoenix for the Christmas holidays. The first thing both wanted was a home-cooked meal. The whole family loves my wife's cooking, but on this special welcome-home night, no one appreciated her meal (and chocolate-chip cookies) more than Katie and my other daughter, Jamie. Why? The answer's obvious. When you lose something, you're ever so thankful to get it back. You feel with intensity the loss of what was missing. Isn't it that way in life? Once something is gone, we see much more clearly the value of what we had. That's how the people of Dieppe understand citizenship; they remember having their identities taken away against their will. So as long as the memory of what it was like to be stripped of their individuality is alive, these French men and women will understand the importance of identity and the value of what our Canadians gave their lives for in defending their country. Every November 11, I attend the Royal Canadian Legion's Remembrance Day commemoration. Although those attending are sincere and do want to remember and pay homage to the veterans, I don't believe that most Canadians have any concept of what the people of Dieppe were forced to live through. My hope is that Canadians never fully understand, because the only way they could would be if another country invaded Canada.

Ask anyone who has ever lost a child the sense of their loss. One can only imagine. To what lengths would parents go to get their child back? I can assure you that citizenship is way up there on the scales of value and importance, next to the loss of a loved one and one's health. The people of Dieppe understand this, whereas the bureaucrats of Canada, including many members of Parliament, regrettably do not.

On January 2, promptly at half past two, Garth, Daron, Katie, and I arrived at the Canadian museum in the heart of Dieppe; we were met by five locals, all taking time out of their day to open the Memorial Museum for our personalized tour. The trip to Dieppe would not have been complete without it. We were taken aback by all the mementoes—a 1942 newspaper headlined with news of the Canadian landing, the bell from a sunken destroyer, a German army helmet. It was almost surreal. After the Dieppe elders told us their stories, I told them mine. To say they were horrified (and I truly mean horrified) that Canada stripped citizenship from the soldiers' own children is an understatement. Just as the soldiers of Canada tried to liberate Dieppe, the elders were now offering me their help in getting Canada to recognize the Lost Canadians. These men actually used the word "liberate." They wanted Garth to write a news story, eager to get the word out to everyone in the community about our plight. They wanted something for the museum. Of course, I do not believe my story deserves to be enshrined in their museum; that is a place sacred to our soldiers. But in some small way we all shared the bond of standing on guard for thee, of trying to right historic wrongs, of believing in Canada, of defending the real values of Canada, of being "Canadian."[1,2]

On January 3, we finished filming. Katie and I boarded the train for Paris; Garth and Daron remained behind to wrap up. Katie and I had physically departed Dieppe, but in our minds and in our hearts there would always be some sort of umbilical tie between our Canada and the northern shores of France. It didn't matter that I was fifty-one years old and my daughter was nineteen; we both came away more enlightened because of the experience, and we were better Canadians for it. Never will we forget those soldiers, and never will we ignore them or what they fought for. Over the years, I've looked into the faces of many of these soldiers' Lost Canadian relatives and of many war-bride children. The same thing that was telling me these men would be proud that we haven't forgotten them also told me they'd be ashamed knowing that Ottawa was today disavowing their family members, saying they weren't worthy of being Canadian. The main sponsor of the 1947 Canadian Citizenship Act was none other than Paul Martin's father, Paul Martin Sr., who spoke these words in 1946 to describe the purpose of his new Citizenship Act: "That all of us be able to say with pride and say with meaning: 'I am a Canadian citizen.'"[3]

Nay, not so.

On the flight back to the US, one of the French flight attendants and I got to talking. She had noticed me typing away on my computer while the other passengers slept. Asked why I'd been to France, I explained the plight of the Lost Canadians. Her interest in my story was clearly personal. She was born in Montreal in 1967 and, while she was still a child, her family moved to France and her father became a French citizen. Today, she's married to a Frenchman and has two young French-born children. She believes that she has dual citizenship, as do her two children, but now that she's heard my story, she isn't so sure. To me, there was no question: she and her children, her brothers, and her sisters (and their respective children) qualified to have their names in Ottawa's "Livret de Canadien errant."[4] How sad. She now joins the long list of others who live in a state of uncertainty.

Back home, nothing about regaining my Canadian citizenship was routine; always there was some unexpected twist or turn just around the corner. What began as a lone pursuit for me and my family now encompassed tens of thousands of people divided into various factions of Lost Canadians.

There were people like me, who as minor-aged kids lost their citizenship; there were the children born on Canadian military bases overseas, the war brides, and, of course, their foreign-born children. The truth was that there were many more ways to lose citizenship; I just had yet to discover them. In the colossal chess game of life, CIC, being my foe, wasn't about to divulge much of anything, let alone any unspecified categories still undetected on my radar. Nonetheless, hundreds of thousands more disenfranchised Canadians were looming just over the bureaucratic horizon.

By late January 2006, with the change of guard at 24 Sussex Drive and also Harper's recently appointed cabinet, including newly minted citizenship minister Monte Solberg, I hoped our troubles would soon be over—that John Reynolds's "stroke of the pen" fix would be a sure thing. Not even close.

In February, Katie and I headed to Citizenship and Immigration Canada's world headquarters in Sydney, Nova Scotia. Nine full months had passed since S-2 became law, and the bureaucrats had yet to offer any form specific to Lost Canadians like me with which to apply for resumption of citizenship. We now had a legal right to be Canadian, but having a right and being able to exercise that right are two entirely different things, so Katie and I decided to test the waters. Hooking back up with our two documentary filmmakers, Garth Pritchard and Daron Donahue, we drove from Halifax straight to CIC's Case Processing Centre, more recognizable as intangible post-office-box addresses and toll-free phone numbers than as a genuine place with real people. On this cold winter's day, we were about to discover how warm or chilly the reception would be.

We anticipated that CIC would not embrace the idea of our filming inside its headquarters, so we set up the camera to film from the sidewalk in front of the entrance. Once wired for sound, I was ready to go; CIC's D-Day was about to commence. Feeling like a reporter for *60 Minutes* (the W5 and *Fifth Estate* reporters didn't want this story), I marched across the street, opened the doors, and walked in. There at a desk sat a middle-aged man who looked more like a security guard than a receptionist. He was in charge of screening, giving the green light to those permitted into the depths of this mysterious complex, the red light to those like me. I asked to see Melba Hefferon, a woman who'd been particularly adept at finding ways to turn down Lost Canadians. Her name appeared on many documents pertaining to Charles Bosdet and Magali Castro-Gyr. As the custodian of their citizenship, the person whose signature was at the bottom of their rejection letters, she was, I figured, as good a person as any to start with. But the defensive line-blocker did his job well: after calling upstairs, he said that Hefferon would not be able to see me. I could, however, drop off any papers I might have and he'd make sure they got to her. I explained that I was there not to drop off anything but to inquire, to pick up something, anything really—maybe a form or pamphlet—that would help a Lost Canadian regain citizenship. "Is there an application," I asked, "so that I can apply for citizenship under a law that went into effect nine months ago? How do I apply? What do I do?"

He placed a call to some case processor upstairs. (I suspected it was to Hefferon, who supposedly possessed far greater knowledge and stature than he, and was infinitely more qualified to answer technical questions.) Whomever it was, he or she became aware that the person in the lobby making the inquiry was none other than Don Chapman, someone these bureaucrats had come to know through numerous newspaper articles, applications, testimonies in Ottawa, and letters sent with a return address in Phoenix, Arizona.

Really, I went there to prove a point, and prove it I did: that close to a year after the passage of S-2, CIC had yet to create an application form to process returning Lost Canadians. In the ten minutes or more that it took staff to search for something that would suffice, I had walked back outside to check in with the film crew. With our camera pointing toward CIC's building, we sensed we were being watched. And then the confirmation—our eyes met with those peering out through the louvered blinds of a second-floor window: one of the bureaucrats was indeed monitoring us. In what seemed to be almost a panic, the woman dove to the floor. The blinds gently swayed back and forth, then a few seconds later came to rest, erasing any evidence that some sort of covert spying operation had just taken place. We all broke out laughing, hoping in some perverse way that she had banged her head against the windowsill.

When I re-entered the building, I was handed a manila envelope and told it contained the application form I sought. I walked back out the door, then opened the envelope. The form inside was for those wanting to apply as immigrants for citizenship; it had nothing to do with Lost Canadians. Clearly, there was no form applicable to our situation. Hence, the road leading back to Canada was again uphill and full of potholes.

I had left my contact information with the man at the front desk. Within minutes of having packed the camera and ourselves back into the van, my cell phone rang. On the line was Mark Davidson, director, Legislation and Program Policy, Citizenship Branch, Department of Citizenship and

Immigration, in Ottawa.* He was a bigwig within the bowels of CIC. It seemed that our little stunt had touched the cold bureaucratic nerves. That it took just five minutes after our leaving for Mr. Davidson to call proved that the power of the press (in this case, the camera of a documentary film-maker) really can move mountains. If only the media had been remotely interested before, our situation would have been resolved long ago. Had the Canadian people really understood this ongoing injustice, surely they wouldn't have allowed it to continue. Going forward, CIC's immediate reaction made it obvious that, to win, I really did need the media. But the million-dollar question remained: How did I get them on board?

Mark reassured me that Lost Canadians like me did indeed have a yel-low-brick road on which to return to Canada; it was just that CIC had been extraordinarily busy, and specific forms had yet to be designed. We were to be patient; CIC was working on the problem. For now, if I could just fill out the application given to me while ignoring most of the verbiage pertaining to immigrants—which was what most of the form was about—and submit all the required documents and, of course, pay the $100 filing fee, CIC could then begin processing me for citizenship. Hopefully, in six months to a year or more, I'd be allowed to stand before a citizenship officer, who would administer an oath of citizenship, and all would be well. My yellow-brick road came complete with a detour directly through those same enchanted hallways of the CIC Case Processing Centre we'd just visited. Could it be that the bureaucrat assigned to my file would be the same woman who'd perhaps just banged her head on the windowsill, having the memory of an elephant and the resolve of a woman scorned? She would be well aware that, in the last few minutes, I was the one who had done the scorning.

Walking this road certainly wasn't going to be easy or fun.

Then another thought crossed my mind. Was the peering-out through the louvered blinds just the tip of the iceberg? In the enchanted castle of CIC in Ottawa, could Monte Solberg, Stephen Harper's newly appointed citizenship minister, and the person proving to be our Wicked Minister of the East, be following my every move in his crystal ball? The answer would come a few years later.

Our next stop was Cape Breton University. Dr. Katherine Covell, of the university's Children's Rights Centre, had invited me to be a guest speaker. A few years earlier, I'd been calling all over Canada to every kind of group

---

* In the ensuing years, Mark and I became friends, and he truly cared about fixing the Lost Canadian issue. He was instrumental in Bill C-37, from its conception to eventual passage. Thanks, Mark.

or organization that claimed to be advocating for equality of rights, human rights, women's rights, and so on. Amnesty International, the Famous Five Foundation, LEAF (Women's Legal Education and Action Fund), the Canadian Human Rights Commission, the BC Civil Liberties Association, Human Rights Watch. If you name it, I probably called it, begging for help. The Canadian Civil Liberties Association mission statement is quite typical: "The [association] is a national organization that was constituted to promote respect for and observance of fundamental human rights and civil liberties, and to defend, extend, and foster recognition of these rights and liberties."[5]

Despite such highfalutin claims, few were willing to listen to me, let alone take action on behalf of the Lost Canadians. The pilot side of me wanted to know why, and here's what I came up with: People growing up in the US have been taught since being in diapers that they live in the greatest country in the world, with the greatest people. God bless them. Although everyone else in the world knows this isn't entirely true, Americans really do believe it.* Canadians, not exactly smitten with this snooty quirk of their southern neighbours, recognize the flaw but don't see that, in their own way, they too do the same thing. How so? Canadians love to brag that in this great big world of ours, they are by far the best when it comes to human rights and the rule of law. From an early age, they've been taught that Canada represents peace, order, and good government, with an emphasis on human rights, and particularly Charter rights. Now, picture this guy from a different country, living in Arizona of all places, telling you a wild tale of discrimination and exclusion, the starring role going to the Canadian government.†

If you're a typical Canadian, the first thing you do is question the source. You rationalize based on what you've been taught—that no way could your country ever violate the very essence of what it purports to be, which is a fair, compassionate, caring country that embraces equal rights. Canada would never send in its equivalent of the flying monkeys of Oz—the bureaucrats at CIC—to go against its own people. But the fact is, the country did. And in telling this story, I had become the courier, the guy who is quick to say, "Please don't shoot the messenger."

But I did get shot, or at least my reputation did. Over the years, just about everybody who had listened to my story told me their first impression was that I was some sort of nutcase. During our first conversation, Dr. Covell

---

* Here I go again, calling the people of the United States "Americans." I really don't like doing it, but it's the way Canadians describe their southern neighbours.

† Arizona certainly has no claim to being an accepting "human rights hot spot" of the world.

had her doubts too; but she was different from those at the other organizations in two ways. First, she listened and, second, she acted accordingly. What that meant is that, after paying close attention to what I told her, she checked out both me and my story. To her horror, she discovered my words were true, that her Canada was not exactly what it appeared to be. The Children's Rights Centre, which conducts research and supervises graduate studies on children's issues, like almost every human rights/equality organization in Canada, is perpetually short of money. Katherine couldn't offer anything by way of financial support, but she did get her students involved in letter-writing campaigns. She did everything possible within her limitations. I always appreciated her efforts and, on this day, I was to speak to her students. They were flabbergasted at what they heard.

I vowed to remember Katherine's dedication to human rights, both as co-chair of her university's department for children's rights and as a person who desires to make this a better world for all. She's the real deal, a person who has devoted her life to making our world better through equality and justice. She didn't just toe the line of some fancily worded fundraising mission statement. I witnessed first-hand how different Katherine was from the heads of most every other organization out there—she really did walk the line she preached.

Overall, we had a very good day in Sydney.

Back in Halifax, we got word that David Emerson had crossed the floor of the House and was now a top cabinet minister for Stephen Harper. Just maybe Emerson would carry our torch; after all, as a Liberal, he had listened sympathetically to my story years before. On arriving back in Arizona, I made repeated attempts to contact the new Conservative minister, even going so far as to fly to Ottawa and attempt to communicate with him in person. Yet, once again, another high-ranking politician proved to be a disappointment. Never again did Mr. Emerson correspond with me. Not a single word or phone call. Interestingly, his wife, Theresa Yeuk-Si Tang, was born in Hong Kong. Being Chinese, she probably knew all about the old Chinese Exclusion Act and how hard it was for people like her to gain official status in Canada. In all these years, the only thing we Lost Canadians got out of David Emerson was silence.

In show business, there's a saying, "The show must go on." It does, and so did my crusade. While in Ottawa, I tried meeting with Monte Solberg, who proved over time that everything was merely status quo. Nothing had changed except the name of the political party in charge. In his eleven months as Canada's second most important person guarding the people's citizenship rights (the prime minister being most important), Solberg never once met or contacted me. Nor did Stephen Harper. My once open-for-business senators retreated to their parliamentary bunkers; the doors to the Conservative empire had slammed shut. Promises made were not kept. Even the efforts of John Reynolds, who pressed on advocating inside his caucus for a quick resolution, proved fruitless. Nothing worked.

The beacon of light was Liberal MP Andrew Telegdi. Andrew was a standout, a ray of hope, who, like me, never gave up. His party certainly didn't support him. Instead, it considered him to be a one-trick pony, citizenship his bailiwick. Why did Andrew become so involved with our struggle to regain our identities? It seems that he too had a story.

In 1957, one year after the Hungarian Revolution, Andrew's family fled Hungary. The revolt (and its aftermath) was pivotal not just for the family but for the world. It also helped define the Canada we know today.

The Cold War was in full swing, with Hungary controlled by the Soviet Union, the enforcers being the occupying Soviet military and the state police, better known as the Államvédelmi Hatóság, or ÁVH. The ÁVH was a Soviet appendage that didn't hesitate to use brutality and torture on those Hungarians considered threatening. As a front, but still controlled by the Soviets, a political party was formed; it was called the Hungarian Workers' Party, or HWP. One of its first and most successful moves was to transform the country from large estates to small plots of farmland. In his book *Hungary's Negotiated Revolution*, Rudolf L. Tőkés explains that the party "embarked on a path of forcible collectivization between 1948 and 1950." He goes on: "The regime's campaign to liquidate the Hungarian kulaks 'as a class' was the most coercive aspect of the HWP's political record."[6]

What are kulaks? The word dates back to the Russian Revolution: kulaks were landowners and farmers who resisted turning their land over to the Soviets. As described in *Seventeen Moments in Soviet History*, the "kulaks represented a counterweight to Soviet power in the villages and by their very nature constituted a 'class-alien' element that had to be eliminated."[7] What I'm getting at is that the Soviet psyche hadn't changed since the revolution in 1917, almost forty years before the Soviets' occupation of Hungary. Andrew's father was an architect and town planner; his mother, a draftswoman. His grandparents were landowners—on the paternal side, a mill, and on the maternal side, a farm. That automatically made them and their family Hungarian kulaks and, as Andrew put it, "kulaks were targeted by the state."

Although the Hungarian Revolution, which began on October 23, 1956, lasted just a few weeks, it captured people's attention the world over. It started as a student march through downtown Budapest, then picked up steam and bystanders on its way to the Parliament building. Upward of 20,000 protesters gathered at the statue of Józef Bem, a national hero of both Hungary and Poland. They sang a song censored by the Soviets titled "Nemzeti dal," made famous in the revolution of 1848. Translated, the words are "This we swear, this we swear, that we will no longer be slaves."

After the students arrived at the Parliament building, some were detained by the ÁVH as they tried to broadcast their demands from government-managed Magyar Radio. As the crowds demanded their release, the ÁVH began firing indiscriminately at the people. Many were killed. As far as kick-starting an uprising goes, the Soviets couldn't have done it better if they'd written the manual themselves. The revolt went into high gear and spread across the country.

At first, the Soviets retreated. The Hungarian people, after years of being subjected to Soviet cruelty and oppression, wanted revenge. Pro-Soviet communists and ÁVH members were executed, oftentimes publicly. Former Hungarian political leaders were released from captivity. The bottom line— what the people wanted—is something all humans desire: freedom and identity; to live as they themselves chose, and to do it as proud Hungarians.

The revolution happened at the height of the Cold War and, in Western countries like Canada, people actively cheered for the Hungarians. Sadly, on November 4, the Soviets struck back with a vengeance. It took just four days to squash the protesters. In retribution for the revolt, more than 20,000 Hungarians were arrested and sentenced, 13,000 imprisoned, hundreds executed, and more than 200,000 became refugees, fleeing their country. Most had nothing more than the shirts on their backs. Out of the hundreds of thousands, five of those escaping from their homeland belonged to the Telegdi family. As kulaks, they were prime targets for persecution by the Soviets. Often people like them were executed or sent to gulags. If the Telegdis had attempted to immigrate to Canada just ten years earlier, they would have been unable to get in. Mackenzie King's policy on Jewish immigration was but four words: "None is too many."[8] Andrew's stepfather was Jewish and, upon leaving Hungary, the five lived for a time in a Jewish refugee camp. That alone would have deemed the family "undesirable" to the Canadian authorities.

The Hungarian Revolution marked several milestones in history; the world was never the same. In 1957, the United Nations issued a general resolution condemning the Soviet occupation, calling it a violation of human rights against the Hungarian people. But that was about it. Maybe the lack of a tough stance was because the US feared that, by getting too involved, tensions could escalate between the Western world and the Soviets, possibly going as far as nuclear war. Also happening at the same time was the Suez Crisis whereby three countries, France, Great Britain, and Israel, colluded in an offensive against Egypt. As Richard Nixon said, "We couldn't on one hand, complain about the Soviets intervening in Hungary and, on the other hand, approve of the British and the French picking that particular time to intervene against [Gamel Abdel] Nasser." [9] Hence, for the Hungarians left behind, they were once again slaves of the Soviets. The singing of their song of freedom, "Nemzeti dal," had been in vain.

The revolution also marked a milestone for Canada. Our politicians, so typically unmoved to do "the right thing" of their own volition, decided instead to act, though only after the public, bombarded by shocking images of the deplorable conditions in Budapest, demanded action. In response, Ottawa finally opened its almost-always-closed doors for immigration to people outside Britain or the US. Make no mistake here. It took a responsible media to incite the public and they, in turn, motivated the politicians. *Time* magazine symbolically named the Hungarian freedom fighters its Man of the Year for 1956. And Canadians, still embarrassed about not accepting any of the Jewish refugees from the ship SS *St. Louis* in 1939, made their desire to be more accepting well known. [10]

This shows how much influence the Canadian media wields. When they elect to make an issue well known, they can, and the Canadian people will absorb it. And if, as in the case of the Hungarians, Canadians are outraged, they are quite capable of creating a huge public outcry. Then, and only then, does the government reverse its twisted policies. Simply put, when politicians see the public outcry as a possible threat to their re-election, that's when they bend to the will of the protesters. If only the media had elected to support the Lost Canadians years before, thousands and thousands of our countrymen would never have had to suffer.

In the end, some 38,000 Hungarian refugees made their way to Canada. In Alexandra Zabjek's article commemorating the fiftieth anniversary of the Hungarian Revolution, titled "How 'the 56ers' Changed Canada," she says: "The outpouring of generosity reflected the compassion and hospitality that many Canadians now view as their country's trademark in international humanitarian crises. Historians often say that 1956 set the template for Canada's government sponsored refugee programs that later helped those fleeing Vietnam and the Balkans." She goes on to quote historian Harold Troper of the University of Toronto: "The fact that the Hungarians adjusted so well encouraged the notion in the popular mind that Canada could do well by doing good. And doing good felt good."[11]

Like the Von Trapp family in *The Sound of Music*, the Telegdis had made their way to a new life in a foreign country. Their journey to Canada began by trekking through landmine-laden fields and forests between Hungary and Austria, then crossing through several countries and over an ocean to finally arrive in a land of strangers who, while speaking a different language, clearly communicated a warmth of affection and acceptance to these newly found, soon-to-be Canadian brothers and sisters.

In ensuing years, Andrew became totally Canadian, but he never forgot his roots. Why? Because a person's beginnings play a huge role in who they are and what they become. As evidence of that intense bond, take a look at the shields of our previous two governors general, one depicting tigers and a Chinese phoenix, the other, two simbi water spirits of Haiti. The governors general could no more part from their culture than I could from mine, or Andrew from his. Having witnessed first-hand how boundaries become distorted when blowing in the wrong political winds, especially when a madman goes on a maniacal rampage, as Hitler did in the 1930s and '40s throughout eastern Europe, Andrew knew that his identity was the North Star of his Ottawa compass. It was both his priority and passion. He knew only too well the horrors that befall fellow countrymen when a government begins to flirt with the idea of excluding its own people. Once it starts, just where does it stop?

As an airline pilot from an upper-middle-class family hailing from North America, I probably would have been like others with a similar upbringing, blissfully ignorant of what some people have endured in order to survive. The Lost Canadian saga had begun teaching me more—way more—than any textbook or schoolroom could ever have. I began empathizing, feeling others' pain, a kindred-spirit bonding to all those who had suffered from the loss of their identity or discrimination. I understood why it became so important to the Jewish community to remember, and for American blacks to continue their centuries-old fight for equality. Regrettably, there is no shortage of examples; discrimination exists the world over.

Lost Canadian Rob Miller said it so well: "Home is where home is." I've been to dwellings that looked more like rubble, but, for the people who called it home, it was to them what Auntie Em's Kansas farm was to Dorothy

Gale. The Lost Canadians, each and every one of us, were simply guilty of wanting nothing more than to be welcomed home.

One of my toughest Lost Canadian cases was a man named Hasan Lashai, who arrived in Canada from Pakistan at age three. His first memories were of the abundance of toys Canadian children enjoyed vis-à-vis the kids of Pakistan. From that day onward, he never took his new country for granted. Hasan played ice hockey, moved around Canada with his neurosurgeon father, and was by all accounts a typical Canadian kid. His problem started when his father immigrated to the States and took out US citizenship. Hasan was seventeen and a half years old, which meant that, citizenship-wise, Canada considered him a minor, whereas the US treated him as an adult. Unbeknownst to Hasan, Canada cancelled his citizenship, rendering him stateless. As an adult, he returned to Canada, but without proper documentation he couldn't work and had no medical coverage. It didn't take long before he was penniless. After 9/11, he became an undocumented man of Middle Eastern heritage illegally living in Canada. It mattered not that Hasan came complete with a hockey scar above his right eye, or that he spoke with definite Canadian idioms (you know the ones I mean, eh?). He was looked at with suspicion, as if he were possibly a terrorist. He was forced to take to the streets homeless. The only country this man had ever really related to was Canada; he'd been a citizen since being a toddler, and now Canada had rendered him stateless. It took me the better part of three years fighting for Hasan's citizenship before I received this email, on November 22, 2006:

> Hi Don—Ystrdy.—I took The Oath—to Queen Elizabeth and all her Successors... and became a Canadian Citizen.
>
> I doubt that there has ever been a more appropriate need for the term—FINALLY!... Thanx is not enuf—it could have not been possible without you... with great appreciation... peace... hl.

That email was a far cry from his correspondence a couple of years earlier when I received what appeared to be his suicide note. Hasan had completely lost hope. And how could he not? The government was telling him to bugger off. No organization had come forward offering support. He had no legal status. He couldn't work. No income, no place to sleep—except maybe on cardboard sitting atop a Toronto subway grate, where hopefully in winter it would be a few degrees warmer than the ice-cold sidewalk. No matter how strong a person's resolve, everyone has a breaking point. In the end, Hasan had toughed it out, and on this day his world would change. After multiple decades, he was once again a Canadian citizen, with identity—and hope—restored.

Bill S-2 was indeed beginning to touch the lives of real people. I had become the champion of this cause, and the fate of tens of thousands lay in the balance.

Canadians, and particularly the media, often ask why citizenship is so important to me. How could I not be touched by what I've seen or by the people I've met? I had looked into their eyes and I had felt their pain. Identity and belonging was much more than a sound bite on a national holiday, as from CIC's showcased citizenship ceremonies on Canada Day. Aboriginals clearly understand the connection humans have to their land. Other Canadians don't always value or appreciate this. Maybe that's because they've had it so good for so long—they weren't challenged, and nothing was taken away against their will.

Despite my citizenship woes, after travelling the world, I realized how incredibly lucky I was to have been born in Canada. My good fortune came about because of the sacrifices of so many people who'd come before me, many sacrificing their lives, like the soldiers of Dieppe. I was the recipient: I got all the benefits, yet I hadn't really paid the price of admission to be part of one of the greatest countries in the world. And it was now my turn to pay it forward.

With S-2 now "in the can" of parliamentary legislation, the thrust of my efforts turned back toward the people who were still left behind, including many of the war brides of World War II and their children.

CHAPTER 8

LEST WE FORGET... LEST WE IGNORE

England, Holland, Belgium, France, Greece, Chile, Denmark, Italy, Jamaica, Bermuda, Norway, and even Germany—wherever there was a Canadian soldier it seems there was a Canadian war bride.
MELYNDA JARRATT, LEADING CANADIAN HISTORIAN OF
THE WORLD WAR II WAR BRIDES

WE ALWAYS LOOK back upon our soldiers as heroic. Take a stroll around any capital city and notice the statues. So many are of high-ranking generals. Even our own Parliament buildings sport their fair share of bronze military busts and figures. I'm not suggesting that these top soldiers don't deserve accolades. Most probably do. But things are often far different from what they appear to be. In war, there can be no doubt that a soldier's five senses are tested to limits far beyond what most of us could ever imagine. People and countries tend to portray themselves, and especially those who served in uniform, in the best possible light. But again, there's often more than meets the eye.

Canadians of both sexes have had to battle discrimination and stupidity, but the authorities always seem to take special aim at women. After World War I, Ontario passed into provincial law the Legitimation Act, chiefly because of the born-out-of-wedlock kids being a by-product of the war effort. Through the act, the province was trying to give identities to as many kids as possible. Somehow, maybe conveniently, almost nine decades later, the bureaucrats at CIC had forgotten this act existed. Under its provisions, a child was deemed to have been born in wedlock if his or her parents subsequently married. Today, the percentage of children born out of wedlock is far greater than it used to be. Another difference between now and yesteryear is that today's society freely embraces those children; in the 1940s, people were not nearly as understanding. Over the years, I've heard of just about every scenario a Lost Canadian could have and, for many without the benefit of parents in possession of a valid marriage licence at the time of their birth, the permanent stigma attached to both the mother and child was traumatic. Birth certificates are normally issued within weeks of baby's first breath. In years gone by, some provinces actually stamped the word "bastard" in bold letters across certificates for the unlucky kids born to single mothers. Those innocent children were labelled for life. Melynda Jarratt wrote in her book *Voices of the Left Behind* about the mothers of those unfortunate kids, oftentimes treated with disdain not just by society at large but by their own family as well.[1] Sometimes the baby was raised as a brother or sister of the mother rather than as her child. Growing up, these children often weren't told the truth about who their real mother was. Common too was the expectant mother disappearing for the last several months of her pregnancy, maybe to a different city or across the border to the US, which raises the question of not only just how many children were born in the US to Canadian mothers but also how many children were born in Canada to American mothers. Adoption records were almost always sealed, which made it difficult for parents and children to find one another later in life.

My own brother and sister are adopted, and both were born out of wedlock to mothers who had travelled to Vancouver simply to give birth, put the baby up for adoption, and leave. Today's society is much more accepting.[2] It's the government that remains in the Dark Ages. Gone are the "bastard" birth certificates. But, depending on your year of birth, the discrimination and finger pointing continue.

I'm describing a Canada that most citizens don't know existed. One crisp fall morning in Ottawa, Andrew Telegdi walked me down to probably the most famous statue there, the one commemorating Canada's war dead. At the base lies the Tomb of the Unknown Soldier. It is one of Canada's most sacred places. I wasn't prepared for what he was about to say.

"Did you know that if the unknown soldier had lived, Canada might have deported him?"

"Excuse me? Are you serious?"

Andrew went on to explain Canada's pre–World War I immigration policy. I was aware that, back then, Canada's doors were open chiefly to Brits and those from Britain's white colonies. But what he said next shocked me.

"Countless numbers of those soldiers were recent immigrants to Canada with a strong desire to defend their newly found country. Canada was only too willing to accept their service, but after the war, if they'd been badly wounded, Canada viewed them more as a financial liability, so it deported many of them back to their country of origin."

"Go on," I urged.

"If you died a horrible death where your body was so mangled that it was unidentifiable, you could be buried in the Tomb of the Unknown Soldier and forevermore be a hero of Canada."

Morals, it seems, were not part of the equation. It was acceptable to get your legs blown off fighting for Canada, but become a financial liability and the country you defended might deport you back from whence you came.[3] What an incredible lack of loyalty and support for these valiant defenders of our country.

In 1939, Canada entered World War II by sending soldiers to England. At the time, young British men had already been dispatched to various theatres of war. So the only eligible bachelors in towns across the UK were mostly the young men of Canada. In the ensuing years, training for combat was their priority number one. But during their time off, they eagerly pursued the activities most young men the world over enjoy doing in their spare time: drinking and chasing women. Some fell in love, some didn't, but for the most part, their youthful desires were given expression. On the feminine side of the equation, the Brits appreciated these young men, knowing their prime purpose was to defend their homeland. With families making the soldiers welcome and towns hosting weekly dances—and young women being encouraged to attend—it really wasn't much of a surprise when nature took its course.

Voices of the Left Behind should be mandatory reading for all adolescent women, as it exposes to just what lengths young men will go to get young women into compromising positions. It also explains just how naive most of these women were. From today's perspective, it might be difficult to understand this naïveté but, back then, sex was pretty much a taboo subject, not even talked about between mother and daughter. Sex education didn't exist. Only when it was too late did the reality of the moment become a lifelong consequence called a baby.

The Canadian government knew exactly why these soldiers had been deployed to those towns scattered across the UK countryside, and it wasn't for pleasure. Those men were being trained as fighting soldiers, willing to risk all, to pay the ultimate price with their lives. Tens of thousands did just that. On one day—June 19, 1942—707 of them died during the first Allied strike against the Germans from the sea. It was called Operation Rutter, later becoming Operation Jubilee. Today we know it as either the Battle of Dieppe or the Dieppe Raid, or maybe better stated, the worst planned event of the war. It was the first and by no means the last battle these young men fought to defend our freedoms. They deserve our accolades and everlasting respect.*

Again, our government knew these soldiers would soon meet the war head-on; it was like a fast-moving tornado on the Kansas plains. Hence, a night or two out on the town after the dance was deemed entirely accept-able. Getting married, however, was a completely different kettle of fish. Although the men were technically allowed to marry, getting permission from the government proved incredibly difficult. All sorts of bureaucratic obstacles were thrown into their paths. The end result was that it became next to impossible. Why would the government do this? First, in the belief that it was acting for the sake of the men, it didn't want the soldiers rushing into marriage. Second, as soldiers, the men owed their loyalties first to their country and the regiments in which they served. Third, because the proba-bility of death was so high, Canada knew that it would be on the economic hook to the wife and child of a Canadian soldier killed in action. Putting it bluntly, it was okay to die for your country. But please be patriotic enough not to leave behind an unwanted financial liability.

Canada's backside was covered. On paper it worked, but in real life it didn't, at least not for the soldiers. As it turned out, the Canadian libido was thriving. Thousands of babies with Canadian fathers drew their first breath during World War II. Eric Clapton, David Clayton-Thomas, Senator Roméo Dallaire, and John Ralston Saul's brother are all products of these unions. Eric Clapton was born out of wedlock, and he was a far cry from being the only one.[4]

Now, despite the morals du jour, how could anyone place blame on those young men and women? Each and every one of them lived in a surreal world. Could Hitler emerge victorious? Would Britain be overrun by German sol-diers? How many, if any, young British men would survive? What is real, what you know to be true, is that your country is at war, and it's not going on in some faraway land. They're bombing in your own backyard, and the bona fide question is: Will I live to see tomorrow? As a soldier, you know that

---

* As of Remembrance Day 2014, CIC and the government of Canada still deny citizenship to some soldiers and children of World War II.

soon you're off to war. The rifle you're carrying isn't for fun—it's to shoot, or be shot. You know the odds. Before the action starts, before the blood and guts begin to fly, you have a momentary solace, a love in your heart, a young woman, and a desire. Some may have entertained the idea of a child. You may be going off to die, but life, and your chance to be a part of it, to continue on, if you will, was possible by having a baby.

As a young woman, you might really be in love. It might be that you've spent several years with your beau; the two of you frequently requested permission to marry. But every time the top brass responded by saying no. Coming to grips with the fact that you might never see the love of your life again, what would you do? A baby would be a connection, forever a part of your life and a reminder of the soldier. Maybe you'd be granting a potentially dying man his last request? Would spending an evening with a person willing to go off and die for you and your family be too much to give?

In war, there are no clear answers. The long-term horizon often means surviving into the next day. When you have but a fleeting instant in time, love and passion have a way of stealing the moment.

The Canadian combatants did their job. Sadly, over 45,000 paid the ultimate price. For those who did survive, the government capitulated, allowing them to marry their brides at war's end. And they did it in droves— almost 65,000 women and children came to Canada on war-bride ships paid for and sponsored by the Canadian government. It was one of the largest subsidized waves of immigrants in Canada's history.[5]

Today, one in thirty Canadians has a war bride in his or her family. In truth, the war brides' narrative is the story of Canada, as these women spread out all across the land. As time pressed forward, their families grew. These women were not just a vein of our heritage but an integral artery in which Canadian culture and society flowed forth.

And that's just from World War II. Not mentioning the war brides of World War I would be doing them, and our country, a huge disservice. They too made their indelible mark on Canada's heart.

Gwen LeFort was just sixteen when she came to Canada in 1918 to become a war bride. She tells her story:

I went to school in England until I was 14. And then, of course, the First Great War broke out, so I quit school and went to work. I was delivering milk. The men were all gone to war, and the women were doing the men's work. It was conscription in England at the time. My dad didn't have to go because he had a large family, [so] he was able to stay home. But the majority of the men were at war. The only young men around were like the Canadian soldiers who were stationed in Shorncliff, which is about 84 miles from Folkestone. A lot of Canadian soldiers. And there were a lot of wounded Canadian soldiers that used to come into town, because Shorn-cliff—there was a big military hospital there. So, we were very attracted to Canadian boys because we loved their accent. I always say I fell in love with an accent.

My father had a restaurant, and there's where I met my husband. He was in hospital, and he was in my dad's place, and I met him there, took him home. My mum felt sorry for the boys from Canada because they were so far from home. So that's where we met. And when he had to go back to France, we were corresponding. And then he came out to Canada once he was discharged. I didn't follow until a year after…

He wasn't wounded. He was shell-shocked. The effects of the war, being in the trenches, had worn down his—his nerves were gone. He was very, very nervous. He was discharged on those grounds. In fact, he got a pension for that reason… He dwelled on what had happened. I used to say, 'It's not happening now. Why not try and forget it'… And he did [dwell on it] for years after. In fact, I was living in Cheticamp [Cape Breton], married, and I had about 8 children—I had 11 altogether—and he had a nervous breakdown, and it was the effects of what he had gone through during the war. Mentally, he was wounded. (And yet you wanted to be with him.) Well, of course, he was my husband. (But even before he was your husband, you'd met him and he'd already…) Well, yes, met him, took him home. Like I say, my mum took pity on him, I guess, because he was so far from home. And I suppose she thought: Well, it could be one of my sons. So, took him home, and in the English fashion gave him cups of tea and things like that, you know, made him welcome. (What about yourself? You were attracted to him.) At that time, he didn't show it as much as he did in later years. In later years—oh my stars, when we were living in Cheticamp, he would sometimes jump up in the middle of the night and say that somebody was coming after him, and he could hear horses. Oh, it was terrible there for a year. For a year, he didn't work at all, his nerves were absolutely gone. And it's all the effects of World War One.[6]

Gwen's story is typical of the wives and families of returning soldiers. Life was never the same again for them.

Some 650,000 Canadians enlisted in World War I. Of those, 418,000 were sent overseas, where more than 68,000—over 10 percent—died in action; 156,000 more were wounded.[7] This means that more than half of all Canadian soldiers sent overseas came back wounded or dead—that was almost 3 percent of the entire population of Canada in 1918.

In 1919, the government of Canada passed an order-in-council offering free passage to the dependents of those Canadian soldiers; over 54,500 foreign-born war brides and their children took them up on that offer.[8] They arrived in Nova Scotia and New Brunswick, and when the St. Lawrence thawed, others went to Quebec. Their fare was for steerage class, with some steaming over on the *Olympic*, sister ship of the ill-fated *Titanic*. Far from the ravaged, war-torn continent from where they came, Canada was a morning ray of hope for these families. They integrated well into their new country and, in their own way, became nation builders.

Same thing with the war brides of the next world war, twenty-seven years later. The stories of those 43,454 women who made their way, along with their 20,997 children, from foreign shores to Canada after World War II are legendary. Like a rainbow on the tail end of a rainstorm, they were a welcome sight when they began arriving in 1946 at Pier 21 in Halifax. It seems that just about everyone got in on it. Starved for good news, the media in Canada couldn't get enough of the war brides. Coast to coast, in every newspaper, there was some snippet about these families. As their predecessors did before them, the war brides spread out across the country. In 1946, they made up 80 percent of all the immigrants allowed into Canada, although they weren't immigrants, they were Canadian citizens.

Or were they? As the head of the Lost Canadians, I had always thought so. But in 2006, our CIC bureaucrats were rejecting many of these women and their children, saying no, they weren't Canadian, and I'll be damned if I could get our elected representatives in this new century of tolerance and understanding to stand behind the political promises and bureaucratic acceptance of yesteryear. Topping that off, getting coverage from an interested media en masse was nothing short of an exercise in futility. Lindsay Lohan got more coverage.

Once again, I'm getting ahead of myself. Back to the past:

In August of 1946, Prime Minister Mackenzie King boarded the *Queen Mary* in Southampton, England, to sail back to Canada along with 1,837 British war brides. On board, before their arrival at Pier 21, he gave a speech to all the women gathered on the deck. As reported by the *Queen Mary*'s onboard newspaper *Cunard Ocean Bulletin*, Mr. King congratulated the war brides, "who won the hearts of Canadian soldiers, the men on their choice of brides, and Canada on the splendid addition being made to its citizenship."[9] Next came a pamphlet titled *Dock to Destination*, published and distributed to the women by Immigration Canada, that stated (as you may recall from Chapter 6), "As soon as the ship docks Canadian Immigration officials will come aboard. These men will complete the formalities for your entry into Canada which automatically make you a Canadian citizen." As with the women of World War I, the Privy Council had issued orders of acceptance, although this time declaring the war brides and their dependent children had the same status as their Canadian husbands and fathers respectively.[10]

It was a magnificent moment for both the war-torn families and for Canada. Going forward, life in this new land would be far more promising and secure than that which these families had left behind in Europe. Canada was a fresh start in a country of newly found hope. Really, how could anyone not be moved to tears when recounting that journey? You left a country ravaged by death and destruction and, somewhere in the midst of that chaos, you discovered love and maybe gave birth to a child. Going further, Canada is so enthusiastic about wanting you that its own Privy Council extends its collective welcome by issuing orders to get you here. The Canadian wives adjunct of the Adjutant General's Office of the Canadian Military Headquarters in London then processes and arranges everything needed for your passage, followed by the government of Canada paying for absolutely everything. At this point, the prime minister personally accompanies you on the transatlantic crossing, making certain you feel accepted in your new homeland "as a citizen." And if that were not enough, the national broadcasting network, CBC, films your entire voyage, and in its news clip refers to your child as "Johnny Canuck Jr.," then concludes by saying, "To its new citizens, Canada extends the hearty hand of welcome."[11] Honest to goodness, it just doesn't get any better than that.

Clearly, these women received this red-carpet treatment partly because of the great success of their predecessors, the war brides of World War I. Everybody had come out ahead—the women, their veteran husbands, their children, and the country. Remember Gwen LeFort saying that she had eleven children? In the quarter century since the end of the Great War, Canada's population had grown by more than 4 million, with fewer than 2 million of those through immigration. What this means is that Canada, a country of enormous magnitude in terms of landmass, was sparsely populated and desired more people. The war brides of World War I had been wonderful at procreating. And now, with a new batch of women entering Canada at the height of their child-bearing years, the government was delighted—it had done its part. In 1945, it even passed the Family Allowance Act, which introduced the family allowance, better known as the baby bonus.[12] It was now time for these new couples to do their part. Besides, what else was there to do on a cold winter's evening on the Saskatchewan prairies?

Of course, that was for those who stayed. A small percentage of the women, around 4,500, returned to the country they had come from, and more often than not took their children with them.

As I said, the world was starved for good news, for feel-good stories that could take one's mind off the aftermath of the war. And there was nothing better than war brides and their babies reuniting with Daddy back home. That's what made headlines. In Paul Harvey fashion, there often was a story behind the story, one that wasn't so warm and fuzzy.*

Only in recent years have nations been able to comprehend more fully what Gwen LeFort understood only too well: post-traumatic stress disorder, better known as PTSD. The mystique of wartime romance is often portrayed as though it were a fairy tale. In real life, it can be just that: nothing but a fantasy. It's estimated that 25 percent of returning soldiers suffered in one form or another from the mental stress of war. In October 1945, a man I knew named Will Allister returned from Japan after being a guest of the Japanese Army for almost four years. He had been one of the 1,685 Canadian soldiers—my dad's best friend, Jack Rose, being another—taken as a prisoner of war in Hong Kong on Christmas Day 1941.[13] It took Will more than forty years to write his book *Where Life and Death Hold Hands*, published in 1989. In a way, writing it was therapy, a part of the healing process that allowed him to come to grips with his experiences almost a half century earlier. In turning those feelings into words, he did something few vets are able to do, and that was to vent. Soldiers, the ones who really have seen battle, usually keep a disconnected silence between themselves and society, even their own families.

Will describes his feelings just after liberation:[14]

I reviewed the lightning changes of the past few weeks ... I was shocked by the luxuries, the food, the way they had turned the war into a fun thing. How in the world could we expect people to understand?

And the bloodthirsty reporters ... hungry for stories. Pressing me to describe a beating. Disappointed at my version of how Yamanaka beat me, bloodied me, drew his sword threatening to decapitate me.

[Reporters:] "Is that all?"

---

* Paul Harvey was an American radio announcer for the ABC Radio Networks, known for his *News and Comment* program, as well as for his *The Rest of the Story*.

[Will:] "Well—I thought that was enough..."
[Reporters:] "No, no, don't you have anything with more kick to it? Something really gruesome?"

Will (after arriving back in BC):

Then the five day binge of wild drinking and partying and violent mood swings. Ecstasy, depression, anxiety, hilarity, unreality. And the therapy of the streets: just an orderly row of happy houses, solid, permanent, unscarred... windows, doors, shutters, painted and bright... a revelation. A proof that life could go on, without any cyclonic threat from the holocaust that had crippled half the world.

When talking about the then love of his life, a young woman named Evelyn, a girl who had not escaped his mind, this is what he had to say:

Would she be waiting? If I could have peered into a crystal ball I would have seen our meeting in New York, a strange day fraught with tensions, groping through the darkness of four years estrangement: the sad account of how she'd fallen in love with a GI who was killed... how she couldn't write, not wanting to lie or cause pain. The abyss was too wide by now, unbridgeable, and I was to end up marrying someone else within a year.

And his thoughts on returning to his family?

Home... I walked slowly from room to room with the family following silently... Everything in place, breathing peace and contentment, the end of strife. I wanted to linger over every detail, but not with this well-meaning but obtrusive audience. We sat down around the dining room table for tea and honeycake... the distance between us was frightening. They seemed so unaware, their problems so tinsel-textured. It seemed all just words. More song without melody... the barrier between us was insurmountable and seemed to grow wider with each passing hour... The more I strove to become part of this setting, the more it eluded me. Along with this awareness came an undefined anxiety that gnawed at me as though some furry tarantula had slipped into my brain and was creeping about with soft threatening steps. This was to be the hallmark of former POWs in the years ahead... I nursed a mad desire to be back in 3D [the Japanese POW camp], where everything really *existed*—away from this glowing make-believe. I had to get away—to see Bob [a fellow POW], now. They couldn't understand.

Regrettably, Will's tale was not uncommon. And neither was this: many of the husbands of war brides found their solace in drinking to excess with their war buddies at the local Legion. I had two Uncle Georges. Both were deeply immersed in their war experience. The first never spoke a word about it. The second became an alcoholic, and his marriage to my aunt failed. Not long before he died, his adult daughter engaged him in conversation. He'd been asked by some buddies to go hunting, and she asked her father if he would go. The reply? "No, I've killed too many people in my life."

How does one respond to that? In the decades before, he had never uttered one word about his involvement in the war. And after this shocking revelation, he never spoke another. And that one sentence was one more than what you heard from other similar war-ravished Canadian vets.

From hamlets to hilltops, Canadian war brides were everywhere. There had been 48,000 marriages, producing 10,000 more children born overseas than those produced by their American counterparts, proving that Canadian soldiers had been occupied with firing more than just guns and bullets.

In the decades that followed, the war brides assimilated well into Canada. Their children grew up and, like every other youngster from the 1940s and '50s, became a slice of Canadian life. They were typical kids of their era. Ian Munroe and Peter Brammah grew up and joined the navy. Marion Vermeersch became a social worker. Jackie Scott worked for the Township of Scarborough and later as a secretary for a barrister who then became a judge. Their mothers and fathers were like every other Canadian mother and father: They voted and sat on juries. They got Canadian passports, they paid taxes, and they lived the good Canadian life. In every way, shape, and form, they had become the quintessential Canadian. Mackenzie King would have been proud. History would show that the vision of the government in the 1940s had been worthy in its acceptance of the families of these Canadian soldiers. Indeed, like their predecessors from World War I, these war brides and their children too were nation builders.

LIKE PREPARING for daylight savings, it's time to spring forward from the 1940s by turning the calendar almost sixty years ahead. The year is now 2005, and there are several months to go before the federal election in January 2006. At this point, the Liberal government had opposed the Lost

Canadian issue with a vengeance. It made absolutely no sense. What possible public good was being served by denying us our citizenship? But deny us it did. Fresh from their defeat over s-2, the triple forces—the bureaucrats, Citizenship Minister Joe Volpe, and, above him, Prime Minister Paul Martin—were all in sync. When an occasional case concerning a war bride, or one of her foreign-born kids who'd been fortunate enough to have been born in wedlock, crossed their desks, they pressed forward, sometimes quietly rejecting the person's citizenship, at other times making backroom deals. There was no real consistency except for the not-so-lucky, the born-out-of-wedlock kids who were still being denied. The triplets in power were forcing us back into the trenches of all-out battle. It seems the cic of 2005 had decided Canadian citizenship did not begin until January 1, 1947, and, because the war brides and their kids had not been officially naturalized, they really weren't citizens after all. The previous sixty years, according to cic, had been a lie. cic's printed words back in 1946—"As soon as the ship docks Canadian Immigration officials will come aboard. These men will complete the formalities for your entry into Canada which automatically make you a Canadian citizen"—were explained away as being a simple misunderstanding. Which means that when Mackenzie King stood on the deck of the *Queen Mary* and welcomed the war brides, assuring them that they were all "Canadian citizens," he didn't know what the hell he was talking about.

How unbelievably arrogant and presumptuous for present-day politicians to question the meaning behind a former prime minister's words, especially a prime minister who had led Canada through very difficult times of war, and who was able more than anyone to place proper value on the survivors of that conflict. According to the bureaucrats, to Joe Volpe, and to Captain Steak or Chicken Paul Martin, "citizen" really wasn't what the prime minister in 1946 had meant. The triplets, having had a change of heart—a cold, frosty, frozen change of heart—were not nearly so accommodating as Mackenzie King had been to the war brides.[15] Mr. Volpe later stood in front of our rolling Lost Canadian camera and stated that, since he had to become an immigrant, so should we. He was drawing a line in the sand. To the war brides and their kids, the battles of World War II had not yet ended. The new front line of combat was now going to be in the federal courtrooms of Canada. For these present-day elderly Canadian women and their middle-aged children, their battle to be Canadian citizens remained but a dream, still years from resolution. Some would die before being recognized. As for the rest, they were about to discover that their fair, compassionate, human-rights-advocating country wasn't even vaguely as advertised.

PART 3

LOST CANADIANS UNDER THE CONSERVATIVES

CHAPTER 9

CHANGING OF THE GUARD

The storm of an election loomed just over the Ottawa horizon.
With Prime Minister Paul Martin about to face a vote of non-
confidence in the House, the political tides were about to change.
DON CHAPMAN, NOVEMBER 2005

I CLEARLY UNDERSTOOD the importance of the media when it came to the
unpredictable motivations of Ottawa politicians. From my days before Bill
S-2, I had befriended a CIC insider who, from her vantage, spotted many
anomalies within the confines of the department. That source proved to
be invaluable. Thanks to her, I often knew what was coming down the pike
long before the media or politicians had been tipped off. A lawyer who had
helped me in the pre-S-2 days called my emails to him "the best computer
game in town." At times I knew the "scoop du jour" long before the media
did. Not just issues pertaining to citizenship but also many rumours and
facts. I had become an Ottawa-insider outsider. By the end of 2005, I had
many political friends. And with citizenship being more or less a non-partisan issue, my contacts didn't feel threatened about talking. Indeed, they
often spoke with little to no restraint. This included the top brass at parliamentary security, legislative assistants in both the House and the Senate,
interns, senators, MPs, bureaucrats, even some investigative journalists.
There was hardly any slice of the Ottawa pie that I hadn't tasted. I got to
know which hotels and which restaurants were political hangouts, and often
happened to be in the right place at the right time to join a gathering of top

politicians for an impromptu get-together. On a moment's notice, I could pretty much get into the office of any of the various MPs whose support I needed.

The constant exceptions were the prime minister and leaders of the opposing political parties. They never proved easy nuts to crack. But there were channels into those offices.[1] I would have thought that for any member of the parliamentary press, it would have been akin to dying and going to press corps heaven having an inside contact like me. That's why the laziness of the Ottawa media, and of journalists all across Canada, never ceased to amaze me. They really didn't seem to get it. Not just in misunderstanding our issue but in failing to grasp the potential good fortune of having an insider who was willing to feed them the odd story here and there. In the States, I'd been interviewed for my expertise on aviation safety by ABC's *20/20*; I'd been quoted in the *Wall Street Journal*, *Newsweek*, and *Business Week*; and I even submitted testimony to Congress. As a pilot, I'd taken all sorts of psychological tests to establish that I was of sound mind before being handed the keys to a $200 million Boeing 747. None of that seemed to matter in Canada. The media's level of caring wasn't nearly as strong as their desire to write a quick article and be finished with their day's work. I was sitting on a Woodward-and-Bernstein-type story. But that sort of investigative journalism took time, and time was money. So often there were corporate bosses who, in spite of having fancy corporate mission statements about the public good, seemed much more cognizant of their bottom lines than of the morals of doing what is right.

Good pilots know their limitations, both what they can do and what they cannot do. Engaging my skills of patience and discretion in Ottawa, I filed away interesting tidbits in my mental filing cabinet.

I had paid my own way through university by working for an NBC television network affiliate and for a radio station in Tampa, WFLA. I had taken many classes in journalism and, after several years of being employed at the news studios, I came away not a complete novice from the backwoods. But in Canada, I was often regarded as some sort of lunatic. Sometimes from the get-go, a reporter or bureau chief's suspicion made me feel like a character from the *Blues Brothers*. I hadn't echoed Jake and Elwood's claim that they were "on a mission from God," but, as with Andrew Telegdi, the media viewed me as a one-trick pony. Sure, they had a slight understanding that some sort of citizenship problem did indeed exist, but their journalistic senses had not been titillated. Remember Will Allister's comments upon returning from Japan, where he had been a POW?

And the bloodthirsty reporters... hungry for stories. Pressing me to describe a beating. Disappointed at my version of how Yamanaka beat me, bloodied me, drew his sword threatening to decapitate me.
[Reporters:] "Is that all?"
[Will:] "Well—I thought that was enough..."
[Reporters:] "No, no, don't you have anything with more kick to it? Something really gruesome?"

The story of the Lost Canadians just wasn't brutal, violent, or sexy enough to appeal to the Ottawa press corps' insatiable craving for more flamboyant tales of excitement. Decapitating one's identity through denial of citizenship wouldn't sell newspapers or boost television ratings with the same gusto as would a Romanian stripper scandal. Nor was our issue capable of embarrassing the politicians, it seemed.

As if in a perpetual game of political positioning, the MPs' objective was to bring favour to their party at the direct expense of the competition. Although there are some individual exceptions, most MPs seemed to be in Ottawa not so much for the benefit of Canadians as they were, to use my mother's description of the impetus of war, for money, power, and prestige. The political actors of Ottawa didn't so much play on a world stage as cater to their own homegrown audience. They very much cared about their images and how they were perceived by Canadians, which, at some later date, would hopefully translate into votes. Their universe rotated around the ballot box. Image mattered more than reality. The truth could be stretched or defamed. What became clear was that ascending the political ladder of success was at times more a direct result of ripping apart the competition than of being a superlative standout. President Kennedy had his own thoughts on the matter: "The great enemy of the truth is very often not the lie—deliberate, contrived, and dishonest—but the myth—persistent, persuasive, and unrealistic." He certainly knew how the game was played.

No question about it: a destructive cycle existed in Ottawa. The media had no problem feeding on the carcasses of wounded politicians, and the politicians had no problem undermining their opposition. The spin doctors were alive and well in Ottawa, supported by a complacent media.

As has become all too common, the human factor wasn't as important to the media as profits. Sexy stories sell, bastard war-bride children don't. It was a tough lesson for a kid from the "peace and love generation," but I pressed on, believing in the lesson I learned in the 1960s, that one person really can make a difference. Jeff Wan used to describe me as "always plotting and planning, plotting and planning." His perceptiveness could be uncanny.

On Tuesday, November 29, 2005, in a vote of 171 to 133, Paul Martin's government succumbed; Canada was going to an election. It was historic in that never before had the government fallen on a simple vote of non-confidence. It was only the fifth time the country had ever held winter elections.

Maybe with a touch of smugness, and with John Reynolds championing our issue within the Tory ranks, along with his assurances that a Harper victory meant our issue would be settled, I found that rooting for a Conservative victory was not hard to do. Besides, the Liberals had shown such an incredible lack of support, almost a disdain for the Lost Canadians, that I had come to view the Liberals as a party of hypocrites, one certainly, among other things, not willing to defend the Charter.

Granted, there were sympathetic MPs representing each party. And now I could donate to various campaigns and write letters of support, as an official, legal landed immigrant in Canada. (I had very reluctantly become an immigrant, in March 2003, as did my wife and three daughters; it was my last-chance option, the only choice available. For me the entire process—read "debacle"—was expensive, humiliating, degrading, and morally repugnant. No matter, I finally realized that it was my *only* way home.)[2] Meili Faille of the Bloc, Bill Siksay of the NDP, John Reynolds and Diane Ablonczy of the Conservatives, and Andrew Telegdi of the Liberals, all were Lost Canadian supporters, and all had my support.* Again, citizenship belongs to all Canadians and should never be a partisan issue. But when it comes to getting elected, all bets are off the table.

The Conservatives were fully aware of my wanting them to win, not because I'm a huge fan of theirs but because the old Liberal brand was stale and needed replacing. In a sense, it reminded me of a line from the old Lee Marvin movie *Paint Your Wagon*. The scene takes place about twenty years before our own confederation. It's the mid-1800s, and the setting is California at the beginning of the gold rush. A Mormon man with two wives arrives in a small mining town whose 400 residents are all male. The two wives don't much like each other, and the men don't much like one man having two of something the others have none of. Soon the suggestion pops up about putting one wife, Elizabeth, up for auction. Eager to get out of the marriage, she agrees. Her husband says, "Elizabeth, you don't know what you'll get."

---

* Of these five MPs, two got their citizenship as immigrants.

"But I know what I've got," came the reply.

That's the way I felt. I had met Harper in the hallways of Centre Block a few months earlier, and in true lobbyist fashion, I walked up and introduced myself as the person behind the Lost Canadians. He was accompanied by his security detail (maybe they were legislative assistants), and the four of us stood there as I shook his hand and looked him in the eye. As we clasped hands, I thought, *You're as boring in person as you are on TV.* A mortician's smile on his face, he at most uttered just a word or two. I sensed a discomfort but really wasn't certain. The only standout thing was the incredible lack of emotion he showed. It was a unique experience for me. I've met all kinds of politicians and celebrities over the years, but I have never come across such a lack of personality. Was Harper having a bad day? Was an unplanned encounter not his bailiwick? No matter. If the Lost Canadians had any chance of becoming citizens, we had to jump on board the boat captained by Stephen Harper.

TWO DAYS before Christmas 2005, the shopping malls bustled with last-minute shoppers. Toddlers held tight to their mothers' hands while waiting patiently in line to see Santa Claus. Grocery stores were running low on holiday hams and turkeys, university students headed home for a much needed break, and children waited anxiously for the big day. For others, a different big day was approaching: Canada would soon be heading to the polls.

On December 23, 2005, I fired off something I had written to chronicle a bit of history on our issue, a Lost Canadian timeline if you will, to some faceless person out there in cyberspace. His name was Brian Hunter. He was with the Conservatives, and Stephen Harper still remained our best shot at ending this citizenship fiasco. Playing to my audience, I targeted Paul Martin, at times quoting his many statements. Here's part of my email:

> **February 2005:** Paul Martin in the House of Commons: "Our laws must reflect equality not as we understood it a century or even a decade ago, but as we understand it today. If we do not step forward, then we step back. If we do not protect a right, then we deny it. My responsibility as prime minister, my duty to Canada and to Canadians, is to defend the Charter in its entirety."
>
> **May 2005:** Conservative-sponsored Bill s-2 becomes law, supposedly allowing the Lost Canadian children the right to reclaim their citizenship.
>
> **September 2005:** Prime Minister Paul Martin gave a scathing

assessment of the United Nations, telling world leaders it was "too often" filled with "empty rhetoric."

October 2005: Paul Martin talking about the softwood lumber issue: "We will not negotiate a win."

November 2005: Minister Volpe talking about the enormous backlog of 700,000 prospective immigrants: "We have to start thinking about the Immigration Department as a recruiting vehicle for Canada's demographic and labour market needs... We are the lungs of the country." Within days, Mr. Martin's government announces: "The federal government is about to mount a campaign to persuade Canadians who have left to return home."

December 2005: The Lost Canadian children are still being denied their citizenship and the right to return to Canada. Unlike his stance with the Khadr family, Paul Martin remains silent, allowing this human rights violation to continue.

December 2005: Paul Martin Jr. is doing to the Lost Canadian children what the US is doing with softwood lumber, ignoring both the law and the win.

It seems that Santa and his elves weren't the only ones busy as bees preparing gifts that surprise. So too was the Conservative campaign machine. Wherever they were located, the top dogs and staffers were buzzing with election fever. I had been told by a party insider that the Conservatives were interested in taking out a full-page campaign ad in the *National Post* to talk about the Lost Canadians. Or, to be more specific (as I came to understand later), about the impotence of Paul Martin. Being only too happy to get the word out, regardless of who won the election, I knew that a full-page ad in a national paper would bring significant credibility to the issue. Besides, whether or not Mr. Martin got re-elected, he'd at least know his unwillingness to solve the Lost Canadian problem had been noticed across the country, and quite possibly know too that, if he *did* get re-elected, the opposition would use his embarrassing lack of achievement against him in the future. Surely he'd be motivated to do something, even if just a wee bit, because anything was better than nothing, and nothing is what he had accomplished so far.

I was also told the ad would not cost me anything. Finally, something I didn't have to pay for. Post-9/11 was traumatic for everyone, for many reasons, but few felt its financial toll worse than airline pilots. United had scaled back our wages, and not just by a few percentage points. It had extracted huge pay concessions. In my case, the cut was a whopping 65 percent of my salary. To top it off, the company now wanted my hard-earned pension back. Funding an ongoing war against a bottomless-money-pit government had not been easy. I often wondered what would happen if Bill Gates were Canadian and the government tried to cancel *his* citizenship. Wouldn't that be quite the battle? But that was fantasy, and I lived in the real world. That's why having a political party so moved to correct the issue that it would eagerly pay huge amounts of money for a full-page campaign ad on the subject seemed like a godsend.

When my fairly mundane email to Brian Hunter arrived on the desk of one of his staff, it was quickly passed up through the ranks. The first stop, it appears, was with Sheryl Hughes, who I imagine was Hunter's secretary. She in turn forwarded my email to a Carol Young, with this note attached:

> Hi Carol,
> Here is another email from Don Chapman that you can forward on to the appropriate people.

Four days later, after Christmas and Boxing Day, Carol wrote this response to Sheryl:

> Thanks for the information. I hope you had a Merry Christmas.

Five days later, the day after New Year's, Sheryl sent this back to Carol:

> Here is a revised version of the national post ad.
> Thanks
> Brian

One day later, on January 3, this is what was sent to me:

> Dear Don,
> Please see the revised version of the National Post Advertisement.
> When it is convenient could you please call Colin* on his cell phone.
> Regards,
> Carol Young
> Davies Advocates

---

* A Conservative Party lawyer.

Attached to the email was a copy of the ad. Eagerly, I downloaded the PDF. And there it was. At the top, a caricature, in colour, of Paul Martin standing on one of his Canada Steamship Lines container ships, which was, of course, flying a flag of convenience; below, the caption "If you won't protect the Charter of Rights and Freedoms then you have no business to become the Prime Minister of Canada, says Paul Martin."[3] Below that, in block letters, centred on the page and in all caps, it read: "LOST IN MY OWN COUNTRY."

Below that were seven bullet points about the Lost Canadians. In one, Magali Castro-Gyr was referenced as being "exiled" by the Liberals, denied citizenship, and sent out of Canada because she refused to sign their gag order. The next point, referred to as "fact," was that there were 85,000 people who, like me, were Lost Canadians. The Liberal bureaucrats and their "no" attitudes were mentioned, and that many Lost Canadians were approaching retirement age. The ad wrapped it all up by highlighting how Paul Martin's government was streamlining immigration for foreigners while ignoring s-2 and the Lost Canadians.

At the very bottom, again in block letters, centred and capitalized:

CANADIANS DESERVE THEIR RIGHT TO CITIZENSHIP
THE CHARTER OF RIGHTS AND FREEDOMS MUST BE PROTECTED

Just one of many attack ads, this one was intended as a one-two punch, hitting directly at the Liberal jugular. The problem? I was adamant about keeping citizenship a non-partisan issue. It had to be. History is littered with the skeletal remains of former one-party regimes that wrote the rules of allegiance. Feeling as I do that citizenship must belong to all Canadians, never to just one political party, I began to ponder the alternatives. What would happen if Paul Martin, or Stephen Harper, won? By hitching my cart to the Conservative campaign wagon, my days of easily jumping out of one political window and into another might be over. I'd be labelled as a Harperite, which I wasn't, and forevermore be looked at with suspicion by the Liberals. And I wouldn't have blamed them. With a Martin victory, Martin would control both the House and the Senate, whereas I'd be a single pawn on a chessboard facing unlimited queens, bishops, knights, and rooks—while the king controlled the rules. As much as I wanted it, I couldn't support the ad. I had, of course, expected there to be some sort of bias, given that it was produced by a political party, but I had still hoped that it would get behind me and my cause. Those hopes were dashed upon seeing the ad, which was written not for the benefit of Lost Canadians but for the sole purpose of getting Harper elected. Through an email I said I would not support the ad and didn't want my name associated with it. Never again was I contacted about it, and in the end, the ad did not run.

By withdrawing my support, just maybe and without realizing it, I violated three Harper-Conservative code-of-honour rules: (1) never question the boss, (2) do whatever is asked of you, and (3) do whatever it takes. I'm still not certain if my refusal to endorse the ad was the reason for what happened after the election. I doubt it. But once Harper became prime minister, the Lost Canadian issue got relegated to the back shelves of a Siberian filing cabinet, or at least that's how it seemed. My gut has always told me that there was another explanation, that Harper never really cared about us to begin with.

A child who'd been a tad bit difficult but still wanted presents might have reservations about Christmas morning, hoping not to have crossed onto the "bad" side of Santa's naughty or nice list. Earlier, I really had believed what John Reynolds had told me: that Harper would fix our issue "with the stroke of a pen." Over the years, the Conservatives had several times used this exact phrase in committee and on the floor of the House. Three years earlier, MP Darrel Stinson, who sponsored the first of five Conservative Lost Canadian bills, gave this reason for his party's favouring the restoration of our citizenship: "To correct historic wrongs and bring the 2003 act up to current morals and standards of what it means to be Canadian."[4]

Why then wouldn't they keep their promises? It was the right thing to do, and the Conservatives knew it. But this was Ottawa, where doing something because it is morally right isn't exactly in the code of conduct.

The one constant in the universe is that things are always changing. On the grandiose scale of the cosmos, change is usually slow and gradual. In politics, change can be as rapid as a supernova. At the celestial core of Ottawa is the prime minister and, after the 2006 election, the chief energy source was Stephen Harper, who really had not uttered a word about righting our "historic wrongs." Like the difficult child having reservations at Christmas, I too had my doubts about the new government. When we had shaken hands, me standing all of maybe twelve inches from Mr. Harper, I had looked directly into his eyes. In that instant, and from that moment on, I didn't share John Reynolds's optimism. Regardless, with the election now over and the honeymoon period about to begin, it was time for me to step back and allow John to try to work his magic from the inside. Like one of the good kids at Christmas, hopeful with fingers crossed, I remained optimistic about the possibility of us getting our presents.

Topping the list of official duties for a new prime minister is determining the Throne Speech and appointing a cabinet. Both provide clues to the direction of the new government, and to just whom we really elected.

On April 4, 2006, Michaëlle Jean sat in the governor general's chair, the chair reserved just for her, in the Red Chamber—the Senate of Canada—and delivered the Throne Speech. Here are a few excerpts:

> No aspect of responsible government is more fundamental than having the trust of citizens... The trust of citizens must be earned every day... To remain strong and effective, our federation must keep pace with the evolving needs of Canadian society... More broadly, this Government is committed to supporting Canada's core values of freedom, democracy, the rule of law and human rights around the world... [The Government] honours the past efforts of our veterans... the Government looks forward to making this Parliament work for the benefit of the Canadian people.

The speech concluded with:

> May Divine Providence guide your deliberations.[5]

Oh goody, I thought. Still living in Phoenix, I was only too aware of the American obsession with religion. In my opinion, Bush was a whack-job, and the last thing I wanted was a Canada that emulated his holier-than-thou attitudes. After emerging the winner on the day of the election, Harper finally sported a real smile. I haven't yet forgotten the closing words of his acceptance speech, almost interchangeable as they were with those Jr. Bush had used to conclude his speeches: "God bless Canada." Only the name of the country had changed. Once again Harper smiled. I didn't.

With the recent cabinet appointments came Monte Solberg, the newly minted minister of citizenship and immigration. Anxious to work with him, I nonetheless waited a few weeks before calling. Fortunately, my Rolodex contained tons of contact information for previous ministers and their staff and, by now, I knew that the one relatively constant thing in Ottawa was the phone system. People came and went, but telephone numbers remained the same. I could have done it in my sleep: from my home in Phoenix, I dialled the minister's number from memory. The receptionist at CIC's Laurier Avenue office in downtown Ottawa answered. To her, the voice on the other end was all too familiar. I also recognized her voice; the only real difference was the greeting. No longer the "office of the Honourable Joe Volpe," it was now the "office of the Honourable Monte Solberg." I didn't expect to speak directly to Solberg. But I did want to let his chief of staff know about the Conservative promises to fix our problem and that, on the other end of the issue, were real human beings desperately in need. Offering my expertise, I reiterated my feelings: "Please, I would love to work with Mr. Solberg's top people to correct a blemish on Canada's past, to 'right an historic wrong.'" I made it clear that I was available any time convenient to them. I was even willing to fly to Ottawa, at my own expense, to meet in person. Whatever was needed, they could count on me.

The receptionist took my message and said that if they were interested, they'd get back to me.

"I sure hope so," I said. "I tried unsuccessfully to work with Mr. Volpe about the citizenship status of the war brides. Recently, a gentleman was forced to file a lawsuit against your department regarding him being a born-out-of-wedlock war-bride child. The suit should never go forward. Not only will the government lose, but you'll look stupid defending it. There's a lot more at stake here than Volpe ever imagined. Please, it's imperative for us to talk. Minister Solberg needs to be briefed, especially if he wants to correct this issue."

"Thank you, Mr. Chapman. I'll pass along the message."

Her reply wasn't reassuring. Even Joe Volpe, who was no prize, at least allowed me access to his deputy chief of staff and director of communications, Stephen Heckbert. And together, we did get some things accomplished. Could the receptionist's brush-off be an omen of things to come? I certainly hoped not.

But it was. My fears of Harper were coming true. After he announced his five top priorities to Parliament, none of which had a hint of anything to do with citizenship, I felt a little betrayed. Worse, I saw a prime minister who wasn't willing to "do the right thing."

Although the Liberals stood in opposition to the three previous Lost Canadian bills, and they certainly weren't rushing to get us back after the passage of s-2, they at least worked with me to help several people entangled in the fishing nets of the bureaucratic waters. Stephen Heckbert and I met, talked, or emailed each other more than a dozen times between February and August 2005, specifically about the war brides, their children still in limbo, and the people captured under s-2. I was always discreet when giving him names and associated details, getting the okay from the individuals involved before handing over their personal information. At times, there was an element of life or death to the situation. I received this email from one of the war-bride children in 2005:

I have been applying to immediately go to Canada to see my mother, who is in the hospital with cancer of the spine. She was given heavy drugs on entry into the hospital (her second cancer, breast removed earlier, two years ago) . . . we the family are getting our head into the fact she might not live more than a week.

Heckbert worked with me in cases like this, moving these Lost Canadians up in the queue. He too was trying to reunite these families, hopefully before the loved one died. One of the people I brought to his attention was Marylin Fong,* and it was only thanks to Heckbert's direct intervention that Marylin was able to look into her father's eyes as he lay on his deathbed and say, "Daddy, I'm Canadian." I will never forget talking with Marylin just after her father's death. Tearfully, she explained how she had held his hand and, when hearing how Canada had finally accepted his daughter, his weak grip got a tad stronger. He died just a week later, knowing that his little girl, after more than four decades of trying, at long last was a citizen of Canada.

There's a twist to this story in that Marylin's citizenship denial for all those years was unequivocally the result of discrimination against her father and his race. The family is Chinese, and her father, who grew up in Vancouver's Chinatown, desired a Chinese wife. But this presented a special problem because there were many more Chinese men than Chinese women in the country. Apparently, white Canadian servicemen weren't the only ones capable of producing kids, and our government knew this only too well. Chinese women immigrating to Canada would undoubtedly mean Canadian-born Chinese babies and, oh my God, that would be terrible. Given the taboos at the time against interracial courting, a young Chinese man was pretty much forced to travel to China to find a wife. On top of that, the Canadian government often changed the re-entry rules for Chinese Canadians, sometimes at a moment's notice. Who knows exactly what the government's motivation for this was, but the idea that if a man stayed in China, Canada would have one less Chinese inside its borders, is not a stretch of the imagination.[6] After all, years ago, Canada was not even close to being an accepting country for outsiders.[7] Anyway, off went Marylin's father to China, where he fell in love with a young woman. To his dismay, it was next to impossible getting his bride into Canada. The roadblocks were numerous—head taxes, strict immigration quotas, that sort of thing. So he moved his fiancée to Detroit, while he settled in Toronto. A long-distance

---

* A pseudonym.

courtship began and a pregnancy ensued. Nine months later, Marylin was born in Detroit. Three weeks after that, her parents made it official and tied the knot.

It seemed not only that CIC's tentacles impeded the born-out-of-wedlock war-bride children but also that the bureaucracy was quite good at exhibiting equal contempt against non-war-bride kids, just as long as they were born between 1867 and 1977 and in Canadian law considered nothing but "bastards."

In the end, Marylin got her citizenship, but there was no way of knowing how many other people were like her, qualified but unaware that CIC had opened up a temporary, three-and-a-half-month window of acceptance in May 2004. You may recall from Chapter 5 Charles Bosdet's and my testimony before the Senate regarding Bill S-17. The day after we spoke, CIC's then acting director general, Integration Branch, Patricia Birkett announced that CIC was shunning the unanimous Supreme Court decision *Benner v. Canada*. Truth be told, that wasn't the only court decision "offensive" to CIC's delicate sensibilities. *Benner* allowed in-wedlock, foreign-born children of Canadian mothers the same right to citizenship as in-wedlock, foreign-born children of Canadian fathers had. Another case, *Augier v. Canada*, set a precedent for granting equal citizenship rights to foreign-born, out-of-wedlock children of a Canadian father or mother. When Birkett, in what I considered a sneaky way, explained to the Senate how the court's rulings were "transitional"—setting August 14, 2004, as the termination date—she opened up a three-and-a-half-month window in which foreign-born, out-of-wedlock children of a Canadian father and foreign mother (people like Marylin Fong) might be granted citizenship by application. CIC's grudging acceptance of these children was simply the minimum required to satisfy the court decisions. And even then, it could be argued that it wasn't enough. Its roundabout ways of thwarting justice went unimpeded under the tutelage of citizenship minister Judy Sgro, and then, like the Olympic flame being passed from one athlete to the next, CIC's torch of discrimination was passed on to her successor, Joe Volpe, who took it and ran with it.[8]

Augier dealt specifically with the born-out-of-wedlock children. The concluding court order 5(2)(b) stated:

The Minister shall grant citizenship to any person who…
(b) was born outside Canada before February 15, 1977, of a mother or a father who was a citizen at the time of his birth, and was not entitled,

immediately before February 15, 1977, to become a citizen under subparagraph 5(1)(*b*)(i) of the former Act, if, before February 15, 1979, or within such extended period as the Minister may authorize, an application for citizenship is made to the Minister by a person authorized by regulation to make the application.[9]

Let me put this legalese into layperson's terms. If you were born prior to February 15, 1977, in or out of wedlock, and if one of your parents was Canadian, then so were you.

To CIC, the offending order was 5(2)(b).* That's what it wanted to get rid of.

In keeping with the Liberals' stance against the Lost Canadians, Joe Volpe had gone back to the old ways of discrimination based on gender and family status.[10] Hence, children born outside Canada in wedlock pre-1977 to Canadian mothers and foreign fathers were once again denied citizenship, whereas children born outside Canada to Canadian fathers and foreign mothers were welcomed. The only difference was gender: if your father is Canadian, you're in; if your mother's Canadian, you're out. For out-of-wedlock kids, the acceptance or denial was reversed. Mother's Canadian, you're in; father's Canadian, you're out. And if that was not enough, the intolerance didn't stop with gender—the prejudice now extended to encompass born-out-of-wedlock kids.

As I mentioned, when CIC opened up its one and only window for people like Marylin, the window of opportunity for acceptance was short-lived, just three and a half months—assuming they knew of the provision and submitted the required application. At the time, Marylin was practising law in California. One day out of the clear blue, she noticed that CIC had posted a notice on its website, saying that if you'd been born out of wedlock outside Canada to a Canadian father and foreign mother, you had until August 14, 2004, to apply for citizenship. The announcement was posted for just a short time, and it was left entirely up to the individual to become aware of it. Now, think of the numerous people affected, people hoping for something helpful, who didn't regularly visit CIC's website. If you were fortunate enough to know of the announcement, you had two choices: (1) apply for citizenship and be guaranteed acceptance (but there was a catch: the citizenship didn't extend to your kids—this is exactly what CIC had done to Lost Canadians like me under Bill S-2) or (2) apply for yourself and your kids; in

---

* Offensive only if you are CIC or one of the many ministers against born-out-of-wedlock kids.

doing so, you waived any right to a judicial appeal if CIC denied any one of you and, further, CIC would accept your application only if accompanied by a signed CIC-produced form admitting you had never been Canadian. That admission could later be held against you. That was it. There were no other options. To apply, you had to jeopardize your future chances. Through strong-arm tactics, CIC forced you to hold your nose and do as demanded. Marylin signed both the application and admission form and sent them to CIC.[11]

Although Marylin did get her citizenship in 2005, her children remain excluded from Canada ten years later. CIC has never explained why this is so, despite our numerous queries. Seems that Supreme Court decisions aren't the only thing the bureaucrats sometimes ignore.

What we do know is that, even today, CIC steadfastly refuses to recognize Marylin's children. In what's become typical bureaucratic anti-acceptance behaviour, they follow their own rules made from scratch from one day to the next. Consistency inside the department and well-versed case processors weren't priorities. CIC recognized Marylin's citizenship before her father died only because of my access to Stephen Heckbert and his intervention. Although my association with the minister's office wasn't an adoring, joined-at-the-hip rapport, it was cordial and productive for all. We definitely played from different handbooks, but the communication channels always remained open.

Kind of like putting the jumper cables on the wrong battery terminals, you instantly know your mistake. Why had I thought that the Conservatives would be any better? The nanosecond Monte Solberg took over CIC's reins, my relationship with anyone in the department became null and void. The silence was deafening.

And so it went. My "two steps forward and one step back" progress had been reversed. Topping the queue during the Volpe administration were the war brides and their children. Under Solberg, they'd been trashed. My mother, now in her nineties, always has snippets of wisdom on the tip of her tongue. She told me of a cherished saying of one of the smartest minds ever to have graced our planet, Louis Pasteur: "Fortune favours the prepared mind." Indeed. But what does one do in my position? On the one hand, you have aging World War II Canadian soldiers and their war brides, and on the other, you have a minister slamming his door shut, doing exactly what I used to do on a pilot layover, hanging the Do Not Disturb sign on the doorknob.

Because of Solberg's silence, I began calling several contacts inside the Conservative Party to inquire about just what was going on. My first call was to John Reynolds. John didn't seek re-election in 2006; instead, he became a "businessman" in Vancouver, which was probably code for being a lobbyist. From my vantage, he was no longer the Ottawa insider he had once been. But the reality was that he frequently met with the prime minister. So his influence was definitely alive and well, and just maybe thriving. John offered up no explanations but, frankly, my gut feeling was that he had had enough, and although he might on occasion mention the Lost Canadians in passing, it would not have been his priority when dining with Harper. During the election, John, along with his good friend and political ally Doug Finley, had gone full force trying to get Harper elected. Finley was the Conservative campaign chairman, and I presume Reynolds was second in charge.

I'd be doing John a great disservice if I didn't make it clear that the Lost Canadians would never have been recognized under S-2 or the bill that came later without his efforts. John remains to this day my friend and supporter. However, just after the election of 2006, and after more than thirteen years as a federal MP, he took a much needed breather, retiring from the public sector. Whatever sort of influence John still had, it had no effect. Monte Solberg said and did nothing.

So I went to the number two politician regarding citizenship, an MP hailing from Weyburn, Saskatchewan, Ed Komarnicki. I liked Ed from the get-go, but with his boss being so aloof, I entered his parliamentary office reticently. We chatted about Joe Taylor, a man who had just filed for a judicial review against CIC and who would become a central character in the Lost Canadians fight.

Joe was born an out-of-wedlock war-bride baby and brought to Canada from England in 1946. His father and mother were typical, falling in love before being separated by the evils of war. Many times his father applied to his commanding officer for authorization to marry, but the Canadian government knew only too well what was likely to happen. Permission denied. Being normal and healthy young lovers, they did what any normal couple would do on the "eve of destruction." The result was young Joe. Shortly thereafter came deployment; Joe's father was off to the front. His position? Flamethrower.

In war, just about everyone has an unpleasant job, but being a flamethrower is one of the most gruesome. On your back are two gas cylinders; in your hand is a type of projectile gun connected by hoses to the cylinders. It's your job to pull the trigger, shooting flames thirty to fifty feet in front of you. Whoever is in your way, other soldiers and possibly civilians, gets scorched beyond recognition. The smell of burning human flesh fills the air. You're a killing machine. And whenever you go to work, whenever the trigger is pulled, there's nothing but death and destruction on the other end. Now picture being an opposing soldier. What's the first thing you take aim at with your rifle? For Joe's father, the reality was simple. Kill or be killed.

How could anyone come out of that experience unscathed? If you didn't suffer from PTSD, you almost couldn't be human. A good friend of the elder Taylor died a violent death as the two stood together on the battlefield. After the war, the soldier's experiences translated into alcohol and anger. On the receiving end, of course, was his new bride, who had travelled from her home country of England to be with the man she'd married shortly after the war ended, and after receiving the blessing of the Canadian government. It didn't take long for her to discover his new personality. The person who left to go to war, a kind, loving man, had come back an abuser.

During my Lost Canadian expedition, I began to see just how much more there was to this story than citizenship. Joe's father, mother, and Joe himself had all been unwilling victims. Joe's father hadn't been killed, but the man he'd been, the happy, gung-ho young man, was dead. The family had paid quite the price for his involvement in the Canadian forces, for his service to Canada.

Just weeks before January 1, 1947, Joe's mother snatched her baby into her arms, took what little belongings were hers, and headed back to England. For various reasons, but mostly because of abusive husbands, around 4,500 Canadian war brides returned to their homeland. And who could blame them? With a slow-falling mist, nothing stays dry. In one way or another, each and every Canadian was affected by World War II.

For young Joe, life was good. He grew up in the UK. He was an only child, raised by his mother and grandparents. He never really knew his dad, but he did know of his Canadian roots. After spending his working years as a successful accountant in England, he opted for a change in retirement. Longing to embrace the connection to his father and to Canada, he began the upstream struggle to return. The problem? CIC puts out no fish ladders, so more often than not, Joe felt as though he were attempting to jump from the water below, up and over Niagara Falls.

His quest began just after the new millennium, at Canada House in London, where he was formally declared to not be a citizen. It came as a shocking surprise, since Joe and his mother had been told they were Canadian citizens—their original entry into Canada was with Canadian passports. He truly believed he was Canadian. His dream was to one day return home.

It wasn't that Joe was an indigent, not even close. He had a tidy sum saved and, with his UK pension, would be set for life. His obsession for Canada had nothing to do with draining the welfare system. His desire, his love of Canada, was intangible. And, like a salmon returning to the stream of its birth, Joe was drawn to his beginnings.

CIC continued its insistence that Joe was not Canadian and had absolutely no claim to citizenship. No matter, he still embarked on the almost 8,000-kilometre journey to Vancouver Island, retracing his path of sixty years before. Joe found his father, but like for so many other kids whose family was ripped apart because of the war, it was too late; his father had passed on. Joe sat by his father's grave, in Port Alberni's veterans cemetery, and pondered what life would have been like in Canada growing up with his dad. How very different it would have been from his childhood in the English countryside. Later, he learned that he had a large family of stepbrothers and stepsisters in Canada, all Registered Indians.

The bureaucracy had it all wrong. It maintained that Joe's quest was about money, insisting that he simply wanted to be on the Canadian dole. This might be said of a small number of people trying to return to Canada, but it certainly wasn't the case with Joe. Nothing could have been further from the truth. A simple exploration of his financial situation would have established that. Joe just wanted to go home; Canada was where he belonged. But CIC said no. Now, no thinking person could possibly believe that everyone wanting to return to Canada wished to do so only for the financial or medical freebies, and probably no one in the bureaucracy actually believed that either. It was simply a convenient excuse to justify the barbarous treatment of people like Joe. CIC had adopted a cruel, blanket condemnation that should go down in history as infamous. It should stir embarrassment and disdain from any feeling Canadian.

I tried to help, but no matter what I did, no matter how high my connections went with all the King's horses and all the King's men, I just couldn't get Joe Taylor back to Canada again.

Ed Komarnicki, the new parliamentary secretary to the citizenship minister, listened as I pleaded for his government to recognize Joe and the other war-bride children. Joe was even willing to apply for a section 5.4 citizenship grant, something CIC accepts all the time, but the government—or better stated, the new Harper government—wasn't about to budge. That left just one way forward. Joe was going to court.

CHAPTER 10

ON THE SCALES OF JUSTICE

*Human progress is neither automatic nor inevitable... Every
step toward the goal of justice requires sacrifice, suffering, and
struggle; the tireless exertions and passionate concern of dedicated
individuals. Injustice anywhere is a threat to justice everywhere.*
DR. MARTIN LUTHER KING, JR.

TRUDY HELLER OWNED and operated a quaint coffee shop in Gibsons. In
2004, Trudy's son-in-law, Jason, helped me come up with the name "Lost
Canadians." Despite the Canadian media showing little interest in these
disenfranchised people, I saw it as my duty to get the truth out to the public.
The Internet was obviously the future, and for us to gain any kind of wide-
spread recognition, we needed to be on it. My knowledge of the World Wide
Web was pitiful. All of my daughters, even my youngest, knew more about it
than I did. I could fly a Boeing 747-400 anywhere, through crowded skies
around the world, landing at all kinds of fast-paced airports, from London's
Heathrow to New York's JFK, from Frankfurt to New Delhi, but the Internet
I found intimidating.

I had mentioned to Jason that I wanted a domain name and, the next
day, he came back with a list of candidates. I chose "Lost Canadians" and
we registered it. From that point on, I never knew what might turn up when
I turned on the computer or answered my home phone. By 2006, people
were beginning to share their stories with me, particularly the war brides
and their children. A year or two earlier, a man had called me at home in

Arizona and told me his tale: he'd been born outside Canada on a Canadian military base, and CIC had not made it easy for him to get any kind of status in Canada. For some time, I remained mostly unaware of the bigger picture that included those like him, the military brats. In passing, he said that there were about 10,000 others like him that he knew of. I filed this away in my memory and continued on. With the change of guard in Ottawa in 2006, my focus remained pretty much on the World War II crowd. Little did I realize the accuracy of his estimate. Nor was I aware of the huge storm clouds forming on the horizon.

At the time, my website was being run by a retired man in Phoenix named Don McMahon. He was the one who organized and posted anything that went onto the site. There was a problem with this arrangement. Don wasn't Canadian, and he was unfamiliar with Canadian culture, with Canada's politics, and with what sort of people Canadians were. Don just couldn't understand how a country—any country, even the worst of them—could deny citizenship to its own people, especially the children of military vets who had served their country in wartime. Americans looked at our situation with suspicion, wondering just what the government had done to us. Canadians, on the other hand, as I've mentioned, looked at us with a large dollop of doubt, unsure of what we had done to deserve our fate. Put another way, south of the forty-ninth parallel, the government was at fault; north of the forty-ninth, the blame went to the individual. It was always challenging talking about the issue with Canadians because I sensed an awkwardness; they silently wondered what dastardly deed I was guilty of to force the government into defending the safety of the Canadian people by denying my citizenship. And every Lost Canadian I have ever encountered felt as I did. Often, to avoid humiliation, those Lost Canadians just kept their mouths shut.

My four original war-bride kids were Stuart Martin, Joe Taylor, Sheila Walshe, and some guy named Woody in London, England. Woody was a mysterious chap who years earlier had been deported from Canada. Why, I didn't know, but I had assumed it was because Canada didn't recognize him as being Canadian. It seems that Woody had found my website and, in turn, had contacted my other three war-bride children.

Sheila Walshe was the first war-bride child to contact me through the website. When Sheila was almost nine, her British war-bride mother gathered the kids up one morning from their Ontario home and headed back to the UK, telling them they were going on holidays. Their father was at work, unaware of what was happening. On their arrival in England, the mother told the kids that their father had been killed in an accident and that they'd be better off staying in the UK. The family was wretchedly poor; Sheila remembers nothing but pain and sorrow in England. Times were tough after World War II, and the locals looked down on the Walshe kids as foreigners. Sheila's own grandfather used to call them his "little bits of Canadian dirt." One night, he threw Sheila, her brother, and her mother out onto the streets, forcing them into homelessness. You can sense the intensity of her pain even now, fifty years later, when she talks about it. She equates her upbringing to that of Oliver Twist, with one difference: "His oatmeal was warm; ours was always cold."

As an adult, her younger brother made his way back to Canada to find his roots and, while in BC, made a shocking discovery: his father was alive. Their mother had lied. The kids had been abducted. The father had never known what had happened to his family. Now that contact had been made, everything changed. Sheila, once a "daddy's girl," longed to return to Canada. Pooling her savings from her wages as a registered nurse and her husband's savings, she returned to Canada with her husband in 1991, buying a little house right next door to her dad's. Yet CIC refused to recognize her citizenship, despite its admission that Sheila had been a Canadian citizen (an abducted Canadian citizen, no less). Without the proper documents, it was illegal for her to stay in Canada.

For the next twelve years, Sheila and her husband, Jim, were forced to go back and forth between the two countries, and had only visitor status in Canada. In 2003, CIC finally allowed Sheila an extended stay in Kelowna on the condition that she did not work or even volunteer. This, of course, meant that Sheila's skills as a nurse were being wasted. She and Jim had no medical coverage, and their only means of support were Jim's UK pension and their retirement nest egg. For Sheila, what mattered more than anything was being back home, living near her father. Twelve years earlier, she'd discovered she had a stepsister, who accepted Sheila with open arms. For the first time in four decades, she felt a sense of family, of belonging.

The father, daughter, and extended family couldn't have been happier, except for one thing—a big thing, mind you—that stood as a roadblock before them. The government insisted that she wasn't Canadian despite being born in wedlock and brought to Canada as a child of a war bride. At best, her stay in Canada was tenuous and temporary. For fifteen years she'd been filling out bureaucratic forms, remitting fees, doing everything CIC asked of her, hoping that one day it would capitulate and give her back her citizenship. The dilemma now was apparently her age. She was over fifty, and the department considered her too old to be desirable as an immigrant. In 2003, she and Jim were allowed to move to Canada, but only by way of an extended visitors permit. They immediately packed up everything in the UK and headed west. While legal, they remained uncomfortable. At a moment's notice, CIC could rescind their permit. Every six months she had to pay more fees, fill out more forms, and regain authorization to stay. Would life always be this way, living from day to day, hoping to make it through? What would she do if CIC turned her down? Would she stay regardless of its decision? And if so, how long before she was detected by CIC's deportation radar? Her father needed her more than ever now, as his health was failing.*

But that didn't interest CIC. Quite frankly, it didn't care. And neither did the politicians. For them, bringing in elderly parents of immigrant Canadian citizens from halfway around the world—folks who could potentially be a huge drain on the health and welfare systems of the country—was a vote-getter. But the reverse, reuniting an elderly Canadian father living in Kelowna with his abducted formerly Canadian daughter, was not important. Always on Sheila's mind was the fear that the government could be so mean as to rip her and her father apart. The way she saw it, only two things could do that: his death, or an encounter with CIC's bureaucratic thugs. Both haunted her on a daily basis. Only time would tell.

Stuart Martin had been born in wedlock and, like Sheila, was brought to Canada as a child, landing at Pier 21 with his parents, receiving the CIC pamphlet, and being told by the government that he was now a Canadian citizen. The family's experience wasn't unique—nearly all of the tens of thousands of war brides and their kids came to Canada this way. The family first went to Sydney and later to Glace Bay. His brother at age six slipped off a snowbank, landing directly in the path of an oncoming car. His little body was buried at a local cemetery. Losing a child is probably the worst thing that could ever happen to a family. Although the pain gets masked as time marches forward, it never really goes away. The family needed a change. So they packed up their belongings and returned to England. Stuart had come to Canada as a five-month-old, and now, at age twelve, he had no choice but to leave. Three years after his arrival in England, at age fifteen, Stuart enlisted in the British Army. Years later, after retiring, he longed to return to his roots in Canada. Believing he was Canadian—after all, he had a passport

---

* As a nurse, Sheila could potentially save Canadian taxpayers huge sums of money by caring for her father herself.

from years before that said he was—he headed to Halifax to visit the places of his former life, reminiscing at his primary school and old playground, amazed at how some things had changed and how others had not. He went to the cemetery and paid his respects at his brother's graveside.

Like Sheila, he pondered what life might have been like in Canada. Thumbing through the phonebook, he remembered his childhood girl-friend from so long ago. What were the chances of finding her, let alone that she'd be single, he wondered. The stars must have been in alignment, because, amazingly, he did find her, and all those years later, they experienced another flame of romance. Stuart was here to stay; he was home. Or at least he thought so. In the bureaucratic hallways of CIC's processing centre not far away in Sydney, the case analysts were saying, "Not so fast."

In the ensuing years, Stuart, not having status, was not allowed to work. He became a part of the theatre community of Halifax, but that didn't translate into putting food on the table. Like Sheila, he was forced to live off his savings and, like all the others in citizenship purgatory, he thought that he was the only one in this position.

It was my website that allowed Lost Canadians for the first time to press forward, fighting back together, as a pack. Credit goes to so many people who have been instrumental in helping me, from powerful top politicians to judges, academics, and even people who in passing offered their suggestions. The result was a combination of all manner of support from hundreds of people. Most remain hidden from public view. That's how it's been with the Lost Canadians, and we couldn't have done it without the Internet. For the first time, people from Timbuktu to Kalamazoo had a way to find one another: through the website.

In February 2006, I again met up with documentary filmmakers Garth Pritchard and Daron Donohue, this time in Halifax (as mentioned in Chapter 7). That's when Stuart Martin became much more than just a voice over the phone. We met, had eye contact, shook hands, sipped coffee, and shared stories. Frequently when meeting in person for the first time a Lost Canadian who was a war-bride child, I'd be shown pictures of his or her father in uniform, sometimes even a binder containing Dad's medals and military citations. Stuart's father must have been an outstanding Canadian soldier—his awards of merit were exceedingly impressive.

Before our get-together, I had been fond of Stuart. But upon meeting in person, me laughing at his British-Canadian humour and witnessing first-hand his stellar personality, we bonded. We were going forward on our citizenship journey together. The pack was growing.

If I were Stephen Harper or Monte Solberg, Stuart was exactly the sort of person I'd want in Canada. The country needed more Sheilas and Stuarts and all the others like them. I kept thinking, *Where the hell is Harper's "stroke of the pen"?* It just didn't make sense.

As more Lost Canadians began identifying themselves to me through phone calls or emails, my salutations changed. I began welcoming them to the club, equating their situations to being on death row. None of us had aspired to be in this position—no one wanted his or her citizenship taken away—but, on the bright side, although our collective identity had been incarcerated in some obscure bureaucratic detention centre, we were fast becoming an interesting, diverse group, our ranks expanding daily. Each one of us had a unique story. Regrettably, though, the judges, jurors, and executioners of our fate remained, as always, the Ottawa politicians.

With the Nova Scotia filming a wrap, we hurried off to Ottawa, hoping to get our share of politicians on camera. Unfortunately, we arrived during a down week—the MPs were back in their home ridings. But with the help of one of my parliamentary security contacts, we were allowed to film directly from the floor of the Senate. Usually, a filming request must be submitted months in advance. It then goes through all the necessary channels, any one of which can give it a thumbs-down. By now firmly on the frequent-Ottawa-visitor list, I had got to know several of the security guards; they, in turn, had become familiar with the Lost Canadian issue. Supporting what I was doing, they allowed us to bypass the time-consuming request process, allowing us instead immediate access to inside Centre Block for filming.

Contacts like those security guards who granted us such favours were starting to materialize with some regularity. I was like the stray mongrel that kept showing up at the front door. Parliamentary staffers began coming out of seemingly nowhere to feed me juicy tidbits. As they began to understand what I was trying to accomplish, they grew more and more sympathetic. They'd all witnessed incredible abuses in the immigration system, with Canada welcoming just about everyone (and their brother and brother's brother) except us. So when Lost Canadians were being escorted to the exit, they felt sympathy, which translated into wanting to help in their own individual ways. My inside contacts were varied and even included customs and immigration agents. I could call and ask them to check the status of one of the Lost Canadians. And soon I'd have the answer. I had no idea if what they did to come up with the answer was legal, and I didn't ask. My attitude was rather laissez-faire. When the political leaders of a country take aim at its own people, we do whatever we have to do to correct it. Many a Jewish family are alive today because of insiders who bucked their governments, caring more about doing what is right than about pleasing morally corrupt politicians. I was thankful to all my insiders; in spirit we were united, as all Canadians should be, fighting in our own "underground" ways to right these terrible wrongs. The Ottawa insiders weren't themselves Lost Canadians, but we had captured their hearts and they eventually became some of our staunchest allies. Each one was a hero to us.

There's a framed saying hanging prominently on the wall at Canada Place in Banff: "Canadian history has been defined as much by the accomplishments of individual Canadians as by the great battles on foreign soil and momentous changes to our society or constitution." How true. To all those who stepped forward and helped, from the bottom of my heart, I thank you.

For the past several years, Joe Taylor and I had been regularly communicating via Skype, email, and telephone, and together we'd arrived at the same conclusion: the only sure path forward was through the courts. Half a year had gone by since Joe had submitted his request for a citizenship certificate and, as the months passed, we grew impatient. I picked up the phone from my home in Phoenix and called one of my insiders to inquire about Joe's status. What we wanted was a simple answer to a simple question: Was he or wasn't he a citizen? We obviously hoped the response would be in the affirmative. But even if it was "no," we'd at least have our answer. Delay seemed to be a calculated part of CIC's tactics. In an almost systematic procrastination, the bureaucrats would sit more or less endlessly, apparently doing nothing, while the applicant—the unwilling victim—had no avenue of recourse; he or she could only do as in the movie *Casablana*—wait, and wait, and wait, and wait. Not ever wanting to take advantage of my inside contacts, I called upon them only on a strictly as-needed basis. Now, I inquired about Joe and, lo and behold, his application had indeed been sitting for the last six months, to use the words of my insider, "on a bureaucratic shelf in Sydney collecting dust." I relayed this information to Joe and together we made it official: he filed for a judicial review by the courts.

Before the hearing, I constantly pleaded for someone—anyone—of importance to listen. But Mr. Solberg had severed his lines of communication. His parliamentary secretary, Ed Komarnicki, was cordial if not himself sympathetic. But, not being the lead dog, he was powerless to do anything. The abuse continued coming out of CIC, with Mr. Harper and his new citizenship minister Monte Solberg not showing one sliver of compassion. Only the names had changed after the election—from those of Liberal MPs to those of Conservative MPs. The attitudes hadn't. For the bureaucrats, it was business as usual.

I have no doubt that Harper knew about my tenacity. And through John Reynolds, he had been briefed about our court challenge. One of the first things the new prime minister did was cancel the Court Challenges Program (CCP). For decades, it had operated as a national non-profit organization providing financial assistance to people so that they could bring forward important court cases regarding Canada's new constitution.

Originally founded in 1978 under the Trudeau Liberals for language rights cases, after the adoption of the Canadian Charter of Rights and Freedoms in 1982, the CCP expanded to cover equality-of-rights issues. In 1992, the Conservatives axed the program, only for it to be restored under the new Liberal government in 1994. With the Conservatives back in power in 2006, the funding once again was to be cut. Was it just a coincidence, or were the Harper people well aware of what we were about to do? Did they target us for pressing forward with a constitutional question on justice? About that we could only surmise. What was certain was that Joe Taylor would have to finance the court case on his own. Magali Castro-Gyr, in her court challenge, had sought assistance through the CCP and been approved for $39,000 of the $59,000 it cost to go up against the government. Without that help, what could a primary schoolteacher like Magali do? Her salary wouldn't have supported a constitutional confrontation of this magnitude, not even close. A private individual going up against the government's unlimited access to public funds was next to impossible, dooming that person from the get-go. And what would happen if the courts awarded costs to the government? Magali would literally have been rendered stateless and bankrupt on the same day. And this was Canada, advertised worldwide as a fair, compassionate, human-rights-upholding country. It made absolutely no sense. The solution was so simple, so morally right: acceptance. But that's not always the principle on which governments operate, not even Canada's, when dealing with their own people.

I always had a sneaking suspicion that Harper understood that the Lost Canadians' last-chance opportunity for justice was through the courts and that, at best, his government stood on precarious grounds denying us citizenship. So, as a backdoor solution, it looked to me like his simple and easy way to eradicate any resistance to his agenda was to deny CCP money to anyone challenging the federal government. If John Reynolds had forewarned the new prime minister about my persistence, and I imagine he did, it wasn't inconceivable that our issue had indeed been a factor in the CCP's going on the chopping block.

In 2006, just as Joe's turn through the revolving Lost Canadian door of the federal courts was about to commence, Harper abruptly cancelled funding to the CCP. He did it as an executive decision and, in so doing, avoided any debate or ratification vote in the House. Harper knew exactly how to play the games of politics—precisely which allies to hook up with, which opponents to challenge, and which ones to avoid. Above all, he was incredibly adept at inflicting damage on his opponents. Voices-Voix, a "nonpartisan coalition of Canadians and Canadian organizations committed to defending our collective and individual rights... encouraging respect for our democratic rights and values, including free speech, transparency, and equality," said this about Harper's gutting the finances of the CCP:[1]

Implications and Consequences:

Equality: Access to justice in equality rights cases is severely limited and is available mostly to those with the financial capacity to pursue them.

Equality: Canada's global reputation of being a leader in human rights is greatly diminished by the elimination of a unique program admired around the world.

Democracy: Discriminatory laws and practices remain untouched and unchallenged for much longer.

Equality: Programs to provide protection from government discrimination such as LEAF for women, DAWN, for women with disabilities, Egale for gays, lesbians, bisexuals and trans-identified people are limited in their ability to protect individuals as effectively.

Equality: The cancellation of the CCP diminished the disability community's access to justice.[2]

By cutting the funds for the CCP, Harper was eliminating much, much more than adversaries like the Lost Canadians or other individual Charter challenges. More than anything, the big-picture item was the courts. Our government has several branches: executive, legislative, and judicial. The courts are supposed to provide a check and balance to the entire system, with particular emphasis on watching over the government, making certain it stays on track with regard to rule of law. By eliminating the CCP, Harper was in effect reducing the ability of the court's power as a watchdog while increasing his power to do things as he saw fit. He was, in so many words, diminishing the checks and balances on government that have served us so well in the last 148 years. The beneficiary, of course, was Mr. Harper.

Without Lost Canadians contributing financially, Joe's chances of success would have been about the same as the Bloc Québécois's sweeping to power in Alberta. By himself, Joe would be broke the day he filed his lawsuit: good lawyers don't come cheap. Once again, Jeff Wan, who had won a unanimous decision in the Supreme Court with *Benner*, stepped up to the plate and offered his advice pro bono. So too did Donald Galloway, a law professor at UVIC and one of the few lawyers in Canada who understands citizenship law (most lawyers understand immigration; citizenship is a completely different beast). And our elusive war-bride child Woody kicked in by offering what he'd turned up in his research—he was great at camping out at libraries in and around London. All in all, we put together a small but formidable team.

From the start, we pressed the government to settle. We hoped that it wouldn't force our hand. I warned of the consequences; I explained that CIC had no concept of how big our issue was, nor how far the tentacles of the court's decision would reach. I was direct, not mincing my words. "For the sake of everyone," I pleaded, "don't wade out into those waters." Other than with my insiders, my only contact with anyone even remotely connected to the department was Ed Komarnicki, parliamentary secretary to Monte Solberg. He was always amiable, but offered nothing more than a few minutes of his time and a warm smile. With Ed tethered to the Conservative sled, he was a passenger, simply along for the ride.

I turned for help to my local MP, newly elected Liberal Blair Wilson. In the recent election, he beat Conservative John Weston for the seat vacated by John Reynolds, whose departure was quite a blow to our cause.

As I've said, it's drilled into us pilots to use all available resources. During the election campaign, both candidates had met with me. And I sensed, at least during the campaigning season, that they wanted to be seen publicly around a mover and shaker. Both not only expressed empathy for my work but also quickly pledged their support "if elected." But by now I was wary of all campaign promises. My attitude was: *yeah, yeah, yeah—been there, done that, heard that*. Neither candidate came close to playing in the big leagues of Reynolds. I had reservations about both of them, but felt particularly reserved when it came to Wilson.

Blair Wilson struck me as a good-looking guy with the smile and depth of the stereotypical politician. I'd just got off the ferry (as a walk-on passenger) in Gibsons and was heading home. There, sitting in a van waiting to get onto the ferry—with "Wilson" boldly painted on its side, there was no mistaking who the van belonged to—was Blair. He saw me and swiftly jumped out to make small talk, telling me all the wonderful things he could do for the Lost Canadians "if elected." Oh, by the way, he also needed a political donation. I hated that about our elected representatives, always having their hand out, but what can you do? That's how the game is played. "Okay," I said, "where do I send it?"

"Give it to so-and-so."

And that's just what I did the next day—$200 cash. I had no idea that giving a contribution in cash wasn't kosher. It took a few years after the election, but Blair ended up being forced out of the Liberal Party for what it perceived to be a number of questionable practices, one of those being his alleged acceptance of cash donations during the campaign without providing receipts. I discovered only later how frowned upon this was by Elections Canada. I gave the money to someone in the party, who may or may not have told Wilson and who may or may not have reported it. I really didn't know. For all I know, the person could have pocketed the money themselves. I was beginning to get an education about the ins and outs of political elections.

Tory John Weston had been courting me for several years. The few times I stopped in at his law practice in downtown Vancouver for a chat, he always showed sympathy, indicating that, "if elected," he could really keep the ball rolling forward as the conduit between me and his party. I forked over $300. This time I paid by cheque, and the recipient was the Conservative riding association.

After the election, Weston came to me, saying that he was great friends with Monte Solberg. Wilson, on the other hand, now my new MP, disappeared behind the camouflage of his politician's personality. He remained useless to the cause his entire time as an MP, despite later becoming a member of the Standing Committee on Citizenship and Immigration. He did, however, start referring his constituents who were having citizenship problems to me. I wasn't even living in Canada. I'm a private citizen. No one out there is helping me financially. And the duly elected member of the Canadian Parliament, with a sworn duty to do what is best for the people he supposedly represents, instead of pursuing answers and solving problems for his own constituents in issues of citizenship, and using his own staffers who are paid to handle them, decided that the best way to deal with these cases was to refer them to me. I'd get an email or phone call asking if I wouldn't mind contacting the problematic constituent from the very

MP who was supposed to be helping me. And here's the story of John Raymond (MacKay) Sullivan, the man it happened to, exactly as he wrote it in his email to me describing his experience:

I was born on May 14, 1942, in the city of Liverpool. There is a lot that I don't know about my mother and father and that's what makes my story so complicated. I will try to explain it the best way I know how.

I believe that my mother was not married when I was born and I think she did something which may have seemed wise at the time, but it's a decision that has come back to haunt me.

On my birth certificate, my mother, Elizabeth Rice, falsely entered her name as Elizabeth MacKay. I believe she did this to give the appearance she was married to my biological father, Paul MacKay. My mother's decision to cover up my illegitimate birth is at the root of all my problems with Canadian citizenship.

I don't know how my mother and father met and I don't know anything about him except that he was a serviceman. I also don't know much about my mother's family in England because they were very secretive about their background and once we were in Canada my mother didn't want to talk about the past. It didn't help that when my mother passed away[,] all of her paperwork was stolen, leaving me with many unanswered questions about her own status when she came to Canada as a fiancée of a Canadian serviceman.

I do know that she was born Elizabeth Rice in Belgium. My mother was an electrician's helper during the war. She was a ½ inch too short to join the Air Force and they would not let her in. While the war was on my mother met a Canadian airman, Stanley Nelson Sullivan, and they fell in love. I know that she met him when I was still an infant because there are pictures of the three of us together. Where Mr. MacKay ended up is anybody's guess. Were they actually married? Was she a widow? I don't know. As I mentioned before, I do not have any of my mother's paperwork so I do not know whether she knew Stanley Sullivan as Elizabeth Rice or Elizabeth MacKay—the [sur]name on my birth certificate. If she wasn't married it makes sense that she used MacKay to avoid embarrassing questions about my paternity.

My memories of the Second World War are those of a child fascinated with things to see and do in my neighbourhood. Within a few short years I was quick to explore the Chinese store just down the street from my grandmother's house where soldiers would give me candy and, in rare cases, the odd pair of silk stockings saying, "Go ahead, lad, give them to your mom."

There were a few girls nearby who I used to hang around with and we were known as "The Dead End Kids." We hung around bombed out areas where you weren't supposed to be and the Home Guard would run us off blowing their whistles. When the war ended Stanley was repatriated to Canada before my mother and he could get married. This was common at the time. Marriage was a complicated process in wartime and Canada's Department of National Defence was in a hurry to get its troops home. In that regard, I always understood that my mother came to Canada as a fiancée of a Canadian serviceman under the war bride transportation scheme. As a fiancée, she had no priority in shipping and since space was at a premium, it was some time before we could sail for Canada. On September 30, 1947, we found ourselves aboard the *Aquitania* with other war brides and children sailing out of Southampton bound for Halifax.

The ocean voyage was terrible, stormy weather with giant waves. It was so bad that they battened the hatches and sealed up the entire ship. You had to stay in your own area and all of the portholes were locked. My mother became very ill at sea and was unable to care for me so I was looked after by a Sergeant in the Canadian Army who was coming home with his comrades. The trip was very frightening. Finally one day everything was quiet, they opened the portholes and the sunshine flooded the passage ways. The ocean was calm, the gulls were squawking. We were safely in Halifax Harbour.

Next, we boarded a train for the 3,600 mile journey to Vancouver. I don't remember most of the ride because I slept a lot, but I recall coming through the Fraser Canyon. There was ice and rocks pushed down by slides most of the way and the soldiers on the train had to clear the tracks all the way to Hope. We finally arrived at Vancouver on October 11, 1947, where I met the man who was to become my father.

My mother and stepfather were married and we lived for the first couple of years in a rural area of Vancouver before moving to North Surrey where we started a small goat farm. Goat's milk was at a premium in those days and hospitals used it to treat patients with chronic illnesses. We had Saanan goats, Bantam chickens and bees. We also grew our own vegetables and pretty much looked after ourselves.

In March 1956, when I was 14 years old, my stepfather formally adopted me and my name changed from John Raymond MacKay to John Raymond Sullivan. In order for my stepfather to adopt me, my mother, who was by now Mrs. Sullivan, was advised by the lawyer to sign as a petitioner along with Mr. Sullivan; in essence, my mother had to adopt me as though she wasn't my biological mother. I believe the reason she followed the lawyer's advice is because her name on the English birth certificate was falsely entered as MacKay and her legal name at that time was Rice, not MacKay. Did she go along to avoid telling the truth about her past? I don't know.

By this time I had been in Canada for nine years and I recall that both my parents were very concerned about my citizenship status. To complicate matters, in England, they said they had no paperwork indicating I had even left the country so as far as the English authorities were concerned I was still in England. I can still remember my father saying, "What is wrong with these people?"

My parents tried everything in their power to get this sorted out but it was all just a confusing mess and it was never properly dealt with by anyone in authority. Over the years they wrote to the Canadian government, the British government, they talked to different politicians trying to get my citizenship resolved. All my parents got was a bunch of promises and a lot of times they didn't even get a call back.

I was only 14 years old but I remember that my parents were very frustrated about the whole situation. Since it seemed that there was nothing they could do but since nobody was knocking on the door trying to kick me out of the country, we just went on with our business. I received a small allowance for doing chores, fencing, feeding and milking the goats, and clearing brush. On Saturday afternoon I would walk into Whalley and see the matinee at the Cameo Theatre.

One Saturday I decided to stay for the evening performance at the theatre and on the way home, walking along the King George Highway I was run down by a very large car. My back was broken in several places, my pelvis crushed, skull fractured, ribs, arms, and legs were broken. I spent several years in the Royal Columbian Hospital in New Westminster. I healed but had missed so much school and I had to go back to the 7th grade. By this time I was so much older than the other kids and I didn't want to go back.

My life became a blotter of meaningless jobs, low paying fly-by-night construction jobs, farm work in Alberta and Saskatchewan. I even got into the Canadian Armed Forces for a while. I was married, had four children and divorced. I'm now living with a fine lady for over 36 years. Because of the injuries I suffered as a teenager, I have lived with arthritis for over 30 years and am in extreme pain every day. I take lots of medication but it doesn't help much.

Last year when I turned 64, I thought I would do some advance work on my application for Old Age Security pension from the Canadian government. In the application form it says "If you were not born in Canada, you must submit proof of your legal status in Canada such as citizenship or immigration documents." You can imagine my reaction to that. All I could think of was my poor mother and father and how they tried so hard to get my Canadian citizenship.

I want to get this issue sorted out once and for all. I have lived in Canada since I was five years old. I was brought here by my mother under the war bride transportation scheme for servicemen's dependents and I am Canadian through and through. I have appeared before the Parliamentary Committee on Citizenship and Immigration to put my story on record in the hope that someone will help me to get to the bottom of my citizenship problems.

I am not a rich man and I do not have a great education. You practically need a degree from university to fill out these forms and it is expensive to order all the documents that they want you to provide, such as birth certificates from England and wedding certificates from Canada. I am confused with all the legal gobbledygook and I don't know what to do. I just wish that someone would help me to make my way through the process so that I can get that little piece of paper that says I am a Canadian citizen.

And so it seems that, in the half-century saga of John Sullivan's quest to be recognized, Blair Wilson, John's MP, could be added to the list of politicians who turned and walked away. The file was now in the hands of a US citizen and pilot who didn't seek out this journey but had found himself deeply imbedded in it. And I, for one, was not going to turn my back on John. Hell, he had served in the Canadian Armed Forces. I had to step forward. No one else had.

I got in touch with John and, as it turned out, he lived in Gibsons, just down the street from the IGA on Pratt Road.* I'd driven past his house

---

* As it turned out, the owner of the IGA, Bob Hoy, was also a Lost Canadian. He was affected by the *Benner* decision but, since CIC was no longer abiding by the court's decision, he was being denied citizenship simply because he had been born in Washington State, in wedlock, to a Canadian mother and American father. Lost Canadians were turning up everywhere.

hundreds of times. I arranged for him to testify before the parliamentary committee—and he did it not by going to Ottawa but, rather, by writing his story, which is what appears above, word for word exactly as the committee members received it.

In Ottawa, once an election is over, the political jockeying commences, which, at the beginning of 2006, meant that the Liberals went from the party in power to official opposition, with the places and positions changing accordingly on all the various House committees. On the Citizenship Committee, Andrew Telegdi, my staunch ally, went from being the chairman to being just another member of the Liberal Party sitting on the committee. Even in opposition, the Liberals didn't know how to use their MPs properly. They bypassed Andrew as the new critic by appointing Maurizio Bevilacqua, who had never before had anything to do with citizenship matters except for his becoming Canadian as an Italian immigrant. So, therefore, he at least attended one citizenship ceremony: his own. Bevilacqua was appointed as the party's critic chiefly because he was a former cabinet minister who needed to be put somewhere. Apparently, Ralph Goodale, the new interim leader of the Liberals, decided Citizenship was a good place to stick in a beginner (I was told through one of my contacts that Goodale's sister was a Lost Canadian). We had just boarded a flight piloted by a captain who had never before flown a plane. Thank goodness Andrew was there, otherwise our issue would have been DOA.

In many ways, I felt as if I had become a bystander. It was truly painful watching the government of Canada decimate the lives of real Canadians like Sheila, Stuart, Joe, and John. The Conservatives just weren't budging. Harper busily worked on getting his five priority items passed in Parliament, and citizenship was maybe number 500, just below "Make opposition parties happy."

Not willing to give in, I called John Reynolds. I called all my contacts in the other parties. I called John Weston. He had bragged about his friendship with Solberg, so I asked him to intervene. Whether he did remains a mystery to me. What I do know is that Solberg's silence was eerie. Did he ever talk about the Lost Canadians among his staffers and bureaucrats? Every time I saw Weston he would smile, telling me what a great thing I was doing for Canada. I sensed Weston was a tree that had fallen in Solberg's forest, lying there on the ground, motionless and useless, with no one around to have heard it fall, or at least no one willing to listen. But the one thing the government couldn't ignore was Taylor's court case, rapidly approaching, like a train coming at you head-on.

Just a few short months before the trial, I was invited by Professor Donald Galloway to talk at the University of Victoria law school. I had left the afternoon clear for the event, and upon arriving at the university, asked him for how long he wanted me to speak. His answer caught me by surprise—I thought he'd say something like thirty to forty minutes. "Two or three hours," came his reply. So the students and I immersed ourselves in the story. Little did I know how important that talk would turn out to be. Joe Taylor was there as well; probably for the first time in their schooling, the law students were able to talk directly with the very people who were challenging the government, people usually known only by their names attached to the top of old court documents or mentioned in footnotes. The students connected Joe's name to a real person, the denial of citizenship to actual faces. They witnessed the pain, the decimation, the toll it took on its victims. Like so many others who offered their support, they too began feeling empathetic.

On May 30, 2006, just as I had done years before for Magali Castro-Gyr and her court hearing, I caught the 6:20 a.m. ferry from Gibsons to Horseshoe Bay, boarded the bus to downtown, got off at Granville and Georgia, crossed the street, entered the Federal Court building, and rode the elevator up a couple of floors. There I met Joe and his lawyer, Rory Morahan. It was like déjà vu; the proceeding was even taking place in the same courtroom.

The hearing commenced, and both Morahan and the government lawyer, Peter Bell, made their opening statements. The judge, Luc Martineau, immediately grasped the enormity of the case. He addressed Bell, telling him that the government was essentially asking the courts to declare all 67,000-plus war brides of World War II and their children not Canadian citizens. There's no transcript of the hearing, so I can't quote verbatim, but it went something like this:

"Are you aware that the possible outcome of what you're asking is to render the war brides and their children—all of them—not Canadian citizens?"

"Yes, sir, I am."

Judge Martineau then said that he wanted everyone to go to lunch—everyone but Peter Bell. He told Bell to call his superiors in Ottawa and warn them of the dire consequences of what they were seeking.

As soon as the hearing resumed, the judge asked Bell what his superiors had said. "Do they really want to go ahead with this?" he queried.

"Yes, they do."

"Okay," replied Judge Martineau.

And so the hearing got underway. Frankly, I wasn't impressed with either lawyer. Regardless, between them and the judge, the fate of 67,000-plus Canadians was on the line. From my vantage, it was astounding just how mean the government could be—putting on trial the citizenship of tens of thousands of innocent women. It also spoke volumes about Stephen Harper. A prime minister is supposed to work on behalf of the people, not against them. But that didn't seem to be Harper's way. He was completely detached from the reality of what the Liberals had started, but, by God, he was going to finish. Harper refused to intervene. He sat back and did nothing, allowing his government to argue why it was okay to kick out the war brides.

The hearing lasted the better part of the day. When it was over, the waiting for the judge's decision began, and not just for Joe. Immediately, CIC began sending out letters to anyone who, like Joe, had an application pending, saying that with the matter now before the courts, a citizenship request could not be processed. Sheila Walshe and Stuart Martin both received the letter. Dr. Martin Luther King Jr., legendary leader of the civil rights movement in the US during the 1960s, once said, "A right delayed is a right denied." He knew only too well what he was talking about. Lots of American blacks died while waiting for their civil rights to be recognized.

After fifteen years of going back and forth between Canada and the UK attempting to get status, Sheila Walshe was shattered. Her elderly father's time remaining was limited. The pain of being abducted—of all those years apart—could be mended only by getting her citizenship restored. Without it, the government could, on a moment's notice, deport her, reopening her old childhood wounds. Her sanctuary had been destroyed once already, and now she lived in fear that it would happen again. Not until she had an official document saying that she was a Canadian citizen would she be able to rest at night. Only that would bring peace, the security of knowing the government could not tear her and her father apart. For Sheila, the waiting was almost unbearable.

For Stuart Martin, his years back in Canada fighting the government had been costly. Being unable to work, he was forced to live off his savings. He went through all of his $100,000 nest egg.

John Sullivan, having no proof that he was Canadian, found the government withholding his Old Age Security. The government also made it difficult for him to obtain medical insurance. He and his wife became destitute. One morning they crammed whatever belongings fit into their car and drove off. Their most important possession, their house in Gibsons, had gone into foreclosure—without an old-age pension, John and his wife couldn't pay the mortgage. Worse, they couldn't afford his pain medications. For John, the agony of being refused citizenship was excruciatingly real, both mentally and physically. To CIC, he was but a statistical blemish—just one of thousands of war-bride children being denied.

Joe Taylor was also forced to dig deeply into his savings. Living under a blanket of uneasiness, he was afraid that the government would go further than just deny his claim to citizenship. He understood that, like John Sullivan, the government could break an individual. Would he be able to keep his home in Victoria? Joe's fate, and the fate of some 67,000 others, was at stake. He would not know anything for another three months.

CHAPTER 11

DOG POOP, FARTS, TOADS, AND BRITNEY SPEARS

---

*And of course the country is founded on the double standard—that's our
history. We were founded on a very basic double standard. This country was
founded by slave owners who wanted to be free. Am I right? A group of slave
owners who wanted to be free. So they killed a lot of white English people in
order to continue owning their black African people so they could wipe out
the rest of the red Indian people and move west and steal the rest of the land
from the brown Mexican people giving 'em a place to takeoff and drop their
nuclear weapons on the yellow Japanese people. You know what the motto ... of
this country ought to be? You give us a colour, we'll wipe it out. You got it. So
anyway, about eighty years after the Constitution is ratified, eighty years later
the slaves are freed—not so you'd really notice it, of course. Just sort of on paper.*
GEORGE CARLIN[1]

WALKING ALONG THE Sydney shoreline at Darling Harbour—that's what I
was up to one sunny spring afternoon after a flight from Los Angeles. In foreign lands, I often discovered things not found back home. This extended
to more than just the food. There are differences in the art, music, movies, books, innuendoes, even the lingo. ("He's my mate" means something
entirely different in Australia and New Zealand than it does on Davie Street
in Vancouver.) On one layover in Australia, I watched the movie *The Castle*.
Brimming with Aussie humour, it's the fictional story of a lone man challenging the federal government. Its message was: your home is your castle.

Yes, it is. And so is your country: there is a bonding between people and the land, the sights and smells, the markets, the foods, the humour. In this vast world, citizenship is every individual's title of ownership, the legal document that says *You are one of us*. It's your licence of belonging.

While in Australia or New Zealand, there was never a time I wasn't thinking, *I love it here, but my heart—my home—is in Canada*. These were British Commonwealth countries; both were at one time bound by the same British-made, outdated laws of identity that I was fighting in Canada. But our southern-hemisphere cousins were light years ahead of us in correcting them. Putting it mildly, they made Canada look like a banana republic.

On my walk, I chanced upon a local bookstore, where I came across a copy of *Down Under* by Bill Bryson. (In Canada, the book is titled *In a Sunburned Country*.)

At the beginning of Chapter 1, Bryson tells of his going to the library and looking up "Australia" in the *New York Times Index* for 1997 to see just how many references the newspaper had made to the country. He discovered that "the *Times* ran 20 articles that were predominantly on or about Australian affairs."[2] In comparing that with how many times the newspaper had run stories on other subjects, Bill came to this conclusion: "Put in the crudest terms, Australia was slightly more important to us [the US] in 1997 than bananas, but not nearly as important as ice cream."

Reading this, I laughed out loud. I couldn't help myself. Bryson had put the truth into such oddball terms that his point was clear: the US wasn't (at least in 1997) all that interested in anything much past its own borders. For me, it worked. I liked the absurdity of it.

Many young folks are today getting their news from comedy shows and networks like Comedy Central.[3] *The Rick Mercer Report*, *The Daily Show with Jon Stewart*, and *The Colbert Report* are all examples of the new medium. It's good in that, at the very least, people are being exposed to various news sources; it's bad in that nothing about the story gets too profound. Walter Cronkite's style of journalism has gone the way of the Edsel. Regardless, comedy is fast becoming the avenue by which young people get their news.[4] And while there was nothing funny about going to court, at times the only way to tell a story, or be a Lost Canadian and live the nightmare from day to day, was to view it all through the lens of comedy, which often involves nothing more than an analysis of the absurd.

Such was the case when in May 2006, 67,000-plus war brides and their children had gone on trial in a Vancouver federal courtroom, their citizenship hanging in the balance. Was there anyone out there, other than the Lost Canadians, the judge, and a few other insightful people, who had contemplated what would happen if the government argued successfully and won? The government had paid for the war brides' passage to Canada in the 1940s; would they now in turn pay for the journey back? Would tens of thousands of now "grandmother war brides" be crammed aboard ships, exiting Canada, bound for Mother England? What would happen to the extended families? Would their spouses, children, grandchildren, and maybe even great-grandchildren all stand at Pier 21 in Halifax waving goodbye? How would that look to the BBC, or worse, to the Queen? On docking in Liverpool or Southampton, would the UK treat them as Canada had, placing them under judicial review and explaining that their British status and all rights that went with it had been lost when they went to Canada? The situation was so ridiculous that it bordered on the bizarre. Could our politicians really be doing this? Well, yes. In Canada, they were. In citizenship law, relative not just to our southern Commonwealth cousins but to much of the world, it seemed as though we were stuck in the Dark Ages.

One might ask where the Canadian media were when all this was going on. The answer is that they were busy covering other stories, which meant that the *Globe and Mail*, *National Post*, *Maclean's*, *Toronto Star*, Canwest, Corus Entertainment, Shaw Media, *Global National*, CTV—you name it— just didn't see us as much of a story. So now, in true Bill Bryson fashion, let me put the Lost Canadian story in terms of the absurd.

The name "Canadian Press" implies that the news service focuses on issues and events having to do with *Canada*. One in thirty Canadians has a war bride in the family; 45,000-plus of the old ladies and 22,000-plus of their middle-aged children (including bigwigs like Senator Roméo Dallaire) were having their status as Canadians challenged by a bunch of bureaucrats who were given the go-ahead by the citizenship minister, who certainly wasn't being held back by the prime minister. And almost no one in the Canadian media cared enough to write about it, which meant that, for the most part, the Canadian people were completely in the dark. On the Canadian Press website, I searched how many times various subjects had been covered by its reporters as news stories. As a reminder, the Taylor case went into judicial review in May 2006. This was what I found:

In news stories by the Canadian Press for 2006: Lost Canadians, zero.

Okay, a bunch of old women wasn't important, at least not according to the Canadian Press. If the women weren't newsworthy, what was?

During the same period, Lindsay Lohan had 89 stories written about her. Britney Spears, 132; Paris Hilton, 124. Céline Dion, a mere 87. The first three alone—America's naughty twentysomethings—commanded the attention of the Canadian Press 345 times versus zero for the war-bride old ladies and their kids in Canada, all of whom had often been described as Canadian nation builders by historians and politicians alike.

From 2002 through to December 5, 2011, the Canadian Press covered these subjects this many times:

CATS: 4,896

PORNOGRAPHY: 2,517

SPAGHETTI: 599

MARILYN MONROE: 440

PAPER TOWEL: 433

TOILET PAPER: 430

PAMELA ANDERSON: 384

ORCA WHALES: 295

TOADS: 117

FARTS: 51

LOST CANADIANS: 31

DOG POOP: 22

How telling is that? Hey, at least we were ahead of dog poop. Measured by the number of times they were covered by the Canadian Press, cats were about 158 times as important as the Lost Canadians, and Lost Canadians were just one-fourteenth as important as toilet paper. Even a Hollywood starlet who'd been dead for almost half a century beat us by a ratio of 14:1.

Joe was feeling not only rejected but dejected. How could he not be? His father had put his life on the line to defend Canada as an infantry flame-thrower, and his life was never the same, damaged forever by the horrors of war. In return, his son was now being told he wasn't worthy of being a citizen of Canada. Simply put, our government didn't feel Joe deserved it because he'd been born out of wedlock. Not getting to the church on time meant the family hadn't shown a strong enough connection to the country. Joe was being punished, if you will, because more than half a century earlier, Canada knowingly and regularly opposed the marriage of its soldiers who actively sought permission for it, simply to avoid the potential post-war financial burden caused by the arrival in Canada of any widows of Canadian soldiers killed in action. It's a contradiction that's become a lasting shame of our country, especially when the government has in 2015 defended its old vicious policies hostile to its own soldiers and these soldiers' children.

On that dreary May 2006 day, I sat with Joe in the courtroom. Like him, I wasn't a citizen. My CIC sin was that I'd been born in wedlock, not far away at Vancouver General Hospital, to two Canadian parents. Now that Bill S-2 had passed, I could at least get my citizenship. But even if I did give in to CIC's blackmailing ways, I wouldn't be able to bring my kids. Still, it was something. Joe had nothing. He had no other avenue but the courts. And CIC was fighting him until only one of them was left standing.

The obvious and simple solution remained too elusive and difficult for CIC and Harper. Because Joe and I were rowing from inside the same leaky dinghy, I knew exactly how he felt. I also had a good dose of anger, sensing that, for the most part, of those in Canada who knew about the issue, none seemed to care. Certainly, the media didn't. Seriously, how would you feel if your father put it all on the line for Canada, and now some sixty years later you're being told to get out? Doesn't military service to one's country in times of war mean anything? What about Remembrance Day? Or is that just a hypocritical day of prime minister and governor general show-and-tell? Isn't what George Carlin says in his comedy routine on double standards in the US just as applicable to Canada?* And, to make it worse, as a Lost Canadian, you know that you're far less important to the Canadian media than farts, and just a tad more important than dog poop. Welcome to our world.

There's a popular saying: "Flying by the seat of your pants." It comes from early aviation parlance and, for pilots, means "deciding a course of action as you go along, using your own initiative and perceptions rather than a predetermined plan or mechanical aids." Maybe another way of saying it is that we recognize gut feelings, the instinct that tells us something doesn't look right, as important signals, often indicative of things to come. I've mentioned that, before an accident or incident, someone in the cockpit almost always says, "This doesn't look right" or "I'm uncomfortable with this." I vowed, as a professional pilot, that if I ever heard those words spoken in my cockpit, I'd react immediately, and not just to ask what the person meant but to listen as though my life and the lives of my passengers depended on it, which might very well be the case.

Throughout the whole Lost Canadian escapade, nothing ever felt right. And I certainly wasn't comfortable with what the government was doing to all these people, nor with the media's lack of coverage. When Joe and I walked out of that Vancouver courtroom, our stomachs were churning because, flat out, what was happening wasn't right. Harper and his

---

* An extract of which is the epigraph that opens this chapter.

henchmen had lined up on the wrong side of the moral question. And so it seems had the media, except for one newspaper, the *Vancouver Sun*.

Several years earlier, I had attended a stage production my daughter was performing in. Sitting next to me was another proud parent. During the intermission we introduced ourselves to each other. She turned out to be Patricia Graham, editor-in-chief of the *Vancouver Sun*. When I heard this, I said something like, "Do I ever have a story for you." Of course, she'd probably heard that line a million times, but that didn't stop her from asking me a little about my story. She later hooked me up with one of her star columnists, Daphne Bramham, to whom I began feeding story after story on the Lost Canadians. If it weren't for the *Sun*, Joe's case would have had as much exposure as the dark side of the moon. In a sense, the *Vancouver Sun* was a ripple. Slowly, over time, others would follow, even the Canadian Press.

A few years back, Magali Castro-Gyr had told me about the German philosopher Arthur Schopenhauer, who is credited with saying, "All truth passes through three stages. First, it is ridiculed. Second, it is violently opposed. Third, it is accepted as being self-evident."* I knew my stuff, and I knew Canada was doing some pretty heinous things against its own people. I also knew that one day I'd be vindicated. But in 2006, with so many people in the Canadian media blowing me off as a nutcase, I still had to press forward. Sometimes I did it in odd ways. Pilots plan far into the future, creating backup contingency plans, just in case. This describes me to a tee. Over time, the truth often gets exposed. So my prodding away at seemingly dead-end leads in the media took on a different meaning, including my constant attempts to get CTV in Vancouver on board. I had a good idea beforehand of the outcome, but nonetheless, several times over the years I marched into the CTV studios on Burrard near Robson Street, took the escalator to the second-floor reception, and asked to see a news producer. By now it would have been surprising—almost shocking—if CTV actually showed interest in our story. If it weren't for my ulterior motive, what I was doing would have been nothing but an exercise in futility. Yes, I wanted the station to do a story—I needed it to be on board—but the reality was that it didn't care. So, in a sense, my going into its downtown offices was a bit of a game. And I was keeping score to see just how many times the professional newscasters at CTV could look directly at a fabulous national Woodward-and-Bernstein-type story and, like a broken record spinning out the same words over and

---

* That this originated with Schopenhauer is disputed.

over, tell me to vamoose. If this were an Olympic sport in the upcoming 2010 Vancouver Games, they would have won gold. The receptionist would pick up the phone and call the newsroom, uttering a few words—whether it be about Magali's court appearance or Joe Taylor's or anything in between—to the person on the other end. There would be a moment of silence as the receptionist listened to the response, which was always a brush-off, then hung up the phone. Then I'd give my contact information. Invariably, that's when CTV's position was clarified to me: that if anyone in the newsroom deemed the Lost Canadians important enough, if CTV wanted to go further with a story, someone would get back to me. No one ever did. It was the classic "Don't call us, we'll call you."

Over the years, I'd done a handful of CTV broadcasts, mainly on *Canada AM*, but in Vancouver, my hometown, my persistent knocking and calling was for naught. Maybe it was because a talk-show host from CKNW doubled as the evening newscaster for CTV. His name is Bill Good, who by this time I had nicknamed Bill Bad, because when it came to turning its back on our issue, no news organization in all of Canada even came close to being as rude and nasty to me as CKNW. For whatever reason, CTV in Vancouver really didn't see the Lost Canadians as a story. Could it have prejudged its audience, thinking viewers wouldn't care? Or could it be that there was pressure from the top telling it not to cover the issue? I don't know. It didn't make sense. I knew that, in citizenship law, what you didn't know could hurt you. And I knew that, as a public broadcaster, as a condition of the Canadian Radio-television and Telecommunications Commission allowing it access to the public airwaves, it was obligated to broadcast programs and information that served the Canadian public.[5] I also knew that by largely ignoring our story, the Canadian media were doing a great disservice to hundreds of thousands of Canadians. Over time, many of the uninformed would themselves be caught in CIC's tangled web of citizenship denial—and yet it was all so easily preventable. The prescription? The public had to be informed. The only antidote was knowledge.

When something goes wrong, we pilots always want to get to the root cause—what happened and why—which includes the not-so-obvious. After more than a decade of trying to get the Canadian media on board, I still can't come up with a valid reason why they took our issue so lightly.

Although the World War II war brides didn't measure up to CTV's journalistic standards, on March 8, 2006, just a little more than a month before Joe Taylor went to court in Vancouver, CTV news in Toronto started gearing up for a showy event. In the first of a series of stories, it reported several brand-new inductees into Canada's Walk of Fame, which honours Canadians who have excelled in, among other things, sports, music, film, and television, as well as in the literary, visual, and performing arts. Here's part of that story:

CTV.ca News Staff
Date: Wed. Mar. 8 2006 4:31 PM ET
The newest inductees to Canada's Walk of Fame were announced today, with a list that includes Canadian icons Pamela Anderson and Alex Trebek.

The remaining inductees are singer-songwriter Jann Arden, actor Brendan Fraser, singer Robert Goulet, comedian Eugene Levy, musician Paul Shaffer, and the legendary Olympic ski team known as The Crazy Canucks. Members Steve Podborski, Ken Read, Dave Irwin and Dave Murray will share the star.

Anderson, who will host this year's Juno Awards, became famous for her role as a lifeguard on Baywatch, while Trebek is the veteran host of trivia show Jeopardy!

The event will be held on June 3 at the Hummingbird Centre in Toronto, and will be hosted by wrestling star Trish Stratus.[6]

Canada seems to have a fascination—almost an obsession—with honouring our famous Hollywood actors, musicians, and artists. The list of those presented with an Order of Canada (OC) is filled with them. In fact, many OC recipients have also been recognized by Canada's Walk of Fame. I don't see a problem with this. But I do find it interesting that many of the new members from both camps were actually Lost Canadians. The fact that this was happening, and the government and the media not realizing it, proves just how out of touch with their own citizenship laws the government was and how totally disinterested in the tragic facts the news organizations were, because I certainly was doing everything in my power to tell them. Their wounds of ignorance had been self-inflicted. Several of the Walk of Fame inductees mentioned in the above article were questionable (meaning, were they really Canadian?), or had close ties to someone questionable. Pamela Anderson left Canada as a young woman, taking up residence in California. She had two children born in the states to a non-Canadian father. For Pamela, her citizenship would not be in question; the problem was with her kids. There existed the possibility that they could one day be told they weren't Canadian.

The list of inductees read like a who's who of Hollywood and included Brendan Fraser, Alex Trebek, Paul Shaffer, Eugene Levy, Matthew Perry, Kiefer Sutherland, Keanu Reeves, Jim Carrey, Dan Aykroyd, Michael J. Fox, Neil Young, Paul Anka, Morley Safer, Peter Jennings, Mary Pickford, Christopher Plummer, Norman Jewison, James Cameron, Yvonne De Carlo, Raymond Burr, William Shatner, Percy Faith, Art Linkletter, Ann Rutherford, Jay Silverheels, Lorne Greene, James Doohan, Glenn Ford, Gene Lockhart, Jack Warner, Louis B. Mayer, Mack Sennett, Harold Russell, and Robert Goulet, among many others, all of whom, like Pamela Anderson, had headed south, making their careers and babies in the US. Looking at what's under the leaf rather than its more visible topside, one might find that some, possibly many, of these stars and/or their children were Lost Canadians. But when I tried to tell this to CTV, it showed no interest. The war brides were basically ignored, while the more exciting, showy Canadians had their faces broadcast from coast to coast. The pressing question remained: Were the recent inductees really Canadian? By the same standard that was being applied to the war brides, some of them were not. But, while the war brides were being seriously abused, the inductees were being lauded as outstanding Canadians.

A FEW months later—it was summer by now—my wife and I were in the living room of our home in Gibsons when the phone rang. My wife answered it. She said hello, then, eyebrows raised, glanced over at me with a this-is-for-you-and-you'll-never-guess-who-it-is look.

"Yes, he's right here. Hold on, I'll get him."

She passed me the phone. I took it and said hello. The voice was unmistakable. In that deep, rich tone of his he said, "This is Robert Goulet. I understand you might be able to help me get my Canadian citizenship."

By now I had started to understand the bigger picture: that many thousands of people were having citizenship problems, affected in their own peculiar ways. My CIC insider always let me know what the department was up to behind its iron curtain, often giving me the name and contact information of a Lost Canadian. Robert Goulet, it turned out, had been born outside Canada to Canadian parents; for him, a pressing CIC question put his fate in the balance: Where was he on his twenty-fourth birthday? This because of CIC's age-twenty-four rule, the requirement for foreign-born Canadian kids to be domiciled in Canada on their twenty-fourth birthday in order to qualify for Canadian citizenship (discussed further in Chapters 12 and 13).

Can anyone tell you precisely where they were almost fifty years earlier, even if it was the day they turned twenty-four? Were you domiciled in Canada? If you were foreign-born to Canadian parents, it mattered—CIC could come after you, out of the clear blue, to deny your citizenship. It didn't matter that you spent most of your life in Canada or that you voted, paid taxes, served on the school board, or sat on a jury. The fact was, you could now be denied citizenship if you couldn't prove where you were the day you turned twenty-four. The day before or the day after didn't matter.

This is what Senator Roméo Dallaire faced when, in 1973, he was denied not just a passport but also his underlying citizenship, just because he was out of the country on his twenty-fourth birthday. And guess what he was doing during his absence? Serving in the Canadian Armed Forces. He had to dig up records of his life in Canada, then go before a citizenship judge to be declared Canadian. To use the good senator's own words, "I think it's an absolutely inhuman process."[7] That story appeared in July 2006 on CBC. Its reporters hadn't exactly shown up in droves to cover Joe Taylor during his court ordeal, but when a celebrity came forward, hey, that was newsworthy. Granted, Senator Dallaire is a Canadian hero, but isn't our country supposed to take care of all its people, regardless of stature? Sadly, I was proving, one victim at a time, that despite our lofty ideals, despite what we've been taught, Canada doesn't always work for the benefit of its people.

Mr. Goulet was indeed an icon, not just to Canada but to the world. In the 1960s, he'd been invited as a last-minute replacement for Burt Bacharach to sing the US national anthem to open one of Muhammad Ali's championship boxing matches. It was broadcast across the country, from New York to Hawaii, and Americans everywhere had tuned in. Goulet took the mic at centre stage and began singing. Half a century later, his rendition still ranks as one of the most memorable of all time: he forgot the words. Americans were appalled. Later it was explained away by his being Canadian by birth. But was he? The reason for his phone call to me was that he wanted my help in getting his citizenship. Ironically, as CTV filmed the unveiling of his stylized maple-leaf star on the sidewalk in Toronto's theatre district, Goulet turned to the cameras and said, "What I really want is my citizenship." Mr. Goulet himself told me this later. The man he said he had appealed to was none other than Prime Minister Stephen Harper. But it was not to be.

Goulet, it seems, might not have been in Canada on his twenty-fourth birthday, and the burden of proof lay entirely on his shoulders to substantiate that he had indeed been here. The government did not have any sort of reciprocating burden to prove that he wasn't. Guilt came before innocence, and it was up to the individual to verify to some faceless bureaucrat that on the day of his twenty-fourth birthday, he was, irrefutably, domiciled in Canada. Amazingly, with the help of many people, including his good friend Senator Tommy Banks, Goulet secured an old photograph of a theatre in Edmonton, along with a newspaper article about his performance there. The article was dated and the theatre's marquee showed his name. Bingo. He had his evidence, proof positive, that he had been performing at that theatre the day he turned twenty-four.

How many people would be so lucky as to have a picture from a newspaper establishing their whereabouts on a particular day forty-nine years earlier? Mr. Goulet died just over a year later, on October 30, 2007. On the day of his funeral, his name was featured on every marquee of every casino hotel on the Las Vegas strip. People there loved and embraced him. Canada, on the other hand, did not. He died without being officially recognized as a Canadian.

Why? Because CIC never got around to verifying his conclusive proof. Goulet sent all the required documents, signed forms, background checks, and grade-school recess reports (Did you or did you not pull on Sally's pigtails in fourth grade?). Given CIC's snail pace at processing applications it didn't like, it could take years for the paperwork to be done. To once again quote Roméo Dallaire, "It's an absolutely inhuman process. The current situation makes no sense." He's right. It's Canada's shame.

On June 14, 2006, the *National Post* ran an article about Mr. Goulet and his new star on Canada's Walk of Fame. The paper had ignored my many calls and emails, and made no mention of his citizenship woes in the article.

Summers were usually a bit of a reprieve for MPs and senators as they returned to their cubbyholes scattered around the country. For the most part, though, this break became a non-stop unofficial federal election campaign. Rumours constantly floated in and out of news stories, with everyone guessing when Canadians would next be headed to the polls. There was no mistaking it; ever since the closing words of Harper's acceptance speech as prime minister, "God bless Canada," our country had definitely become more American; Jr. Bush and his Republican clan were indeed exerting their influence north of the border.

While the politicians went around conducting campaigns-lite, I spent my summer in warfare mode, preparing for their eventual migration back to Ottawa.* I tried my best to solicit, maybe even embarrass, the media and human rights groups into helping us. At best, I was but a constant gnat flying around the faces of our political elite. I spent time on my boat, at times going out on the water with John Reynolds. Many of the MPs were aware that I was in Gibsons, and several enjoyed an inexpensive holiday there (well, inexpensive for them, anyway). I'd take them boating; many stayed at my mother's place right by the water; I'd loan them a nice car. Life was good in Gibsons and they knew it. Visitors came from all over, even lost and found Lost Canadians. By now, some had been captured through Bill s-2; the majority, however, remained lost. It had been just over a year since the passage of s-2, and many Lost Canadians were contacting me, saying that CIC had not yet processed their applications. They were, like Robert Goulet, Canadians. The problem was that they couldn't prove it. Years before, I sat with my daughter watching a Discovery Channel nature program filmed in some foreign land with crocodiles. The announcer made a profound statement: "Nature doesn't care if you live or die. The reality is, nature is indifferent." It stuck with me because that's how I would describe the way Minister Monte Solberg viewed Lost Canadians and their citizenship struggles.

The judge in the Taylor case, Luc Martineau, had given both sides a Friday, June 9, deadline to get further information to him. Behind the scenes, emails were flying between me and Ed Komarnicki, parliamentary secretary to Mr. Solberg. I would then coordinate with Joe Taylor and his lawyer and my want-to-be MP John Weston (the Conservative who had lost to Blair Wilson). Once again, to use pilot lingo, it was "use all available resources." Whatever it took, I was willing to try. The objective was to correct this mess. On June 6 at 1:18 in the morning, I fired off this email to Mr. Komarnicki:

> Ed: Regarding the Joe Taylor case, this is what is happening, as well as what we need...
>
> Joe Taylor MUST have a response from Mr. Solberg by Friday morning; a federal court in Vancouver is waiting for the answer. Judge Martineau wants your office to clarify the position of the war brides and their children. I explained what is needed in a letter sent to John Weston, who will be forwarding it to Jason Kenney. It offers a perfect solution to the war brides, to their children, and to Joe Taylor. If you have any questions, then

---

* I called it "campaign-lite" after lite-beer. Fewer calories but nonetheless beer. The parliamentarians weren't officially campaigning, but really they were.

please call me. A letter of clarification must be received by the court on or before Friday morning.

This is what I got back at 9:03 a.m.:

Thanks for your email. I have read it and contents. Bringing it to the attention of the minister.

My question wasn't just about Joe, but rather, how did the citizenship minister view *all* the war brides? Were they or were they not recognized as citizens of Canada on January 1, 1947?

When Joe and I were sitting in the courtroom, watching his life being examined, Judge Martineau asked this same question. But it was directed to the government lawyer, Peter Bell. Let me quote from *Vancouver Sun* reporter Gerry Bellett's article of May 31, 2006:

Judge asked to rule on status of war brides, kids
"This is not a street fight; the outcome of this goes beyond the interests of Mr. [Joseph] Taylor. It has huge consequences," Justice Luc Martineau warned Crown lawyer Peter Bell, who was representing the immigration minister.

Martineau said if he accepted the government's argument that the son has no Canadian citizenship status, the same would apply to all those like Taylor and his mother, who came to Canada as spouses and dependents of Canadian servicemen who served overseas in the Second World War...

Morahan then produced a letter from former Liberal immigration minister Joe Volpe saying that in fact war brides were granted citizenship in 1947 pursuant to the Citizenship Act.

Bell said using the letter would "not be correct in law" as it was not a statute.

"No, but it answers my question," said Martineau.

If you want this court to say all these persons are in limbo because the minister got it wrong—this is what will flow if you are right..."

Martineau decided to give both sides 10 days to produce documents concerning what happened to the citizenship status of war brides and dependent children after the 1947 Citizenship Act was proclaimed.[8]

The judge had been given a letter I had in my possession. It had been given to me by the NDP citizenship critic Bill Siksay. In August 2005, Bill wrote to the then citizenship minister, Joe Volpe, asking him to clarify whether the war brides and their children had become citizens on January 1, 1947. Here's Volpe's reply, dated September 25, 2005:

"The Canadian Citizenship Act, which came into force on January 1, 1947, automatically granted Canadian citizenship to women who were married to Canadian soldiers overseas before that day. Children born to these couples also obtained citizenship automatically, by birth on Canadian soil or though their father, if born outside of Canada." [9]

Despite this admission by Mr. Volpe that Taylor, and all the war brides and kids like him, were Canadian citizens, he still forced Taylor into court, saying out of the other side of his mouth that no, Taylor wasn't Canadian. And if that were not enough, Volpe's successor, Monte Solberg, took the same position. The government had no problem telling Taylor to get lost. Nor did it seem to care if he went bankrupt.

In the meantime, emails continued to arrive in my inbox. It seemed that the age-twenty-four rule, the requirement for foreign-born Canadian kids to be domiciled in Canada on their twenty-fourth birthday, was doing to Lost Canadians what electric bug zappers do to flies. Tons of folks got annihilated. From June 8:

I, like so many others, have tried several times to claim Canadian Citizenship and have been denied. My Mom met Bill whom I have called Dad since I can remember.

They married in London in 1942. Dad was a Canadian serviceman stationed here in the UK. But he was sent to Italy. Mom got a letter from the War Office saying he was lost in action and presumed dead. His brother Ron remained here in London. I understand that Ron and Mom had an affair and that I was a result of it. Bill was not killed in action after all but returned to my Mom only to find that she was pregnant. I did not know of this till I was in my 40s. I can reveal all later if you wish. But, to cut a long story short, Mom and me were on the *Franconian*. And we went to Canada to live with grandparents and Dad as I knew him. I went to school till I was 9 years old. But, in 1953, Mom became homesick, and wanted to return to England. Dad brought us back. Although I never understood then that I had been adopted by Bill. Since then, both my parents, Canadian Citizens, have since passed away. I decided to find out all that I was never told about who my real father was etc., etc. I went to Canada and found a way to remain there for 3 years. In that time, I searched out all my Canadian relatives and everything else I could regarding my legal status. I applied 3 times for my citizenship and was turned down. I have since tried at Canada House here in London with still no success.

Well, this is just a little about me and my strong feelings about this issue; I wonder if you might like to add my story to the vast list. Or maybe you might be able to advise. Thanks in advance.

Yours truly,

William J. Thomas

Later, this arrived:

Happened to run across your website and read with interest your presentation to the Standing Committee. My brother also lost his citizenship. He was born in 1941 in England. Our father was serving in the Canadian Army. My mother was a war bride and travelled on the *Queen Mary* in 1946 with four children (my youngest sister was 5 months old) to Halifax, and made the train trip to Fort William (half way across Canada). We were raised in Canada. My father died in 1953 of cancer leaving my mother and then 5 children alone with no friends or family.

When my brother was 21, he was studying for his chartered accountancy, and went to live in Bermuda and work in an accounting firm (correspondence course with Queen's). When he went to have his passport renewed, he was told he was not a Canadian, and never had been. They tore up his passport and said he should never have had one in the first place.

As you can imagine, this was a shock, considering that his father served in the war for Canada, etc. Brian went to live in England and never returned to Canada. I think it was a loss to Canada. Someone with a professional degree who would have made a contribution to Canada was summarily rejected. He has now died but has a child who could be eligible for citizenship if Brian's citizenship could be restored. I asked a CIC person why he wasn't told when he was given his passport that he had to do something about retaining his citizenship. And I was told that there would have been newspaper ads and he should have known.

When you consider yourself a Canadian, why would you read an ad that says you are not, even if you happened upon it by chance? In any case, it is rather like the *Hitch Hiker's Guide to the Galaxy*—the information was there—but you didn't go looking for it so it is your own fault. Why didn't Veterans Affairs make an effort to contact their troops?

I was very sorry that this has happened. If my brother had his passport after his twenty-fourth birthday, he would have found that he had to apply for a citizenship card to be OK.

I wish you luck with your quest.
Yours sincerely,
Olivia Jackman[10]

This was followed three days later with some good news:

Hi Don.
Just wanted to extend my thanks to you for your efforts on behalf of the
Lost Canadians and Bill s-2, etc. I took the citizenship oath this morning
after applying for resumption June 5, 2005.
Sandra Brown

In the whirlpool of life, I was trying my best to prevent Lost Canadians
from being sucked down by the unfeeling currents of Ottawa. I had become
their lifeline and, for the most part, their only hope. How could I walk away?
I was piloting the plane that they happened to be on and, by God, I was
going to get them safely back home.

My main contact at CBC was Gary Symons, but I was in Gibsons and he
was in Kelowna. Gary connected me with Curt Petrovich at CBC Vancouver.
Curt did a couple of interviews, which aired just after Canada Day 2006,
featuring Stuart Martin, Roméo Dallaire, and Joe Taylor. All told compelling
stories. But Dallaire's comments were the ones that stood out:

"Being born to a Canadian father in those days meant that I automatically became a Canadian citizen. [Otherwise, I would not be so favoured.] ...
I mean that's a near impossibility to imagine—[going] from being a citizen
to being a non-citizen."[11]

Petrovich went on to say that Dallaire was "caught [in] a change in law
that required people not born in Canada to take steps to retain their citizenship. But the change was never explained to war brides or their children."[12]

Petrovich then talked to Melynda Jarratt, Canada's leading expert on
the World War II war brides. Melynda always had a unique way of cutting
to the chase. "If Senator Roméo Dallaire is not a Canadian citizen," she said,
"let's just go shoot the Easter Bunny." She followed that with: "The Harper
government inherited this problem, the Harper government did not create
it, but the Harper government better damn well fix it."

Yes, but easier said than done. The comment "being born to a Canadian
father in those days meant that I automatically became a Canadian citizen"
is but one instance of many that show just how complicated the citizenship
laws were. One would think that a senator, particularly one who doubles

as a Lost Canadian, would have an intimate knowledge of the laws. But he didn't. His statement went to the same issue Judge Martineau was trying to figure out: Were the war brides and their kids citizens on January 1, 1947, or not? How pathetic, really, when something as basic and fundamental as citizenship gets so complicated that it becomes a court issue, maybe even having to make its way right up to the Supreme Court, to settle who is and who is not a citizen of Canada. The best description of what was happening in this maze of convoluted citizenship law came from Jeff Wan, the lawyer who won a unanimous decision in the Supreme Court of Canada in *Benner v. Canada*. "It's like a barnacled creature which has grown another barnacle, which in turn grows yet another barnacle, ad infinitum." Like a mobile you hang above a baby's crib, the laws of citizenship and the mobile are always moving, blowing with the prevailing winds. Not only were senators like Dallaire confused but even our citizenship ministers had no clue as to the laws' many nuances. Professor Donald Galloway, one of the only people in all of Canada who studies citizenship law, stated that it has got to the point where no one really knows just who is or is not a citizen.

Then, in the middle of this storm, something completely unexpected blew in through the front door, and it had nothing to do with citizenship. People began writing to me, mainly from England, in search of family connections or long-lost friends:

Dear Sir,

I found out about 20 years ago that my father was named Jack Goodall, and that he served over here in England in the RCAF. And in 1943, he was stationed in Sussex, before going over to Sicily, I believe. He met a young lady named Gertie Lumsden whilst stationed in Sussex in 1943 and, as a result of their relationship I was born in Dec. 1943. I have tried for the past 20 years to track down any details about Jack Goodall to no avail. Public Records Office here in London have no strong records which enable all RCAF personnel to be determined by their movements in Southern England during 1943. RAF records cannot determine even which RCAF personnel were stationed at a given time.

I have met with a brick wall when asking Veterans Affairs in Montreal as I cannot prove Jack Goodall was my father because his name does not appear on my birth certificate.

Where do I continue my search?

Regards,

Paul Vider

I am trying to trace Mr Charles Docherty or any of his relatives or anyone who knew him. The last address I have for him is 81 ½ Kenilwoth Avenue, Hamilton, Ontario which was in 1945/1946. He was stationed in or near Croydon, England during the Second World War and I would greatly appreciate any information.

Thank you in anticipation,

Mrs. Jenny Noble

Good Morning,

I am hoping you can help me or redirect me to the appropriate people. I do not have much information. Just that my husband's brother is the son of a Canadian solider stationed in Sussex (near Groombridge) during 1943–1944. Only information I have is Raymond Douglas or Douglas Raymond is his name. I know it is a long shot but I have to try as his son is now 62 and anxious to trace the whereabouts of his father.

Thank you for your time,

Ann Muil

I am writing on behalf of the television program "Memories," a production by the Dutch public broadcast channel KRO.

"Memories" is about people and their memories of friends from the past. Viewers can contact our program with a request to search for the friend they lost sight of and would very much enjoy to meet again. If we manage to track down the lost friend, the reunion is always a joyful event for both parties. An episode of our show with English subtitles can be viewed by clicking on this link. http://memories.kro.nl/international.

KRO Memories has recently received a very special letter from a Dutch viewer by the name of Virry de Vries Robles. Virry de Vries Robles (1932) is a survivor of Transit Camp Westerbork. Virry, a Jewish girl, was imprisoned at Camp Westerbork starting late November 1943. Because of a coincidence she avoided being transported to Germany and stayed in the camp until it was liberated on April 12, 1945.

Virry particularly remembers one Canadian soldier, who visited her family regularly and taught her some English words. Virry was 12 years at the time and she remembers how much he liked her mom's apple pies. She considered him a friend and made two rings out of "airplane glass" (Plexiglass from fighter planes). One had a metal plate carrying her friend's initials: S.R. The other ring, which she gave to the Canadian soldier, had her own initials: V.R. Virry estimates S.R. was about 20 years old at the time and that he was in the Westerbork area for about two weeks.

Virry now is a volunteer at Remembrance Centre Camp Westerbork (a museum), where she tells visitors about her experiences in the camp. Earlier this year Virry donated the remaining ring to the museum.

When Virry mentioned how often she still thinks of him and how much she would like to know what became of him, museum staff decided to help her locate this man (or his family). Unfortunately, very little is known about him.

Since S.R. was in Westerbork for two weeks, it seems unlikely that he was with 8th Reconnaissance Regiment or the South Saskatchewan Regiment. They first moved on within an hour of liberating the Camp. The SSR had moved on by April 14.

Next, Capt Connolly 230 Det. C.A. took command (230 Detachment Civil Affairs). This makes it likely that S.R. was part of this unit.

If you have any information that can lead us to Virry's Canadian friend, please contact me.

Sarah Hol

Requests like these began to come in with regularity. I generally passed them over to Melynda Jarratt, who always gave so generously of her time. Occasionally, a connection would be made—after half a century, the war still had repercussions. Often the reunions went well. These family members of Canadian servicemen were not seeking Canadian citizenship, but I imagine that they were, in a sense, a threat to CIC. Everything always seems to boil down to money. Our government was afraid of opening up this can of worms, thus denying citizenship to middle-aged children who, like Sheila Walshe, just wanted to be with their dads.

For the most part, the summer of 2006 was like any other summer for me. I worked like a fiend, trying in any way I could to help anyone and everyone who made themselves known to me. Joe Taylor and I waited anxiously for the court's judgment. And then, on September 1, it came. Joe called me immediately after receiving the news from his lawyer. He had won. We were ecstatic but also reserved, knowing only too well the government's propensity to appeal. But for the moment, Joe was deemed to have been a Canadian for all those years. And it went further, much further. The judge ruled that the government had violated all kinds of Joe's rights, from those covered by the old Canadian Bill of Rights to current Charter rights. His decision read like an encyclopedia of government violations aimed smack dab at its own people. The war brides and their kids could now safely go to sleep in their Canadian beds, in their Canadian homes. It was the second time the government had declared them to be citizens. Sixty years earlier, Mackenzie King, along with Immigration Canada's government bureaucrats, had welcomed them to our shores as "Canada's newest citizens." In 2006, a federal judge was able to do something that went far beyond the abilities of our current politicians and bureaucrats: he declared them all to be "Canadian citizens." How ironic that just short of four months later, with the new year being ushered in, 2007 would be declared by six of our provinces the Year of the War Bride.[13] Like a spoilsport ruining a lovely party, our federal government wanted no part of it. For the time being, though, that didn't much matter to Joe. All of a sudden, life was good—very good: he had even got some of his court expenses reimbursed.

Back in England, Joe was once again interviewed by the *Vancouver Sun.* "I can't wait to be there—Canada's my home," he said.[14]

His elation didn't last very long. The Harper people decided they didn't much like the good judge's decision. So, almost as fast as a bolt of lightning, Monte Solberg appealed it. At great Canadian taxpayers' expense, we were heading back to court. Keep in mind, judicial decisions usually get appealed because of some significant mistake made by the judge. But in Joe's case, what was significantly wrong with restoring his rights? Why not just finally leave the poor guy alone? Was the government making a feeble attempt to save face?

If only Joe had been a Hollywood star, or maybe in the porn business with a bunch of cats. Then his story would have commanded the Canadian media's attention. But as a lone warrior against an army of bureaucrats and disinterested politicians, fighting for not just himself but also for tens of thousands of elderly women and their children, well, it just wasn't sexy enough to garner their attention.

The Canadian Press 2006 scoreboard ended this way:[15]

Cats, porn, and Hollywood stars: 302 mentions.

Lost Canadians: 0.

HON. ANDREW TELEGDI P.C., M.P.,

LIBERAL ASSOCIATE CRITIC FOR CITIZENSHIP AND IMMIGRATION

BILL SIKSAY, M.P.

NDP CRITIC FOR CITIZENSHIP AND IMMIGRATION

AND

SENATOR ROMÉO DALLAIRE

WILL HOLD A PRESS CONFERENCE

TODAY AT 3:45 PM (OCTOBER 4, 2006)

IN THE CHARLES-LYNCH PRESS CONFERENCE ROOM

SUBJECT: THE CASE OF JOE TAYLOR AND THE CITIZENSHIP ACT

ON SEPTEMBER 1, 2006, MR. JUSTICE LUC MARTINEAU OF THE FEDERAL COURT ALLOWED THE APPLICATION OF JOE TAYLOR FOR CANADIAN CITIZENSHIP AND DIRECTED THE MINISTER TO ISSUE MR. TAYLOR A CERTIFICATE OF CITIZENSHIP. MR. TAYLOR IS THE SON OF A CANADIAN WWII SOLDIER (BORN OUT OF WEDLOCK).

MARTINEAU BASED HIS ORDER ON HIS FINDING THAT THE SECTIONS OF THE CITIZENSHIP ACT UPON WHICH MR. TAYLOR'S ORIGINAL APPLICATION WAS DENIED CONTRAVENE SECTION 1 OF THE *CANADIAN BILL OF RIGHTS* AND SECTIONS 7 AND 15 OF THE *CANADIAN CHARTER OF RIGHTS AND FREEDOMS*.

THE MINISTER IS APPEALING THE DECISION. THIS IS AN OUTRAGE.

THE CITIZENSHIP COMMITTEE OF THE 38TH PARLIAMENT OF WHICH MR. TELEGDI AND MR. SIKSAY WERE MEMBERS, HELD HEARINGS IN ALL PROVINCIAL CAPITALS, AND IN VANCOUVER, WATERLOO AND MONTREAL.

AT THE INVITATION OF THE THEN MINISTER OF CITIZENSHIP, THE COMMITTEE WROTE THREE REPORTS TO PARLIAMENT, THE LAST OF WHICH WAS CALLED *UPDATING CANADA'S CITIZENSHIP LAWS: IT'S TIME.* IT MADE RECOMMENDATIONS TO MAKE OUR CITIZENSHIP ACT CONFORM TO PROVISIONS OF THE *CANADIAN CHARTER OF RIGHTS AND FREEDOMS*.

CHAPTER 12

AND THE WINNER IN THE
STUPID CATEGORY IS...

*All too often we hear stories of veterans who are ignored or
disrespected by government. What a shameful way to treat men
and women who risked their lives to defend Canada.
This shame will end with the election of a new government.*

STEPHEN HARPER, 2006 ELECTION CAMPAIGN

OCTOBER 4, 2006. The former chairman of the Citizenship Committee
under the Liberals, Andrew Telegdi, who'd been the parliamentary secretary to Citizenship and Immigration Minister Elinor Caplan and who now
was the Liberal associate critic for citizenship and at all times my staunch
ally, was outraged by Monte Solberg's resolve in going forward to appeal
Judge Martineau's decision against the government. His anger was directed
not just at the current government but also against his own party. It too had
opposed Taylor. By his side was former Lost Canadian and Liberal senator
Roméo Dallaire, as well as Bill Siksay, the NDP's citizenship critic. Together
they held a joint press conference in the Charles-Lynch Press Conference
Room, located in the bowels of Parliament. The topic was Joe Taylor, or,
better and more broadly stated, all the war brides and their children. But it
went even further in that Canadian citizenship itself had come under attack.
As you may recall, Andrew was one of the Hungarian '56ers. His family had
lost everything when, as refugees, they fled their homeland for Canada.
Identity and belonging were etched into the very fabric of his being. It was

also etched into mine. And that's how the two of us had become inexorably joined at the hip, so to speak, in our quest to right these terrible wrongs.

The *Vancouver Sun* and *Toronto Sun* were on top of the issue. The *Globe and Mail* wrote a couple of stories, then basically went into journalistic hiding. That was about it. The press conference really didn't produce much press coverage. Too bad, because coming from this trio, the quotes were to die for. Although most of the Canadian media remained on the sidelines, one unlikely company put its coverage out on the Web. About 1,500 kilometres south of the Canadian border, based in Sunnyvale, California, Yahoo Corporation released the story. Here's an excerpt:

The judge, upon hearing of the government's appeal of his direction, suggested the government drop its case because, if it won, the citizenship status of every WWII bride and their offspring would be in jeopardy—all because Joe had been conceived before his parents married. Instead of complying, the Harper government is going ahead with the appeal.

"This is insane," said Kitchener-Waterloo MP Andrew Telegdi, Liberal citizenship critic and chairman of the Standing Committee on Citizenship and Immigration who often contested his own government's strange policies on the issue...

Dallaire said it was "absolutely nonsensical" for the government to appeal. "There is a term called 'bureaucratic terrorists'—that's the gang in the middle of the system that has this power trip of authority and interpret things, not for the benefit of the citizen, but for the benefit of the government... That is not their duty. Their duty is to make sure that the government is compliant with laws in order to help citizens—not the other way around."[1]

Leave it to a no-nonsense lieutenant general to pull no punches. *Bureaucratic terrorists. The government is not compliant with laws. Absolutely nonsensical.* Next to speak was the NDP's Bill Siksay, who didn't just expand the issue by introducing one more group of Lost Canadians, but also talked about Harper's decision to deliver Joe a "double whammy" in the same week—the appeal of his court case and the elimination of the Court Challenges Program. It meant that, financially, Joe Taylor was on his own. Bill's statement: "Mr. Taylor's situation is but one example of the importance of the Court Challenges Programme, a programme that made it possible for Canadians to fight for their rights, especially when they were up against the seemingly unlimited resources of the government."[2]

He went further: "Weeks ago I urged Minister Solberg to forgo an appeal and, instead to set the Department to work addressing the serious issues Joe Taylor's case raises. We need a government and department willing to fix the problems of Canadian citizenship."

Bill also brought up another lingering problem, that of the military brats, children born to Canadians overseas with the Armed Forces or diplomatic corps, or those just working overseas: "Due to a bureaucratic foul-up, many of them have discovered that they have not been registered as Canadians. Many have been told they have to apply to be a permanent resident and then apply for citizenship. There is no excuse. Record[s] exist to prove that they were entitled to Canadian citizenship. The government must move immediately to solve this citizenship problem too. As... one of the advocates working on this issue says, 'This stupid error must be corrected immediately.'"

"Insane," "stupid," "nonsensical," "bureaucratic terrorists," "not compliant with laws"—these were the qualifiers top Canadian MPs and a senator were using to describe their own government. You'd think it would have got the journalistic wheels turning. This wasn't said at some wacky question period gone awry; it was a well-thought-out, scripted, multi-party press conference with MPs and a senator. And it represented two parties in the House of Commons. That alone was a rarity.

As a pilot, listening to language like that would raise all kinds of red flags. You'd think it would have tweaked the journalistic curiosity of the Ottawa Press Gallery. But it didn't. It was telling that a US organization broadcast the story—a Canadian story—to the world, yet the Canadian media showed little interest. After a plane crash, investigators immediately go to work searching for the two black boxes. One is a voice recorder, recording everything uttered in the cockpit during the last thirty minutes of flight (although thanks to Richard Nixon and the Watergate tapes, the forensic investigators are now able to go back further than thirty minutes). And the second box contains all kinds of digital data, often with more than a hundred inputs. The objective is to find the cause—what made the plane crash? The investigators painstakingly put all the pieces together, like a massive jigsaw puzzle. Thanks to advanced technology, they can take the data recorder and plug it directly into an aircraft simulator. They then basically sit back and watch as the simulator recreates every detail of the final moments before impact. They get to see and hear exactly what the pilots in the cockpit did. Borrowing the message from John Lennon's song "Imagine," can you "imagine" this happening in Ottawa, political investigators immediately discovering what went wrong and how to correct it? In the world of make-believe, anything is possible, so for a moment, "imagine" that just after a "political accident," investigators plug the press conference quotes noted above into a political simulator. Then throw in my repeated warnings for Solberg not to oppose us, suggesting he would probably lose way more than he could even imagine, add in the court's ruling that the government had contravened the old Canadian Bill of Rights as well as having violated sections 7 and 15 of the Charter of Rights and Freedoms, and, faster than greased lightning, the investigators would know exactly what went wrong. Cause of accident: Captain Stephen Harper and co-pilot Monte Solberg ignored all repeated warnings. Case should never have gone to trial. Gross incompetence.

Another difference between aviation and politics is that, in the former, when mistakes of this magnitude are made, people die. Pilots are usually the first to go. In politics, nothing much happens to the politicians in charge. When major problems arise, the offending minister gets a new portfolio. In Ottawa, Solberg seemed ready, willing, and able to inflict further damage. He wasn't spending his own money on this nonsense. He was spending the Canadian taxpayers' dollars.

Two days after the press conference, Andrew stood in the House of Commons during question period and, looking directly at the citizenship minister, asked, "Mr. Speaker, Joe Taylor, the son of a second world war Canadian soldier, was born in England in 1945. He and his mother became Canadian citizens when they landed in Halifax in 1946. When the marriage failed, he and his mother returned to England. When Mr. Taylor moved back to Canada several years ago, he was denied citizenship rights because he was born out of wedlock. Does the minister really believe it is justifiable in this day and age to discriminate against children born out of wedlock?"

Solberg replied, "Mr. Speaker, I have to say that I am very sympathetic, like all parliamentarians, to people who find themselves in situations that the act did not anticipate and we want to sort those out. However, when there is a situation where there is a court decision that has implications for hundreds of statutes, dozens of departments and could cost tens of billions of dollars, we have a duty to appeal."

Andrew's response? "Rubbish . . . On September 1, Federal Court Justice Martineau ruled sections of the Citizenship Act unconstitutional and ordered the minister to restore Mr. Taylor's citizenship."

Solberg once again reiterated the statement: "We cannot stand idle when court decisions threaten dozens of statutes and could cost the government billions of dollars. In a case like that, it is our duty to stand up for the Government of Canada and the people of Canada."[3]

Talk about screwing up. Solberg had just announced to anyone listening that, because he continued the previous minister's court challenge against Joe Taylor, Canadian taxpayers might now be on the hook for "tens of billions of dollars." To keep one man out of Canada only because he'd been born out of wedlock, Solberg and Harper had gambled the farm and lost. Put into other terms, the amount of money he was suggesting equates to $600 for every Canadian man, woman, and child on the planet. Setting aside the ethical considerations of cancelling 67,000-plus people's citizenship and looking at it only in terms of money, that's a colossal blunder. In aviation, a mistake of that magnitude would have left dead bodies strewn all over the place. But this wasn't aviation, it was politics. So Solberg was allowed by the prime minister to press forward.

The next day, Andrew Telegdi issued a press release: "The Conservatives need to realize we are in the quantum age and not the stone age; it is wrong to discriminate against someone who is born out of wedlock... Canadian war brides and their children do not need the Minister's sympathy. The government's responsibility is to defend the rights of these Canadians and not discriminate against them."[4]

Peter Worthington of the *Toronto Sun*, one of my few allies in the media, responded by writing an article titled "A Foolish Appeal." In another column he wrote, "They [the Conservatives] put the government over the individual. They put a price tag on individual rights, on Charter rights."

Indeed they had. Morals, ethics, equal rights, and doing what is right, it seems, had a price tag.

And then, in true hypocritical fashion, a few weeks later, Monte Solberg was out there telling Canadians to celebrate, of all things, Citizenship Week. CIC's own internally generated press releases intimated that it was to be a festive week, a time for all Canadians to rejoice and reflect on what it means to be Canadian. The icing on the cake came next: Mr. Solberg made his very public statement announcing the theme for Citizenship Week 2006: "Canada: We all belong."

As he smiled to the cameras he said, "Although we cherish our differences, we gain strength from what we hold in common. Like our values—freedom, justice, equality, respect for diversity and peace."[5]

FOR THE Lost Canadians and particularly for Joe Taylor, it was all just a slap in the face. But life goes on, as does politics, and our battle. And did I ever have something up my sleeve.

Pilots, and especially international pilots, are briefed daily as to what's going on in the world regarding threats and safety. When I began my career,

I could bypass security just by wearing my uniform and showing a company ID badge. It didn't matter much what I happened to be carrying. Over the years, I'd carried just about everything on board. Once my wife wanted real New York pizza. So I called ahead to United Operations at La Guardia and asked that pizza be delivered to the gate upon our arrival, so I could take it back with me on the return flight. Then there was the time I showed up with my golf clubs. I waved my ID at the security agents and was let through. And the time I had a hockey game in Denver and brought my hockey equipment as carry-on. Another time it was Rollerblades.

Life for us changed severely after 9/11. A colleague was once flying (the plane, that is) from London to Los Angeles, and he bought a box of chocolates, sealed in plastic wrap, at the gift shop next to the boarding gate: the transaction took place in the secured area. But that mattered not to the gate agent, who refused to let him take the chocolates on board, saying that some might have liquid centres that could be liquid explosives. The regulations had moved far beyond the absurd. But that's the point. In bureaucracies, at times things can and do get out of hand. In aviation after 9/11, probably some bureaucrat who never before had any experience in airport security was now its supreme commander. And, by God, everyone and everything was suspect, even the pilot and the chocolates. To make matters worse, the new policies were being administered by the gate agent or some brand-new homeland security screener who, just six weeks before, had been unemployed and watching reruns of *I Love Lucy*.

Pilots are briefed on the latest missives from Washington, so I knew well in advance about upcoming changes to US-Canada border crossings. I began to lay out my battle plan. The new security requirements between Canada and the US, part of the US government's Western Hemisphere Travel Initiative whereby travellers to and from Canada, Mexico, Central and South America, the Caribbean, and Bermuda would be required to present a passport to enter or re-enter the US, were taking effect on January 23, 2007. Hence, this would be the target date for our D-Day invasion of Ottawa. I got in touch with one of my behind-the-scenes Lost Canadian experts, a CIC worker. Next I phoned a brand-new Lost Canadian, then Gary Symons of CBC. Together we were about to storm the Hill, where Stephen Harper resided.

A few years earlier, another contact had come a-calling. I received an email from Dr. Barry Edmonston, one of Canada's leading experts on demographics. The acts of opening my email and answering my phone always held an element of fascination for me: Was it some name-brand politician, a top journalist like Peter Worthington, a singer-actor like Robert Goulet, or an academic like Barry? Barry's call was a game-changer.

Barry's father had emigrated to Canada from Scotland as a young man. During the war, he taught Canadians and Brits how to drive convoys at night undetected. Their practice ground was Kingston, Ontario. Barry was born there in 1944, in wedlock to a Canadian mother. His sister came along in 1946. After the war, the family moved to the States and, when Barry was a teenager, his father took out US citizenship. Barry became a Lost Canadian and so did his sister.

At the time, Barry was teaching at Portland State University. Over the years, he taught at the University of Toronto and Simon Fraser University, and as I write this he's at the University of Victoria. Barry wasn't only one of Canada's leading experts on demographics, he was also a member of the Statistics Canada advisory board, with a special focus on Canadian immigration. He frequently dealt with senior people inside Citizenship and Immigration Canada. And now he was dealing with me. He crunched all the numbers, sometimes using information directly from CIC, and he and I were the only ones in Canada privy to his estimates of how many Lost Canadians there were in each of several categories. Even CIC didn't know, nor did the citizenship minister or any of the standing members of the Citizenship Committee. For the time being, I held on tight to the information.

I had just left a war-bride friend living in Qualicum Beach, BC, by the name of Eswyn Lyster, and was heading down the island highway to Victoria to see Joe Taylor. Stopping at a phone booth, I called my contact at CIC. What she said left me flabbergasted. When CIC decided not to honour the Supreme Court's rulings, specifically by getting rid of its order 5(2)(b) having to do with children born in or out of wedlock—or foreign-born children of a Canadian mother and foreign father—having equal rights to citizenship, the effect was to re-establish the old loss provisions, as you may recall from Chapter 9, in my discussion of acting director general, Integration Branch of CIC, Patricia Birkett negating the Supreme Court decisions of *Benner* and *Augier*. In other words, there were now many more ways to be stripped of your Canadian citizenship. In Wall Street terms, the bureaucrats denying people citizenship had become a growth industry.

One of the many documents produced in the Taylor case was an internal CIC memo in which CIC admitted to rejecting citizenship for an average of 392 Canadians per year between 1998 and 2004. I have no doubt that most of the government's records, and especially the more damning ones, went missing long ago. But let's extrapolate from those numbers we do have.

Sixty years at about 400 people per year equals 24,000 ex-citizens. Many Canadian towns aren't this big. Imagine every occupant being deported. But doing it all at once wasn't CIC's way. No, its technique mirrored nature's method of carving out the Grand Canyon—slowly and over time. For CIC, it had taken six decades. The Lost Canadians were singled out individually, case by case.

But the tides were about to change. And no matter how much the bureaucrats resisted, the assault had begun far from Ottawa. A woman by the name of Barbara Porteous wrote to Peter Worthington of the *Toronto Sun*, and he in turn emailed her story and contact information to me. Here's the email:

Today I received a copy of your column which appeared in the *Toronto Sun* Sept 8, 2006, re Joe Taylor's Citizenship case. This helped explain why I have had no success in my appeal for attention to a similar citizenship problem. I have had the constituency and a senator from our area intervene, with no appreciable results because of this pending court case. I think the Judge's decision was correct and I don't understand the appeal or on what issues they are appealing.

My Story: I was born in the USA in 1936. My father had Canadian citizenship until nationalization in 1943. My Canadian husband and I were married in the States... our homes were 20 miles apart, divided by a "friendly" border. In 1959, I was 23 yrs old and pregnant with our second child. We moved to the US to run a business purchased by my father. We signed and returned green cards of Canadian Citizens living in the States each year. We had Canadian passports issued at the US consulate in Vancouver where I also had a Loss of Nationality registered for my US citizenship when I voted in Canada. We returned to Canada in 1965. All dealings with the Immigration and Customs people at the border, who we knew personally, never informed us of any change in my Citizenship status. We were welcomed back. I was able to use my certificate for verification when registering for CPP and Canadian Pension and Medical coverage.

In Feb 2006, I applied for a renewal citizenship card to CIC Nova Scotia. On July 30, I received a letter that I had lost my citizenship June 14, 1960 because I was living out of the country and had not indicated I wanted to retain my Canadian citizenship by age 24 (but after age 21). I had never received any information about this stipulation. I was informed that if I lived out of the Country 10 years, I would lose my Citizenship.

I have lived as a conscientious, community minded Canadian citizen, active in political issues, voting in every election. I have been a Poll Clerk,

Returning Officer and Census Taker for the Federal government and a member of the Reform Alliance, Conservative Party for the past 15 years. That life is over. To add insult to injury, the letter from CIC stated I should contact Immigration on how to "regularize your status and obtain permanent residence in Canada." After one year residency, I could reapply for Citizenship.

Thank you for taking an interest in reporting Mr. Taylor's case and it seems there is hope if the Judge's recommendations and findings are upheld . . . I may not live long enough to see the results, but perhaps I can handle the stress of this situation if I know something is being done and this would never happen to anyone else ever again.

I am enquiring if there is any update on when this appeal may be going ahead or information that may help me. Living stateless at 70 years of age is not fun, and fear of losing pension and medical benefits terrifies me so I do not want my name used at this time.

I immediately contacted Barbara, explaining what I was planning in Ottawa, and she agreed to be the lead person in our frontal attack.

On August 5, 1981, the US president had set a new course that changed the world, and many would say not for the better. Ronald Reagan fired the striking air traffic controllers, in effect busting their union. It set off a tsunami of union busting, corporate layoffs, and different wage scales for old and new employees doing the same job. What happened over the subsequent three decades was that the rich got richer, the middle class shrank, and the poor got poorer—all traceable back to that one day in 1981. Union busting was now alive and well. And over the ensuing years it began to thrive in the US. When Reagan was first elected in 1980, the percentage of union workers in the US was just a tad over 20 percent; by 2011 it was below 12 percent.[6]

While not as dramatic, the same trends are visible in Canada. It was the start of a worldwide phenomenon, and it began in aviation. As a pilot, I witnessed it up close and personal. But it didn't apply just to my industry. Wage declines spread like a cancer throughout the world. Air traffic controllers and pilots were affected first, then lower-wage earners, and, today, it's affected almost everyone, from architects, middle managers, and doctors to teachers, public servants, and book publishers—except for those in the top 1 percent. Some professions were hit harder than others and, in the field of journalism, no one took it in the shorts more than investigative reporters. A thorough, well-researched story takes time, and time is money. Besides, stories of cats and young Hollywood starlets sell much better than that of a stateless seventy-year-old woman from Osoyoos, BC. For the publishers— the owners of the media, people like Rupert Murdoch—the content of the news isn't really their concern. What matters, what trumps other stories and motivates today's media barons, is what sells.

Walter Cronkite could not accomplish today what he did not all that long ago. Everything in the media has changed. I liked Cronkite's style and his credibility. I like the old-school journalists. As a college student in 1973, I sat glued to the television screen watching the Watergate hearings. I admired like heroes the investigative journalists as they uncovered the facts. That was then. Today, young pretty girls are often hired to read the news and, of course, are paid a pittance compared with their yesteryear counter-parts. News reading has become a contest, a hanging branch connected to a tree called entertainment. Most everyone in the media has been affected, even our very own CBC, as it too began competing against its private-sector counterparts for a share of those almighty advertising dollars. Our national broadcaster, like the rest, was cutting back, a victim of Harper's obsession with controlling his environment.

My friend, Gary Symons, belonged to the old school of journalism, and his reporting of the news reflected that. Over the years, I fed Gary all kinds of stories on the Lost Canadians. In turn, he pitched them to the many out-lets inside CBC. I appeared on *The Current* several times thanks to Gary. Although Gary's forte was radio, on occasion he crossed over into television. Like anyone who first hears my wild tale of the Lost Canadians, Gary had doubts initially. But he did what reporters are supposed to do: he checked out my story to confirm its accuracy. By the time 2006 was winding down, we had a multi-year history of working together. I'd never given him any-thing but credible stories backed up by bare-knuckle facts. So when I called Gary from my home in Phoenix in November, asking if he wanted the story of my attack on Ottawa, he did what any good journalist would do: he lis-tened attentively.

I spilled my guts, telling him about my inside sources. I mentioned Dr. Edmonston, Barbara Porteous, my CIC insider, and the upcoming passport requirements. For the first time I was divulging secrets, opening up to allow him to verify the facts with his independent sources. I told him about the many other ways to lose citizenship. Like any top-notch reporter, he could smell a story. However, he still had bosses to report to. With dollars for investigative journalism hard to come by, reporters were, to a certain extent, forced to become salespeople, pitching the story's merit to superiors, who in turn had been mandated to keep expenses to a minimum. It was a tough sell. But Gary succeeded. My attack had just moved from the planning stage to the implementation stage. The stars were lining up and, as with a space mission, everything was a go.

We planned to go to Ottawa and blow the lid on the Lost Canadian story, and we had but two months to prepare. First there was the sorting out of the new Lost Canadian categories (listed below), which I discovered mainly through my contact at CIC and from people calling me and explaining how they had lost their citizenship. Then I had to find someone to represent each group. Gary began his research, coordinating with a colleague in Toronto named Susanne Reber—another twenty-plus-year veteran CBC investigative reporter. Gary's first stop was Victoria, to see Dr. Barry Edmonston, who ran the numbers and came up with estimates of how many Lost Canadians belonged in each category. Gary contacted my CIC insider, arranging for her to get a CBC cell phone. Thus, when her phone rang, it was either Gary or Susanne; if she dialled out, the person answering was Gary. That way, the calls were not traceable on CIC's phone records.

Here are CIC's previously hidden methods of cancelling unsuspecting Canadians' citizenship:

PARTIALLY FIXED WITH BILL S-2:
As a minor child, one's father took out citizenship in another country.

CURRENTLY KNOWN:
- You are a foreign-born Canadian and on your twenty-fourth birthday weren't domiciled in Canada.
- You are a war bride who never became naturalized.
- You are a war bride's child who never became naturalized.
- In certain circumstances, your connection to Canada came through a woman rather than a man. This mainly affects foreign-born, born-in-wedlock children to Canadian mothers and foreign fathers. Once again, the *Benner* decision applies.[7]
- You were born out of wedlock to a war-bride mother.
- You were born to a Canadian serviceman outside Canada (i.e., you're a military brat).
- You are a woman who married a non-Canadian prior to 1947.
- You took out citizenship in another country prior to 1977.

NEW CATEGORIES:
- In certain circumstances, you are a second-generation born-abroad Canadian and didn't reaffirm your citizenship by your twenty-eighth birthday.
- You were a border baby (most were born in the US mainly because the nearest hospital was in the US rather than in Canada) and never properly registered. People from Quebec are particularly affected.
- You are a born-in-wedlock child of a woman who married a non-Canadian prior to 1947. It doesn't matter that you've spent your whole life in Canada.
- You are a child of an S-2 Lost Canadian.

WHAT A difference a year makes.

What a difference it makes being the party in power versus being in opposition.

And what a difference there is between making election campaign promises and actually being in power and making good on those promises.

You'll recall also from Chapter 9 that, during Christmas 2005, Harper's people were anxious to run full-page campaign ads featuring the failed policies of the Liberals, at the bottom of which, in all caps, were the lines:

CANADIANS DESERVE THEIR RIGHT TO CITIZENSHIP.
THE CHARTER OF RIGHTS AND FREEDOMS MUST BE PROTECTED.

A mere twelve months later, at Christmas 2006, the Conservatives had become the Ebenezer Scrooges of campaign promises. Monte Solberg retreated into silence, akin to the famous Mrs. Calabash of Jimmy Durante fame—no one knew who or where she was.[8] That's why Joe Taylor and I began referring to Solberg as "the cardboard cut-out."

On December 21, just before Christmas, Joe got a present. Not from Solberg or anyone connected to CIC, mind you, but from the Federal Court of Appeal in Ottawa:

Court File No. A-417-06—Order of Mr. Justice Létourneau
MCI v. Joseph Taylor.
After a careful consideration of the parties' submissions, I am satisfied that the test developed in RJR-MacDonald v. Canada (AG) [1994] 1 S.C.R. 311 is met and that a stay is justified in this instance. Accordingly, the Order of Martineau, J., rendered on September 1, 2006, is stayed pending the determination of this appeal.

In plain language, the government was granted an appeal, which meant that we were heading back to court.[9] For Joe, it was devastating. He would have to prove everything all over again, and at his considerable expense. Still, the court's notice felt like a stay of execution. He would, at the very least, be allowed to spend his holiday in Canada. It took a federal judge's order, but Solberg and his CIC thugs were forbidden from rounding up the "bastard" and deporting him. Yes, this was Canada. That was how we ushered in the new year.

January 1, 2007. For me it was like the countdown to a moon launch: T-minus twenty-two days and counting until the new border regulations came into effect.

As always, the lines of communication were wide open between Andrew Telegdi and me. In movies, the president of the US has a red phone—a hot line—which rings only when the possibility of armed conflict looms. One phone line at my home in Phoenix had become the designated line for Lost Canadian business. When that phone rang, I knew it was important. I also spent a great deal of time trying to solicit help from others, hoping again that some organization would step up. I wasn't after its money, and I didn't need much of its time. I needed its voice. If only a group—any group, but ideally a non-profit organization (one professing to help people on equality of rights or human rights issues)—would come forward and speak out, it would make a world of difference. And it would have helped so many people. Organizations were always great at asking for donations, saying they spoke out about equal rights, but they didn't on our behalf. I expected these charitable foundations that are supposedly out there for the public good to step up to more than just the collection plate—I needed their voice. At the very least, they should have been writing about our plight in their newsletters. The stark truth was that, in part because of these organizations' collective silence, Canadians remained largely unaware of the issue. I had become like a beggar, with no pride, willing to take help from anyone, from whomever or wherever it came. The list of Canadian organizations I approached, pleading for support, was truly a who's who of Canadian charities. Pretty much none came forward. Lost Canadians weren't just being turned away by our own government; Canadian human rights groups had turned their backs on us as well.

Landing an airplane in rainy and gusty conditions is always a challenge. Your hands and feet are constantly moving the control yoke and rudder pedals. In military terms, a constantly changing situation such as this is referred to as being "fluid." This describes our preparing for Ottawa. I forewarned

Daphne Bramham of the *Vancouver Sun* and did my best with the *Globe and Mail*, *Maclean's*, *National Post*, CTV, and *Global National*, among others.

CBC had recently declined to air the Lost Canadian documentary. Claude Vickery of CBC's *Fifth Estate* wrote to say that he didn't feel the Lost Canadians was their kind of story. Brett Mitchell at CTV's *W5* echoed these sentiments. Bottom line: few in the media had any interest whatsoever. *Canada AM* would occasionally have me as a quick-segment guest. I called and spoke with two of their people—Marilyn Mazurek and Kristin Wever. While I was appreciative when I did get on the show, I found the producers to be about as flaky as one could get. I'd arrange to do a show and then, at the last minute—maybe if Lindsay Lohan had been arrested the night before—I'd get a call informing me that my segment had been nixed. It had become crystal clear that, not for a lack of my trying, the only journalism cart we could hook up to was Gary Symons at CBC.

The first bombshell for us came on January 4. Monte Solberg was out as citizenship minister; Diane Finley was in. The situation was indeed fluid—as fluid as whitewater. Finley had been an MP for just two and a half years. Given that she was rather new, I didn't know which way she'd blow: with the bureaucratic winds or in the opposite direction, more toward the Supreme Court decisions that said we had a right to citizenship? With any new minister, there's a honeymoon period during which you give him or her the benefit of the doubt. Typically, I'm more than happy to do that. But our attack was like the start of the Soap Box Derby: we'd just left the gate and were picking up momentum. Too many players had prepared, and none more than Gary Symons and Susanne Reber, who had devoted the previous couple of months to the story. It was to be full speed ahead. After dealing with so many incredibly rock-bottom citizenship ministers over the years, I obviously had reservations about Finley. But no matter, she was the new minister. Besides, she'd have to be better than Solberg. So while I remained hopeful about Finley, I wasn't about to call off the dogs. Once again, I phoned the citizenship minister's office to introduce myself. Gone was the receptionist's salutation "Office of the Honourable Monte Solberg" and in was "Office of the Honourable Diane Finley." Same person answering the phone, but now with a different greeting. And, as I would soon discover, a different attitude.

CHAPTER 13

TORA! TORA! TORA!

Never in aviation chastise someone in your crew for their input. We
ALWAYS check and recheck until everyone in the crew is satisfied. After
we verify the issue, even if one crewmember was originally wrong, they
get treated with respect. One day they might be the one who saves us
from a bad situation. In many careers, a newly hired worker's opinion
or concerns may be ignored by the thirty-five-year veteran whose pride
or ego cannot handle the idea of a junior employee being right. In
aviation, we always want input—egos don't matter. USE your crew.
CAPTAIN BRUCE RICHARDS, UNITED AIRLINES BOEING 767 PILOT

THIS WAS HOW it began:

CBC Radio One—*World Report*
January 22, 2007
In: Barbara
Time: 2:12
Out: Ottawa

Announcer: "You can hear more on this story tonight on the *World at Six*."
   [Background: church music. Singing.]
   GARY SYMONS: "Barbara Porteous considers herself as Canadian as
maple syrup and hockey pucks. The daughter of a local farmer, she's the
organist at the Anglican church. She even worked for Elections Canada."
   BARBARA PORTEOUS: "I've worked as a poll clerk, as a deputy returning officer, and as a census taker."

SYMONS: "So, Porteous thought it would be no problem when she applied for a passport. Instead, she got a letter saying she is no longer Canadian. The problem dates back a half century to when she worked in the US for five years. Under the laws at the time, anyone living outside Canada on their twenty-fourth birthday would lose their citizenship, unless they signed a document to retain their status."

PORTEOUS: "I never had any information about having to apply to retain my citizenship. How do you apply to retain what you have?"

[Music fades.]

SYMONS: "Barbara Porteous is just one of thousands of people who have lost their status as Canadians when they apply for passports. All due to provisions of the 1947 Citizenship Act that the federal government is still applying today. The minister of citizenship and immigration admits those laws are unfair and discriminate on the basis of age and gender. But Diane Finley will not commit to changing those laws."

FINLEY: "Overhauling the act is a major, major effort, and quite frankly it's more than we could take on to help these people at this point in time."

SYMONS: "Finley does say, in an exclusive interview with CBC News, that she will change policy. Rather than requiring people to apply as landed immigrants, she plans to issue grants of citizenship to those who qualify. But that takes eight months. And Barbara Porteous also says it does nothing for people who may lose their citizenship in the future. She's urging the minister to change the law."

PORTEOUS: "Do I not come under the Charter of Rights and Freedoms that everybody else has? What does it mean to be stateless in the land you lived in for forty-six years?"

SYMONS: "Gary Symons, CBC News, Ottawa."[1]

And so it started. The first wave of offensive attacks had begun; we had landed on the beaches of Ottawa and were ready to storm CIC's headquarters. While its commander, General Finley, was a greenhorn, the commander-in-chief, Stephen Harper, was by now a seasoned Ottawa combat veteran. But on this day, for the first time ever, we had the media flanking our positions. It was the one thing out of Harper's control, and alone it could wield huge influence in the world of public opinion—and that terrifies politicians.

For legislators, their being in Ottawa generally isn't about you or me; it's about them and, more specifically, their jobs. Ex-politicians, and particularly ex-prime ministers, generally go back from whence they came, making great speeches and writing memoirs. In the States, since being in politics is tantamount to being in the entertainment business, they also make lots of money. Sarah Palin proves the point. In Canada, ex-prime ministers basically retreat into relative obscurity—unless, of course, they become paid lobbyists, which, at best, isn't done for the greater good of the people. Brian Mulroney proves that point.

At the beginning of 2007, at the ripe young age of forty-seven, Stephen Harper was in no way thinking about retiring. And he wanted nothing to stand in the way of his keeping his job. Fortunately for Harper, citizenship-wise, the opposition parties were complete nincompoops. Yes, some individual MPs were fabulous and they stood up for us: Meili Faille of the Bloc; Bill Siksay of the NDP; Andrew Telegdi of the Liberals. But overall, the MPs were ignorant, uncaring, and incompetent. We were hoping that, if word leaked out around the world as to what Canada was doing against its own people, it might embarrass the living daylights out of the MPs and motivate them into action. After all, Canadians love to boast about their human rights record. Maybe we could shame them into action.

That was part of our plan. The assault began with a piece by Gary Symons and Susanne Reber, first broadcast in Newfoundland during the wee hours of the morning and, hour by hour, making its way west, finally being broadcast from CBC Victoria—that was but the first of a multi-phase offensive. At CBC's Ottawa radio studios, Andrew Telegdi and I took turns taking shifts inside the soundproof booth. You wear a headset and speak into the microphone sitting on a small shelf in front of you; outside in the control room, an operator connects you to various live CBC shows across the country after CBC's morning report airs. Each gives you maybe five minutes to tell the story; in this way, the story makes its way from city to city, from coast to coast. At long last, the Lost Canadians were getting their story out over the national airwaves. *World Report* has about a million and a half listeners each morning, and these listeners were being directed to a CBC webpage to read Gary and Susanne's more in-depth coverage, which explained the many categories of Lost Canadians.[2] At the top of the webpage was a photo of a hand holding a Canadian passport, with this caption: "A passenger readies his Canadian passport before boarding a flight to the U.S. CBC has found that more than 200,000 people are at risk of losing their citizenship—and denied passports—because of out-of-date laws." Not only did the webpage give estimates of how many Canadians might unknowingly fall into each group, but the write-up on each group featured the story of a corresponding Lost Canadian caught in the bureaucratic nets of CIC. Going further, the journalists stated:

> Citizenship is something most Canadians take for granted—and it is arguably the most important right a nation can confer. But for thousands of people, many of them born in Canada, or born elsewhere to Canadian parents—citizenship has become an elusive goal.
>
> Although the federal government says it is aware of about 450 cases of people who have lost their citizenship, a CBC News investigation found there could be more than 200,000 people living in Canada who could potentially lose their citizenship, under sections of the 1947 Citizenship Act that are unknown to most people.[3]

Here were the categories and their corresponding numbers, as reported:

- Chattel children: up to 20,000 living in Canada; 85,000 in the US. They were people like me who lost their citizenship through no fault of their own as minors when the "responsible parent" took out citizenship in another country.

- Border babies: minimum 10,000 living in Canada. They were people born in the US, usually because the nearest hospital to them was in the States.

- War brides: potentially 25,000 to 35,000 in Canada.

- War babies: between 6,000 and 20,000 living in Canada.

- Born abroad after 1977 legislation: up to 42,000.

- Illegitimate Canadians: up to 30,000 Mennonites. They were people born, or supposedly born, out of wedlock. (More on this below.)

- Military brats: 110,000, mostly in Canada.

That evening on *The National*, Paul Hunter did a segment featuring the newly minted citizenship minister, Diane Finley. The only thing that could have made things better was for all the Canadian media to jump on board.

Not for a day or a month, but until the situation was corrected. Other than that, we couldn't have asked for more. It was as good as it gets. And as it turned out, it was also the pinnacle of the Lost Canadians media blitz.

Like the Japanese attack at Pearl Harbor, the media story came as a complete surprise: CIC and Harper didn't see it coming.

They immediately jumped into their foxholes and began firing back. Not at me or at individual Lost Canadians, but directly at Gary Symons and Susanne Reber.

The sun hadn't reached high noon before the phones at CBC's Toronto offices began ringing. The caller? CIC. The message was clear and to the point:

1. TWO rogue CBC reporters are doing a story about Lost Canadians using false information.

2. WE admit to there being around 450 Lost Canadians, not hundreds of thousands.

3. THE two reporters bought into Don Chapman's unfounded claims, and they aren't just wrong but grossly incompetent.

And so it seemed that, if you can't shut down Chapman, shut up the messengers. Before the day had expired, even the Prime Minister's Office weighed in. At the time in Ottawa, the only way not to leave some sort of trail that could be traced back to the source was pinging with BlackBerry. Only because of Gary and Susanne's investigative journalism backgrounds and extensive contacts were they able to discover just where the pings had originated, and, by goodness, they had come directly from the commander-in-chief's offices. Whether Harper was the man behind the onslaught remains a mystery. But the fact was, cannons were being fired from his command centre. And did CBC ever feel the heat.

Cathy Perry was the person Gary and Susanne reported to at CBC Radio headquarters in Toronto. Immediately skittish, Cathy retreated. Instead of standing behind her reporters, she caved in to her superiors at CBC, who elected to pull the stories. Sadly, if they got away with it, the unsuspecting public would continue being left completely in the dark, and just maybe to their own peril. Above Cathy, the government threats weren't just made but carried out. Yes, the media were the one thing out of Harper's control—journalists from all the various news organizations were free to jump on board and report the story if they wished. Indeed, we were counting on their strong support. How naive. The other Canadian journalists and media outlets continued to watch from the sidelines (though the Canadian Press finally did do a story). The Harper government was proving the existence of real limits to a "free" press, at least when it came to reporting something that displeased it.

At the time, it had been just over sixty years since Canada rolled out the 1947 Citizenship Act, and Harper's people had planned quite the celebration. As a Lost Canadian, I always found it insulting that Canada observed Canada Day by swearing in immigrants around the country as brand-new Canadians, to show off how welcoming the country was to newcomers. All the network channels were highlighting an upcoming or ongoing citizenship ceremony. A favourite tactic was to single out a family and ask members how they felt becoming Canadian, especially on such a memorable day. For the media, what a delightful way to portray our country—always accepting of others. For the average Canadian it worked; they felt good about themselves and their country. But to the hundreds of thousands of us being denied (and who were not being asked how we felt), it was a slap in the face. Year after year after year, that's how we spent our typical Canada Day. Because we didn't vote we didn't count.

What mattered was that the masses loved Canada Day celebrations and, for politicians, it was the perfect time to be seen participating in these feel-good moments. And then, thanks to the media, who never missed broadcasting such events, the Conservatives would be seen as being well received in the public eye. To politicians in a minority government, this meant a great deal, because the special celebrations—the feel-good moments of 2007—were to be ongoing, lasting much longer than just one day. After all, it was the sixtieth anniversary of the year in which Canadian citizenship began, according to the bureaucrats, and the festivities could potentially continue for quite some time, maybe right to the eve of another election. It was simply the picture-perfect opportunity to make political hay, showing off the gracious Harper government, especially to those in the immigrant communities, many of whom wanted to get family members into Canada. More than anything, those people represented votes. It would be an extraordinary, possibly year-long photo opportunity. The Harperites loved it and enthusiastically threw their collective weight behind it.

But on January 22, 2007, a monkey wrench abruptly halted the cogs of their political engines—me being the chief monkey. Having 200,000-plus Canadians basically being told to pound sand put a crimp in the government's plans. What came next was surprising, even for those already skeptical of Harper and his ways. Gary Symons told me that the government cancelled several million dollars' worth of promotional advertising to CBC and called off the celebratory event. It seems our Lost Canadian news blitz got in the way, and the Conservatives' public relations plans got the kibosh. Instead of simply admitting the problem, correcting it, and moving forward with the celebration, the Harper-folks abandoned it altogether. For CBC, an already cash-strapped network mostly dependent on government funding, the cancellation was more than detrimental. Perhaps not insurmountable, but definitely disturbing in that whoever controls the purse strings also influences content, even if it's subtly. In the future, when the next round of government funding came up for debate, would the Harper-controlled regime look favourably on a defiant CBC?[4] The top decision makers at the Canadian Broadcasting Corporation caved, doing exactly what the Conservatives wanted. The Lost Canadian stories were shelved and Gary and Susanne discredited.

What had been planned as another Lost Canadian frontal attack on the next day's morning news, once again first airing over CBC airwaves in the early morning in Newfoundland, were put on hold. Gary and Susanne spent the night of the twenty-second arguing their position to the CBC powers that be, explaining who Dr. Edmonston was and his expertise, how they got their facts, and the basics of their other informants. Just 300 seconds—five minutes—before *World Report* hit the eastern airwaves at 6 a.m., CBC's top muckety-mucks capitulated, giving the go-ahead to a watered-down version of the story.

It seems Joe Taylor wasn't the only one on trial. Gary and Susanne's professional reputations were now on the line. Their having over forty years of combined experience, as well as various accolades, awards, and merits, meant nothing to their detractors. The CIC wonders that be had treated them as rogue reporters and the Prime Minister's Office had got involved, wanting their heads; to CBC brass, that was all that mattered.

But, Gary would later say, "Harper's mistake was forgetting that I was an investigative journalist." (And, after dealing with Gary for so many years, let me add, "and a damn good one.") Gary stayed with our story, later accompanying me back to Ottawa. He knew that the facts we had reported were accurate yet saw the intense opposition we faced. His journalistic nose sniffed a much bigger story, and he began working behind the scenes too. Almost immediately, he started filing freedom-of-information requests. It took a while for the "investigation of his investigation" to come to light, but eventually the truth emerged. In the meantime, I went back to work advocating for the Lost Canadians. But even that wasn't easy because many in the Ottawa media were ignoring me altogether. The reason eluded me. And I wouldn't know why until Gary had concluded his covert investigation.

One person I worked with, just after our Ottawa offensive, became an integral part of our machine. Christopher Maughan was a young man not long out of journalism school and a freelance writer for the Canadian Press. I had figured the Canadian universities, and particularly their schools of journalism, which I approached constantly, would have enthusiastically put me in touch with a couple of their outstanding students. They didn't. So I tried in every way I could to solicit an aspiring young journalist on my own. Sadly, in Canada, promising star students like that could be named on the Worldwide Wildlife Fund's endangered species list. They are few and far between. Fortunately, I eventually met up with Chris. He had two wonderful qualities: he was one of those just-out-of-school hungry journalists, and he was very good at what he did. In February, Chris wrote a story that went viral worldwide thanks to the power of the Canadian Press. Rarely did the Canadian Press jump on board, but, when it did, it sure made a difference. No question about it, there was a direct relationship between media coverage and the fate of Lost Canadians. The more we made the news, the more of us got into Canada.

Despite Harper having some success at stifling CBC, he wasn't able to control the media outside Canada. The stories of our wacky citizenship laws were picked up by the US media, and criss-crossed that country from New York to LA. Even my local television station in Phoenix did a story. But the coverage was scattered and brief. What helped us more than the spotty US coverage was coverage by the international community. The CBC story had caught the attention of Clive Cocking, a Vancouver-based reporter for the prestigious *Economist*. It had also piqued the interest of the editors of the United Nations' magazine *Refugees*.

On February 7, 2007, the Lost Canadians were featured in the *Economist*, in an article titled "Lost in Kafkaland," complete with a caricature of an old lady being booted out of Canada. Next up was the United Nations' *Refugees* magazine. It was devoting its entire September issue to the subject of statelessness, which would be titled "The Strange Hidden World of the Stateless." In it would be documented the various countries around the globe—the offenders—that had made people stateless. As it turned out, Canada (or more specifically, Canada and the Lost Canadians) was featured on a two-page spread, dead centre in the magazine. No reader could miss it. But that wasn't to be published for another seven months. I put this knowledge away in my back pocket, thinking that down the road it might help me shame Canada into doing the right thing. Not that I wanted to embarrass Canada. I love this country, and I take no pleasure in discrediting my homeland. But if that's what it took to get politicians to embrace equal rights in citizenship law, then so be it. Not because I wanted it to, but this battle had escalated into all-out warfare, and I was pulling no punches.

By the end of the week, after the assault, I headed back to Phoenix and turned my attention to coordinating future Ottawa hearings. Because of the extensive news coverage, my email inbox was overflowing. Attempting to answer each message as it came in, plus having to make a living, kept me busy as a beaver. And, of course, no one was paying for my expenses. Money poured out of my pocket by the tens of thousands of dollars. Harper made me understand exactly what it was like to go up against Goliath.

Because of the complete disappointment of Monte Solberg, my relationship with Diane Finley began with a great deal of skepticism on my part. Fortunately for all, that's not how it ended. My gut tells me that John Reynolds played a big part in greasing the wheels for our going forward, because one of his very good friends, the man who headed up Stephen Harper's 2006 election campaign, was Diane's husband, Doug Finley. While he's never confirmed it, I do believe that credit is due to John for this.

Back in Arizona, I was gearing up for hearings before the Standing Committee on Citizenship and Immigration. On February 19, Diane Finley was to appear. I spent most of the month scraping and preparing. Andrew Telegdi and I talked often. He would ask me if there were any witnesses who should be heard and, in turn, he'd advocate from inside the committee, asking that they be called to testify. He also wanted my input on the committee's direction and what it should be advocating. The one difference between us was that, despite Andrew having to do battle within his own party over citizenship issues, he remained a die-hard Liberal, whereas I did everything to keep politics out of my considerations. He would be quick to lash out at the other parties; I was rather standoffish.

Four days before Diane Finley was to appear before the committee, Paul Hunter did a citizenship story for *The National*. Although festivities for the sixtieth anniversary of citizenship had been cancelled, one activity was still on: the swearing-in of several families, at the Supreme Court no less, ironically the very institution CIC was ignoring. Finley was there. For Lost Canadians, it was more than insulting. For example, take Barbara Porteous. She grew up in Canada, was a citizen, married here, had babies, worked for Elections Canada, and paid her taxes. But because she was just a few kilometres from Osoyoos, BC, right across the small-town border in Oroville, Washington, on her twenty-fourth birthday, Canada had made her stateless. She was now seventy years of age. Canada turned its back on Barbara. Yet, for about eighteen immigrant families from around the world, CBC provides a feel-good moment where politicians are able to show off and tell the public that the country is welcoming and accepting. And the guy who orchestrated it all was CBC's Paul Hunter. The following day I got several emails from furious Lost Canadians.

> Hi! Saw the 2-minute clip. So, CBC is covering the celebration commemorating the 60th anniversary of CDN citizenship... talking about how millions of "us" take it for granted that we are Canadian. Are we taking it for granted? HELL NO! ON THE CONTRARY! We are showing more spine, energy and non-complacency than most Canadians! Paul Hunter also mentions the "18 or so families brought in from around Canada, who can trace families from across the world, being sworn in as new Canadians." OK! What have I missed here? What about our families being brought in to commemorate our Canadian heritage dating back to AND within Canada, at least the mid-1600s!!! So now CBC is talking about citizenship as if they have THE TAKE ON IT. WHAT HAVE YOU BEEN SAYING ABOUT PAUL MARTIN SR., THE CITIZENSHIP ACT AND DIEPPE SINCE HOW LONG NOW?!! AND CBC DOESN'T WANT ANYTHING TO DO WITH OUR DOCUMENTARY? FUCKING HYPOCRITES IS ALL I GOTTA SAY ABOUT IT NOW!

The other day, a former MP in the Mulroney government came to see me (he knew my husband's family well), and told me that even his own constituency caucus do not understand the trauma the loss of citizenship causes... He's now 80 and we agreed, it's not like the good old days... and who you know doesn't mean a thing. He can't believe what's happening to me and that his own party has done nothing to help me.

Today, Canada celebrates 60 years of citizenship at the Supreme Court. Last night *The National* did a long segment on citizenship. But nowhere did anyone mention a thing about people losing their citizenship. It was all fluff and wonder. The only analogy I can think of is a great ceremony of white people thrilled to honour the invention of the drinking fountain. The problem, of course, is that their fountain is only for whites, and I happen to be black. That's how it felt watching CBC's program last night.

When you get kicked·in the guts like that it takes time to recover enough
to make a pertinent comment—I have just put up with a triple whammy:
  Thought of *The National* last night.
1. Finley has a "Let's celebrate 60 years of WONDERFUL Canadian
    citizenship."
2. Harper will fund Juno beach for the next five years.
3. CBC put out a CIC bureaucratic publicity broadcast!!
    Can I just go crawl under a stone now?

From the people who are fighting the hardest for the rights of Canadians,
The National did a horrible job last night!

And those comments were just the tip of the iceberg. The remark that
hit the nail on the head was that CBC really had done a CIC bureaucratic
promo. From a news perspective, there wasn't any balance. I too had found
CBC's coverage disgusting.

Two days before Finley's appearance in front of the committee, I wrote
an email to Roy MacGregor of the *Globe and Mail*:

The Parliamentary Committee on Citizenship and Immigration has called
hearings to discuss what went wrong with the 1947 Citizenship Act. Testimony will begin on February 19, then reconvene again on February 26,
March 19, and March 26. 200,000 people in Canada are discovering that
they are no longer Canadian. I mentioned to you that I would break the
story on the 23rd of January, which I did. It's now garnered worldwide
attention. Newspapers all over the US, some US television stations, Fox
News Network, the *Economist*, CBC's *The National*, *World Report*, *Canada
AM* (Monday the 19th and 26th) have all done stories. Even the *New York
Times* is doing an article for next week. Toronto's Peter Worthington has
called this a "national travesty, as Canada's shameful debacle." Why is
it that your *Globe & Mail* has not even printed a single word about this?

Almost immediately I got this reply:

There's no conspiracy, Don. My hunch, which may be wrong—and certainly isn't right, in another context—is that there's been so much on this
the Globe feels it's familiar territory and, therefore, doesn't bother. It's not
about suppressing anything. It's just a psychological thing that happens in
newsrooms that editors will hear something, know they've heard about it,

and then pass on it without ever thinking about whether it appeared in our paper. It happens everywhere. You have had amazing coverage—I've seen it here in Ottawa—and I personally think it's in the bag. An oversight that, obviously, will be repaired. Best of luck with your issue. Have no fears that it will be resolved satisfactorily.

Roy.[5]

As I pen these words in 2014, almost seven years after receiving the above email from Mr. MacGregor, some Lost Canadians still remain disenfranchised. Hence, I can say unequivocally that Roy was wrong. The fact that I'm still fighting proves that Canada's little oversight wasn't "in the bag."

Two days later, the hearings commenced. Diane Finley was the first to testify. Usually the Citizenship Committee met in a not-so-fancy room in the West Block. But not today. Because of the media coverage—hell, even the *New York Times* sent a reporter*—the room reserved for Finley's appearance was one of Parliament's best. Located in the more picturesque Centre Block, Room 253D, situated just back from the main entrance, on the right side of the oversized hallway leading toward the parliamentary library, and more frequently used for special gatherings like entertaining heads of state, was today reserved for the Lost Canadians.

Obviously, when the media actually does what they portray themselves as doing (which is reporting the news), parliamentarians pay attention. It makes all the difference. I was sitting at the back of the room when Finley walked in with her entourage, which included the bureaucracy's top person, Deputy Minister Richard Fadden. With about three minutes to go before the show began, I introduced myself. It was the first time Finley and I had met in person. She was cordial but businesslike—I had, after all, not made the first days of her job very easy. We exchanged pleasantries, and then she promised to get in touch with me later. Then the meeting, televised on CPAC, began.[6]

THE CHAIR (Mr. Norman Doyle (St. John's East, CPC)): We'll bring our meeting to order.

... Welcome to our meeting. I want to welcome the minister to our committee meeting today as we begin our study on the loss of Canadian citizenship for the years 1947, 1977, and 2007...

---

* Ian Austen was the *New York Times* reporter.

TOP: My great-grandparents' family, c. 1890s; the family had already been in Canada for generations.

BOTTOM: My parents' World War II wedding; dad is in his Canadian military uniform.

JUNE 1962
BANFF
CHAIRLIFT
0899
PROPOSED SITE
1968
WINTER
OLYMPICS

ABOVE: 1962, high above Banff; I'm sitting between my parents. After my folks moved to the United States, family holidays were spent back in Canada.

RIGHT: With my grandma, 1950s, Vancouver (by Canadian photographer Foncie Pulice).

TOP: My wife, Brenda, and daughter Katie at Lake Louise. After starting a family of our own, we made certain our kids also learned to appreciate the sights and flavours of Canada.

BOTTOM: With Katie at a hockey exhibit in Calgary just before the Olympics.

TOP: Brenda with Katie and Jamie in front of the B.C. legislature.

BOTTOM: Daughter Mindy makes three!

TOP: My mum and her grandchildren at the beach in Kitsilano, Vancouver, where she grew up.

BOTTOM: Grandpa Jack Rose, a former Canadian POW held by the Japanese in Hong Kong during World War II.

TOP: On "Take Your Kids to Work Day" my daughters went with me to Germany in a Boeing 747-400.

ABOVE LEFT: My girls standing with John Reynolds on the day I first met him. It was a game-changer in Canadian citizenship history.

ABOVE RIGHT: Our daughter Jamie, suited up to win!

TOP: In Parliament's restaurant, May 5, 2005, celebrating the passage of Bill S-2, our very first Lost Canadians victory. Mum is in front, Andrew Telegdi (Liberal) is on the left, John Reynolds (Conservative) is in the centre, and I am on the right.

BOTTOM: The most sacred spot in Parliament is the Memorial Chamber, dedicated to the sacrifice of our Canadian war dead. Sadly, our government keeps insisting that these World War I and World War II soldiers were not Canadian citizens. This is historically erroneous.

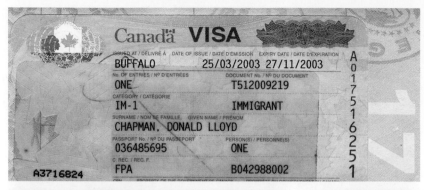

TOP: My "immigrant" certificate. It didn't matter that I'd been born in Vancouver to Canadian parents—I still had to go through the entire immigration process.

CENTRE: Stephen Harper with Barbara Porteous. Unknowingly, she was stateless for almost half a century. Harper had promised to fix the remaining Lost Canadian issues. After eight years, we're still waiting.

BOTTOM: The House Citizenship Committee "dream team." Left to right: Bill Siksay (NDP); Meili Faille (Bloc); Andrew Telegdi (Liberal); Diane Ablonczy (Conservative).

ABOVE TOP: The day we won with Bill S-2. Sitting in the prime minister's chair: my family; Lost Canadian Magali Castro-Gyr (second from left); standing is Andrew Telegdi, Melynda Jarratt (war brides expert), and MP Meili Faille.

ABOVE BOTTOM: The day my family became Canadian for the first time and I became Canadian for the second time. Citizenship judge George Gibault presided.

TOP: In Pugwash, Nova Scotia; Katie standing at her great-great-great-grand-parents' home, now a National Historic Site known as Thinkers Lodge, home to the 1995 Nobel Peace Prize.

BOTTOM: Katie in front of the Canada Post building in Antigonish, named after her great-great-great-uncle William Alexander Henry, a Father of Confederation.

ABOVE TOP: Bill Norwood is the Jackie Robinson of collegiate football; he was United Airline's first line pilot of colour. Standing with him is Velma Demerson, a Canadian made stateless for marrying a Chinese man.

ABOVE BOTTOM: U.S. newscaster Gwen Ifill, Asa Herring, Larry Jackson, and me, decked out in our Tuskegee Airmen jackets. Larry was our chapter president, and Asa was one of the original Airmen.

"In Flanders fields where poppies grow"

TOP: Laying the Burma Star wreath with one of my heroes, Herb Lim. The Chinese-Canadian war experience is not widely known.

BOTTOM: An original photo of poppies in Flanders Fields, taken by Canadian World War I soldier Charles Bosdet. Seriously wounded, he was hospitalized for nearly a year. Decades later CIC insisted that not only was Nova Scotia–born Charles not a Canadian citizen, neither was his grandson Charles III, born to Canadian parents in Winnipeg in 1952.

New citizenship minister Diane Finley spoke next. Sitting next to her was CIC's deputy minister (the top CIC bureaucrat), Richard Fadden. Finley began by expressing her gratitude for being able to talk about citizenship, something "so fundamental to Canadian identity." She mentioned how moving the recent citizenship ceremonies at the Supreme Court had been, saying that citizenship wasn't just about rights but also about responsibilities.

Yes, I thought, *but rights and responsibilities are a two-way street: individuals in regard to their country, and the government in the way it treats its people.* After all, the entire reason for government is to protect its citizens and, if possible, make life better for them.

Her focus centred on approximately 450 people who, she said, hadn't really lost their citizenship but, rather, their proof of citizenship. Equating the document to a birth certificate, she said that if a person loses it, he or she must apply to have it replaced. Finley was adamant that the number of people affected was around 450.

After her speech, the MPs were allowed comments and questions. Andrew Telegdi began, saying that there were upward of 200,000 Lost Canadians and that clearly the 1947 Citizenship Act was discriminatory. Canada welcomed 300,000 immigrants per year; why not first extend the welcome mat to people with rock-solid Canadian connections and backgrounds? He also brought up the issue of the Mennonites, noting that upward of 30,000 folks had lost citizenship simply because CIC discriminated against people married in a church abroad.

Conservative MP Barry Devolin then spoke about one of his constituents who had been born in Canada and had an Ontario birth certificate, yet years earlier had unknowingly lost his citizenship. His wife, someone born in a different country, sponsored him to become a Canadian citizen. Devolin pointed out the complete absurdity of the situation.

Finley, being the latest newbie minister and not yet spooled up to speed on the portfolio, countered, "Basically anyone who is born in Canada is a Canadian citizen."

Well, I'm not, I thought.

Liberal MP Jim Karygiannis brought up Statistics Canada's estimates of Lost Canadians numbering far more than 450.

A constant with citizenship ministers is that there is always a huge demand for their time; without question, their portfolio is incredibly challenging. Finley was forced to excuse herself from the hearing for a prior engagement. That's when I stepped in to testify. There's a really funny scene in the movie *My Cousin Vinny*. Vinny is the quintessential New York lawyer, defending his cousin in a murder trial taking place in a small Alabama town. As it happens, it's Vinny's first trial ever. Being pretty much an average guy off the streets, it took him six attempts to pass the bar exams. Totally inexperienced, he has no clue about judicial protocol. When the prosecuting attorney concludes his opening statement, Vinny stands, looks at the judge, then says, "Uh ... everything that guy just said is bullshit." The district attorney immediately counters, "Objection. Counsel's entire opening statement is argumentative." The judge fires back, "Sustained. Counselor's entire opening statement ... with the exception of 'thank you' ... will be stricken from the record."

This was to be my *My Cousin Vinny* moment. I walked up to the microphone to rebut the minister, and although I did not use Vinny's words, the same point definitely came across: I intimated that everything Minister Finley had just said was bullshit.

I had already mentioned to the MPs present how it had been forty-six years since I had lost my citizenship, all because my father—not me—had taken out US citizenship. Now I said: "The punishment here doesn't fit the crime. I didn't do anything wrong. I'm guilty only of being a very proud Canadian."

Karla Homolka is an infamous Canadian serial killer. Arrested in 1993 for the murder of three women, one being her own sister, she served out her prison sentence and on July 4, 2005, was released. Hmm, let's do the math. Three young girls murdered, twelve years in prison. That's four years for each murder. My crime is having a father who took out citizenship in the US when I was all of six years old, and now, sitting before the committee forty-six years later, I was still not considered Canadian. That was my point: that all of the hundreds of thousands of Lost Canadians were being unfairly punished.

It was both fascinating and sad that Diane Finley knew little to nothing about the problem. Although, to her credit, she appeared to be a fast learner, and unlike so many of her predecessors, she actually took an interest. Just a short time before Finley became citizenship minister, Marion Vermeersch, a war-bride child from Finley's riding, went to her local constituency office and asked for help. The government was denying Marion citizenship because, like Joe Taylor, she'd been born out of wedlock. It turned out that Finley didn't understand the problematic intricacies of war brides' citizenship issues. Not understanding one's portfolio was just so typical in Ottawa—cabinet ministers without a clue. You'd never knowingly board an airplane as a passenger with such an inexperienced pilot. But this wasn't aviation. It was politics, where the coveted cabinet promotions were often assigned not because of one's knowledge but because of one's loyalty to the prime minister. Since the election of 2006, your devotion to Stephen Harper, your being faithful, and where you sat inside the Conservative lobby had become inextricably intertwined with your chances of advancement.

The very next day, by golly, something amazing happened. The *Globe and Mail* at long last wrote a story on us. It was all of 457 words, which was about one word for every Lost Canadian CIC erroneously claimed was out there. The writer, a relative newbie by the name of Alex Dobrota, quoted Finley's 450 estimate exactly. But what really stood out was the title: "'Lost' Canadians Get Citizenship: Finley Uses Discretionary Power to Help Mennonites, War and Border Babies."

If that were true, there'd be no need for more committee hearings. The war brides and their children would have been citizens. The Taylor appeal would have been resolved. The border babies, the Mennonites, the age-twenty-four people, the age-twenty-eight people—they too would all be citizens. Certainly, I wouldn't have kept hanging around Ottawa. Nor would I have been able to add more chapters to this book. Seven years later, I'm writing because there are still Lost Canadians out there; indeed, in 2015 there remain way, way more than 450, as the laws have not yet been corrected satisfactorily.

As for Mr. Dobrota, I have no idea where he is today. But I do know that the *Globe and Mail*, despite having a new editor-in-chief, pretty much continues to watch from afar. Could Roy MacGregor have been accurate when he wrote, "My hunch, which may be wrong—and certainly isn't right, in another context—is that . . . it's familiar territory and, therefore, [the *Globe*] doesn't bother. It's not about suppressing anything. It's just a psychological thing that happens in newsrooms that editors will hear something, know they've heard about it, and then pass on it."

I find his statement concerning. Cats, pornography, and Hollywood starlets constantly make "the news," never seeming to be passed up by the media just because they've heard about these subjects before. In fact, the media, with its insatiable appetite for sexy stories, jumps repeatedly on the sensational ones, especially those about the rich and famous. And it regurgitates them almost word for word, day after day, ad nauseam.

Regardless, the *Globe and Mail* had finally devoted a whole story to us. Just one, mind you, on the hundreds of thousands of disenfranchised Canadians, and, in the process, just happened to get all the pertinent facts wrong.

Lock, stock, and barrel, it bought into the government's dribble. When I called asking that a correction be printed, the *Globe* refused, then pretty much walked away from reporting on the remaining 200,000 Lost Canadians altogether. For the *Globe*, it seemed that our issue was for the most part over. As for the readers who purchased the paper to keep abreast of the news, they certainly didn't get what they paid for.

On a bigger note, any kind of acquiescence to the government by a major newspaper or news organization would be reminiscent of the Soviet Union's *Izvestia*, where the publication could print only what the government approved and nothing more. Remember how strenuously Canadians, the US, England, and the rest of the "free" world condemned the Soviets for such practices? Was this actually happening in Canada? From the Lost Canadians' vantage, it sure seemed like it.

For now, round one was over, with both sides retreating to their respective corners. With the next bell we'd again be back in the boxer's ring swinging. The next hearings were scheduled for exactly one week later.

CHAPTER 14

MR. SMITH GOES TO WASHINGTON; MR. CHAPMAN GOES TO OTTAWA

No man can know where he is going unless he knows exactly where he has been and exactly how he arrived at his present place.
MAYA ANGELOU

I'd just like to say that my Canada includes me.
WILLIAM SMITH, LOST CANADIAN

— I —

FOR THE NEXT year, the time I spent in Ottawa didn't seem a whole lot different from what I would have spent had I been an MP or senator—the big difference was that MPs and senators were paid, they had staffs, and each weekend they could travel back to their riding at government expense. In the entire year, I never saw a politician staying at the Travelodge. Compared with the other Ottawa hotels, it was much less expensive and quite a bit less fancy. I got free coffee and corn flakes for breakfast. Our elected representatives had a food allowance. I was solely focused on correcting some very discriminatory laws, whereas most of the MPs hadn't even heard of the Lost Canadians. And didn't want to.

Moving back to Canada from England had been a lifelong dream for John Erison. After his mother died in 2001, as he and his wife, Dawn, sorted out her belongings, they discovered his British birth certificate. On the back was an Ontario government official stamp that read: "Family allowances Ontario region." John was the by-product of the union between Canadian World War II private Albert "John" Erison and Violet Hamilton, a sergeant in the British Army. Albert John had trained at Camp Borden, in Ontario, and during the war was stationed at Borden Camp in Hampshire, England, the place from which the Ontario army camp derived its name. John's father, also known as Canadian Military Forces ID#1397158, delivered tanks and heavy equipment; his mother was a clerk. They met at the Darby army camp and married. In 1943, young John was born. In June 1946, the family arrived at Pier 21 in Halifax with plans of making their life together as productive Canadians. They settled in the London, Ontario, area, where John attended preschool.

It's amazing how John's early impressions of Canada lasted a lifetime, and he always longed to return to the Canada he remembered as his homeland. It was like that with Lost Canadian families everywhere. Many children, despite being infants when they left Canada, nurtured an inner identification with Canada for the rest of their lives.[1] Often within the same family, some kids cared a great deal about their Canadian past, whereas others could hardly have cared less. My elder brother and sister didn't have a burning desire to be Canadian, but I did. In 1948, news came from England that John's grandmother—his mother's mother—was dying of tuberculosis. It meant that her younger children, John's aunts and uncles, would be put into an orphanage. The family in Canada knew they had to return to England so, in 1948, they reluctantly left Canada. In this regard, the Erisons weren't unique; several thousand war-bride families moved back to England. The family's Canadian saga had begun with their arrival in 1946 and, for John, now in England, returning home to Ontario became his lifetime quest. His wife, Dawn, explains it best:

I knew how badly he [John] wanted to return to his beloved homeland and we had already decided to try and emigrate. We looked at what was involved and quickly realized that we were getting older and were losing points in the points system on a yearly basis. I decided that the only way was for me to go to University and work for a Degree. We looked at the National Occupational Classification lists online and realized that the best Degree I could work for was for an Environmental Scientist as that would give us around 35 points with a Bachelor of Science and that Degree and job skills which were high on the N.O.C. list. So back to school I went in the Fall of 1999. But money was tight with fees to pay and a mortgage, so I had to keep my job going and work nights—going to Uni in the daytime and sleeping in between. I would take an occasional vacation day when I needed to do assignments—or catch-up on my sleep. The day that I sat for my finals [June 28, 2003], after four years of hard study, the Immigration laws changed. I could no longer get 35 points for my endeavours.

We had no option but to apply for a Charitable Worker's Visa, which we did on August 11. I came to Canada [in 2003] to work as a volunteer. This meant we were not taking employment that a Canadian could do—as it was unpaid.

Once we were here we engaged an Immigration Lawyer in Montreal, who had us fill out mountains of CIC forms, and in turn we provided a mountain of documents. The lawyers were certain our application would succeed. They told us to stop worrying, and even encouraged us to make plans for our Canadian future. In September 2006 our application came back—refused ... and no reason was given (apparently CIC doesn't have to give a reason.) ... To say we were devastated was not even scratching the surface. John felt betrayed and rejected by his homeland that his father, grandfather and ancestors had farmed, worked for, fought for, and died for. He was heartbroken.

That meant we had to renew our Visitor Visa, which meant we had to leave Canada by the 24th of March. Literally, we could not even reapply as we had to have a relative here in Canada (not for sponsorship) but to have "a connection." The only one who CIC would accept was John's uncle, who passed away whilst our application was being processed.

So, [afterward we learned that] the day that Diane Finley [then citizenship and immigration minister] had said that no one who would be Canadian with Bill C37 should have to leave Canada—we were on a plane returning to England. A few months passed and we were unaware when a friend emailed us and told us that Bill C-37 was happening. I contacted folks and was soon given Don Chapman's phone number and contacted him. By this time John had been diagnosed with bladder cancer, was recovering from his first surgery, and due for chemo.

Don continued to keep us updated by email and phone during this process and it was this that gave John the reason to keep fighting for life. More surgery and further treatments later and we watched with bated breath as Bill C-37 passed its way through to fruition. John could return home!! Such joy... which was short-lived as John failed to thrive after all these cancer treatments. In July of 2008—before Bill C-37 was ratified—John suffered from kidney failure from all the drugs and treatments for his cancer. He passed away disenfranchised from his homeland.

When you've got tens of thousands of war-bride families, even though the situation of each is unique, collectively they become a kaleidoscope of sorts. John's mother, Violet, was no different from the hundreds of thousands of young patriotic British women who enlisted, volunteered, worked in factories, worked on farms, or became firewomen, paramedics, mechanics, pilots, you name it, during the war. With the men off to combat, for life to continue with any semblance of normalcy, it was imperative for the women to step in. At the start of my battle, I had thought only about citizenship. But the further I delved into the Lost Canadian "fight from hell," the more people I met, and the more I heard their stories, the more evident it became that the issue was a great deal bigger than merely citizenship. It was also about women's rights or, more specifically, equal rights for women. The laws in 1947 were terribly biased, and that didn't sit right with me.

Another category of people rarely mentioned was that of the women who married foreign men. About 1,000 enlisted Canadian women were stationed in England, and many fell in love with foreign men. After the war, some husbands came to Canada, and some Canadian women stayed in Europe.

Like their British counterparts, Canadian women at home volunteered and were involved in many if not all aspects of the war effort. It's disappointing that the war stories of women are not more widely known. Kaye Fremont, born in Vancouver, enlisted in the Royal Canadian Air Force Women's Division, in 1941. As the parliamentary hearings progressed, and as a Lost Canadian herself, she contacted me (just one of the hundreds who did), asking if there was some way I could help her regain her citizenship. As I became more familiar with other Lost Canadians, I came to appreciate that they represented every person and group in society. Another faction was the English soldiers, tens of thousands of them, who trained all over North America, including in Canada. Some fell in love; their Canadian war brides later left to make their lives in Europe.

As the next of several committee hearings commenced on February 26, 2007, World War II raged on. Not in Europe but in the backrooms and hallways of Ottawa. A few weeks earlier, I had begun conversing with Diane Finley's new chief of staff, John Weissenberger. It had been just over a year since the election but still fresh in my mind were the Harper campaign promises, one of those being no patronage appointments. John was a geologist who had befriended Stephen years earlier when both were university students. They became best friends. Not only had John introduced Stephen to his wife, Laureen, but he was best man at their wedding. After being burned in Ottawa with incredible regularity, I was skeptical about John. But unlike with the regime of Monte Solberg, who had slammed his door and kept it shut for his entire eleven-month reign, at least now there was renewed communication. And, like it or not, it was the Conservatives who were the kingpins, the Ottawa elite, and it was them I had to deal with. But Weissenberger wasn't just any ordinary Ottawa contact; he had an umbilical connection to the grand fromage himself. Despite my skepticism, I wanted to meet him.

On February 18, I emailed John to say that I was in town and suggested we get together. Thus we began what would become a year-and-a-half-long relationship. Despite his chief-of-staff position being an obvious patronage appointment (the closest connection it had to his geologist background was that changes within CIC happened about as fast as glaciers melted), I liked John from the start.[2] We arranged a get-together for the twenty-fourth—just two days before the committee hearings recommenced. Here is John's email:

"Hi Don, Just a note to confirm that I will meet you at 2 PM this afternoon in the Starbucks in Chapters—just east (down the hill) from the Château Laurier. I'll be wearing a bulky grey coat with the name "Schlumberger" on it. See you then. JW."

Starbucks, with its relaxed, easygoing atmosphere, was a welcome change after the rigmarole of visiting a minister at Laurier Avenue. In fact, it was the exact opposite of going to the minister's offices on Laurier, where you enter the building through a rotating door, stamp your feet a couple of times to get the snow off your shoes, undo a button or two of your outer coat, loosen the muffler around your neck, then walk up to the security desk and tell the guard who you want to see. He in turn asks to see your ID, which, of course, is in your back pocket, underneath your heavy wool overcoat, suit jacket, and sweater. You basically have to strip down to get at it. Eventually out comes your driver's licence, which you hand to the guard, who in turn picks up the phone to call upstairs. Some security guard at the other end of the line asks a few questions to the guard downstairs, who then tips his head down to cast a quick, dubious glance at you above his reading glasses. He looks directly at you, then mumbles a few words into the receiver, and finally, only after both are completely satisfied that you are who you say you are, yet another person is dispatched from the twenty-first floor to the lobby, with the sole intent of accompanying you upstairs. Precautions are so extensive that you must be escorted to the bathroom. Outside the loo, someone waits for you to do your business, then escorts you back. And if that isn't enough, the humiliation continues as everyone working on the damn floor watches as you leave for the washroom and again witnesses your return. After years of being a regular twenty-first-floor visitor, I'm certain it was logged into their computers precisely how long it took for me to pee.

So to say that it was indeed a pleasure getting together with John at Starbucks, where I could actually go to the john, is an understatement. Looking back, I should have tested my theory and disappeared into the men's room. On my return it would have confirmed just how much CIC knew about me if John had said, "You took a few seconds longer than normal."

The meeting went well. Very well. And it was productive in that John and I laid the groundwork for going forward. He struck me as a man who could get things done. The citizenship hearings had been going on for quite some time, and we both knew they would not let up but would continue well into the foreseeable future. It was a relief to know that John supported the spirit of those hearings. The mood at CIC had definitely changed. The stormy Solberg winds from the north had become gentle Finley trade winds favourable to the direction in which we were sailing. We agreed that when I got back to Phoenix we'd set up a conference call between me, John, and the minister.

Before Parliament's summer break, ten meetings specifically to do with the committee's study were held.[3] The first started promptly at 11:05 a.m. on February 26. Chairman MP Norman Doyle began: "I want to welcome the witnesses today to our committee hearing on the loss of Canadian citizenship for the years 1947, 1977, and 2007."[4]

Bill Janzen and Mary Boniferro of the Mennonite Central Committee began by explaining how Mennonites had been particularly affected by the legislation that came into force both in 1947 and in 1977. These acts were filled with wacky in- and out-of-wedlock provisions. Since Mexico didn't recognize the Mennonites, their church marriages were never government-sanctioned. That meant the children of those unions, under Mexican law, were born out of wedlock. And then, in a one-two punch, the 1977 act stated that all second-generation, foreign-born children must reaffirm their citizenship by their twenty-eighth birthday. But, of course, CIC isn't known for alerting people about obscure rules.

Translated, tens of thousands of people lived in Canada as legitimate Canadian citizens, holding official certificates of Canadian citizenship, but on their twenty-eighth birthday, unless they'd reaffirmed their status with CIC, their citizenship became null and void. Around 30,000 Mennonites were directly affected. Janzen and Boniferro explained to the MPs how one citizenship certificate could affect upward of 200 people, which meant that the number of people at risk was much greater than it might appear on the surface of things. Boniferro cited an example:

> Recently I had a case where the local immigration office took a family... There were eight children and the father who were not Canadian, but the mother and the eight children had come in as Canadian citizens, and she had sponsored her husband to become a landed immigrant. Now they find out that she's not Canadian, and all of those certificates had to be returned.

She noted a common CIC trait, that of regularly doling out inaccurate information, to the detriment of the individual:

> Unfortunately... when the first ones became 28 and... went to the local CIC offices, they were often not given accurate information. For example, in one southern Ontario office two siblings went in, because they had the letters and they knew they had to retain before they were 28... the officer told [them] "Once a Canadian, always a Canadian."
>
> We have people... asking why they should believe me, when someone in a CIC office has told them there is no such thing.

(In time, non-Mennonites in the same boat began contacting me. Often they could no longer work: no legal status meant no job and no income. To give more context to the February 26 hearing, here's the story of a Mennonite man, Johan Teichroeb:

> I was born in Mexico in February of 1980. My parents moved to Manitoba when I was six months old. They applied for citizenship for me, and I received it on November 6, 1980. I grew up in Canada. I went to school here. I joined the workforce when I was 16... and became a truck driver. It was always my dream to become a truck driver.
>
> Then I heard that I was in the category to renew my citizenship before I was 28... I sent in the application late in 2002. One year later, I received a letter stating that I had never been a Canadian and I could not retain my citizenship because my grandfather was born out of wedlock.
>
> That was shocking for me. I've always been in Canada. For over 20 years I've been here. I got married here. I have two Canadian-born kids here...

It was just hard to believe. They were telling me I wasn't a Canadian...
I couldn't cross the border, and the company couldn't supply me with
Canadian runs, so I was out of a job.

... I lost a lot, all due to the fact that there was a marriage certificate
made 75 years ago stating that my grandfather was born out of wedlock.
He was not technically born.[5]

Mr. Teichroeb began to cry.

I lost everything, including the house. I was down to renting a house.
Money-wise, I was borrowing money to buy groceries for the kids... My
wife was depressed and started taking antidepressants. There was no news
of getting anything back.

So I went from job to job, trying to support the family, trying to keep
everything I had... I'm still trying to pay off what I borrowed four years
ago.

... This should never have happened. I was in Canada, and for something like a marriage certificate... I mean, they had a marriage in church,
not a civil marriage. That was what was keeping me from my citizenship...

The law said that because I was born after February 1977, I had to
retain my citizenship before I was 28. But the thing is that if I had been
born three years earlier, I would have never had a problem. Everything
would have been fine.

Think about it: How many Canadians could prove, with all the required
documents, the legal status of their grandparents' marriage, especially if the
wedding was close to a hundred years ago, and particularly if that marriage
took place in another country? But the real question to ask was why: Why
was this a requirement for retaining one's citizenship?)

But back to the hearing. The committee heard next from David Choi, a
director of the National Congress of Chinese Canadians. His statement was
in support of the Lost Canadians. It was also to the point:[6]

Compliance with the laws must also mean compliance with the... Canadian Charter of Rights and Freedoms. Compliance would mean giving
equal rights to all Canadians.[7]

Next up was Christine Eden, talking about children born outside Canada
on Canadian military bases—military brats:

I represent the adult children of the Canadian military who were born during the period of 1947 to 1977...

From 1950 through 1977, there were over 110,000 babies born on Canadian military bases throughout Europe, in France, Germany, England, Belgium, and Holland. They were registered by the required registration of birth abroad...

In 1977 the registration of birth abroad was cancelled and replaced with a citizenship card. The problem is that we were never advised of this requirement. Prior to the computer era, we had no problem obtaining passports or any government identification with the documentation we had...

The registration of birth abroad was a handwritten document that in many cases is 60 years old, so obviously it is not going to be in good physical condition...

What's happening now is that many of us who are applying for passports and citizenship cards are being told ... we are not Canadian...

To tell a military person when they are close to retirement age that they are not Canadian is very offensive. It's something that should not happen...

I have two cases that I find somewhat sickening. One is a retired RCMP sergeant, and the other is a Canadian army major, who are now unable to renew their passports because they do not have a citizenship card. When they went to CIC, both were told that they're not Canadian...

In the next five years, you are going to find these individuals coming forward to apply for Canada Pension. Without proof of their Canadian status, they are not even going to be able to apply for welfare while you fix it ...

I know people who, as late as last Friday, have gone to CIC or Passport Canada to apply for a passport and who have been turned away and told they're not Canadian...

I have people who cannot even get an updated driver's licence.

How ironic that, in 2014, Canada was studying its veterans charter, deciding what benefits to extend to its vets. From Christine Eden's testimony, it's apparent that Canada has often disregarded its "sacred obligations" to our military folks. Imagine having spent your life serving in the Canadian Armed Forces and now you or your child being told that you are not—indeed, never have been—Canadian.

It was my turn to speak. Being blunt, I said, "Come on, folks, this is common sense." I then challenged the parliamentarians. Since CIC was in hot pursuit of Lost Canadians, I said that MPs should be the first people to have to prove their citizenship. I continued:

> It shouldn't take major brain surgery to fix [the act] ... It's a waste of tax-payer money. It is a real waste of money to go on witch hunts like this ... We're here because parliamentarians didn't do their jobs in 1947, 1977, and with the Benner case. They threw it back and now we're back to square one again. Fix this thing.

One of my heroes, Magali Castro-Gyr, the schoolteacher forced out of Canada, spoke next. Her situation was just like mine: she was a minor child when her father took out US citizenship. Now, she talked about the unprofessionalism of CIC, to what great lengths it went to make you prove your worthiness, and, echoing Mary Boniferro of the Mennonite Central Committee, how it all too often gave out false information:

> We were informed that because I was a Canadian, I could sponsor my husband. That is what I did. We came to Canada and two months later, I received a letter from Citizenship and Immigration Canada, further to my applying for citizenship cards for myself and for my children.
> ... Upon reading this letter, you will note that it contains four spelling mistakes as well as a number of factual errors. The letter notes the following:
> When your father acquired U.S. citizenship in 1958, you were a dual national (Canadian and French).
> Because I was a minor child, I lost my citizenship.
> It's interesting, because first of all it was not in 1958, it was in 1975 ... I was born in 1959, so I could not have been a dual citizen in 1958; I was not even born yet.
> There are also spelling mistakes in this letter. One of the first is that the woman who signed this, Beverly Foggoa, spelled Canada as "Camada." She spelled my children's names wrong. She spelled our family name wrong. This is the kind of bureaucracy I've dealt with—sloppy ...
> When I received that letter, I took on a lawyer. I spent $27,000 of my money bringing this case ...
> I had a judicial review going on for two years. I then was sent an "offer" ... in May of 2003 that stated nine different points of things that I needed to do if I wanted to stay here. I had to leave, I had to come back as an immigrant, I had to stay another year, I could then apply to resume citizenship, and more importantly I had to not divulge the terms of this

agreement. I could not go public with the terms of this agreement. I had to be silent.

That was a gag order. At that point, I decided this was very wrong and I went very public. That's the reality of what I was living with here. I was given a gag order. It was absolutely unsettling. We didn't know if we could stay or not stay.

Publicly this was happening, yet privately CIC was telling me, "You're just the kind of person we want to have here in Canada."

Magali refused to sign the gag order and, consequently, CIC forced her to leave the country. Several months later, the government capitulated and granted her citizenship, but by now she was living in Switzerland. What's ironic is that her father had regained his Canadian citizenship and was living in Canada with her mother. Magali's brother, Thierry, was still caught in CIC's web, and worse, he was stateless.

Next came Rod Donaldson:

I was one of these people also born out of wedlock in 1959. What had happened was that my father—and this is the dirt coming out—was already married to another woman. He was a police officer in the OPP, stationed out of Barrie, Ontario. My mom was a nurse in Orillia. They happened to meet; things happened, even as they do in modern times... and my mother became pregnant with me.

My mom came from a very well-off family in the Port Severn area. To avoid embarrassment, through a nurse friend down in the Windsor area they ended up somehow in Detroit, Michigan, at Sinai Hospital, where I was born.

Through my formative years I'd always been told I was born at Mount Sinai Hospital in Toronto...

... I applied for my birth certificate, because I realized I didn't have one; back then you didn't need anything other than your driver's licence to cross the border.

I got a letter back... I remember reading it and saying, "Gee whiz, mom, they're saying I've never been born. The Canadian government checked five years before my birthdate and five years after, and they have no Rod Donaldson born on that date."

With that, mom suffered a little bit of embarrassment. A couple of days later she took me into the family dining room, sat me down, and proceeded to tell me the story I've just told you.

I wondered how I came to Canada. What had happened was that she had left me behind. I was left in Warren, Michigan—to the best of my knowledge—with someone who I know was [a] notary public. I think her husband was a lawyer, but when my mom handed me my birth certificate, which happened to be a fictitiously named American birth certificate, she asked me never to contact the people who had notarized that certificate, so that's why I'm thinking those thoughts.

Two years later, my parents were together. Dad had left his previous wife. My little brother had now been born, and I guess they decided they'd better go get Rod Junior. They went across the border, and mom was literally at the front door... talking with the husband and wife, and my father snuck in the back door and stole me out of their house and brought me to Canada.

On the trip to Canada, dad, being a police officer and thinking they were going to be looking for this car, dropped my mom off at the border, and she pushed me over. I asked her, "How did I get here?" She said, "Literally, I pushed you across the border in a baby carriage, and dad came around in the car and picked us up later."

I have fallen through many loopholes, all just because people know who I am. They know I'm Rod's boy, so I must be a Canadian.

Probably because of the news coverage of this hearing and subsequent embarrassment to the politicians if they didn't act on this, it wasn't long before Rod got his citizenship through a 5.4 grant. For him, the issue had been resolved. For other folks in this quagmire, CIC maintained its old ways of denial.

The hearings continued, and on March 19, sitting member of Parliament Marlene Jennings spoke. Jennings had been fervently opposed to the Lost Canadians years earlier. Now, however, she was having a change of heart as her own citizenship came into question. She began by explaining her conversation with CIC:

I was simply asked whether I was born in Canada, and I answered yes. Then I was asked whether I had always lived in Canada, and I answered yes. The woman then told me I was a Canadian citizen. However, she quickly changed her mind and asked me whether I had ever obtained the citizenship of another country, and I said yes. She then asked me under what circumstances that had occurred, and I told her that it was in connection with my marriage in 1974 to an Italian citizen who was a permanent resident of Canada at the time. She then told me that she didn't know whether I had lost my citizenship.[8]

Until then, Marlene hadn't told the case processor that she was an MP. Once CIC was made aware of that, the Registrar of Canadian Citizenship stepped in:

I was told that my file was quite complicated.

The person on the other end of the line asked me if it was okay with me for them to send an email with all the information to the Nova Scotia office so that real experts could study the case. Subsequently, I received a telephone call from the [r]egistrar of [c]itizenship. He asked me several questions. He said he thought I was a Canadian citizen, but that since the act was very complicated, he would have to check everything to do with my obtaining Italian citizenship... in order to verify whether or not I lost my Canadian citizenship...

... At that point there were serious doubts as to whether or not I was a citizen. When you have the registrar of citizenship saying, "I think you're a citizen, but I have to go back and study the law"—he's the expert—that shows you how complicated this law was and is.

At that point, I realized that if I was told I was not a citizen, then I was no longer a member of Parliament, because a precondition to be qualified or admissible as a candidate for election to Parliament is that you are a Canadian citizen. I immediately made an appointment with the Clerk of the House in order to sit down and say that I was questioning the propriety of my continuing to sit in the House, to take part in debates, and to be in committee...

... As a result of my going public about the doubts as to my own citizenship, I've received calls and emails from many Canadians across the country saying that their situation is similar and they are now having doubts as to their citizenship. They're afraid to call the hotline in case they are told they are not a citizen...

I will end with one last point. Mr. Chapman and I have had many discussions over the last weeks and months. He is suggesting a series of amendments to the legislation that would provide citizenship retroactively to every Canadian who lost their citizenship through no act of their own. I've had an opportunity to review it, and I support it wholeheartedly and I hope the committee will as well.

It was always interesting how people changed from being complacent to being in almost a state of panic when they realized their own status was in peril. In Marlene's defence, she never asked for special favours or consideration. My CIC insider told me that, without question, Marlene had lost her citizenship when she obtained Italian citizenship in 1977. CIC had turned a blind eye. I never revealed this to Marlene.

At the March 26 session, Wendy Adams spoke:

By virtue of several circumstances, my brother and I are lost. We are considered to be lost Canadians...

Our parents met in 1960 in Cold Lake, Alberta. Our mom was serving in the Canadian Forces as an MP, and our dad was in the U.S. Air Force. They married in 1961 and our mom left the Canadian Forces to be with our dad. Being in the military, our family moved often. In 1963 my brother was born in Peru, Indiana. I was born five years later in Colorado Springs, Colorado. In 1970 our dad left for a one-year tour in Vietnam and we moved to Canada to live with my mom's family. When he returned we moved to Omaha, Nebraska. Then in 1972 we moved to Spokane, Washington.

Knowing that the next orders my dad would receive could possibly be another isolation assignment where he would have to be away from us for another year, he decided to retire from the air force. With my mom's desire to live near her family and my dad's love for fishing, we moved to Canada. We arrived in the small oceanside town of Powell River, British Columbia, in 1973. I was five years old. We've lived in Canada for the past 34 years, and amazingly, for the most part, in one place. As children, when the topic of citizenship arose we knew we were born in the U.S. and held U.S. citizenship, but we had always been told by our parents that we were entitled to dual citizenship because our mom was Canadian.

At one time my brother even registered to vote... Aside from being left out on election days, we found that the citizenship papers were unimportant to us, as we could travel quite freely across the border at that time with photocopied documents, papers, birth certificates, and immigrant papers. Then September 11[, 2001] came. The photocopied documents became a thing of the past and we would need passports and permanent resident cards to travel.

We decided it was time to apply for Canadian citizenship [proof of citizenship]... [We] had our documents verified for certificates, etc., and paid our fees, $200 each. Our applications were mailed in fall 2004. Then we waited and we waited. After several phone calls and a year later we finally were able to talk to somebody in the immigration department. We were told our application had not yet been processed. Then we waited some more. Finally, in November 2005 we received a letter stating that our applications were denied and we had missed the August 14, 2004 deadline. We didn't even know there was a deadline. Our applications were received in October 2004, so we had missed the deadline by a few months... We felt defeated. [She was referring to the scc *Benner* case, now being ignored by cic.]

For 32 of the past 34 years that my brother and I have lived in Canada we thought we were Canadian. Imagine our shock when we were told that we had missed a deadline. What deadline? We didn't know there was a deadline.

... We were educated, we worked, and we paid taxes in Canada. We are married to Canadians and our children are Canadian. We really felt that becoming Canadian citizens was just a formality. Now we have been asked to pay yet another set of fees, to wait 12 to 15 months, and to take a test. Our only alternative is to apply for our permanent resident cards, which means yet another set of fees and time off work... Three weeks ago... we learned of these hearings and the Lost Canadians Organization. We didn't realize there were so many others like us.[9]

I was the next to speak:

It should be noted that six days ago there was a Federal Court decision very similar to Wendy's—Babcock v. Canada. It was a gentleman in the same position—a Benner case—who applied in July 2004 and they sent him a refugee package, not anything to do with citizenship. So he missed the deadline of applying [under] Benner by one month, and he won last week in the Federal Court of Canada, defending himself. This is a decision already determined by the Supreme Court.

Soon, it was Charles Bosdet's turn. cic wrongly thought he was a Mennonite. Maybe for that reason, or maybe because his father took out us citizenship when he was a minor child, cic cancelled his citizenship. He began by explaining his background—a former editor of a major legal publication who dealt with various companies and compliance audits, as well as with corporate and government compliance matters, Charles was extremely well versed in bureaucratic technicalities and nuances. He too was a Lost Canadian who, as it turned out, had been wrongly denied. He talked about CIC's rejection:

> I understand policies and procedures and so forth, but it got to the point that what I was receiving in letter after letter from my evaluator didn't acknowledge the stuff that I was sending ... It didn't acknowledge, in some cases, secondary evidence that the citizenship policy manual plainly states is acceptable and will be accepted in lieu of primary evidence.
>
> In my case, I believe the evaluator thoroughly violated the proscription against placing an undue burden on an applicant ...
>
> There was also a certain lack of professionalism. This evaluator sought to disprove my own citizenship by applying a foreign nationality law to one of my ancestors. In a subsequent discussion, it was very clear that this evaluator did not understand—was completely ignorant of—the fact that there was a difference between this foreign nationality law and Canada's ...
>
> What bothered me wasn't that she was ignorant of the law; what bothered me more than anything was a complete lack of interest in learning anything new. I expected her to say she would check [or] ... consult with somebody. There was none of that ...
>
> There followed a series of disingenuous and misleading request letters that looked fine if all you knew was what you read in the letters, but in truth many of the things that appeared in these letters were belied by a stack of evidence sitting on her desk, evidence that she was pretending wasn't there ...
>
> On appeal, it didn't stop there ... My case eventually was taken over by an evaluator in Ottawa. The case processing centre evaluator on my file apparently misrepresented my case to the Ottawa person, and this came to light when the Ottawa evaluator called me, and a whole raft of things came to light. She had been misinformed [or not informed] about the nature of the evidence in the case.

That ancestor Charles was referring to was his Canadian-born grandfather, who'd fought in all the major battles in World War I, including Vimy Ridge. The case analyst concluded that his grandfather and father weren't Canadian, so therefore neither was Charles, who had been born in Winnipeg to a Canadian mother post-1947.

It was all so crazy, especially considering the considerable number of shady people Canada was allowing into the country. Charles went on to say that severe problems existed at the Sydney case-processing centre, which to this day have not been rectified. He ended his testimony with this:

> The onus should not be, in my view, on a citizen whose resources are far more limited than the evaluator's are to overcome every single objection. In many instances, those objections seem to have no bearing whatsoever on the case at hand. The denial letters, if they're issued, should inform people of what the recourse is...
>
> I would propose to the committee that it might consider putting expiry dates on challenges to official documents issued by the Canadian government. If you issue a passport in 1942, somebody 60 years later should not be able to come along and, for no reasons they disclose to you, say this is not acceptable.

Now speaking was Melynda Jarratt of www.canadianwarbrides.com. She explained how the war brides and their children had been so warmly welcomed into Canada, and now, after more than sixty years, the current government was questioning their status. It was, she said, "a bunch of malarkey," particularly since "the archival evidence [to the contrary] is so astounding." She went on to say how the minister of veterans affairs in 1946 specifically stated that the war brides were Canadian citizens. She then said this:

> Princess Alice, the sister-in-law of Queen Mary,... was married to the Governor General of Canada at the time. She had been asked to write a foreword to the welcome to war brides. It was printed in 1944 by the Department of National Defence and the Wartime Information Board. In it she says... "Coming from the British Isles to become a new citizen of Canada, you will have..."

Melynda's point was that given a previous government's acceptance, and declarations, that the war brides were Canadian citizens, why should the current government be denying it?

The next to speak was William Smith, a border baby—someone born in the US to Canadian parents, then brought to Canada as an infant. People living in Quebec and Manitoba were particularly affected, as the nearest hospital for many of them was in the US.

Smith explained how his parents brought him into Canada three weeks after his birth in the States, and how the immigration officer's comment was

"Oh, you have a new Canadian." Because of William, his family qualified for the federal baby-bonus program. Yet today, after spending his entire life in Canada, the government says he isn't a citizen. Because of this, Smith can't work. In his own words, after years and years of battling CIC, "I'm now financially destitute."

Christopher Veeman was a lawyer representing a different border baby. Of the many children of the Clark family, all born in the US and brought back to Canada immediately after their birth, only one was being denied a 5.4 grant. The reason? He had a criminal record—which brings me back to the *Benner* case. *Benner* wasn't just about gender rights; it also dealt with criminality. Benner's past was shady, yet the Supreme Court said it wasn't a factor with regard to citizenship. He might not even be close to the type of person you'd want as a citizen but, nonetheless, he was still a citizen. The court was stating that, as with family members, you don't always get to pick and choose. When C-37 came into effect, the last remaining Clark son got recognized.

To the committee, I pointed out that, despite the government's claim of 5.4 grants being a catch-all for people not quite fitting neatly into a Lost Canadian category, the grants more often than not didn't work. The Clark family's situation proved this. What is certain is that when politicians or bureaucrats have free rein to decide just who is or is not a citizen, individual rights often get sacrificed. Charles Bosdet, Magali Castro-Gyr, Rod Donaldson, Wendy Adams, William Smith, me, and countless thousands of others were all veterans of the unfairness of it all.

— II —

THE HEARINGS NOW turned to the masters of their respective fields. Dr. Barry Edmonston, our expert on Canadian statistics and demographics, was the first to speak. He too was a Lost Canadian, and one of my insider sources, having frequent dealings with senior people inside CIC. Before the committee, he verified everything I had said, which also corroborated the numbers Gary Symons of CBC had reported. Never before had we put Barry in the limelight.

Donald Galloway, professor of law and a leading expert in citizenship law, followed. He made a couple of profound statements:

> I want to propose to you, first, that there is a very simple and very thin conception of citizenship that underlies our Citizenship Act and the various

acts that identify the rights of Canadian citizens, such as the Canada Elections Act and the Immigration and Refugee Protection Act.

The simple idea is this: a Canadian citizen is a person in whose name the government of Canada acts and whose interests the government of Canada has undertaken to promote. It is these two facets, these two principles, that underlie the Citizenship Act and its predecessor, the Citizenship of Canada Act.

How do we distinguish between a citizen and a non-citizen? It is not that the government has no obligations to non-citizens. Whether somebody is a permanent resident, a temporary resident, a foreign national, or an enemy combatant in war, the government has an obligation to respect the human rights of these individuals. The obligation to Canadian citizens is greater than that. The government has undertaken to look after the interests of Canadians and to promote them, not just to respect them. Similarly, the government claims to act not in the name of permanent residents or foreign nationals; it claims to act in the name of us citizens.

When did the government of Canada start acting on behalf of Canadians? Was it in 1947, or was it much earlier? The answer, I think, is obvious.[10]

He then asked:

Is the government living up to its undertakings to look after the interests of Canadians and to promote them? If we look at the Citizenship Act, I think the answer is no. In the first part of my brief I try to argue that this is a continuing failure. We're not just dealing with historical anomalies concerning people who have arrived in Canada and are being mistreated or people who were born here and were mistreated. It's something that continues.

Christina Godlewska spoke on behalf of the BC Civil Liberties Association. She mentioned how citizenship was a fundamental right, not a special dispensation. In her words, "It's more primary, more conceptually primary in a lot of ways than some of the other rights that are enumerated in the charter."*

Christina talked about the age-twenty-eight rule; Joe Taylor and the war-bride kids; Taylor's court challenge; and how the government's approach to

---

* In the years to come, the government would publicly claim that citizenship in Canada was nothing more than a legislated privilege.

the issue was adversarial, suggesting it needed to fundamentally change the way it dealt with Lost Canadians.

In a subsequent session, John Ralston Saul spoke. He is the husband of former governor general Adrienne Clarkson. His mother was a war bride, and his brother was born overseas during the war and brought to Canada as an infant. I was rather amazed that, after all the years of my attempting to woo his wife to speak out on our behalf, which she never did, he spoke freely about me. His words were flattering, but as time marched forward, I never saw any follow-through in his actions.

Yet other meetings followed, with more Lost Canadians coming forward. I'll end with the story of a man—an old man—who touched the hearts of everyone in the room. He'd had a stroke, which deprived him of the ability to speak. His daughter did the talking.

Guy Valliere was born in 1926 in Montreal to an American father and Canadian mother. During World War II he served as a Canadian soldier. He had suffered a stroke, and the government refused to pay for his medical expenses. Why? Because unlike Joe Taylor, Guy had been born in wedlock. As a younger man, for a few years, Guy was employed in the States. He had the right to because his father was American. Under Canadian law, his mother was chattel of the father, and because they were married before 1947, she lost her Canadian status. In a nutshell, our government refused to recognize Guy as being Canadian.

It was difficult watching an old man weep. In the testimony, his daughter said that without identity he felt alone, like a nobody, almost less welcome in the country than a terrorist. Knowing his time left was limited, he just wanted to die in peace—*as a Canadian*. After putting his life on the line as a World War II soldier, didn't he earn at least that right?

At the end of the testimony he looked my way, then shuffled toward me, arm in arm with his daughter. When he extended both his arms to me, I put my hands into his, and he burst into tears. Then so did I. In fact, there wasn't a dry eye in the room; even the MPs were sniffling. Gary Symons walked over to Diane Finley to ask about Guy's status. She assured Gary that Guy would be recognized.

He never was.* In the meantime, his medical bills mounted. I was able to raise some money to help him offset his costs, but I couldn't help but wonder why in the world a country would treat one of its vets so poorly. I still

---

* Diane Finley turned Guy's file over to the bureaucrats, who never followed through on it. So much for political promises du jour. As the old saying goes, they weren't worth a plug nickel.

can't answer that. Nor can I find words to describe how shameful it is that this wonderful country of ours, which boasts about being compassionate, wasn't at all compassionate, not by any stretch of the imagination. Instead, it was being ruthless, heartless, conniving, and uncaring. Regrettably for Guy, that wasn't the end of his ordeal. In time, it got a lot worse.

Of the ten hearings, two were sessions where the only witnesses were bureaucrats. I attended the first but, being exhausted, retreated to Phoenix for the second, which I could view on my computer through the CPAC website. The morning of the hearing, I sat back and watched the live proceedings. Or at least I did until the MPs began questioning the witnesses. I thought Andrew Telegdi forgot to ask something, so I emailed him the question. I saw him glance at his BlackBerry. Just moments later, he posed my question.

In that instant it dawned on me: knowing the email addresses of various MPs, I could have sent all kinds of text messages, asked all kinds of questions. I could have got the MPs fighting with one another, emailing one provoking question to a Liberal and then emailing an equally provoking question to a Conservative. But that wasn't my way. It got me wondering just how many lobbyists actually run government meetings from afar. I bet it happens with some regularity. Think of this the next time you watch CPAC and see an MP glance down at his or her mobile device.

Ottawa's annual Firemen's Ball was held at the Delta Hotel that year. Every politician and his or her brother seemed to be there. Andrew Telegdi knew the room would be full of all kinds of political big shots, so he'd asked if I'd like to accompany him. Outside, I came face to face with Monte Solberg, who intimated that, if he hadn't been replaced as citizenship minister, he'd have resolved our issue. I got the impression he blamed me for his ministerial demise.

Inside, I met many MPs, including senior cabinet minister Vic Toews, who just happened to be a Mennonite born in Paraguay. Like Mexico's Mennonites, Paraguay's were at risk in Canada. I brought up Marlene Jennings's case, saying that he could be like her, having his citizenship questioned. I later heard through the grapevine that he didn't take what I said lightly. Yet, I never heard him voice an opinion on Lost Canadians and our issue, not even once. As for Marlene Jennings, I suspect CIC recognized her citizenship because not doing so would have blown our issue wide open. Even the tight-lipped Canadian media would have to cover a scandal as big as a sitting member, and a Privy Council member at that, who was not a citizen of Canada. Had she been booted out, the media would have been all over it, and the question raised, could a Privy Council member actually be a Lost Canadian and thus not a Canadian at all?

CIC was good at granting special favours, recognizing certain individuals while denying others in exactly the same circumstances. Again, Marlene did not ask for special favours. She was willing to go with the hand that CIC dealt her. Dr. Barry Edmonston was like me, a minor child whose father took out US citizenship. Barry lost his Canadian status. Yet, in 2002, CIC sent him a Certificate of Canadian Citizenship. Why to Barry and not me, or to the other 85,000? My guess is that he was a bit of a CIC insider, and it would be embarrassing to the bureaucrats if they were to get rid of someone even they had considered to be Canadian. That was the beauty of doing things on a case-by-case basis. CIC could do as it pleased, without much accountability. To be blunt, it was free to discriminate up the yin-yang and no one would be the wiser. It was a disastrous recipe for the likes of Magali Castro-Gyr or, for that matter, all Canadians. Charter rights—equal rights— are at the core of our identity. To discriminate so blatantly against one group set a terrible precedent. It really meant that all Canadians' rights were at stake, and it cheapened citizenship for everyone.

Also at the Firemen's Ball was Jack Layton. He always talked about people's rights, going so far as wanting to be known as the leader of the party that stood up for the little guy. He sported a perpetual smile, yet he too never once called me, met with me, or personally went to bat for any of us.[11] I might revise the saying "As silent as a lamb" to "As silent as a Layton." Although Bloc MP Meili Faille was one of our champions, her boss, Gilles Duceppe, was as talkative as Layton was on our issue. He also never spoke out publicly, despite his father being a British home child. Home kids too would find it next to impossible to provide the proper credentials needed to satisfy CIC's insatiable appetite for documents.[12]

After the summer recess, things picked back up in the fall, but not with the same gusto as before. Earlier in the year, I did have my phone meeting with Diane Finley and John Weissenberger. It went very well, and I then gave them a copy of the changes in law needed to solve the issue. (What they didn't know was that the person who wrote the material was my CIC insider.) I believe it provided the seeds for change. Finley had made it clear that, for any legislation to go forward, it needed to have the unanimous support of the committee.

As I had come to expect, the Canadian media went back to covering Hollywood starlets and stories du jour—meaty issues like ours didn't command their attention (and especially when they couldn't be told in 600 words or less or, in the case of television, in just a minute or two). On November 2, the Federal Court of Appeal in Vancouver issued its ruling regarding Joe Taylor.[13] It agreed with the lower court that Joe had been a citizen of Canada but then went further, saying that because he hadn't been domiciled in Canada on his twenty-fourth birthday, he had subsequently lost his citizenship. Immediately, Finley stepped in, offering Joe citizenship through a section 5.4 grant. But that wouldn't go into effect for another couple of months. We had the right to appeal to the Supreme Court. But without the help of the Court Challenges Program, taking a case to the high court could easily cost us over $100,000. For the government, its "tens of billions of dollars" gamble worked, at least for now. In the coming years, it was to be tested further.

This chapter opened with the tragic story of John Erison, the son of a Canadian private and a British sergeant. John died waiting for Bill C-37 to be ratified, but his wife, Dawn, was still eager to return to Canada to bury her husband in his homeland. She writes:

> Don Chapman contacted me and began asking if I intended to return to Canada. I told him I would if I could. Don spoke to someone in CIC Ottawa and I was instructed to phone him (his name was Blair Fraser), which I did. I was then told I was not John's wife (long pause—for effect) but his widow (another long pause for effect) and therefore I could not return to Canada, as John, who would have been Canadian by the following April 17th, was dead (another longer pause for effect), so I was no longer able to return. John had been dead for only a few days and the funeral had not taken place—but I knew John had to be buried in his beloved Canada. This was not the time to mention this ... I phoned Don Chapman back and he said "Leave it with me," and within 25 minutes he had phoned me back and instructed me to phone another number and ask to speak to Ruth Wiseman. She was actually most helpful (as she clearly had been instructed to be), it felt like all her help was "through gritted teeth," but she did help, and was thorough and guided me through the process for me to return to Canada which I did on the 18th of October, 2008. I was given a Temporary Residence Permit [T.R.P.] for two years. Ruth Wiseman instructed me to apply for Permanent Residence after the New Year of 2009, which I did. It was refused in 2010: I was told I had applied too soon! I have since renewed my T.R.P. by October 2010, for 1 year as my UK passport was due to expire this year and there is a time limit about how soon it can be applied for in advance. I applied for my renewal of my (hoped for) current

T.R.P. from the 18th of October, 2011. I still await this from Vancouver. I also applied for my permanent Residence this last summer too. There is a 20 month wait the last I heard.

Remember, John had been a Canadian citizen. I did get Dawn into Canada, where she buried her husband in the family cemetery.[14] I then turned my attention back to the many other Lost Canadians. With Christmas 2007 fast approaching, citizenship to them was still just a disjointed dream. As best I could, I was trying to make it a reality.

On December 6, the Citizenship Committee issued its official findings. The all-party unanimous recommendation was that we should all be Canadians. It issued a statement that war-bride children, regardless of being born in or out of wedlock, or being born before or after 1947, should all be recognized.[15]

On December 10, 2007, Diane Finley once again sat before the Citizenship Committee, announcing a new government bill just for the Lost Canadians, Bill C-37. It would, she said, fix 95 percent of all the problems. It was a godsend; there was light at the end of our tunnel. What a coincidence: December 10 just happened to be Human Rights Day, which just so happened to be the sixtieth anniversary of the United Nations Universal Declaration of Human Rights, which just so happened to be authored by Canadian human rights advocate John Peters Humphrey.

Or maybe it wasn't a coincidence at all.

CHAPTER 15

THE RIGHT THING TO DO
FOR THE RIGHT REASONS

The scene: Just before the infamous Selma,
Alabama, civil rights march in 1965:
*"We've waited a long time for this to happen in Selma. Our people
have been through sit-ins at lunch counters and had to force themselves
to the front of the bus. This is the most important step."*
"Mrs. West, if I may, how have you been able to keep the faith all this time?"
"It was that or giving up. Giving up is easier, but it doesn't feel as good."
FROM THE FILM *SELMA, LORD, SELMA*

THERE WAS ALWAYS a direct correlation between news coverage and the plight of the Lost Canadians. More published news meant more folks got their citizenship. I spent the better part of my 2007 Christmas holidays preparing Joe Taylor for his citizenship ceremony. For whatever reason, Joe had commanded decent news coverage, and I wanted to keep surfing it, like the crest of a wave, for as long as possible. In a sense, his ceremony would slingshot our issue forward in the parliamentary legislative process, and hopefully keep the earlier springtime momentum going.

As the ball fell in Times Square and couples kissed and shouted "Happy New Year!" the Lost Canadians, for the first time ever, had real hope that it might indeed be a happy year.

The House of Commons wasn't scheduled to sit until January 28. Joe's ceremony was on the twenty-fourth.[1] I arranged for all kinds of people and groups to be there; even Diane Finley wanted to attend. As a last-minute substitution, she sent her parliamentary secretary, Ed Komarnicki. Meili Faille of the Bloc was there; so too was Andrew Telegdi of the Liberals. The only federal party not represented was Jack Layton's NDP. Several of the Chinese World War II vets attended—they knew only too well the feeling of being treated as non-citizens. The ones who survived the war were recognized with full Canadian status. (The catch was that they had to survive. Pay the ultimate price and die fighting for Canada, and they'd go to their graves as non-Canadians.)*

Also in attendance was Chief Kim Recalma-Clutesi of the Qualicum First Nation. Roy Miki, an Order of Canada recipient for his part in obtaining redress for Japanese Canadians interned during World War II, was there.[2] In addition, there was Howe Lee of the Vancouver Chinese community. Flying out from Fredericton was Melynda Jarratt, Canadian war-bride historian. After Bill S-2, she became my partner, advocating and helping almost on a daily basis (now, there's somebody else who deserves the Order of Canada). Eswyn Lyster, British war bride and author of *Most Excellent Citizens*, came in from Vancouver Island, while Scottish war bride Zoe Boone, president of the New Brunswick War Brides Association, came along, wanting to witness the historic moment.[3]

Jackie Scott also attended. Her situation was just like Joe's, born out of wedlock to a war bride. How ironic that Joe was being recognized whereas Jackie got denied. The hypocrisy was incredible—the head bureaucrat for Case Management was a guy named Stéphane Larue, who, at the time, had the title of director general, Case Management Branch, Citizenship and Immigration Canada. How in the world he could justify accepting Joe while turning his back on Jackie was beyond me. Larue had flown in from Ottawa (at taxpayers' expense) and, when he met Jackie, she explained her story to him in person. He indicated his support for her, yet, when he returned to Ottawa, where he didn't have to look Jackie in the eye, he sent her a rejection letter. What audacity. The wording was typical: "The legislation that was in place at the time of your birth stated that British Subject status could only be derived through the father, if born in wedlock." By doing it that way, Larue didn't have to witness up close and personal the upset and devastation his letter caused. By being a good CIC manager, by doing his job well, he actually stood to gain a promotion and corresponding pay raise. It didn't

---

* By non-Canadians, I mean not Canadian citizens, because that's what the government is now saying.

matter that by his forcing an issue to court, it might cost the Canadian tax-payers millions, or even "billions."

As always, Daphne Bramham of the *Vancouver Sun* was there; so was CBC. I had asked for one particular citizenship judge to preside, Sandra Wilking. Over the years I've been to a lot of ceremonies and, no question, Sandra was the best. Everything about the day went very well. Chief Recalma-Clutesi made Joe an honorary orca whale, considered by her people a significant honour. I left the ceremony hoping it indicated our home stretch to the finish line. We had indeed begun the new year on a high note.

Regardless of how smooth a flight appears to be, the pilot always has backup plans, and always keeps in mind alternate airports at which to land in the event of an unforeseen emergency. One just never knows. That's how I approached Ottawa: swinging on a star but prepared to bounce off the atmosphere. At any given time, on a moment's notice, the government could be defeated. When that happens, all legislation still on the table gets wiped off. Election fever was like a constant thick blanket of smog over a city, and I wondered, if the government did get defeated, would the Conservatives pick up the Lost Canadian pieces if they emerged victorious? What if the Liberals won? They had vehemently opposed us until now. I wasn't interested in Ottawa's political jockeying; my time was spent dealing with the many people who, like Guy Valliere, were elderly, with not much time left to regain citizenship. Going to an election was the one thing I could do nothing about. But just in case we did, I turned to academia.

In a sense, students resemble a swarm of bees. If they're focused, they keep stinging. That's what it was like years earlier when the now Speaker of the Senate, Nöel Kinsella, taught at St. Thomas University in Fredericton. By engaging his students, he could much more easily facilitate change—his specialty being human rights. Taking this lesson to heart, I knew that I needed to get students on board. After years of failing to spark their interest (several times I'd been a guest speaker at individual classes),* I began to solicit an entire university. Trying to woo universities by appealing to morals didn't always succeed, so I donated money, hoping that by doing it this way, they'd at least be forced to listen. My work in Ottawa was so intertwined with their courses—women's rights, social justice, political science, human rights, equal rights, law—the list went on and on. Occasionally,

---

* The students at Cape Breton University's Children's Rights Centre being the exception; they began a letter-writing campaign after my visit there in 2006.

a professor showed interest, but not the university as a whole. The most responsive academic institution was, amazingly, in the States. Kudos to the University of Washington in Seattle. On the north side of the border, Simon Fraser University (SFU) deserves accolades, though its involvement lasted but a short time.

My first contact at SFU was Cathy Daminato, vice-president of Advancement and Alumni Engagement. She introduced me to a couple of professors, and then to the university's president, Dr. Michael Stevenson. Before Harper, all the parties had agreed to rewrite the Citizenship Act. Frankly, it's essential to Canada's future. But the Conservatives had cut the already allotted funding. I figured that by getting a university on board, just maybe its student bees would buzz long enough to force the government to revisit the issue. My family sponsored a three-day workshop at SFU's Centre for Dialogue, at which students, academics, and experts from all over Canada gathered to discuss "Being Canadian: The Fine Balance of Citizenship and Identity." In the end, it yielded no fruit, as Harper didn't budge and the students talked mostly about immigration. Canadians don't seem to understand the difference. Regardless, seeds had been planted. My hope was that one day they would grow and bear fruit.

At best, citizenship laws remain a confusing mess. After more than thirty years and all kinds of amendments and countless court decisions, each having its effect in law, even the supposed experts inside CIC were challenged when deciding who was or was not a citizen. Canada desperately needed a well-thought-out, polished, brand-new citizenship act, not just a patchy quilt hastily stitched together in the bureaucratic backrooms guided by the politicians du jour.

I explained in Chapter 6 the long path a bill takes before being passed—from first, second, and third readings in the House, plus committee hearings, to the same process of readings and hearings in the Senate. Only when debated and passed in both the House of Commons and Senate can the bill be signed into law. Usually, the governor general does the signing, but, in his or her absence, a designee—typically a high-ranking judge—affixes his or her signature on the last page, and, poof, the bill is law. Anywhere in the process the government could table it, which is code for putting it on a backroom shelf to collect dust. It's a backhanded way of blocking it from a vote. And let's say the bill gets all the way through the House of Commons and the Senate but has not yet been signed by the governor general (maybe the bill is in transit on its way to him or her). If the government falls, so does the bill. No joke, s-2 really was that close to going down. We were concerned that the Liberals would hold on to s-2 until after a confidence vote.

So, getting a bill through the House and Senate can take a long time, often much longer than a current government can stay in power. Harper being Harper, he wasn't by any stretch of the imagination thinking about Lost Canadians, so if it were more advantageous for him to dissolve Parliament or force a vote of non-confidence, he'd do it. Also, Diane Finley made it clear that she wanted *unanimous* support. It reminded me of another line from the movie *My Cousin Vinny*: "Is there any more shit we can pile onto the top of the outcome of this case? Is it possible?" After all my years in Ottawa, I got to be very good at the political game, and since those were the cards I was being dealt, those were the ones I played. There were no alternatives.

Andrew Telegdi, with his legislative assistants Rachelle Cyr-Kelderman and Reevin Vinetsky, got me an ID badge that gave me unlimited access to the Hill. It was worth its weight in gold. Free to wander, I could meet MPs on their turf (in their offices, or maybe in the cafeteria). I could even show up for committee meetings. Andrew, exactly like me, was focused and forever plotting and planning. We shared the same goal, and together we were like two GPS-guided missiles aiming smack dab at the final target: royal assent of Bill C-37. It was almost as though I had become an unofficial MP, complete with a side-room workplace in Andrew's office. When Parliament reconvened on January 28, I kicked into high gear.

On the Conservative side, my main contact was Ed Komarnicki. With Joe Taylor's battle behind us—his destiny now sealed with his Certificate of Canadian Citizenship—Ed admitted that the government's court case against Taylor had been a mistake. I wondered how his party could have been so blind. Let's say that, just before takeoff of a flight and right in the flight path, a mile from the runway, is a Level 5 thunderstorm, the most severe possible. The tower is reporting high-level wind shear. Any pilot deciding to "go for it" is inviting disaster. Yet that is how the government faced the Taylor case.

It was now over for Joe. Regrettably, because he got his citizenship by way of a 5.4 grant, there hadn't been much precedent set in law, so CIC was able to carry on denying others like Joe, which it was doing on an ongoing basis. Hopefully, C-37 would fix that. Hopefully.

Before our nirvana, it had to make its way through the legislative process, beginning with first reading in the House of Commons. As we were all quite aware, almost anything could go wrong. Would our former arch-enemies, the Liberals, once again battle for our defeat? I didn't think so, but regardless, I worked both sides of the House.

A common problem when dealing with politicians is that they are constantly being reassigned portfolios. As the hearings began, two key MPs were replaced. NDP Bill Siksay was out, Olivia Chow (Jack Layton's wife) was in. Adios Meili Faille of the Bloc, howdy-do Thierry St-Cyr.

Finally on the home stretch with a Lost Canadian bill—it being years and years in the making—and rounding third base for home plate, two parties change their citizenship critics, replacing them with novices. That's like having two experienced pilots fly the plane from London to Toronto, then for landing hand the controls to a couple of student pilots. Or you, the reader, starting this book right here in Chapter 15, then immediately being asked to vote on the legislation. You really wouldn't have any perspective, let alone a gut feeling. You were absent during all the testimony. You never heard one of the witnesses, nor could you relate to their heartfelt stories. If someone had mentioned to Ms. Chow or Mr. St-Cyr the story of a disenfranchised old World War II veteran named Guy Valliere, they probably would have asked, "Who's that?"

I once asked Rachelle Cyr-Kelderman, Andrew Telegdi's legislative assistant, how she would describe a typical MP. "Kind of like a high-school loner who just wanted an audience," came the reply. "In Ottawa, they feel important." Yes, but they really were important. They had the power to shape a country and its people, telling them just who had the right to belong and who didn't. They made all the rules and the laws.

I'd never want unqualified novices flying my plane. But this wasn't aviation, it was bureaucratic Ottawa.

One further question remained: Why would the political forces within the parties keep changing their knowledgeable committee members, particularly when we were down to the final seconds? Except for two distinct years when the four parties each had wonderful, compassionate, smart MPs on the committee, citizenship seemed to be a common starting point for freshly minted politicians cutting their teeth.*

In the moment, none of this mattered. As I said, I had no choice but to play the hand dealt, and Diane Finley wanted every vote to be unanimous.

---

* During those two years, even the MPs called it a "dream committee" when Andrew Telegdi (Liberal), Diane Ablonczy (Conservative), Bill Siksay (NDP), and Meili Faille (Bloc) worked together. It was a pleasure being able to work with them.

In Ottawa, can anyone ensure that, let alone with a Harper-led government? But that was my task, and it was imperative I get it done, despite partisanship seemingly at an all-time high. Inside, I testified again before the committee. Outside, the political winds were blowing, and if the parties thought they could get away with it, together they'd huff and puff, attempting to blow Harper's House down. And, along with it, Bill c-37.

To my astonishment, the bill went through second reading in Parliament at Mach 3 speed, with only one amendment. A revision was added because of the Lebanon crisis, one of the first international incidents on Stephen Harper's watch: in July 2006, war broke out in Lebanon between Hezbollah and Israel. According to CBC, upward of 50,000 Lebanese-Canadians were in the country, half having dual citizenship and living there permanently.[4] As CTV later reported, about 14,000 were evacuated at a cost to the Canadian taxpayers of around $85 million. That's not chump change, and not only did it rile Canadians living in Canada and MPs like Garth Turner (who immediately called for changes to the Citizenship Act), but the questions of dual citizenship, obligations of the state to the individual, and, in turn, the obligations of citizens to the state became hot topics across Canada.[5] The Conservatives' response was the amendment. Otherwise, c-37 was purely a Lost Canadian bill.

The change had to do with second-generation born-abroad children, which was to say that babies born after c-37 became law, if they were born outside Canada to parents who had also been born outside Canada, would not qualify for Canadian citizenship. It was the Conservative answer to solving possible future Lebanese situations. Unfortunately, the way it was written (either haphazardly or deliberately) meant future chaos with a brand-new generation of potential Lost Canadians. I called Ed Komarnicki in February asking to have the amendment taken out. Ed gave me an ultimatum: accept the bill as is or forget it, there would be no c-37.* With the fate of hundreds of thousands of people lying in the balance, I reluctantly agreed to accept it as it was, believing that down the road we could work to correct the flaws. John Erison's death remained fresh in my mind, and I wasn't about to play Russian roulette with the other Lost Canadians still out there.

The one problem remaining was Finley's request for unanimity: in Harperville, MPs went for the jugular. The only unanimity was that of

---

* In fairness to Ed, he did check with his top people—probably meaning Diane Finley or Stephen Harper—and they in turn said the second-generation clause would not be taken out. He did try to appease us. If you're not the lead dog, the view never changes. Ed was not the lead dog.

parliamentarians wanting their party to be a majority. Almost nothing else mattered—certainly not the hundreds of thousands of disenfranchised Canadians.

In the legislative obstacle course, one unmistakable hurdle was MP Jim Karygiannis. A naturalized Canadian from Greece, he was a clear threat to unanimity. Jim was another of my staunch supporters, but he hated the second-generation born-abroad clause. Greece is one of those countries that doesn't confer citizenship merely by birth on soil (*jus soli*), and the potential was there to render children of Canadian parents stateless. Jim was thinking about the ramifications for his future grandchildren, and rightly so. Further, the September 2007 UN magazine *Refugees* article highlighted Canada as an offending country for making its own people stateless.[6] Hard to believe, but Canada's partners in crime—the other featured deviant countries—were Cambodia, Bangladesh, and Zimbabwe. Had those countries instead been Canadian teenagers, I sure wouldn't have wanted my daughters hanging around with them, learning their street lessons on human rights. Canada, on the other hand, didn't seem bothered. I think only Peter Mansbridge of *The National* reported it, and that was thanks to Gary Symons. Hopefully, the Conservative amendment would take the UN's journalistic scolding of Canada to an elevated level.

It was clear that Jim Karygiannis wasn't going to sacrifice his principles, so putting C-37 to a vote in committee could have spelled its demise. It wouldn't pass Finley's litmus test of unanimity. Once again, Andrew was our saviour. Andrew arranged for the committee to vote on a day Jim was out of town. It was done. *Finis.* Now it was on to the third and final reading. Our collective fate was going before all 308 members. How in the world were we going to get them to vote all as one?

We could only hope that the government stayed together. To say that Jim was displeased with the second-generation born-abroad clause being passed in his absence would be an understatement. In fact, for a while, we wondered if he'd try to kill the bill altogether. Out of respect for the thousands it affected, he bit his tongue, and I was able to sleep more restfully.

From there, the bill went like greased lightning. The first reading was just before the Christmas break, when it was announced by Minister Finley on December 10, 2007, which, as I mentioned, also happened to be Human Rights Day. It wasn't a coincidence. When Parliament returned on January 28, the bill went to second reading ten days later. Eight days after that, it passed third reading, which meant that if the Senate didn't add any of its own amendments, our business with the House had concluded. It was a testament to the fact that when the government wants it, legislation really can be accomplished "with the stroke of a pen."

Immediately, I was in contact with Diane Finley's chief of staff, John Weissenberger. At the time, the Senate had a Liberal majority, so for me to get our bill into that side of Parliament, I needed a Liberal senator as co-sponsor. Not knowing if the government would hold, I had to work like an IndyCar driver. A Conservative, Weissenberger was helpless to suggest a Liberal. So Liberal Andrew Telegdi made a few phone calls. Within ten minutes of hanging up with Weissenberger, I called him back, reporting that I had my senator: Lorna Milne. I was even helping to write her speech. The speed with which it happened, my being able to jump from one party to the other with ease, left Weissenberger both amazed and impressed.

Eleven days later, the laborious process of readings and committee hearings was to begin all over again, but this time it was at the first reading in the Senate. Having twice been down the Senate-brick road with other bills, I felt cautiously optimistic. On March 4, C-37 went to second reading, with Senator Wilbert Keon (Conservative) and Senator Lorna Milne (Liberal) making speeches. A few highlights:

Senator Keon:

> Honourable senators, these heartbreaking stories have captured everyone's attention. They are the so-called "lost Canadians," people who ceased being citizens of this great country because of outdated provisions in former legislation ... I thank the witnesses who came before the House of Commons standing committee for telling their stories and for contributing to this historic moment. It took great courage and stamina to do what they did and they deserve our applause ... I remind honourable senators that countless lost Canadians are counting on us to pass Bill C-37. This legislation is long overdue.[7]

He also made this statement, which had great significance in the subsequent years:

> I will be candid and say that as much as this bill will accomplish for Canada and for Canadians, there may yet exist a small number of cases that fall outside its parameters. I am sure all of this will come to light during discussions at committee; but that is why subsection 5(4) of the Citizenship

Act exists and will continue to exist, so that the minister can make a recommendation to the Governor-in-Council that a grant of citizenship be
made where it is warranted.

Senator Lorna Milne spoke next (Lorna admitted to me that her mother
had had her citizenship questioned when her father was mayor of Toronto):

Three years ago, my colleague Senator Cook stood before you and said:
Honourable senators, we have an extraordinary opportunity to right a
wrong and to give meaningful consideration to those individuals who have
been disadvantaged by the operation of the 1947 Citizenship Act...
    It is estimated there could be as many as 250,000 people directly
affected with loss of citizenship...
    In the September 2007 issue of the United Nations *Refugees Magazine*,
Canada was highlighted as an offending country with regard to statelessness with the words: "A few slip-ups in the framing of citizenship law can
have extraordinary repercussions"...
    It must be noted that Bill C-37 is not the long-term answer. In that
regard, only a new and complete Citizenship Act rewrite will suffice. The
problem with a completely new Citizenship Act for the lost Canadians is
that it will take too long for most of them. They are getting older, and many
would not live to see their birthright restored.
    The issue of future generations, who belongs and what is a Canadian,
is for the next rewrite, which I urge should commence as soon as this bill
becomes law. Until then, the solution is Bill C-37.
    To summarize, no longer should women and children be considered as
chattels of a man. We are too great a country to allow this approach to continue. It is now time to show fairness, compassion and regard for human
rights in our citizenship laws.
    Article 7 and 8 of the UN Convention on the Rights of the Child, which
Canada ratified, clearly state:
    You have the right to a nationality (to belong to a country), and you
have the right to an identity.

With that, the bill was forwarded to committee for further study, and,
for the first time in years, I actually had thirteen days in a row off. I flew to
Vancouver for some much-needed downtime on the Sunshine Coast. Taking public transportation from the Vancouver airport to Horseshoe Bay, you
make a transfer downtown. While there, my curiosity got the better of me

and, like I had done so many other times, I walked into the CTV building (this time with suitcases in hand), went up the escalator, and strode over to the reception desk. Within weeks, almost certainly Canadian citizenship law would change, and every Canadian on the planet would in some way be affected. By now I had a track record in Parliament, which, for even a beginning investigative journalist, is easily traceable. I explained to the receptionist how the rights of Canadians would soon be diminished (the second-generation born-abroad clause); like a broken record, the reply came. "If the newsroom is interested, they'll get back to you." Frustrated, I left to catch my bus. For the next several days, I called just about every media outlet in Canada pitching the story—CTV, *Global National*, CBC's *The National*, Canadian Press, *Globe and Mail*, *National Post*, *Maclean's*, CKNW radio. Not one person showed any interest, except, of course, Gary Symons and Susanne Reber at CBC. I couldn't imagine the US legislating citizen rights away without one journalist caring (or, as in this case, only two). The Americans would be outraged. But I wasn't in the States; this was Canada, where citizenship rights—equality of rights—weren't worthy of discussion.

On April 10, I was back in Ottawa to testify. Accompanying me was local Gibsons reporter Cathy Roy. Except for one hitch, it appeared to be clear sailing. The snag came in the form of a woman named Janet Dench, executive director of the Canadian Council for Refugees. Janet was asking the senators to take out the second-generation born-abroad clause. Although I agreed with her position in principle, I knew that C-37 was a go with the amendment and would be DOA without it. Finley's people had made this clear. Why had Dench come forward now, only after the many years it had taken for me to get to the finish line? Why had she never contacted me before? I sensed that her passion wasn't so much for the older Canadians as it was for the younger ones. Not once before or after C-37 has Dench contacted me, yet I've tried to contact her. Frankly, I don't believe she understood that, by arguing successfully, she would have killed our bill and the corresponding last chance for people like Guy Valliere and Bill Doobenen.

Bill was born and raised in Saskatchewan. He attended high school in Kamsack and graduated from the University of Saskatchewan, receiving a Bachelor of Science in engineering physics with distinction in 1959. He joined the Royal Canadian Air Force, becoming a flying officer holding the Queen's Commission. Honourably discharged in 1963, he remained in the Air Reserve, subject to recall in the event of serious national emergency, for the rest of his life. For the next three years he designed sonar and fire-control systems for the Royal Canadian Navy. With his specialized talents, Bill became an integral part of the national defence of North America during the Cold War, which took him to the States. Working on highly classified projects, for security reasons he was required to take out US citizenship. He was quite unaware that by doing so he'd lose his Canadian citizenship.

Bill's story was typical, especially after John Diefenbaker cancelled the Avro Arrow program. A bevy of Canada's best engineers and PhDs went south searching for employment. Lost Canadian engineers, particularly McGill graduates, abounded. NASA, Boeing, McDonnell Douglas, and Hughes were just a few of the beneficiaries of our Canadian talent.

After retirement in 2006, Bill and his wife, Denise, decided to leave California and return to Canada. At the border, to his shock and dismay, he was informed that he was no longer Canadian. Imagine, Bill served in the Canadian military and was still in the Royal Canadian Air Force reserve, which had the power to recall him in a national emergency and require him to serve, and yet CIC is telling him to get lost. That was in November 2007. He responded by doing exactly what I would have done: he claimed refugee status.

In April, just as C-37 was about to become law and welcome people just like Bill back into the Canadian family, his case surfaced before the Refugee Board—which seems to allow all kinds of shady characters to stay in Canada—and instead of approving Bill, it issued an immediate deportation order. That was Bill's dilemma just as Janet Dench testified before the Senate committee. You just can't make this stuff up.

And now, the fate of C-37 was in the hands of the chairman of a Senate committee who got to decide whether to give the bill a thumbs-up or a thumbs-down. Senator Art Eggleton, ironically, had voted against the Lost Canadians years earlier while serving in the House as a Liberal MP. Fortunately, he'd changed his mind. His committee's recommendation was unanimous. Straightaway it headed to the Senate floor, where again it passed unanimously. I felt as though I'd gone to the Land of Oz and back with the witch's broom, hand-delivering it to Diane Finley, the wizard of CIC. The impossible in Ottawa had become possible. We had done it. All that remained now was for the governor general or her designated appointee to sign it into law.

On April 17, 2008, for the second time in my life, I sat in the upper gallery above the Senate floor, along with my wife, in the seats reserved for the governor general or other exceptionally distinguished visitors. These seats are almost always vacant, so when someone is actually sitting in them, every senator notices. Waiting for the proceedings to begin, I admired Lord Beaverbrook's paintings depicting Canadian battles from long ago hung on the walls. Finally, it was read into the official record that C-37 had received royal assent. Hundreds of thousands of Canadians would once again be recognized. Another battle, another story for the history books.

I thought of William Wilberforce, a British MP who, almost by himself, championed the end of the British slave trade. As his long struggle through Parliament commenced, he was ridiculed and alone. But after more than a decade of hard work and persistence, he had turned the majority of MPs around. His story is portrayed in the 2006 movie *Amazing Grace*, in which there's an emotional scene just after the Speaker declares Wilberforce's bill passed. At long last, he allows his emotions to flow. I related.

But all was not over. My attention immediately turned toward the 5 percent left behind.

Remember Conservative Senator Keon's words, "There may yet exist a small number of cases that fall outside its parameters. I am sure all of this will come to light during discussions at committee; but that is why subsection 5(4) of the Citizenship Act exists and will continue to exist, so that the minister can make a recommendation to the Governor-in-Council that a grant of citizenship be made where it is warranted"?[8]

To those words, Diane Finley later added, "If individuals qualify under the new legislation, ... they could apply for the section 5(4) and not wait until the legislation comes into force ... We do not want to hold people up because the law has not yet come into force when we anticipate that it will and it is the right thing to do for the right reasons."[9]

While the getting was still good, I needed to present to Finley a few cases that fit the above description. First, however, there were some formalities to attend to. Minister Finley wanted a photo-op, so together we held a quick press conference in Centre Block. Emerging from the Conservative lobby, we walked straight into a media frenzy. Diane made a quick statement, then it was my turn. My wife stood by my side. What had just happened in law was earth-shaking. For the first time in Canadian history, women achieved equal rights in citizenship law (going forward, anyway; going backward, the discrimination problems remained). The government had finally admitted that affected were hundreds of thousands—a far cry from the number of 450 bandied about just months earlier. In the US, the *Wall Street Journal* reported the events. So did ABC News, Fox News, Bloomberg, and MSNBC. In Canada, where people were genuinely affected by the law, they hardly made the news.

It seems the Ottawa reporters were in a frenzy because of something going on in Mexico to one lone Canadian by the name of Brenda Martin. Our issue had been swept off the media floor. Our thirty seconds of fame lasted maybe all of twenty. You couldn't turn on the television or radio or read a newspaper that day without learning about Brenda Martin. "Guy Valliere" and "Margot MacKenzie" and "Lucy Proulx" might just as well have been names written in Swahili.*

Canadian citizen Brenda Martin left Canada for Mexico in 1998. Her employer was a man named Alyn Waage, who, supposedly unbeknownst to Brenda, was involved in an Internet pyramid scheme, defrauding 28,000 investors from fifty-nine countries out of US$90 million.[10] In 2006, Mexican officials arrested Martin, saying she had shared in some of the dirty money. As Bill C-37 made its final run through Parliament, Brenda sat in a Mexican jail. She'd been put on suicide watch while awaiting the judge's ruling. Canadians were glued to her story, and politician after politician went public with their views. In March, MP Bill Casey from Nova Scotia wrote a letter to the Mexican ambassador, Emilio Rafael José Goicoechea Luna, first requesting that Martin be released, then suggesting Canadians would not want to travel to Mexico if she wasn't.[11]

On March 12, the jailed Martin had a visitor also named Martin, but this one was a former prime minister of Canada, Paul Martin Jr.; who apparently had decided to use his international statesman's status to win her release. The next day's edition of the *Toronto Star* (which, during this same time, didn't cover much regarding the Lost Canadians) quoted one of Brenda's friends, who said, "He (Paul Martin) was the nicest man. He was so kind to her. He hugged her."[12]

On April 22, Mexican judge Luis Nuñez announced that Martin was guilty, sentencing her to a minimum of five years in prison, and fining her what amounted to $3,441. The judge said that she'd been part of the scam. Harper's response? He sent the minister of multiculturalism, Jason Kenney, to Guadalajara to negotiate her release, and, in doing so, the government of Canada paid her fine. The media coverage had provoked the politicians into action and, in the end, it worked. To the delight of most Canadians, Brenda returned to Canada in a chartered jet paid for by the federal government. Who was CBC's reporter for all of this? Paul Hunter, the same reporter who'd been so insensitive to the Lost Canadians with his coverage of the sixtieth anniversary of the Canadian citizenship act.[13] And the cost to

---

* Margot MacKenzie and Lucy Proulx are Lost Canadians whom I'll introduce later.

Canadian taxpayers of the private jet? Just under $83,000.[14] On her return, Brenda was immediately escorted to a taxpayer-subsidized Canadian jail. Released soon thereafter, she's since been a frequent guest of the Canadian penal system, again at great public expense.[15]

Now compare this to the story of a Lost Canadian who lived in Spokane, Washington. Her name is Margot MacKenzie. Just two weeks before royal assent of Bill C-37, she sent me this email:

> Three years ago whilst living in the United States, I was diagnosed with end stage renal failure. In order to have Social Security paid out to me, I learned that I must be a legal resident of the United States. I have lived here since age twenty-five when I gave birth to my daughter. I had worked here for thirty-five years, paid taxes and Social Security, and travelled back and forth across the Canadian border to visit family and friends. So I began the process of getting a legal residency here without giving up my dual Canadian/British citizenship.
>
> Wonder of wonders, apparently someone decided I was not entitled to Canadian citizenship although my father was Canadian with a Canadian veteran's pension until he passed away in the '90s. I lived in Canada since 1946 until I was almost 25, always in Ontario. I also cannot obtain legal residency in the US since I had no legal rights to live in Canada which made my entry to the US illegal!!!!!!! Talk about a rock and a hard place. I have a sister who lives in California since she was eighteen. She is Canadian because she was born there but I am a whole different kettle of fish because I went to Canada at the age of two with my mother who was a war bride who became a Canadian and died a Canadian. I cannot even go home and die! Now what? It is an incredible thought that I am not Canadian, a real shocker. I have always thought myself to be Canadian. In my sixty-five years, I lived in England a total of three years and in Canada, twenty-four years, but am apparently British.

When entering the US forty years earlier, Margot declared herself to be Canadian. And now with Canada saying she wasn't—never had been—it meant that she had obtained her US green card under false pretenses or, better stated, fraudulently. Therefore, the US could refuse to pay for her kidney dialysis, and take her name off the national kidney-transplant list. Cutting to the chase, Canada's refusing Margot's citizenship really could end up being a death sentence for her. Brenda Martin received national news coverage for being on a suicide watch in a foreign jail. Margot too was in a foreign country, but unlike Martin, she had (as I knew from my dealings with her) an outstanding character. And her dilemma wasn't of her own doing. But that didn't matter. Former prime minister Paul Martin certainly didn't fly to Spokane to give Margot a hug. He didn't use his statesman's status to help her get kidney dialysis. In fact, he never once opened his mouth about her. Same thing with Stephen Harper. Margot's situation was desperate and, to me, represented the perfect candidate for Diane Finley's "We do not want to hold people up because the law has not yet come into force. [Granting a section 5.4] is the right thing to do for the right reasons." Doing so would be incredibly simple, and it would completely correct Margot's problem. Unlike Brenda Martin, it wouldn't cost Canadian taxpayers one single penny, not even in health care dollars, since she was planning on staying in the US.

Keep these two stories in mind.

Two years earlier, just months after Harper first became prime minister, in April 2006, he got blasted from one coast to the other for his decision not to fly the Canadian flag at half-mast over Parliament each time a Canadian soldier died in Afghanistan. Everyone was talking, and Harper didn't like the heat. About the same time, the Historica-Dominion Institute started an online petition asking that a state funeral be given to the last remaining Canadian World War I vet.[16] At the time, four vets were still alive. And did Canadians ever respond. It took just three weeks to gather 90,000 signatures online and, on November 21, 2006, at the urging of the NDP MP Peter Stoffer, the following was read in the House of Commons: "Mr. Speaker, there have been consultations between the parties and I believe you will find unanimous consent for the following motion. I move: That in the opinion of this House, the Government of Canada should honour all who served Canada in the first world war by sponsoring a state funeral on the passing of the last Canadian veteran of this Great War."[17]

Once again, the media, including the *Globe and Mail*, were all over it.[18]

One year earlier, I had met with staunch Conservative and close ally of Stephen Harper former MP John Reynolds, at the Waterfront Restaurant in Gibsons. I said, "If you think the flag not flying at half-mast was a big deal, let me tell you about another impending public relations disaster for Harper."

Of course, that piqued his interest. I went on to explain the Dominion Institute's petition. The problem? By now the last surviving World War I vet was Jack Babcock, who lived in Spokane, Washington, and was 106 years old. He left Canada in the 1920s and officially took out US citizenship in 1946. So, legally, as a non-Canadian, he wasn't entitled to a state funeral.

After C-37 received royal assent on April 17, 2008, CIC and Veterans Affairs went into high gear. Not so much for the Lost Canadians but for Stephen Harper. Why? Because it would be a PR nightmare having Jack Babcock, by now 107, die without being entitled to a state funeral. John Reynolds must have listened intently, then reported to the top brass my words of caution. No time was wasted: Veterans Affairs Minister Greg Thompson was immediately dispatched from Ottawa to Spokane, not far from where Margot MacKenzie lived, with the sole purpose of getting Babcock to agree to become Canadian. Margot wasn't Thompson's concern. In the past, Babcock had been indifferent. On arrival, Thompson presented Babcock with a Veterans Affairs award and, shortly thereafter, Backbock sat down and wrote a mere twelve words to Harper: "Could I have my citizenship restored, I would appreciate it. Jack Babcock."

It was profoundly moving for Mr. Harper.

Instantly, Finley got her bureaucrats working at lightning speed to process the paperwork. It then went to Harper, who straightaway got his cabinet to agree to a 5.4 citizenship grant. With almost the precision and speed of the old Strategic Air Command, Greg Thompson set his next mission: fly to Spokane (at taxpayers' expense), this time accompanied by an official who would immediately administer Mr. Babcock's oath of citizenship. Everyone beamed, especially Stephen Harper. No longer was it his concern that Mr. Babcock could die as a non-citizen, thus forcing him to say to a demanding public wanting a state funeral, "Sorry, folks, no can do." Like icing topping a delicious cake, the prime minister not only avoided a PR disaster but, with help from the Canadian media, who were all over the story (some had accompanied Thompson to Spokane), looked like a compassionate soul, doing what is right for his Canadian people.

CTV's national news ran a video saying that Jack Babcock was "Canadian again."[19] I called to say that the government had told the Lost Canadians that citizenship didn't exist before 1947, so how could Babcock be Canadian "again"? I mentioned Margot MacKenzie, saying she lived just down the street from Mr. Babcock. Why couldn't her citizenship have been reinstated at the same time? I asked CTV to cover that story. It declined.

So why did Harper ignore a dying Canadian, yet very publicly show his acceptance to the last surviving World War I vet? Publicity, pure and simple. Harper would have looked terrible if Babcock died without being Canadian, whereas, image-wise, Margot did nothing for him one way or the other. And for poor Margot, it got worse. The government forced her to wait an entire year before recognizing her citizenship. Out of sight, out of mind. Lastly,

CTV felt that my point about the government claiming Canadian citizenship didn't exist prior to 1947 was just a technicality not worth mentioning. Maybe, but thousands of Canadians had been stripped of their citizenship because of that little technicality. In fact, if citizenship didn't exist before 1947, then every World War I or World War II soldier who died fighting for Canada in those wars was never a Canadian.* But what the heck—it's just a minor technicality.

From royal assent to Babcock's being "Canadian again," it took the government just twenty-one days to take stroke-of-the-pen legislation from theory to fact. I guess if the prime minister wants it badly enough...

Ten days after royal assent, on April 27, *Global National* for the first time ever to my knowledge broadcast a story that at least had a little bit of Lost Canadian content. And I do mean a little. *Global National* was doing a story about a group that had gone to Ottawa with the intent of lobbying Finley, trying to get her to relax the rules for foreign strippers trying to get into Canada. Instead of using relevant footage, it spliced in video of the press conference I did with the minister. If you had watched the *Global National* newscast, you would have seen me standing there, along with my wife, as the reporter talked about foreign strippers. We'd been made to look like their lobbyists. Also pictured was Bill Janzen of the Mennonite Central Committee. I called the *Global National* news people, but they refused to broadcast a correction.

Just two days before royal assent, something else had happened not far away. The RCMP, at the direction of Elections Canada, raided the Conservative Party offices in Ottawa looking for evidence of illegal activity during the 2006 election campaign. One top general was none other than Diane Finley's husband, Doug, who happened to be a close friend of both Stephen Harper and John Reynolds. There were questions as to whether the Conservatives had been involved in what is called "in and out" financing and third-party advertising, the first having to do with transferring campaign dollars between the Tory local ridings and national offices, the second being highly dubious, if not downright illegal. The question was, did the Conservatives illegally overspend, thus gaining an unfair advantage in the 2006 election? And if they did, was it deliberate?

Michael Ignatieff stood in the House of Commons on April 15, 2008, and asked, "How did it get to this? An RCMP squad raiding the offices of the Conservative Party...?"[20]

---

* Again, my reference to "Canadian" here means Canadian citizen.

The Conservative response, as reported in the *Toronto Star*: "A raid by the RCMP on Conservative party headquarters is a 'PR stunt' by Elections Canada intended 'to intimidate' the governing party in a civil court case, the Tory party says. The explosive charge was made in an interview with a senior party official following Prime Minister Stephen Harper's comment in the Commons that 'it is unclear in our mind why exactly Elections Canada is undertaking this action today.'" One party insider said, "Quite frankly they [Elections Canada] can continue to search until their face turns blue," implying it would never find anything. He went further, stating, "Ultimately there will be a court ruling on this, and we are confident that that court ruling will be in our favour."[21]

Fair enough. If anything goes wrong in aviation, hearings commence with the purpose of seeking out the truth. If called to testify, pilots are not at liberty to say no.

But this was Ottawa.

Shortly after the raid, many members of Parliament wanted to cross-examine Doug Finley. After all, he was the Conservative campaign manager during the period in question. Could it be that the only way to make the issue go away—and just possibly a contempt-of-Parliament charge with it— was to call an election? Strange things can and do happen in Ottawa.

For the most part, the issue conveniently disappeared when the House recessed for the summer holidays. I spent my time working to secure as many section 5.4 grants as possible. The problem was that 5.4s must first be approved by the cabinet and the governor in council and, during the summer, the cabinet doesn't get together regularly, and sometimes not at all. This meant that securing a 5.4 citizenship during these months was next to impossible.

Like Jack Babcock, Guy Valliere was also a war vet, not of World War I, but of World War II. Unlike Mr. Babcock, Guy wasn't a last remaining survivor. But healthwise, Guy was in a bad way. I sent him $1,000 for medical expenses. I also teamed up with Madame Francine Lalonde of the Bloc when she issued her press release pleading for the government to recognize his status. Some in the media responded, but not enough to profoundly move Harper into action. I sent an email to CKNW's Bill Good, probably more than anything to see if he'd turn his back on a Canadian World War II soldier. He always had great things to say over the air on Remembrance Day, so I wanted to see if his "Good" words actually translated into "Good" actions. They didn't.

Guy was totally up the creek without a paddle, and losing his voice because of a stroke gave him no way to cry out for help. I called John Weissenberger, who was very helpful. I can't thank him enough for what he did. All Lost Canadians owe him a debt of gratitude. But Weissenberger also had to deal with a not-so-cooperative bureaucracy. On June 11, I sent this email to him:

> I have three people for 5.4s, two of whom are close to dying. Time really is of the essence. One qualifies for citizenship under C-37, the other doesn't (although she's a fourteenth-generation woman from Quebec.) The last person is an eighty-six-year-old Canadian-born World War II vet. For the two women, if they aren't approved before the GIC [governor in council] soon, they most likely won't survive to ever be recognized as citizens. Both have the same dying wish—to be Canadians. The 5.4s would be purely for compassionate grounds.
>
> I gave CIC Lucy Proulx's and Margot MacKenzie's names quite some time ago, but I find out today that Blair Fraser is just now getting to their cases. In talking with him, it was the typical dot all the "i's" and cross all the "t's." Only because of their dire situation, I was hoping that they could be considered next week before the GIC meeting.

Despite Weissenberger's intervention, nothing happened. So the next time we communicated, I became a great deal more forceful. I threatened that if CIC continued to ignore Guy Valliere, he would claim refugee status, which could actually bankrupt Canada.

When a person makes a refugee claim, the government has only two choices: acceptance or denial. If denied, Guy would have been deported to the US. If he was, I said, we'd get every documentary maker I could muster to film his death, showing the world just how heartless Canada could be, dropping an old war veteran on a street corner to die. He wouldn't even have the ability to ask bystanders for help. It didn't take a brain surgeon to figure out how disastrous this could be to Harper's image. For sure, dumping a Canadian vet to die in a foreign country would have made news—in Canada, the US, and around the world.

The other option was acceptance, but it had to be done "with cause." Here was ours: Guy would base his claim on having no medical insurance in the US, so his entry to Canada would be justified on compassionate grounds of life and death (which it was).

At the time, 47 million Americans were without health insurance. Now consider that there are just 35 million Canadians in total. I asked John where Canada was planning to park the FEMA trailers (the supposed temporary housing units for the victims of Hurricane Katrina). Any first-year law student would know that accepting Guy because he had no US medical insurance would set a huge legal precedent, one Canada and Harper didn't want.

Within minutes I had my answer. Guy would be accepted as a permanent resident. It wasn't citizenship, but he could stay, and his medical costs would be covered. Unlike Brenda Martin, Guy didn't require jet transportation, and he didn't go to jail. He lived in Montreal with his daughter Michelle until his death. Imagine that. He got to live in the city and country of his birth, and in the country he defended as a World War II vet. Many people take such things for granted—but not Lost Canadians.

Liberal MP Joyce Murray once asked me what the big deal was when people discover they aren't citizens. I really believe she didn't understand. I'll cite Guy Valliere as the answer.

By the end of summer, just as Parliament was about to reconvene, something else began to brew. One of Harper's 2006 campaign promises was that he wouldn't call an election for four years, which meant that, barring a non-confidence vote, the next election would be in January 2010. Here it was, more than two years before that date, and an election was being called. Why? In my opinion, I'm one of the only people in Canada, outside of the Conservatives themselves, with a clue of (at least what I perceived to be) the real reason behind it.

Doug Finley never testified before Parliament. If an election wasn't called when the new session began, the opposition parties might very well seek a contempt-of-Parliament charge. For the Conservatives, the easiest and most direct way to get the potential scandal to go away was to force an election. No worries if you're innocent, but big worries if you have something to hide. Apparently, that early January 2006 Conservative newspaper advertisement for the Lost Canadians was exactly the sort of thing Elections Canada was trying to discover, and I had the evidence.

CHAPTER 16

LUCY IN THE SKY

If they would rather die... they had better do it,
and decrease the surplus population.
CHARLES DICKENS, *A CHRISTMAS CAROL*

I FINALLY DECIDED to begin moving some belongings to Canada. All landed immigrants are privileged to get a one-time freebie transferring personal belongings from our country of origin to Canada. It's about the only thing that's free. For my family of five, I spent well north of $10,000 trying to immigrate, which included fees for lawyers, police reports, fingerprints, employer records, and physical exams. It was as though, in order to get into Canada, you first had to open yourself up to a Citizenship and Immigration colonoscopy of your life. Somehow, it had become completely irrelevant that I was born in Canada and had been a legitimate Canadian citizen. I might just as well have been from Mars. Often during my speaking engagements, I say that I come from the hardest country in the world to get into Canada from: Canada. By September 2008, it had been thirty-six years of trying, and I still wasn't a citizen. I lost it when I was six and asked for it back when I was eighteen.

On September 4, John Reynolds and I anxiously boarded my boat in Friday Harbor, Washington, on a short cruise to Sidney, BC. That's where I would officially declare the boat to customs and, voila, it would be registered. From there we'd shove off to Gibsons, where the *Sea to Sky* would be permanently berthed. I had called ahead so that everything would be in order. At the time, Gary Lunn, MP for the Saanich–Gulf Islands riding, was one of Harper's cabinet ministers. John arranged to meet up with Gary. Again rumours were flying over a possible election, which was called just three days later when, at the urging of the prime minister, Governor General Michaëlle Jean dissolved Parliament.

Hanging around high-ranking influential people is always interesting. You often hear things or get inklings of what is to come. Stopping off at Lunn's house, there was no doubt in my mind that the eastern storm clouds of Ottawa were fast approaching. Hoping Diane Finley would remain as citizenship minister—in more than a decade, she was the only one to really do something for us—on this day I just wanted to get my boat officially registered and be on my way home.

But that was not to be. The supervisor at Canada Border Services Agency said that, in April 2009, a bill would be implemented in Parliament that would retroactively give former Canadians like me their citizenship. So, on his own, he decided to tax my boat as though I were a returning Canadian. It didn't matter that, as an immigrant, I had a right to bring the vessel into Canadian waters duty free; he was going to treat me as a citizen for tax purposes. Revenue Canada's bill? A mere $12,400. I suggested taking the boat back into US waters. But that, evidently, was quite unacceptable.

"Put one foot on that boat and we'll confiscate it" was the elegant way he phrased it, and there was nothing Lunn or Reynolds could do about it except advise me to pay the tax. It was either that or abandon the boat. What a welcome that was—to be taxed according to a levy that hadn't yet been made into law.

Here I was, taking my first official step in the process of finally going home and, instead of treating me with something approaching respect, Canada was demanding money. My rights as an immigrant were trampled on and squashed. It turned out to be an omen of the months and years to come. Not just for me but for other Lost Canadians as well.

The federal election was held on October 14. Since I was being taxed as a Canadian, I wanted to vote. But no. At my local polling station, the officers with Elections Canada decided I wasn't Canadian enough and immediately ushered me out. Consider that when C-37 came into effect in April 2009, Canada was going to recognize my citizenship back to my birth, with no interruptions. Yet, in the here and now, when I wanted to vote, I still had no rights as a citizen. It felt degrading being ushered out in front of everyone as if I were a criminal who had done something wrong. At the very least, soon I would be Canadian. Not so for 5 percent of the Lost Canadians, the ones implied by Diane Finley's statement, "c-37 corrects this for 95 percent of the people." As a pilot, if I ditched a plane in the Hudson River, I'd rescue 100 percent of the people or die trying. Having a hundred passengers means a hundred get rescued. Would Captain Chesley "Sully" Sullenberger be a hero if he had knowingly allowed 5 percent of his passengers to die? No way.

By the end of October, Jason Kenney had been appointed Canada's newest citizenship minister. How surprising, a brand-new captain who'd never before flown a plane. Whenever the pilot leaves the cockpit, he or she briefs the pilot taking over, even though that person knows what's been going on. Then it's a simple transfer of duty, like "You've got the controls," followed by the reply "Okay, I have control of the airplane." On returning, the pilot is briefed, with special attention paid to anything of consequence that happened during his or her absence. Then, once again, "I've got the controls," followed by "You've got the plane. Air traffic control gave us a clearance direct to Gander," for example. On long-haul flights, the briefing may be a great deal more in-depth. Either way, the point is to make certain everyone is clear about who's in charge and what's going on, so that the flight carries on with safety and continuity.

This isn't how Ottawa works. After the election, Diane Finley's top staffers immediately became incommunicado as they accompanied the minister to her new portfolio, minister of human resources and skills development. For the umpteenth time, I was back on the phone calling the new citizenship minister's office, hoping to brief Jason Kenney directly. This time doing so would be especially meaningful, since the new cabinet was now back to meeting with some regularity. Hopefully, I could triage and get some of the Lost Canadians who were in the most dire straits a 5.4 citizenship grant. Fitting the bill were people like Guy Valliere, Margot MacKenzie, and Lucy Proulx. By now a veteran of the parliamentary process, I was certain CIC would erect roadblocks. Hence, it was imperative that I talk to Kenney and persuade him to keep watch over his bureaucrats and personally ensure everything progressed as smoothly for c-37 taking effect as pilots transitioned in the cockpit.

My call was transferred to Kennedy Hong, whose title at CIC was director, Case Management. Eventually, I was granted a meeting with Hong, a couple of other CIC bureaucrats sitting in, but unfortunately, still somewhat fresh in their minds was my showing up with camera rolling at their headquarters. If I'd been a fly on their wall, no doubt they'd all be preparing to swing gigantic fly swatters. Jason Kenney was probably encouraging them to do it. And their fly swatters were designed to bash tigers.

John Erison had just been buried in Canada by his wife. Knowing the incredible pain of his death and of CIC's rejection felt by his widow, I vowed to do everything possible not to allow this kind of thing to happen to one more person or family. But then, I wasn't the citizenship minister; Jason Kenney was. And he'd washed his hands of the issue.

One result of the 2008 election, other than Harper gaining sixteen seats and the Liberals dropping eighteen, was that my MP was defeated. Blair Wilson had replaced John Reynolds when he retired in 2006. Two years later, just before the next election, Wilson's name and reputation were being publicly trashed. Elections Canada investigated and after eight months cleared him of any serious wrongdoing. One question remained: Did the Conservatives plant negative stories about Wilson with the intent of swaying voters? For laymen like me, it all seemed fishy and too convenient, bombshell news breaking right on the eve of an election. Blair was forced to resign as a Liberal MP and subsequently lost.[1]

My new MP was John Weston, who for years had been wooing me for support, always suggesting he had some sort of in with his party. During the campaign, Weston returned all my phone calls. Afterward, he changed his cell number and became a missing person, or so it seemed. Nevertheless, I remained hopeful that his words of support would translate into actions.

On December 25, I became aware of the true identity of the Christmas grinch. Unmistakably, it was Jason Kenney. Not one of my 5.4s had been processed. Guy Valliere's condition was growing extremely perilous. After three months of the minister's silence, I had nothing to lose, so I fired a shot across his bow by writing a letter to the editor in *The Local*, the smaller of the two competing papers on the Sunshine Coast, where I live. I titled my letter "Dead Silence" and wrote about Margot MacKenzie. I couldn't get her out of my mind; she needed kidney dialysis and to be on the kidney-transplant list. This is part of what I wrote:

> Apparently campaign promises don't always translate into actions. I did notice when the Conservatives appeared to be dying on the vine, they did everything and anything to stay alive. However, when it comes to protecting individual Canadians from the grim reaper, they aren't nearly as responsive. Mr. Weston has shown his allegiance and it sure doesn't seem to be with his constituents. Shame on you, John Weston. You could help a woman stay alive, yet you chose to remain silent, DEAD SILENT.

Being nice had yielded no results. Maybe my taking a much more direct approach would wake up Kenney and my MP. It didn't. They reacted, but not as I expected.

In January 2009, I met with the fourth most powerful person in Canada outside the Queen: Senator Nöel Kinsella, Speaker of the Senate.* Kinsella had championed our cause with Bills S-17 and S-2. His office is the largest in the Senate, and I'd met with him several times before. In one corner was the very table where Queen Elizabeth had signed into law the Canadian Charter of Rights and Freedoms. Once, my wife and I sat there. I quite enjoyed the senator, and our relationship was prosperous. This time, however, the mood was different. I first became aware of the change while talking with his chief of staff, Janelle Feldstein. She asked a rhetorical question: Why *should* they help me? Turns out, she was quite aware of my rather blunt letter to the editor regarding their fellow Conservative and my current MP, John Weston. I suspect that neither liked it. Senator Kinsella, as always, was most gracious, but after that meeting nothing of substance ever transpired. I tend to think that the mood swing wasn't so much his as it was Janelle's, particularly since my previous encounter with the good senator was a result of him beckoning me, not the other way around.

Nine months earlier, Andrew Telegdi sponsored a celebratory dinner for the passage of C-37 in the members-only section of the parliamentary restaurant. Several distinguished people were there, including Meili Faille of the Bloc. As I walked out of the room reserved for the Lost Canadians crowd, a familiar voice called out. Looking around, I saw Senator Kinsella with Janelle Feldstein at a nearby table. He'd been following my journey with C-37 and was most complimentary, saying I was a hero of the Senate for my continued battle on behalf of Lost Canadians. I sensed that he was a warm, caring man.

After C-37 received royal assent, most of my former Conservative champions went on to champion other things. Jim Karygiannis, a Liberal, got me a parliamentary ID badge now that Andrew Telegdi had been defeated. Jim was enjoyable to work with and we became good friends. His legislative assistant, Margot Doey-Vick, worked behind the scenes. One time, she ordered the complete file CIC had on me. It was 330 pages and growing daily. My CIC insider once told me that CIC monitored my every move. As a Boeing 747 pilot flying hundreds of people all over the world, I'd had

---

* The top people in Canada, in order of importance politically, are (1) the governor general, (2) the prime minister, (3) the Speaker of the House, and (4) the Speaker of the Senate.

everything about me checked and rechecked: there was no way an odd sort of character would be allowed to pilot an airliner. Who knows, maybe in Canada, getting a bunch of elderly war-bride women their citizenship constituted a high security alert.

In February, word came that Guy Valliere had passed away a broken man. Stephen Harper had refused to intervene, and Jason Kenney snubbed his section 5.4 citizenship grant. As Guy's headstone reads, "You are a man forgotten by your country but acknowledged by your desire to be Canadian." I'm sure Mr. Kenney was too busy rearranging his office furniture to notice. Guy was my second Lost Canadian to be buried disenfranchised from his own country, but my first World War II veteran to be so cold-heartedly disregarded. Ever since, when I spot Harper at televised Remembrance Day ceremonies, I think of Guy. The prime minister's feel-good speeches are nothing but a facade. How could any prime minister, let alone a prime minister wanting to be known for cozying up to the military, willingly ignore a Canadian World War II vet? The Conservatives' shunning Guy was appalling. My resolve to pursue my cause grew only stronger.

Again, C-37 would change citizenship laws on a number of fronts. One area of major concern was the second-generation born-abroad clause, which had huge ramifications for unsuspecting Canadians. There are 2.8 million expats out there and, without their knowledge, after April 17, 2009, not only could their babies be born without Canadian citizenship but a small percentage could actually be stateless.[2] Finley had assured me that in these cases, Canada would grant them citizenship through the 5.4 process, but with Kenney ignoring her other 5.4 promises, we weren't so sure. Still, with only a few months left before implementation of the bill, Canadian couples needed to know what was happening. Dialling media control-room numbers almost by memory by now, I tried as best I could to engage the media to warn them of the consequences. You'd think that after all these years—after two bills go all the way through Parliament and are passed unanimously—they'd know my track record and just maybe they'd listen. Not so. Getting fired up again, I began asking why they were ignoring Lost Canadians. Wayne Williams, news director at CBC News in Vancouver, replied, saying the issue was simply "Don Chapman's passion." True enough. But with CBC's mandate to tell Canadian stories, wasn't it obligated to speak out?

As 2008 drew to a close, the *Globe and Mail* highlighted me as one of its nation builders of the year. If that weren't so pathetic it would have been funny. Its top nation builder was Jean Vanier, who, while deserving every accolade out there, was born in 1928 in Switzerland.[3] Vanier's own citizenship could be questioned. He had served in the British Navy and spent a great deal of his life, if not most of it, outside Canada. As best as I could tell, he wasn't in Canada in 1947, the year he turned twenty-four. My point is, there's an excellent chance that Vanier was a Lost Canadian. Under C-37 he'd be recognized. But the bill hadn't yet taken effect. Being a celebrity whose citizenship could be questioned was not unique. There were hundreds, maybe thousands, of others. While they'd soon be recognized, most remained largely unaware of their dilemma.

I called Keith Morrison, one of NBC's narrators for the investigative journalism show *Dateline*. Keith was married to Hollywood actor Matthew Perry's mother, who just so happened to be Pierre Elliott Trudeau's press aide when our Charter of Rights and Freedoms came into force. What a ceremony they had back in '82, proclaiming that women now had equal rights. Not true, because in citizenship law they didn't. Matthew was born pre-1977 in the States to a Canadian mother and an American father; if it was in wedlock and Matthew wasn't in Canada on his twenty-fourth birthday, then he too wasn't Canadian. Fortunately, C-37 would cover him. Same thing for Kiefer Sutherland. Paula Abdul and Amanda Bynes would be covered, as their mothers were from Canada. Wayne Gretzky, who years earlier listened as I explained the Lost Canadian story to him and then did nothing, had kids who were affected, since they too were born outside Canada. So were children of William Shatner, Michael J. Fox, Neil Young, and Christopher Plummer. Famous Canadian Hollywood entertainers were a dime a dozen, and each and every one of them had children who were affected. Then there were children of former NHL players: Bobby Orr, Bobby Hull, and Mr. Hockey himself, Gordie Howe. Even Don Cherry's kids were born in the US.[4] The key questions for each person were "Where were you on your twenty-fourth birthday? Outside Canada?" If so, they too probably weren't Canadian, just as Roméo Dallaire wasn't. The list of affected famous Lost Canadians was huge, yet I still couldn't get the media on board. Nor were average Canadians much interested—mention citizenship and their faces glazed over. Their reaction was amazing. Sometimes it was downright rude.[5]

Here's but one example. My mother lived at Leisure World Arizona and, together, we got to know Ken and Amber MacLeod. Ken had retired as a federal judge in Saskatchewan and often helped me with legal issues, including Joe Taylor's case. In 2009, with Ken's health failing from Parkinson's, the MacLeods sold their home and returned to Regina. I knocked on the new owner's door, welcoming them to Leisure World. They were from

Victoria. We chatted for a minute or two. I told them of my home in Gibsons. Their reply: "You're a fellow Canadian."

My response: "Well, no, not yet. Canada took my citizenship from me when I was six years old."

The man's reaction was direct and to the point. He asked me to leave, treating me like some sort of deranged pedophile. Feeling humiliated, I just couldn't let it end that way. A few days later, I again knocked on their front door. When the man answered, I handed him some information about c-37, saying I didn't lose my citizenship because of anything I'd done. He handed back the information around his barely open door, then said, "I couldn't care less about your citizenship problems." Sadly, his attitude wasn't uncommon—in Leisure World alone, this sort of thing happened to me four times. It was amazing how badly Canadians could treat one of their own. They were ignorant of the issue, therefore unbelieving. Why? Because people like Wayne Williams at CBC decided not to tell our story. It was like a dog chasing its tail: without mass media coverage, Canadians wouldn't know about the issue, and there'd be no outrage over the way the government treated us. Absent the outrage, politicians didn't care.

In 2008, the *Globe and Mail* teamed up with *Maclean's* to put on an evening forum titled "Canada: Nation or Notion?" They brought in two supposed Canadians to debate the issue: Adam Gopnik and Malcolm Gladwell. Both were journalists in the US. Over the years, I had left both of them several messages. Never once did they take my calls, and both were supposedly Canadian. Or were they? Gladwell had been born to Canadian parents outside Canada and, I believe, was out of the country on his twenty-fourth birthday. Was he a Lost Canadian? How ironic that *Maclean's* and the *Globe and Mail* were sponsoring a debate on what Canada was or wasn't. Yet, when it came to a real issue dealing with real Canadians, they showed little to no interest. I fired off letters to both editors respectively, Mark Stevenson and John Stackhouse, with no reply. I sent a booklet to Colin Campbell of *Maclean's*, explaining the issue. He couriered it back, telling me no one was interested. Whatever I did, whomever I contacted, no one could be bothered.

Just a month before c-37's implementation, my family was scheduled for a citizenship ceremony. We flew to Vancouver, where my wife and two of my daughters had to take a citizenship test, a one-on-one oral examination with citizenship judge George Gibault. My youngest daughter was exempt, being under the age of eighteen, and, as a former Canadian, so was I. If they passed, we'd all be sworn in two days later. When the judge emerged from his office with the exam results, he said that he'd never before had one person, let alone three, get 100 percent. I was proud of my family, knowing they'd make great Canadians.

Although my kids and I were covered under c-37, I wanted them to get their citizenship through the normal immigration process. Bill c-37 was to deem all naturalized Canadians as being "born in Canada" for purposes of passing on citizenship. My gut, however, told me the bureaucrats would be doing this for every naturalized Canadian except the naturalized children of Lost Canadians. Anticipating potential problems down the road—that the issue might one day have to be tested before the courts—I wanted cic to fully understand that the guy they might be squaring off against was me. On March 20, 2009, my family took an oath to the Queen. Standing at the podium, smiling at the 200 or so soon-to-be Canadians, Judge Gibault said, "We have people here today from countries all over the world. India, China, the United States, Brazil, Pakistan, everywhere."

As he went on to another subject I burst out, "Excuse me, but you forgot one country."

"Yes, I accidentally did. Folks, we also have one person from Canada."

Most everyone in the room was bewildered. How could that be? Yes, there really was someone in the room from Canada getting their Canadian citizenship. The week before, India had removed its patriarchal legislation, giving citizenship to the children of Indian-born mothers. Ten days earlier, Bangladesh began allowing men and women to pass citizenship on to their respective children equally. Yet here in Canada, the "human rights" country, I was still in a raging battle over equal rights in citizenship law. As so aptly stated two years earlier in the *Economist*, it was all Kafkaesque.

It should be noted that Judge Gibault was good friends with Jason Kenney. Harper got rid of most, if not all, of the non-Conservative judges, so when I was sworn in, Judge Gibault was the only practising citizenship judge west of Calgary. Like travellers stuck at an airport blanketed in heavy fog, people all over western Canada were delayed in getting citizenship.

On April 17, 2009, I was in Ottawa with several new Canadians. One of them, Will Wilkinson, was an editor for *Cato Unbound*, a publication of the Cato Institute, a Conservative US think tank. Bill c-37 had just become law, with hundreds of thousands of Canadians affected, and Jason Kenney still refused to talk to me. He did, however, invite Will Wilkinson up to his office. Will interviewed Kenney for an article he was writing about Lost Canadians. Later, at the Friday's Roast Beef House in Ottawa, about twenty of us enjoyed dinner together. On my right was newly found Canadian Dean Echenberg, Canada's newest MD. Across the table sat Jackie Scott and Dawn Erison. Jackie had just submitted her paperwork for a 5.4 citizenship grant. Dawn was still grieving over the loss of her husband, John. She showed up in his honour, knowing, in her own way, that he was looking down and sharing in our success.

It was one thing becoming a citizen and quite another proving it. Here I was, privy to the way Ottawa works (or more accurately stated, doesn't work), knowing there could be mass problems for all Canadians, not just us newly found ones, and no one cared. Since the Western Hemisphere Travel Initiative was implemented in 2007, having a Canadian passport or birth certificate didn't necessarily mean you were a citizen. Bill C-37 went a long way in solving that, but problems still existed. For the government, the only real proof was a Certificate of Canadian Citizenship, which cost $75 and could take more than a year to be issued. Although Bill C-37 would make the born-in-wedlock kids of the war brides Canadian, many couldn't prove that they were. And without that proof, the government could deny all kinds of things, like Old Age Security, and it didn't take an Einstein to figure out that many of these people were at or nearing the age of collecting benefits. Instead of advocating for the individual, more often than not, the government defaulted to the deny mode. Lost Canadians were turned away trying to obtain driver's licences, medical coverage, you name it. Some couldn't vote, yet under C-37 they were citizens. From the get-go, fixing this glitch was one of the big things I wanted to meet with Jason Kenney about. The problems were just so easily avoidable. If only he'd been actively involved; after all, wasn't that what he was being paid for? Kenney's ignorance or lack of caring (or both) translated into real Canadians being denied real benefits, even passports. An example:

Dear Mr. Chapman,

After listening to you on the radio recently, I thought you might like to know of this incident. My life story is that my parents met each other while they were in show business in the 1940s. Dad was a professional high diver and Mother, an American, was a professional dancer. They married while in the US and in 1951 I was born in Wheeling, West Virginia. Approx. one year later they decided to move and to live in Canada. Dad was born and raised a Frenchman in Montreal, Quebec. From that point on I lived and was educated in Canada. I of course knew that I was

born in the USA but I was Canadian through and through. At the age
of eighteen I voluntarily joined the Canadian Armed Forces and was in
for almost exactly seven years. After basic training I served as an infan-
tryman, 1PPCLI Calgary for the first few years, then three years as an
Airborne Commando Paratrooper in 2 Commando at Edmonton Greis-
bach barracks. From the week after I was released from the Forces I
commenced the job that I've been with to the present (with the City of
Edmonton's Edmonton Transit System). I've been a Transit operator (bus
driver) for the last going on thirty-three years.

Up until a few years ago you only needed the driver's license and birth
certificate to cross the US/Canadian border, then passports became mandatory. So, as any other Canadian, I acquired the application form. When
the form gets to the part or section that inquires about place of birth and
birth certificate, the whole thing becomes a dead end. I phoned Canada
Place. A lady took my call, and told me that I am not a Canadian and never
was. She also informed me that the only way that I could become a Canadian was to take a course as she had done. I can't even take this any further
other than to tell you how I got my passport. I drove down to the American
Consulate in Calgary. With my birth certificate it only took them a total of
forty minutes for me to acquire a US passport. I will close with this statement, if I'd known at age eighteen what I know now, I would not have
served in the Canadian Forces. My present status is that I am an American
Citizen residing in Canada. The people at the US Embassy stated I am
as American as they are! Whether I like it or not! I guess that I know how
those people who you represent feel.

Bruce Cadieux, Edmonton, Alberta

The fact was, Bruce was Canadian under C-37, and yet a CIC call centre
agent was telling him he wasn't. It was typical, CIC's own people knowing
nothing about their own laws and yet holding the individual accountable.

Another glaring example: Priscilla Corrie is a war bride whose first husband died fighting for Canada in World War II. She had remarried another
Canadian. Now, after C-37, the government was denying her a passport.[6]
She was eighty-seven years old and wanted to go on a cruise, something
she'd desired for several years. It didn't matter that her previous passport
had expired, meaning she'd had a Canadian passport, and in fact, had had
one most of her life. The government steadfastly refused to give her one.

Then there were people being denied Old Age Security:

Dear Don,

I am the child of a British mother and a Canadian father. My parents were married in 1944 and I was born in November of 1945 in Britain. Under the War Brides Act of 1943 I was born a Canadian. When my mother and I came to Canada in September 1946, I supposedly did not go through immigration because I was a Canadian. Thus, there is no record of me entering the country. Now I am applying for Old Age Security and being denied because I can't prove when I entered the country. Fortunately, my mother is still alive and we are hoping her immigration papers will include my name, even though under the Act she was a Canadian too and may not have immigration papers either. I'm wondering if there is any information you could provide that would help me with this problem? I'm ready to take the government to court.

 Rod Burgess

And another:

I am wondering if I qualify as a lost Canadian. This is my story. I was born in Baudette Minnesota USA to Canadian parents. A USA hospital being one mile away and a Canadian hospital was 40 minutes away. I was taken to Rainy River Ontario at three days old. I was at that point given a Record of Birth Abroad from the Canadian government. However after years of wear and tear it has become illegible. And is in many pieces. I have explained this to numerous people and they tell me I have to apply for a Canadian Citizenship card. This will cost me more money and takes 10 months. I have been rejected for a Canadian passport. I have voted in Canada and hold a SIN. Is there anything you can do for me? My name is Anne Hartman. Maiden name Anne Westin.

The problem was that these people were Canadian but couldn't prove it. Hence, the government was wrongly denying their benefits. One story particularly stood out and, for safety reasons, I'll change the names. Liz Ball, like me, was born in Canada and taken to the US as a child. After C-37 she lived with her nineteen-year-old son, Larry; together they were survivors of an abusive husband/father. They could hardly wait until the new legislation became effective because, for them, it meant salvation. They would be able to start life anew in a country where they didn't live in fear. Only because of Jim Karygiannis was Liz able to get her Certificate of Canadian

Citizenship. As they crossed into Canada, the border guards knew nothing about the new law and, in their ignorance, made Larry a refugee. All he wanted was to be able to work and go to Carleton University. He was like any other nineteen-year-old but, without legal status, his dreams were off limits. I called Carleton, asking if it would make an exception, but it wouldn't budge. For almost a year, Larry couldn't do much of anything but sit around hoping a letter would arrive from CIC with a little card inside that read "Certificate of Canadian Citizenship." That would turn his life around, give him equal rights to pursue dreams like any other young Canadian. Keep in mind that his mother was born in Canada and Larry was first-generation born-abroad, so both were legitimate Canadian citizens under Bill C-37. But without proof it meant nothing.

A couple of weeks before his refugee status expired we decided to hole him up at the same Ottawa church Stephen Harper attends. We even planned to have him sit on the prime minister's pew. Again, only because of the intervention of Jim Karygiannis was Larry officially recognized, and it took almost a year. In the end, Liz and Larry moved back to the US, away from two abusers—the husband/father and their newly found country of Canada. Using the word "abuse" fits because that's how they felt it, and I agree.

Lucy Proulx was a fourteenth-generation Québécoise. In fairness, Lucy didn't qualify under C-37, but she should have been considered for a 5.4 grant. Lucy was in California, dying from stage-four breast cancer. In her last days all she wanted—her dying wish—was to be recognized as a Canadian citizen. It was not to be. She became our third potential Lost Canadian to die disenfranchised. Hence the title of this chapter, "Lucy in the Sky." Jason Kenney never even bothered to respond to her or my many letters of appeal.

Now for a six-decade and still ongoing horror story—of another Canadian completely ignored by Jason Kenney:

My name is Donna Lewis. Born Dec. 1946, Colorado Springs Colorado. I came to Canada in Mar. 1947. I was brought here by my birth mother Honorah Joyce (Dennelly) Hulse. She was a British war bride and she came to Canada in 1944. My father was a Canadian citizen and also a Canadian soldier. His name was Jack Hulse and he passed away in Westminster Hospital in London Ont., in June 1946... My mother brought me to Chatham Ont. and gave me to her former neighbours and she returned to the States where she resided until her death in 2007. She had divorced and remarried another American, but she was still being paid $1400 a month from the Canadian government for being a widow to my father Jack Hulse right up to the day she died. This is why I believe that she was still a Canadian.

I was adopted to George and Isabell Jackson both Canadian citizens and even though I have an American birth certificate they are named on it as my parents and their place of birth is also named on my birth certificate. I grew up thinking that I had dual citizenship and as long as I never voted I could work in Windsor and live in Detroit sort of thing, and my adopted mother went to her grave still believing that. I did not find out that I was not a Canadian citizen until 1980 when I was arrested for being here illegally.

The charges were dropped but it started a living hell for me. Here I was with a social insurance number, a job, a new house, a new car, bank payments, and two children to support and I am told by immigration that I have to quit my job. I am no longer able to work in Canada or am I allowed to enter any government building such as the post office or library etc. I can't believe this was happening. My parents got the baby bonus for me and thought I was a Canadian; I attended school till I quit at the age of 13. I went to work full time and worked almost every day until this happened. I have been married three times and have had three children. I received the orphans benefit for my children from Canada Pension and the survivors benefit, so I'm thinking how much more Canadian can I be. Well I was the stupid one. I finally got a working permit from immigration for $50 a year, then later on came Minister permits for $200 a year. Was I ever a proud Canadian. Then I had to pay for and carry a piece of paper with my picture on it in my purse to live in my country. I did everything I was told to do. I went for medicals. I obtained a queen's pardon, and each time I was assured that I would become a Canadian. Well it never happened. I would get depressed and say forget it, I'm tired of the run around. I went for a long time without a health card or a permit. I would get so frustrated that I would go into deep depression; thoughts of suicide were never far from becoming a reality. Then I would pick myself up and dust myself off and start again.

I had a bad car accident in 2001 so I had to get a health card. Well I was told to pay $700 and have my husband sponsor me and they would forego the medical under grounds of compassion ... I still had to pay for a permit and another [operation on] top of that, that was in 2002. I passed the medical and they did not inform me until March 2007, meanwhile there went the health card, the nurse, the oxygen, and all of the people who were trying to get me better... I went to the bottom of the barrel... but no health card, no help from any doctor or hospital. That ended in March 2007, and that's when I received the results from immigration that I had passed the medical in 2002 and they were enclosing a temporary resident permit and told me not to lose it. When I phoned them I was told that they did not enclose the permit, the letter was only for presentation to obtain a health card. I was really fuming over this and was ready to throw in the towel, but I hid my pride and obtained a health card as by this time I was blind with cataracts in both eyes. So since March I have had two surgeries, one for each eye, that I am very thankful for... I can see but I still have no status in Canada.

I am up and moving around; I even go shopping the odd time. So I decided it was time to start my fight again and that's when I learned of the war brides and the children. I also learned that there was a process known as naturalization, and I found your website on the internet by accident, and I truly believe that there are guardian angels who guide us sometimes when the going gets rough, and thanks to you I have renewed my faith in mankind as I always was a loner; I did not fit in as people would laugh at my story and say I was lying, so I don't have many friends, but I heard from some people today who can relate to my story, and I realize I am not alone nor am I the worst case. I learned today that there are people worse off than I am, so I will keep fighting. It's not just me now.

I have other people to fight for. I hope I can help someone as you have helped me. I have documents to prove what I wrote in this letter and there is more but I have covered most of my story. It's hard to remember every detail as I have memory problems from my accident, but everything comes back to me. I have suffered a great deal because of this and I will never forget what I have been put through for just one piece of paper saying I am finally a Canadian, I finally belong, and I hope with all my heart that the other lost Canadians will get their papers too. We have waited a long time. If you need more information please let me know. Thank you again.

Donna Lewis

I got Donna her legal right to stay in Canada with medical coverage, but never citizenship (although she did qualify under c-37). On each and every holiday or my birthday she'd send me an email. She was so appreciative, almost as though I had been the only one in her life to ever give a damn. As

I write this, I still tear up. Her own father died from injuries sustained as a Canadian World War II soldier. But for what? To have his little girl treated so shabbily?

It became clear that Mr. Kenney's interests had little to nothing to do with citizenship. When he became the minister, he added one more portfolio, that of minister of multiculturalism. I viewed it as a conflict of interest—Citizenship, Immigration, and Multiculturalism. Ignore the former, combine the latter two, and you've got a recipe for political success. Kenney became a virtual campaign machine, free to go into immigrant communities, throw money at them, then promise his help in getting their families (such as aging parents) into Canada. And the best part? It was all paid for by Canadian taxpayers. Not a dime had to come out of the Conservative coffers.

Lost Canadians didn't vote as a block and, without rights, they didn't vote at all. Naturalized Canadians, however, were great at voting en masse, and in making their votes count. It was a lesson not lost on the politicians. I've watched videos of Jack Layton wearing a turban and parading around with the Vancouver Indian community. He also knew about us, which raises the question, why the silence? If he really was a man for the people, he should have spoken out. I kept trying to contact the NDP's new citizenship critic, Olivia Chow, who just happened to be Layton's wife, but she didn't return my calls. Same thing with Thierry St-Cyr of the Bloc and with the Liberals' new critic, Maurizio Bevilacqua. Part and parcel, no one cared to do the right thing—everything was about votes. I came to view the opposition as being accessories to Jason Kenney.

In June 2009, the House Citizenship Committee did allow me one last testimony. I took along Marcel Gélinas, a Canadian-born man who had been born in wedlock to a Canadian mother and American father, and thus wasn't Canadian. If only he'd been born out of wedlock. Like Guy Valliere, he's an old man and a World War II vet who'd been lowered to begging for his citizenship. He even had a fleur-de-lys tattooed on his left arm.

My nephew was there to testify, since his daughter was being denied. The reason? Her connection to Canada was through my sister, a woman. On the other hand, the child of my brother's daughter would be accepted because that connection was through a man. For these two cousins, both aged two, everything was identical except for one thing: the gender of their Canadian grandparent. The year is 2009, we're in a post-Charter-rights Canada, and we're telling the committee that CIC is violating unanimous Supreme Court of Canada rulings that people could not be denied citizenship based on gender. Almost everyone on the committee was unaware. Why? Because they were brand-new political appointees rather than informed professionals.

When it was Jackie Scott's turn to speak, she told the MPs that her situation mirrored Joe Taylor's except that she was in Canada on her twenty-fourth birthday. To make it more wacky, the previous committee had issued a unanimous all-party recommendation that all war-bride children be recognized, including the born-out-of-wedlock kids. But the MPs who listened to Jackie, the very ones who are supposedly "experts" in citizenship law, had no clue about their own committee's prior recommendations. The only thing coming out of our appearance was that Kenney's office wrote to Jackie asking her to resubmit an application for a 5.4 grant (it had just turned down her recent request). I mentioned having a list of seventy-one other people in limbo. Olivia Chow felt my request was reasonable, yet afterwards, Kenney ignored it, and so did Ms. Chow.[7]

For the record, I complained about Mr. Kenney and CIC, but when I began to elaborate, the committee chairman, Conservative David Tilson, abruptly cut me off. I didn't sense much compassion. The parliamentary secretary to Jason Kenney, Rick Dykstra, shut me out almost as badly as Kenney. The only difference was that he at least said "hi" to me as we both filled our coffee cups at the back of the room. John Weston, my own MP, met our group before the hearing and asked me to apologize for my "Dead Silence" letter. In the six months since I had written it, two more Lost Canadians had died disenfranchised, and now to patch things up, I was supposed to apologize to him?

Magali Castro-Gyr was the woman who, like me, had a father that took out US citizenship when she was a minor. CIC had cancelled her Canadian citizenship, thereby rendering her stateless and forcing her into a judicial review. You may remember that she was offered citizenship in return for signing a gag order. That bit of misconduct came under the Liberals, with Jean Chrétien as prime minister and Denis Coderre as the citizenship minister. As much as I'm hammering away at the Conservatives, no party was any good with the Lost Canadians. In fact, despite their faults, the Conservatives have been the best. The Liberals were by far the worst. That's as a party. Exceptions are individual MPs like Meili Faille of the Bloc, Bill Siksay of the NDP, Andrew Telegdi and Jim Karygiannis of the Liberals, and John Reynolds and Diane Ablonczy of the Conservatives. By now Magali was again a legitimate Canadian citizen, but under Jason Kenney, CIC refused to issue her a passport allowing her to travel from Switzerland to Canada.

At the very same time, another Canadian by the name of Suaad Hagi Mohamud was having passport problems. Suaad had recently arrived in Toronto after spending three months in Nairobi trying to prove she was who she said she was. Canadian officials denied her a passport, and it was only after DNA testing that CIC capitulated. It made news all over Canada, causing a huge public outcry. As a result, the Canadian diplomat who handled her case got recalled, and Public Safety Minister Peter Van Loan announced an investigation, which ended up as a special summer session before a parliamentary committee. Witnesses were called to testify. Later, Mohamud was awarded legal costs. She sued the government for $2.5 million, and in November 2012 settled out of court for an undisclosed amount. At the time, a question had been raised as to whether she'd been trying to sneak her sister into Canada.[8]

But there was no doubt about the status of Magali. While the Mohamud fiasco engrossed the country, Magali was being denied a passport in Geneva, and her situation was clear—there was no grey area—Magali was Canadian. Why was the government refusing to issue Magali a passport? Granted, she'd testified before the Citizenship Committee, she had challenged CIC by taking it to court, she was now helping me with the ongoing Lost Canadian battle, and Mr. Kenney sure didn't seem to like me or the Lost Canadian situation one bit. It's conjecture, because CIC doesn't always explain why it denies you, but could it have been retribution? And where was the media for Magali?

Remember, while Magali got her citizenship through a 5.4 grant, she now qualified under S-2 and C-37. Think about it. A tenth-generation woman from Quebec is denied her passport—she's not a citizen in any other country—and not only does the media ignore most of the story but so too does the parliamentary committee investigating Mohamud. Thankfully, Jim Karygiannis intervened and Magali was issued a temporary white passport—the kind given to people who are stateless.

Seriously, why did the media largely ignore Magali while going into a frenzy over Mohamud? I'm not suggesting Mohamud isn't worthy of press coverage. Any time a Canadian is denied due process, it's a very big deal indeed. What I'm suggesting is that Magali's situation also deserved media and political scrutiny.

For almost a decade, I'd been trying to get *National Post*-turned-*Globe and Mail*-turned-*National Post* columnist Christie Blatchford to write about the Lost Canadians. After reading her article about Mohamud titled "Turning a Blind Eye," I fired off an email. This was what I said:

Christie,

Just a month ago a tenth-generation Canadian-born woman was denied
a passport in Geneva. There's a nineteen-year-old Canadian citizen currently being allowed to stay in Canada only because he claimed refugee
status in his own country! In February of this year an 85-year-old Canadian-born, Canadian WWII veteran died disenfranchised from his own
country. Right now Jason Kenney is ignoring a unanimous Supreme Court
decision saying that it's illegal to discriminate against women. By not complying with the court's ruling, he is in essence in contempt of court. The
result? A two-year-old girl is currently being denied citizenship.

My story is now a part of Canadian history, and both you and the
Globe and Mail have, to use your words, pretty much "turned a blind eye."
Whether it was deliberate or because of other reasons, you never elected
to tell this unique story. In today's article about Suaad Hagi Mohamud
you stated, "And here we are again, with Ms. Mohamud's case, her release
coming only after the Canadian media gave her plight extensive attention."
I couldn't agree with you more. Without media coverage Ms. Mohamud
probably would never have seen justice. For the hundreds of thousands of
Lost Canadians, many who are still not being recognized in Canada, just
maybe you could make a difference.

Silence is not always golden. As Dr. Martin Luther King once stated,
"History will have to record that the greatest tragedy of this period of social
transition was not the strident clamor of the bad people, but the appalling
silence of the good."

This was how she responded:

I haven't "turned the other way," as you put it. I'm just frigging busy and
disorganized. Haven't a secretary or assistant, do my best, but when you
write five times a week, as I do many weeks (four the other weeks), travel
a lot and sometimes at a moment's notice, things get lost.

I do not ignore Canadians in need; in fact, on my first day back this
week, I wrote about one. But there are lots of folks seeking my help, asking
me to write stories, and I guess I can't do them all ... small as my personal
life is, I can't work 24-7 all the time. I'm sorry your story slipped through
the cracks of my disorganized life.

I can sympathize, in that I too always have a lot going on in my life. But
when I took on the Lost Canadians, I did everything in my power to make

time for everyone. Here I was, not so much fighting for me but for tens of thousands of others, including our coveted war dead. It was about principle and equal rights for all. Instinctively I felt as though Christie Blatchford was ignoring us, probably out of being ignorant of the portfolio, which was exactly why, over the years, I'd wanted to meet with her one on one. I needed to explain. After several no-shows on her part, I moved on.

On October 21, 2009, several of us were in Ottawa preparing for a protest march during Citizenship Week. Inside the House, Marlene Jennings presented a motion on the floor, calling for all the MPs to vote unanimously to grant seventy-one of my remaining Lost Canadians their citizenship. The second she finished speaking, the leader of the government in the House of Commons, Conservative Jay Hill, shouted at Marlene from across the floor, "That's bullshit."[9]

You may remember when Barack Obama was addressing Congress and Representative Joe Wilson yelled out, "You lie." It went viral, all over the world. Wilson later apologized very publicly.[10] Everyone in the States knew about it. You couldn't turn on the TV or listen to talk radio without hearing it being discussed. If you, the reader, are aware, that alone testifies to the force of the US media that Wilson's indiscretion had been so widely covered. Even the *Globe and Mail*, the *National Post*, and *Maclean's* wrote about it. Now compare this to Jay Hill who, just as much as Wilson, had violated the sanctity of the institution. Swearing on the floor of the House is a great big no-no. Although Hill did immediately apologize, in Canada, the media let it pass. While it's interesting that House protocol had been so blatantly violated, it's even more telling that the leader of the government in the House of Commons lost total composure simply because Marlene Jennings was asking the House to recognize citizenship of the people who were highlighted in this chapter. Why were the Conservatives so staunchly opposed?

By now, getting the occasional story into the media had become much more difficult, as they truly believed our problem had been solved. During Citizenship Week, finally a journalist came forward—Terry Milewski of CBC. We had secured a permit to march in front of Centre Block, and we did it at the urging of several Conservatives who supported us, saying we needed to embarrass Kenney publicly. John Reynolds once said that if Harper was shamed, he'd react by firing Kenney. But then, Reynolds was the guy who told me that if Harper became prime minister, he'd fix our issue "with the stroke of a pen." That evening, Lost Canadians Arch Ford, Jackie Scott, and baby Rachel Chandler were featured on CBC's *The National*. No doubt about it, Rachel is one of our cutest Lost Canadians ever. Her guilt was being a second-generation born-abroad child, born to a Canadian father and Chinese mother. She was also the first of several forthcoming stateless babies—all as a direct result of C-37.[11] Like father, like daughter—her daddy, Patrick Chandler, also happened to be born outside Canada to Canadian parents. He grew up in Canada and lived his whole life being Canadian. As an adult, he took a position teaching English in China, where he met Rachel's mother. Going back to Minister Finley, she said that in the case of a stateless baby, Canada would grant the child citizenship through a 5.4. It sounded reassuring when she said it, but in 2009, Canada had a new citizenship minister who had no problem ignoring his predecessor's promise. By doing so, Jason Kenney put Canada into the awkward position of violating three UN human rights conventions at the same time, the Rights of the Child, the Reduction of Statelessness, and the Universal Declaration of Human Rights. It took another year—a long, long time for a six-month-old baby—for Rachel to be rescued, and it wasn't Canada stepping up to help. Her Canadian grandfather had Irish roots, so Ireland, not Canada, gave her citizenship.[12] I found our government's lack of response disgusting. Further, imagine the headache of the Chandler family travelling under their passports. Father's Canadian, mother's Chinese, baby's Irish. Thank you very much, Canada.

That night on *The National*, here's how Terry Milewski wrapped up his interview:

Milewski: "The immigration minister says just follow the process."

Jason Kenney: "Rather than having, you know, press conferences or trying to politicize their application, just make a solid application, make a strong case, and it will be considered fairly on the merits of their case."

Milewski: "But the Lost Canadians say that's just the problem, that they do bring strong cases and still get turned down."[13]

And so our battle continued. Apparently, the powers that be weren't embarrassed enough.

As time marched forward, Lost Canadian rejections became the norm. In response, multiple lawsuits were filed. The taxpayers were again footing the bill for the government lawyers.

As 2009 rolled to a close, the *Globe and Mail* again highlighted me as a nation builder—not because someone at the newspaper had nominated me, but rather because so many Lost Canadians submitted my name that it couldn't ignore it. We closed the year with absolutely no Certificates of Canadian Citizenship in any of my remaining Lost Canadians' Christmas stockings.

For the second year in a row, the grinch won. Harper and Kenney had stolen our Christmas cheer. Let me conclude by saying that Lucy Proulx was a wonderful person, epitomizing the spirit of what Canada should be. She was a real gem. Let me rename this chapter "Lucy in the Sky with Diamonds." May she rest in peace.

CHAPTER 17

THE GOLD MEDAL OLYMPIC GAMBLE

As Canadians, we believe that a government must work in the interests of its people, not the other way around. We believe that countries that respect the rights of their own people are more likely to respect the rights of other nations and be good world citizens.
PRIME MINISTER STEPHEN HARPER WHILE
IN UKRAINE, IN A SPEECH BEFORE
THAT COUNTRY'S PRESIDENT, OCTOBER 2010

Yeah, this was, to say the least, extremely jarring. I felt completely violated, I mean, personally and professionally, you know, and for journalism over-all, because this is not only a violation of freedom of the press—you know, the idea that, you know, the state is going into your papers, your documents, your sources, everything—but also a violation of the public's right to know, because if journalists feel there are things they can't report on, that they'll be detained, that they'll be arrested or they'll be questioned, they'll be interrogated, this is a threat to the free flow of information. And that's the public's loss. That's democracy's loss.[1]

ON NOVEMBER 30, 2009, the above conversation was broadcast all over the US on an internationally broadcast US news program *Democracy Now!* Hard to believe, but the speaker was talking about Canada. Four days earlier, the show's co-host, Amy Goodman, and two of her colleagues had been detained by armed Canadian border guards. They were interrogated and their belongings, including Amy's computers and private papers, were searched.

Amy was travelling to the Vancouver Public Library to speak about health care, Tommy Douglas, Afghanistan, and Iraq. But that's not what the border guards were worried about. Their interest was the upcoming 2010 Vancouver Olympics. If Amy was going to be critical of the Games, she would not be allowed into Canada.

Whether or not one is a fan of the Olympics is beside the point. What happened was a blatant attack on freedom of speech and the right of the media to report the news. One really needs to wonder why the Canadian government would attempt to censor a world-renowned journalist over her like or dislike of the Olympics. If the media doesn't report something, how will the public ever discover the truth? When censorship begins, just where does it end?

I'm uncomfortable with this. The pilot in me was saying, "This doesn't look right." Red flags were everywhere. The issue of censorship is a huge one. CBC reported Goodman's story, but overall, the incident didn't make much news in Canada.

Amy was spot-on when she said, "This is a threat to the free flow of information. And that's the public's loss. That's democracy's loss."

I first heard about Goodman's story through an online news site, the *Vancouver Observer*.[2] I contacted the publisher, Linda Solomon. I explained the Lost Canadian story and asked if the *Observer* might be interested in doing a full series. I'd provide all the contacts and the *Observer* could take it from there. Investigative journalistic dollars being about as plentiful as Siberian tigers, I knew it was a long shot. After all, I was dealing with the Canadian media.[3]

But Linda was different. She listened intently without writing me off as being crazy. Maybe it was because of her background. She had grown up with a world-renowned photojournalist mother, then worked as a journalist in New York City before going north after 9/11. Linda is exactly what I would describe as a perfect North American, combining the best of the US and Canada. She's a no-nonsense journalist, not the kind you'd see on Fox News, and not the professionally complacent Canadian media type either. Linda scrounged up the funding, and the *Observer* Lost Canadian series was a go. The starting date would be just after the Olympics.

In January 2010, for the second time, Jackie Scott filed paperwork requesting a 5.4 citizenship grant. She did it because the bureaucrats asked her to reapply, but only if she'd first pay another $200 filing fee. It appeared that Jason Kenney's people, after rejecting her first application, had a change of heart. Well aware that Jackie and I had met, the bureaucrats also knew I'd adopted the habits of those small frightening terriers that bite down hard on the lips of much bigger dogs. No matter how much the larger dog shakes its head, the bite of the smaller one becomes more and more vise-like. By now you'd think CIC would have figured out that its path of least resistance was granting Jackie citizenship. Besides, it was simply the right thing to do.

This time, however, unlike with Joe Taylor's case, we had a few more tricks up our sleeve.

Both Jackie and Joe were born in England during World War II and out of wedlock. It wasn't until after the fighting had stopped that their respective parents were allowed to marry. One difference between Jackie and Joe was the date they arrived in Canada. Joe came in 1946, Jackie in 1948. As a baby, she needed major medical attention. The doctors had deemed her unfit to travel. Fortunately, there was a Privy Council order saying that, if a voyage was delayed due to medical reasons, the soldiers and dependents like Jackie would remain qualified for purposes of having the same status as the husband or father for citizenship.[4] When Jackie and her mother arrived in Canada, her parents immediately tied the knot. Jackie grew up having no clue that she was, as our government described it, a "bastard" child.

The Taylor case made it clear that Joe had been a citizen of Canada all the way up to his twenty-fourth birthday. Joe lost his citizenship because, on that magic date, he wasn't domiciled in Canada. But Jackie, when she turned twenty-four, was gainfully employed as an administrative secretary in Vancouver. Supporting her claim were Federal Court and Federal Court of Appeal rulings both saying she was a citizen.[5] Now, just as with the *Benner* decision (the unanimous Supreme Court ruling giving women rights equal to those of men to pass on citizenship), CIC decided it didn't like the rulings. Hence, it defied the court by denying Jackie citizenship. But here was our ace in the hole: in 1927, Ontario enacted the Legitimation Act, a direct result of the out-of-wedlock children born overseas to Canadian soldiers of World War I.[6] Basically, the legislation maintained that if you were born out of wedlock and your parents subsequently marry, your birth is legitimized back to the day you were born.

There's more. Not only was there a reference to a child being "legitimized" in the 1947 Citizenship Act, but that legitimization got tested in the Supreme Court in *The Queen v. Leong Ba Chai* in 1954. That case involved a Chinese Canadian who had fathered a child out of wedlock in China. On his return to Canada, he continued providing financial support to the mother and baby in China. In Chinese law, his providing financial support meant that he and the woman were married. Yet, in Canada, the couple needed to be formally and legally recognized as such. The Supreme Court ruled that, despite Canadian law, Canada would recognize the laws and customs of the person's country of origin, which meant that Ba Chai was married. That legitimized his baby, which in turn allowed the child Canadian citizenship.

We didn't know any of this during the Taylor case but, thanks to two people, one of my "found" Canadians, Fred Colbourne, and the other, Robert Addington, whose family was also affected by the legislation, we learned of these old laws of legitimation. Supporting Jackie's position were Federal Court and Federal Court of Appeal judgments, and a Supreme Court ruling. Further, Robert uncovered two letters, one from the Registrar of Canadian Citizenship dated 1948, and the other from the acting commissioner, Immigration Canada, in 1949, recognizing children born outside Canada, out of wedlock, to Canadian fathers and foreign mothers who subsequently married. The legal precedent being so obvious, why would any prime minister or cabinet minister willingly ignore it? But Mr. Kenney did, and Mr. Harper allowed it.

You'd think that admitting in the House of Commons during the Taylor case that, if the government lost, the potential cost to Canadian taxpayers could be in the "tens of billions of dollars" alone would be enough to get Jackie's citizenship papers signed and thereby end the nonsense. Ditto for the handful of other born-out-of-wedlock war-bride kids still out there. But that would be too logical and too simple. Most of these people had lived, worked, raised families, voted, and paid taxes in Canada all their lives. And now, suddenly, they were told to get out. What the hell was Kenney thinking? Surely he wouldn't be so foolish as to repeat Solberg's billion-dollar gamble.

That's what we thought, and that's why we had a good feeling when Jackie sent off her paperwork for her second 5.4 request. It wasn't long before she heard back, and what she got back wasn't at all what we had contemplated.

On February 1, 2010, Jackie received a letter of acknowledgement that CIC had indeed received her application; it was signed by a Michael Sousa, senior general counsel for Citizenship and Immigration Canada. By accident, included in the envelope was a copy of internal email communications between Stella Holiday, CIC case analyst; Paul Yurack, counsel NHQ, Legal Services, Citizenship and Immigration Canada; Paige Purcell, senior counsel and team leader, NHQ Legal Services, Citizenship and Immigration Canada; and Sharon Chomyn, director general, Case Management

Branch, Citizenship and Immigration Canada, which revealed their strategy for dealing with Jackie. Here it is:

"Since it is likely that Ms. Scott's 5.4 request is likely [sic] to be put forward with a positive recommendation by the Minister to the GIC, then I would normally suggest you write to ask her whether she wishes to withdraw/place on hold her request for proof application, until the sec. 5.4 is finally disposed of."

The communications went on, but the gist was clear. They planned to grant her citizenship through a 5.4 while simultaneously turning her down for proof of citizenship. I called my CIC insider, who admitted having never heard about the Legitimation Act. Nor was this person aware of anyone else in the department knowing about it or, for that matter, even discussing it. Here was a real law, on the books, tested in the Supreme Court, which the gatekeepers of Canadian citizenship knew nothing about. Apparently, for decades, CIC could very well have been wrongfully denying all these people citizenship, and it was doing it as a calculated effort in coordination with its government lawyers. For now, all Jackie could do was wait.

In the meantime, people continued contacting me on a daily basis, asking about their status. When Diane Finley departed, so too did the dedicated Lost Canadian call centre, so in a sense I had become the de facto Canadian citizenship ombudsman. CIC conveniently reverted to its old ways, which basically were to ignore us. Frankly, we felt that its method of dealing with Lost Canadians was through attrition. As a group, we were getting older and, if CIC delayed long enough, we'd all be dead. For CIC, problem solved.

A few years earlier, one of our war brides, Eswyn Lyster, wrote a letter to the Queen of England.[7] Eswyn thought she'd be interested to know how Canada was mistreating her war brides. Although the Queen didn't personally respond, Buckingham Palace did—not once, but twice. The second time was when a rabbi in Montreal wrote, saying that Canada had denied him citizenship because of gender discrimination against his mother. Both letters were referred to our governor general. From Rideau Hall, the responses came back: "I've forwarded your concerns to the Minister of Citizenship and Immigration, the Honourable Jason Kenney." Was I surprised or what—yawn, yawn. But that's how Ottawa did things. When Helena Guergis was the minister of state for the status of women, I wrote her a letter, saying her boss, Steven Harper, was actively discriminating against women in citizenship law. I got this back: "I've forwarded your concerns to the Minister of Citizenship and Immigration, the Honourable Jason Kenney." When Rona Ambrose replaced Guergis as minister of state for the status of women, I again contacted the ministry. It blessed me with yet another reply, saying the matter was now in Jason Kenney's hands. Not one case got resolved.

It made me wonder. Instead of being in Canada, what if I were in Germany in the late 1930s? I write a letter to Hitler, saying several of my neighbours have been rounded up and taken away. He writes back, "I've forwarded your concerns to Adolf Eichmann."

On January 25, 2010, I boarded a WestJet flight from Phoenix to Winnipeg. The next day, hundreds of people were gathering to tell their stories at the Canadian Museum for Human Rights.[8] By now, I had a bit of a track record with both the Aspers and the museum. As I've noted, it was always interesting dealing with non-profit organizations. They all made wonderful claims as to the very important work they did but, when I asked them to help Lost Canadians, their enthusiasm waned. A few years earlier, I was at wit's end with the Institute for Canadian Citizenship (ICC). Just before hanging up the telephone after a conversation with someone there, I mentioned that one day I'd expose the institute for not doing what it was claiming. It wasn't long before my phone was ringing. It was ICC's head lawyer, who explained that their hands were tied: in order for the government to give ICC tax status as a charitable entity, it couldn't lobby the government. I understand the rationale, but what if the wrongs committed were being carried out by the government, as was the case with the Lost Canadians? The answer, simply, was that the charitable organizations either weren't supposed to go against the government or didn't want to bite the hand that fed them. At least, that's how the ICC lawyer explained it. Could the Canadian Museum for Human Rights have its hands tied as well? Most convenient for the government. But then, it made all the rules. To challenge it, you pretty much had to head to the courts, something next to impossible after the government cancelled the Court Challenges Program. You were forced to dig deep into your already challenged pockets, then invest years of your time and energy, hoping for a positive outcome but knowing all the while that the government and CIC had a bad habit of ignoring court decisions. And, of course, Lost Canadians were getting older.

We really were between a rock and a hard place. All we were trying to do was secure equal rights for all Canadians, something the government lauded itself for doing. Governors general, prime ministers, MPs, equality-of-rights organizations—they all knew the buzzwords and were fabulous when it came to staying on target with feel-good quotes and slogans the media loved. But their actions, which often didn't become public knowledge, typically told a far different story.

While in Winnipeg, I made a presentation at the Canadian Museum for Human Rights. Among the people listening were Gail Asper and Mary Eberts. Mary is a lawyer who had been deeply involved in the framing of the guarantees of equality in the Canadian Charter of Rights and Freedoms and one of the founders of LEAF. After my presentation, Gail made some comment about my story having teeth. Later, I discovered that the museum put out several videos, one featuring me. Here's what I said: "When you have citizenship, you are a member, if you will, of a family. But if they take it away, you have no right of judicial review to challenge the government, you have no right of a land, a home, protection—police protection. Nothing."⁹

This being a human rights gathering and Gail being Jewish, I was hoping she would finally catch on that the taking away of one's citizenship is a very big deal. Hitler was all too aware of this fact, since it was the first thing he did against the Jews when he came into power. He clearly understood that stateless people have no rights. The museum opened in September 2014, so only time will tell if the powers that be consider equal rights in citizenship law to be worthy of discussion. As of March 2015, they obviously hadn't. There's been no exhibit regarding Lost Canadians, and in searching their website, by typing "Lost Canadian," it says: *There are no items that match your search criteria.* But what the heck, there was a match on "cats." (See Chapter 11, "Dog Poop, Farts, Toads, and Britney Spears.")

Mary Eberts later emailed me, saying she would like to help, but nothing really happened after that. I contacted one of her LEAF cohorts, Marilou McPhedran. She too was instrumental in obtaining women's rights in Canada, and she too kept her distance from me.

In February 2010, my family was in Vancouver for the Olympics. It was a fabulous event. Most people would say Canada winning the gold in hockey was the pinnacle. A split second after Sidney Crosby scored the winning goal, horns blew, fans began screaming, people hugged and high-fived. Absolute euphoria enveloped the city. Sitting in my daughter's downtown apartment, I called my ninety-three-year-old mother in Phoenix. I held the phone's receiver outside the eighth-floor window to let her hear the noise. She told me, "The last time I heard Vancouver erupt like that was the day World War II ended."

Mothers—especially nine-decade-old mothers—can put a spin on things with the wisdom of the ages. I loved the Olympics apart from a few things I couldn't get out of my mind. While I was finally Canadian, the Jackie Scotts of the world were still being denied. At the closing ceremonies, Harper sat with several First Nations chiefs on the opposite side of the stadium from my wife, my daughter, and me. I thought back to when he apologized for the residential schools and for the country's treatment of the Chinese. I fully agreed: apologies were many decades overdue. But how could this man sleep at night knowing he could end the Lost Canadian saga with the stroke of a pen, yet chose not to? I also didn't take to John Furlong, the man in charge of organizing the Vancouver Games, who years before had brushed me off. He talked of the Olympic spirit as "a force that can replace despair with hope and ignite the human spirit."[10] Nice words, but I knew all about his empty rhetoric. I believed the message, not the man. How would Furlong, an immigrant himself, like it if Harper snatched away his Canadian identity?

I also found it ironic that during the closing ceremonies, of the eight people carrying the Olympic flag into the stadium, four were or could have been Lost Canadians, or had Lost Canadians in their families.[11] Most didn't suspect a thing.

The Olympics are indeed special. Canada, like other countries, wants to be a contender. Often, the governor in council offers 5.4 citizenship grants to foreign Olympians—providing, of course, they compete for Canada. It's an ongoing practice with CIC. Canada desperately wanted an image of fairness, compassion, human rights, and winners. Remember the Jamaican-born Ben Johnson? Canada wooed him, granting his citizenship through a 5.4. He went on to win two gold medals. He even set two world records but later was stripped of them for his use of steroids. CBC called it "Canada's shame."[12] Never once did CBC, or any other network broadcaster, say that Canada's real shame was its treatment of its own people, the Lost Canadians, Chinese, Japanese, Jews, Indians, and, of course, women. The list, unfortunately, is long and growing.

I too had made an Olympic effort, and I'd been at it longer than some of the Olympians had been alive. I got no glory and no ceremony (although thanks to *Global National*, for a brief moment I looked like a lobbyist for foreign strippers from coast to coast). And, like pulling the plug in a bathtub full of water, the money being poured into the Lost Canadian issue was constantly going down the drain. At least there was an inner satisfaction, because at least 750,000 Canadians were now secure.

In March, I met with Megan Stewart and Meghan Strain of the *Vancouver Observer*. For two full days I briefed them on the issue. Stewart, who was working on her masters of journalism at UBC, became the lead journalist on the story. Strain worked behind the scenes. For the next several months, we stayed in constant contact.

Journalists generally want two independent sources to verify a story. I knew Harper's folks had put the screws to Gary Symons and Susanne Reber at CBC, but to date I knew of no other interference.

On April 21, 2010, I was scheduled to be a guest speaker for the University of Washington's Canadian Studies Center, in Seattle. At the University of Washington Club, from 2:30 to 4:00 p.m., several students, faculty, and invited guests listened to my story. Several were Lost Canadians themselves—Bob Stacey, divisional dean, Arts and Humanities, and professor of history; and Linda DiBiase, a librarian at UW Libraries. After the Q&A, Professor Nadine Fabbi made an off-the-wall comment, which was backed up by Amy Scott from the university's Office for Planned Giving. Both had received calls from the Canadian Consulate in Seattle asking that I not be allowed to present, as I might not portray Canada in the best light. Bingo, I had my second confirmation of government interference—the first occurring back in January 2007, when the government tried to censor CBC after it broke the story about there being hundreds of thousands of Lost Canadians. Both Nadine and Amy responded to the caller the same way, explaining that the university was an institution of higher learning where freedom of speech was encouraged, not censored. Both said that anyone from the Canadian Consulate who wanted to attend my talk could, and that if they disagreed with anything I said, they were free to challenge it. Nadine and Amy also reassured the caller that I wouldn't be privy to his objection until after my talk had concluded. To my knowledge, no one from the consulate attended. Certainly no one challenged what I said.

The fact was, I didn't make the Canadian government look bad—Stephen Harper and Jason Kenney were doing a great job of that themselves, as had Paul Martin, Jean Chrétien, Monte Solberg, Joe Volpe, Judy Sgro, Denis Coderre, and Elinor Caplan before them, not to mention the ensemble of complicit bureaucrats. Fortunately, my conversation with Nadine and Amy was witnessed by two journalists: Jenny Cunningham from the public broadcasting station KCTS in Seattle, and Megan Stewart from the *Vancouver Observer*.

For years I'd been sending story suggestions to the *Oprah Winfrey Show*. I figured that, with her vast Canadian audience and her personal experiences with discrimination, maybe she'd be interested. She wasn't. Probably ten or twenty of my emails went unanswered. Regrettably, Americans don't often look outside their own borders to notice what goes on elsewhere. If I asked my pilot friends, college-educated world travellers all, what the capital of Canada was and who was the prime minister, they'd pause for a moment, then, with a look of "who cares," maybe respond by saying "Toronto and

Trudeau." Oprah knew her audience, she knew the American psyche. No one in the States cared except maybe one anonymous person who contacted me by email.

Whomever it was who had emailed, he (or she) knew quite a bit about me—stuff not out there in the public domain. It was the only time since taking on the Canadian government that I felt threatened. I believed him to be American, as he'd taken offence at my wanting to be Canadian. It was all quite unsettling.

Given that I was a loud-mouth in Canada, this wasn't the first time I'd ruffled feathers. I was also a union activist and had been quite involved with aviation safety. Over the years I'd appeared on ABC's *20/20*; been quoted in the *Wall Street Journal*, *Newsweek*, and *Business Week*; and submitted testimony to the US Congress. After Bill C-37, I began feeding Susanne Reber stories about aviation, telling her about some airline pilots who made just $5 an hour. We talked about pilot fatigue—that the airlines were now having quite a bit of their maintenance done overseas, where, just maybe, a few fake nuts or bolts might be wending their way into the system.

Looking back, no wonder some in the media considered me a flake—my claims seemed preposterous, like $5-per-hour-pay for airline pilots. But with the Continental crash in Buffalo less than a year later, the world discovered for itself the truth of what I'd told Susanne about the deplorable conditions in aviation.[13] CBC aired its in-depth news coverage, using me as one of its sources.

Sadly, the Canadian media just wasn't of the same calibre as their US counterparts. Investigative journalism south of the border was far superior, probably because they had more money. It also helped that Americans were much more engaged.

That's why it was so thrilling in September 2010 when, in Toronto at the Canadian Online Publishing Awards, Megan Stewart's name was read out as co-winner for best online article, for her Lost Canadian series with the *Vancouver Observer*. By now, she'd partnered with another UBC graduate named Darren Fleet. Their work was indeed impressive. As Megan later told me, it was standing-room-only at the back of the room that night. The judges for her category were from *Esquire* and *New York Magazine*. When the winner's name was announced, she had to make her way through the crowd, down to the floor, and around the front tables where representatives of *Maclean's*, the *Globe and Mail*, the *National Post*, CTV, and CBC sat. The bigwigs of Canadian journalism witnessed the accolades and awards being presented for the very story they had ignored.

What a great moment that was, not just for the *Vancouver Observer* and Megan and Darren, but also for the Lost Canadians. At home in Phoenix, I savoured the moment. That's how I coped, enjoying each victory one by one. I had to do it that way because on a moment's notice, the mood could change. One never knew what lurked just around the corner. The *Vancouver Observer* obviously epitomized the good. As for the bad, well, something terrible had happened to one of my Ottawa-based Lost Canadians, Jan Makins, in June 2010. Here's her story:

I was born and raised in England. I moved to Canada, lived in Louisiana from 1979 until my divorce in 2002, which was when I considered moving to Canada since I had no family in the United States and the rest of my small family were scattered throughout the world.

In 2003 I sought guidance from Canadian Immigration and they suggested I apply for citizenship. They said it would be a simple process due to the fact that my grandfather was Canadian. He was from Cape Breton, had enlisted in the Canadian Expeditionary Force in 1917 and subsequently married my British grandmother in England. I submitted an application for citizenship in October 2003 but it was denied in March of 2005 based on the fact that my grandfather was my maternal grandfather and I was not "born out of wedlock."

I moved to Canada as a visitor in April of 2005 and was able to obtain visitor extensions through December 2010. Meanwhile I applied for Permanent Residence as a Skilled Worker but it was denied in November of 2008. At this point I hired a lawyer which led me nowhere, but he did bring to my attention the Joe Taylor lawsuit and at the same time a friend came across the Lost Canadian website. I contacted Don and later he told me he was planning a demonstration at the Parliament buildings for October 2009. I was anxious to take part, along with my friends who rallied for hours in the pouring rain!! Later that week Marlene Jennings brought up a motion in Parliament to give immediate citizenship to a number of Lost Canadians, of which I was one. The motion was struck down.

Then unexpectedly in March of 2010 John Baird's office (member of Parliament for my area) suggested I apply for citizenship under Section 5.4. Almost two years later, I am told my application is at the highest level, somewhere between the Governor in Council and the Minister. It has neither been approved nor denied.

Unfortunately, in June of 2010 I decided to take a 3 week holiday in England. On my return I was denied re-entry into Canada for one year and deported back to England. This was despite the fact that I had a visitor extension until December of 2010 and an ongoing citizenship application. I owned a residence in Ottawa, was financially sound, healthy, volunteered at the hospital—in other words a model citizen... I moved to Florida, and then returned to Canada one year later on June 24, 2011. Throughout this ordeal Don was in constant contact and doing everything in his power to get me back into Canada.

Jan's crime was being born in wedlock to a mother who was Canadian. If Jan had been born out of wedlock, or if the Canadian had been her father rather than her mother, or if she'd been born on or after January 1, 1947, Jan would be Canadian. Now, if you were an employer and refused an applicant for any of those reasons, you'd be before the human rights tribunal in a New York second. And it would be right in going after you. It's illegal in Canada to deny someone work because of age, gender, or family status. Yet Jan's denial was a combination of all three. When I contacted the Canadian Human Rights Commission, I was told to contact the Honourable Jason Kenney, minister of citizenship and immigration (all roads led to Kenney), and they explained how the commission was prohibited from dealing with issues having to do with government discrimination in citizenship law.

Then, to top off Jan's nightmare, CIC had her deported. She had a legal right to stay in Canada, and yet that right was ignored. Her MP was John Baird; one of his office workers was a woman named Andrea. When Jan and I first began working together, Andrea warned her that, by associating with me, Jan might find her application delayed. And so it was. It appeared that Canada had a "Chapman's list," and Jan's name was on it.

In July 2010, I had contacted Nicole Girard, director of CIC's Citizenship Legislation and Program Policy Division. For the first time ever, someone at CIC officially stated the government's estimates on how many Lost Canadians there were. She admitted there being at least 750,000. That's a far cry from the number Diane Finley revealed to the committee—450. I mentioned that Bill C-37, although correcting nine of the twelve ways to lose citizenship, left three categories untouched while creating three more. I explained that the way the legislation was being interpreted by her department, Canadian-born citizens could actually have fewer rights than naturalized Canadians; how the government was still denying many of the pre-1947 folks; and that CIC was ignoring three Supreme Court rulings. In so many words, discrimination was still very much alive and thriving in Canadian citizenship law. I suggested some very simple solutions to correct the problems. She listened. I wrote and sent her a brief outlining the remaining issues and their respective solutions, then for the next three years she went silent. (In 2013, when it surfaced that Kenney was considering a second-generation born-abroad amendment, we again connected. Our conversation discussing the deficiencies was cordial but businesslike. She thanked me for my input, then once again she went her way and I went mine.)

Earlier in 2010, a bill was introduced in the House dealing with Native women's rights.[14] Like the Lost Canadian situation where women didn't have the same rights as men to confer citizenship on their children, Native women couldn't pass on status. In *McIvor v. The Registrar, Indian and Northern Affairs Canada*, McIvor won; Native women were to be given the same rights as Native men.[15] The courts gave the government a fixed amount of time to bring the laws into compliance, but it missed the deadline. However, C-3 did eventually pass, going from introduction to royal assent in just nine months. Retroactively, Native women could now pass on status to their children. It was ironic for the Lost Canadians; the government was currently doing for Natives what I was asking them to do for us. It meant that some First Nations women now had more rights than non-Native women. Further, Canada could now grant or deny rights based entirely on ethnicity.

At the beginning of November, I was interviewed by the University of New Brunswick's student newspaper. I mentioned there could be as many as 1 million Lost Canadians.* The reporter mistakenly reported it as being 1 million "stateless" people.[16] Of course, that is wrong. I had forewarned him that CIC read everything printed about me. Any doubts he may have had vanished once the article appeared. Jason Kenney finally came out of the closet, writing a letter to the editor in which he accused me of misleading the public about there being 1 million stateless people. Before Kenney even sent his letter, I had contacted the editor, explaining the error. The correction had already been published. Here's what Kenney wrote: "I challenge Mr. Chapman to tell us how he has determined there are hundreds of thousands of 'Lost Canadians.' This figure is sensational and cannot be substantiated."[17]

It was an incredibly easy rebuttal: "Last Mar. 8 during question period on the floor of the House of Commons, you spoke these exact words, as

---

* I was referring to the total number of Lost Canadians—people who at one time or other were deprived because of old, discriminatory laws—rather than to only those currently without citizenship rights.

published in Hansard, 'This government, Parliament and the Liberal Party adopted Bill C-37 in the last Parliament to correct the Citizenship Act to welcome back to Canadian citizenship hundreds of thousands of lost Canadians.' You, Minister Kenney, you are my substantiation."[18]

That same month, Katie Hewitt of the *Globe and Mail* emailed me, asking me to submit my bio for the newspaper's Transformational Canadians series.[19] I explained that the *Globe* had been terrible in its news coverage of the Lost Canadians and, besides, the issue wasn't about me. She replied that highlighting me would in turn highlight the problem. Although I didn't much care to be in the newspaper, I cared greatly about the issue. Looking back, I shouldn't have bothered. The best the *Globe* had ever come up with was an old article that I had complained about almost four years earlier because it got all the pertinent facts wrong. The *Globe* refused to print a correction. The title alone was a joke: "'Lost' Canadians Get Citizenship."[20] Obviously, we hadn't, and the numbers were a tad bigger than the 450 figure the *Globe* had reported.

As 2010 came to a close, once again the holidays were filled with talk of an election, and I was more than willing to jump into bed with someone other than Stephen Harper. It had been one year since Jackie Scott had filed for her second 5.4 citizenship grant, and two months since I had requested a Certificate of Canadian Citizenship for my grandson. The fight raged on, another stateless child surfaced, and all of us sat waiting in the deafening silence from CIC.

By the end of March 2011, only one story dominated the news. Just six days after the spring equinox it became official: Canadians were heading back to the polls. And with that, for the first time in my life, I became actively engaged in trying to get someone elected, throwing my support behind Liberal Daniel Veniez. I liked the man, and he embraced our issue. Suddenly, red signs were gracing my fence. Years earlier, they were blue, for John Reynolds. The election was telling. By now, all four party leaders knew about the Lost Canadian issue, but none spoke out. I had a public encounter, caught on camera, with Michael Ignatieff, who said "95 percent isn't good enough when we're talking about rights ... and citizenship."[21] He was referring to the folks not covered under C-37. Ironically, Bloc leader Gilles Duceppe's father was a Lost Canadian, yet Gilles didn't speak out. Melynda Jarratt and I were asked to participate in an NDP town hall meeting. We submitted questions on Lost Canadians, but Jack Layton ignored them. Citizenship-wise, not one leader attempted to hold Harper accountable. In the end, my riding went to incumbent John Weston, who later was appointed to

the Standing Committee on Citizenship and Immigration. I called, asking
him to be an advocate. I wanted to testify before the committee, and to have
a face-to-face meeting with Jason Kenney. Neither happened.

Shortly after that, I met with Gary Symons, and did he ever drop a bombshell. He was talking about the 2007 fiasco where Harper and CIC had
gone after him for broadcasting the Lost Canadian story. Through his freedom-of-information requests, he had discovered that while the bureaucrats
were suggesting the numbers of Lost Canadians out there numbered only in
the hundreds, behind closed doors they were admitting that my estimates
were spot-on, and they were talking about me by name. In other words, they
were publicly slamming me, indicating I was some sort of nutbar, yet they
knew full well that my words were true. After the government called the top
CBC people, telling them they had two rogue reporters, it went further by
contacting several Ottawa media folks, intimating that if they did any story
about me or the Lost Canadians, they could be taken off the government's
Ottawa press corps list. Governments have the ability to direct stories, and
reporters love being on the inside. No one wants to be taken off the preferential list.

Apparently, I had been both blackballed and publicly discredited. No
wonder I had been so shunned by the media.

What a way to run a country.

The April 18, 2011, online issue of the *Globe and Mail* included a story
titled "The Harpers Go Bollywood in GTA Battleground" and featured a
photo of Laureen Harper dancing with Akshay Kumar, the famed Indian
movie star:

> The Conservative Leader appeared at a Brampton, Ont., movie theatre
> to rub shoulders with Bollywood superstar Akshay Kumar, an Indian per-
> former with a huge fan base in Canada.
>
> Mr. Kumar's arrival was greeted by adoring and shrieking fans.
>
> The film star offered an effusive endorsement for Mr. Harper before
> a debut showing of his new movie—a gesture the Tories are hoping will
> help them win Greater Toronto Area seats with big Indo-Canadian
> communities.[22]

Harper, the consummate campaigner, obviously wanted the Indian
community's vote, and here was a way to get it. Parade around with a huge
Bollywood star and let him endorse you to his adoring fans.[23] The strategy
worked. In return, Kumar wanted Canadian citizenship, and it had come to

the media's attention that he might get it through a section 5.4 grant. They were investigating a possible conflict of interest.

There's power in being able to grant citizenship more or less on a whim, almost with a snap of the fingers or the stroke of a pen. In the end, both Harper and Kumar were happy. The media wanted to know all about the 5.4 process. They contacted me, mentioning that there had been some objections to Kumar's grant within Harper's cabinet itself. They wanted hard evidence. I responded by saying that what goes on inside the cabinet is private, meaning there is no public evidence. Unless there's a leak, what happens inside Harper's cabinet stays inside Harper's cabinet. Further, I explained that granting citizenship for special favours was not new in Canadian politics. Lost Canadian Frank Gehry got his in just over twenty-four hours when Jean Chrétien extended the offer to him, Elinor Caplan's cousin; she was citizenship minister at the time.

No question, granting citizenship for political favours is ripe for abuse in Canada. Put money in a Swiss bank from an unnamed source and quite possibly get citizenship. With such little oversight, the possibilities are endless.

In the end, Harper was prime minister and Kumar a new Canadian. It wasn't exactly trading citizenship for pizzas or Romanian strippers who help your campaign, but it was close. Could "substantial connection" to Canada be defined as someone who actively helps the prime minister get elected and prominently dances with his wife? Yes, I think so.

Meanwhile, Lost Canadians without a huge Canadian fan base—Jackie Scott and the others like her—were forced to wait for their 5.4 grants, knowing they might never get them. Some were in failing health, and if relief didn't come soon, they might not be around if or when it did. As with Joe Taylor, it was time to head back to the courts.

Recall Monte Solberg's words: "We cannot stand idle when court decisions threaten dozens of statutes and could cost the government billions of dollars. In a case like that, it is our duty to stand up for the government of Canada and the people of Canada." So why was the government once again gambling taxpayers' dollars over something it had already lost? Why not just give these people citizenship and be done with it? Didn't it learn anything from the Taylor fiasco?

Who knows?

But for the second time, with certainty, the Conservatives under Mr. Harper were about to gamble the Canadian taxpayer farm.

CHAPTER 18

PLEASE, PUT ME OUT OF BUSINESS

There is no crueller tyranny than that which is perpetrated under
the shield of law and in the name of justice.
CHARLES DE MONTESQUIEU

IN THE ELECTION of 2006, I had reluctantly wanted Stephen Harper to win. In 2011, although I favoured Ignatieff, I had reservations about him. He had been the second leader of a political party who took a supportive position regarding the Lost Canadians. But it wasn't in Ottawa or anywhere most people would notice.[1] Iggy did it when I asked him about it in a public Q&A during the election campaign, and it would be hard to imagine *any* political leader standing before a crowd and saying, "Yeah, let's get rid of the bastards."* Of course, he had to give me his support. But I was already disappointed in him because, in all the years leading up to the election, he had never uttered one word in the House of Commons about our issue despite my many calls and emails pleading for his support. After losing the election, he retired from public life and retreated to teaching at the University of Toronto, probably with a focus on human rights.

Support for our cause was drying up. I talked to Bob Rae during the summer of 2010. He too listened politely and, in a surprised tone, indicated that his brother might have been a Lost Canadian. Other than his emails to me saying that he supports the issue, his party has remained rather silent. Jack Layton obviously had his health problems after the election. So,

---

* I say "bastards" because that's the term many born-out-of-wedlock war-bride kids use when describing how the government has made them feel.

in his absence, I called the NDP House Leader Libby Davies, whose Vancouver Downtown Eastside people promptly shut me out. The Bloc had disappeared, and what remained in the Conservative Party was the same ministerial disappointment who, for almost three years, had refused to acknowledge my existence. It had reached the point where I felt a similar disdain for Jason Kenney as I had for George Bush Jr.

After Kenney became citizenship and immigration minister, he added to the mix one more portfolio: multiculturalism. Maybe in a previous life Kenney was the guy who stood outside a nightclub, assigned to woo in customers. Running a political campaign has all sorts of specific job descriptions but, to me, Kenney was the guy doing anything and everything to try to seduce voters into supporting the Conservatives.

Shortly after the election, I watched a CBC reporter interview Kenney about his role in the election, suggesting he had been the main person responsible for Harper's win. What the reporter said validated my thoughts about the man and his role within the party. Yes, I thought, Kenney had indeed stacked his ministerial deck of cards so that Harper would be at the election table with a royal flush. I questioned the ethics of so blatantly using a portfolio, which really ought to be about the public good, simply as a vehicle for harvesting votes. In the CBC interview, Kenney proudly stated he'd been attending upward of forty functions per week all over Canada as he visited the many different immigrant communities. At each, he gave a speech (both an entrance and an exit one). Throw into that his travel time "all across Canada" and then do the math. It means that, at minimum, he was cozying up to immigrant groups twelve to fifteen hours per day, every day. So just when did he have the time to do what he'd been elected to do—represent *all* Canadians. What about his own constituents? I would love to be paid as a full-time pilot and be able to skip work to do whatever suited my fancy. Obviously, playing hooky is realistic only in the world of politics, and only because the public is accepting of such behaviour. Granted, all parties do it, but to me, it sure doesn't seem right. I vote for people to represent Canadians, not themselves.

The CBC interview reminded me of Jason Kenney's testimony before the House Committee on Citizenship in 2009 where Liberal citizenship critic Maurizio Bevilacqua posed this question: "Minister, I just want to follow up on Ms. Wong's question. I found interesting the whole notion of multiculturalism and immigration coming together. Just for interest's sake, on your workload, what percentage do you spend on your immigration duties versus your multiculturalism duties?"

"It's hard to say precisely, but I would say probably 70 to 30 immigration to multiculturalism, in terms of my time."

"Doesn't that make you a part-time minister of citizenship and immigration and a part-time minister of multiculturalism?"

"It makes me very tired, is what it makes me."[2]

By his own admission, Kenney was spending zero time on citizenship issues (70 percent immigration plus 30 percent multiculturalism equals 100 percent of his time). In aviation, there are several distinct phases of flight. Takeoff and climb; cruise; descent and landing. I'd hate to ride on an airplane where the pilot completely checked out of one of those phases. But so it was with Kenney. His job title began with "citizenship," yet that's not at all what he was doing. Even my CIC insider confirmed it. Citizenship was not his priority.

In the post-9/11 world, passports are needed for international travel. That meant the citizenship side of Kenny's portfolio was desperately in need of attention. A lot of Canadians would soon suffer the consequences of his inaction. I tried telling this to the media, to no avail. Kenney's lack of active participation in citizenship haunted Lost Canadians, but in time they wouldn't be the only ones feeling the pinch.

During the spring of 2011, I got a call from Lin Crosbie-Marshall, a writer in Newfoundland who had been assigned to do a story about the Lost Canadians for *Downhome* magazine. She featured three people who had been denied citizenship; all were war-bride children. Two were covered under C-37; the third, at least according to CIC, wasn't. That person's name was Audrey Poole, and this is her story:

> I was born abroad pre-1947, in wedlock, to a Canadian mother, but under the present rules, am not entitled to claim citizenship under Bill C-37. However, if I had been born to a Canadian father under the same circumstances, I would receive Canadian citizenship automatically. My mother was born in Canada and met my father there before the war. They were to marry and live there as soon as my father left the Royal Navy. Unfortunately, the war intervened, and he was sent to Malta, where the marriage took place. So that I could be born in Canada, my mother booked passage home in August 1940, but on reaching the UK, she was informed that the ship (the SS *Geraldine Mary*) had been sunk in the Atlantic by a German U-boat. She therefore had to remain in the UK, spending most of her time volunteering to help her own countrymen, sent to a local nursing home taken over for treating wounded British and Allied servicemen.

In August 1946, we wanted to return to Canada but my father was badly affected by the war (with what today would be called post-traumatic stress) and felt he could not leave England.

Consequently, we had to return to England and it was not until I was 21 that I was able to return to Canada. I was told that because my mother was Canadian, not my father, I would have to emigrate to Canada, which I did, and was in Canada on my 25th birthday.

When Bill C-37 was introduced, I had hoped that Canadian women would be included and I would be able to apply for citizenship as the official Canadian Immigration Commission stated: "People who would obtain citizenship included people born abroad before 1947 to a Canadian parent." Unfortunately, although it states "Canadian parent," it still only applies to Canadian fathers—effectively denying the same rights to Canadian mothers. Although the government has righted this discrimination for First Nation Canadian women, it has failed to do the same for other groups such as mine.[3] It is difficult to understand why. Canadian fathers have the right to pass their citizenship down to their children, while my mother, whose family have lived in Canada continuously for over 300 years, cannot. Many of my ancestors fought and died for Canada in both world wars, and their names are recorded in "The Books of Remembrance" in Ottawa. I would sincerely like to move closer to my family, and hope that you can do something to convince the present government to give equal rights to Canadian women so as to change the present gender discrimination.

Too bad Audrey hadn't been born out of wedlock. I find her situation fascinating when looking at it in terms of Newfoundland, the last province to join Confederation, on March 31, 1949. One of the conditions for entry was that Newfies be recognized as Canadian citizens, back to date of birth or date of domicile. Earlier I mentioned that we'd discovered that for the children like me, whose fathers took out citizenship in another country and hence lost our citizenship under the 1947 act, we had every right to return as Canadian citizens. Within the act was a provision for our return. CIC, on the other hand, based its denial on a provision of the 1977 act, which instead made us immigrants required to qualify. Basically, the government was cherry-picking. Judging us on the 1947 act, it should have given us its remedy. But that's not what it did. Instead, it judged us by the legislation in 1947 while giving us the remedy of 1977. It was the only way it could deny our rights. In a sense, CIC was now doing this to the Newfies.

Audrey and her family were domiciled in Canada on January 1, 1947. So, having a British father, she should have been recognized as a citizen. If she was a citizen, then Bill C-37 restored it, since she was out of Canada on her twenty-fourth birthday. Second, her family moved out of Canada and back to Newfoundland, where they resided in March 1949. Therefore, given the condition of Newfoundland becoming a province of Canada, they should have been recognized as Canadian. But once again, CIC was cherry-picking—to the detriment of the individual Canadian.

I wanted to meet and explain this to Mr. Kenney, but he refused to see me. And trying to correct the Lost Canadian issue was next to impossible when the person in charge wouldn't speak or publicly defend his position, but rather always retreated behind the heavily guarded fortress of CIC. In doing so, the remaining 5 percent become easy prey for the deeply entrenched bureaucracy, with its well-stocked arsenal.

Soon another woman came forward with one of the most heartbreaking stories I had heard in all my years fighting for Lost Canadians. Her name is Velma Demerson, and she's in her early nineties. She was born in Canada in 1920. It seemed that, according to the government, by 1939, Velma as a young teenage girl had committed two offences. The first is that she fell in love. The second is that, after Eve and Mary, she was the third woman in the history of mankind to get pregnant out of wedlock. To make it exponentially worse, the father of her child was Chinese (not Chinese Canadian, but Chinese Chinese).

Unbeknownst to most Canadians, there is a particularly offensive piece of legislation dating from the late 1800s called the Female Refuges Act of 1897.[4] Getting pregnant out of wedlock was one way to be labelled "incorrigible." Another was being involved with someone outside your own race. Velma was guilty of both.

Her punishment? Jail. Velma was imprisoned, where she gave birth to a cute little baby boy.

It gets worse.

The government practised medical experimentation on Velma, and the drugs it gave her affected her baby.

Most Canadians remain unaware that our own government had been in the same business as Josef Mengele, the infamous Nazi doctor of Auschwitz, although not with the same intent. Regardless, for the crime of having a child out of wedlock with a Chinese man, the government of Canada experimented on Velma and her Canadian-born child.

In Velma's own words:

It was 1948 when I entered the Canadian citizenship office in Toronto to apply for a passport. I was born in Saint John, N.B., in September of 1920. I was told I wasn't a Canadian, I was Chinese. I lost my Canadian citizenship as a result of marrying an alien in 1940. I went to the Chinese Embassy in Toronto and was again denied citizenship. I became stateless.

The law changed in 1947 and any Canadian-born woman who lost her citizenship through marriage was entitled to get it back. Why the immigration officer didn't give me Canadian citizenship in 1948 I don't know.

In May 1939, I was eighteen years old, 3 1/2 months pregnant and living with my Chinese fiancé when the police came to our home. I was arrested, charged with being "Incorrigible" and sentenced to one year in the Belmont Home. Soon thereafter the Home closed down and forty-seven incorrigible young women including myself were transferred to the Andrew Mercer Reformatory for Females in Toronto and put in cells. Many years later the offence "Incorrigible" was declared to be illegal.

My son was born in 1939 while I was in the Reformatory. I was not married and he was a Canadian citizen. I married the father of my child when I was released in 1940. In September 1949 I sent my son, Harry Yip, a Canadian citizen, to Hong Kong to learn the Chinese language. He was nine years old. Due to racial prejudice he could not assimilate into Canadian society. I could not accompany him as I did not have a Canadian passport. On his arrival in Hong Kong he was beset by reporters. During the trip his eczema had broken out, the result of an experimental drug used on me during pregnancy. Reporters weighed the mixed-race problem. It was deplored that a Canadian boy was sent to Hong Kong with its lower standards of hygiene. The publicity embarrassed the Chinese community in Toronto. I felt like a complete outcast—I attempted suicide.

It was decided I would apply for a passport in my maiden name. There was a 5-year penalty for falsely obtaining a Canadian passport but I was desperate. I was successful in obtaining one and left Canada on a Danish freighter in May 1950. But I was unable to obtain suitable employment in Hong Kong—my son's name was Harry Yip, mine was Demerson. I was afraid it would be discovered that I had broken the law. I managed to survive by teaching shorthand and elementary English but my wages were insufficient. After a year I sent my son back to his father in Canada. He would be removed from his father and become a ward of the Children's Aid.

I also broke the citizenship law when I worked for the federal government as a non-citizen [under] my single name in 1949. Over the years I voted in elections. Many women, I believe, have broken these laws not

knowing they were non-citizens. I obtained my Canadian citizenship when
I applied in 2004. I was 84 years old.

Velma lived in BC the better part of her life, always with the fear that
if her "lie" was discovered, the government could actually throw her back
in jail. Remember, being stateless, she wouldn't have been allowed to
work, and being stateless was a direct result of being married to a foreigner.
Because she lied about her marriage, Canada could legally throw the book
at her. Her punishment could have been up to five more years in jail. Her
story breaks the bounds of decency in terms of how this country treats its
citizens. It's so off the wall that it sounds unbelievable. But it's true. Velma
Demerson spent more than six decades without benefit of having a country
all because she got pregnant out of wedlock and took a Chinese husband.

If Velma's son were alive today, he too could be denied citizenship under
Jason Kenney's rules, although, most likely, Kenney wouldn't notice.

Back in the 1970s, my father gave me some advice: "If you make a
mistake in life, make it because of love, not hate." Velma fell in love with
someone and, as a result, had a beautiful baby boy. That was seventy-five
years ago, and she suffered not because what she did was wrong but because
she fell into a bureaucratic quagmire in a non-accepting country. She
deserves a full government apology. So do all Lost Canadians. And Velma
brought up a very good point: How many other women married non-Canadians prior to 1947? Could they be stateless? Would they be like Velma, who
for all those years was afraid to speak out, fearful of possibly being thrown
into jail? Because the bureaucrats and Mr. Kenney elected to ignore the all-
party, unanimous recommendation of the Citizenship Committee to not
attach a retroactive drop-dead date, C-37's acceptance went back only to
1947.[5] That means the discrimination continues for people born before this
date. How many Velma Demersons arc still out there?

During the summer parliamentary recess, I learned that the Liberals
had appointed a brand-new citizenship critic, Kevin Lamoureux, and he
would be speaking at two locations in the Vancouver area. Jackie Scott and
I attended, as did a reporter from the *Vancouver Observer*. I walked up to
Lamoureux and asked him if he knew about the Lost Canadians. While I
didn't like his answer, I admired his honesty. He had heard about people
having citizenship problems but, other than that, no. What a surprise—a
new appointee to the Citizenship Committee without a clue. I had talked
about the issue one on one with Bob Rae, the new interim leader; his predecessor calls Lost Canadians a human rights violation; the previous Liberal

citizenship critic issues a press release about us; and now the Liberal Party appoints a novice with absolutely no understanding whatsoever.

Pilots are extremely well trained. Rarely is there a bad apple, let alone two. Your chances of getting on an airplane with two weak pilots in the cockpit is infinitesimally small, pretty much the same chances of getting two knowledgeable, competent politicians together on the Citizenship Committee. Once again the opposition parties were useless in providing proper oversight, allowing Jason Kenney to go about his merry way of denial. Lamoureux went so far as to say that if we couldn't explain the Lost Canadian issue in one page or less, he wasn't interested. Imagine the pilot flying your plane having read only one page from the training manual on how to fly. Would you be comfortable having that person as your captain? For Lost Canadians, we were stuck with incompetent MPs, be they citizenship critics, citizenship ministers, or prime ministers.

I met with the NDP's newly appointed citizenship critic Don Davies but, by 2014, we had had just two meetings in his office. Not much else happened. He admitted having a Lost Canadian family member. Then, just as Davies was spooling up on our issue, his party took him out of the portfolio, replacing him with yet another newbie, Jinny Sims, and just as Sims was spooling up, she was swapped out for Lysane Blanchette-Lamothe. The decade before Blanchette-Lamothe was born I was trying to regain my citizenship. It was like musical chairs, always with the Lost Canadians getting stuck without a chair.

The Canadian Bar Association (CBA) held its annual convention in Halifax during the summer. Before the meeting, I talked with the chairman of its Equality Committee, Aleem Bharmal. He was very receptive and agreed to raise the issue at the convention. It was quite a coincidence that Governor General David Johnston was one of the guest speakers at the convention. Having a passion for law, he pulled no punches in hammering at the lawyers. The governor general's message was that Canada needed to become a smarter and more caring nation, especially with the country's 150th birthday fast approaching. He talked about the ethics of law, and how very few lawyers had spoken out in advance of the financial collapse of 2008, despite their insider knowledge of what was about to happen. Turning to law schools and how potential students are vetted, he suggested they examine not just their "demonstrated intelligence," but also perform an extensive evaluation of their personal relationships, their "wisdom, judgment, leadership," and their "ethical sensibility and depth." Furthermore, as reported by the *Globe and Mail*, "he criticized lawyers for their role in adding unnecessary delay to legal cases and not doing enough pro bono work," saying that "the percentage of pro bono work done is minuscule."[6]

When Mr. Bharmal returned from the convention, I contacted him. We had a pleasant conversation. But I was left with the feeling that, although he personally agreed with me, the Canadian Bar Association had no interest in the Lost Canadians. At the very least, you'd think the CBA would be shocked by our government's ignorance of citizenship laws and complete disregard of several court decisions, including from the highest of them all, the Supreme Court of Canada. But then, just maybe the CBA was also ignorant of Canadian citizenship law. Other than its one short statement to the House Citizenship Committee in 2014, I can find no record of it ever speaking out on Lost Canadians.

After confronting the establishment for so many years, on October 15 I joined about 5,000 others for the Occupy Vancouver rally. There could be no question, something has gone terribly wrong, all around the world. In country after country, leaders have stopped representing their people. Like the others, I too desire a better country, which to me would be one that puts its people first. My grandson had just turned two. We were together that day, and while he was having a great time running among the crowds, I was thinking about his future. He had his own citizenship problems. With C-37, his Canadian status was questionable simply because CIC was now allowed to treat some children differently from others. My grandson is one of those on the short end.

At the same time, an interesting situation was happening south of the border. There, a ninety-five-year-old Canadian-born man named Leland Davidson in Centralia, Washington, had recently discovered, of all things, that he wasn't a US citizen, despite having been born to American parents. He'd been living in the States since age five. With the tighter rules regarding border security, his citizenship problem surfaced when he tried to get an enhanced Washington driver's licence. It seems his parents had neglected to register his birth abroad, so technically he wasn't a US citizen.* So far his story sounds awfully familiar. In trying to prove his connection to the States, he came up against the federal bureaucracies and his paperwork was delayed. Being ninety-five, the time left to him was not exactly abundant. But here is where things get radically different in terms of how the US and Canada handle this type of thing.

KOMO TV is Seattle's ABC television affiliate, and Leland decided to

---

* If Mr. Davidson wasn't Canadian, despite being born in Canada, then he'd been stateless—a man without a country—for ninety-five years, all thanks to the Canadian government.

contact the station. It immediately solicited the help of Senator Patty Murray, and soon the *Seattle Times* did a story that got the bureaucrats moving. It was as if a magician had pulled a rabbit out of a hat. Leland was quickly scheduled to attend a citizenship ceremony in Seattle, where all kinds of media broadcast the event from coast to coast.[7] Twenty-eight family members attended, all five generations of Davidsons. The news caught the eye of the *Vancouver Sun*'s Brittany Wong, who teamed up with *Seattle Times* writer Lornet Turnbull to do a full-page article in the *Sun*, on the front page of section B, which happens to be titled "Canada/World."[8]

So let's compare. In Canada I call the media and they mostly ignore the situation; if they do write a story, it rarely motivates CIC into action. Citizenship seems to matter a great deal more to Americans than it does to Canadians. North of the border, there appear to be two distinct citizenship drinking fountains. A well-kept one for Canadians, and the other, a run-down fountain with weeds at its base for Lost Canadians. That's really how it feels.

In November, CBC ran a story on *The National* about Alice McKay, a woman in BC whose situation somewhat mirrored that of Leland Davidson in the States. Alice, however, wasn't so much interested in driving as she was in getting a passport. It seems Alice was born in the US and was brought to Canada as a two-year-old in 1929 by her parents. She grew up in the Ottawa area.

Alice's family planned ahead for a 2011 gathering in Hawaii, so, in October 2009, they applied to CIC for proof of Alice's citizenship. As her son said, "We're already over two years since we applied (for citizenship)...The frustration is there is nobody you can talk to. There isn't anybody that I can pick up the phone and say there is an injustice here." Dan was referring to CIC's Case Processing Centre in Sydney, Nova Scotia—the same one that for decades had been giving Lost Canadians citizenship fits. As a veteran of its inefficiencies, I was hardly surprised that the McKay family had discovered that dealing with CIC wasn't much different from beating your head against a brick wall. Alice's son was obviously frustrated. "When you are told in October to call back in May—they obviously don't have any idea how long it will take. So they just pick numbers and dates out of the air."[9]

And now compare this with the story of Lost Canadian rabbi Schneur Rabin from Montreal. Earlier in the spring, Canada, in an instance of gender discrimination against his mother, denied Rabin citizenship. He contacted CIC's counterpart in Australia because he happened also to be a Lost Australian. Keep in mind, these citizenship laws were written by the British, so they graced the books of many countries in the Commonwealth. Canada appears to be the lone holdout in fully correcting the deficiencies. As mentioned earlier, several years ago, Australia welcomed back its lost citizens (ironically, its laws became effective on July 1, 2010, our Canada Day). Schneur qualified, so he sent in his application from Montreal. It took just ten days for the Aussies to process his application, immediately sending him his Certificate of Australian Citizenship. Other countries have made their process relatively easy, advocating for the rights of their citizens. In Canada, it can easily take more than two years.

Mr. Kenney, as "citizenship" minister, where were you?

Over the years, I'd warned the media several times about the issue of waiting times and proof of citizenship certificates. Can you imagine being turned away from medical treatment, Old Age Security, a driver's licence, or a passport; not being able to vote; and for some, not being able to live in Canada, simply because you couldn't prove you were Canadian? But that was the reality for many Lost Canadians.

Let me quote again from the CBC story: "Figures from Citizenship and Immigration Canada show that while many more applications are coming in to the Sydney processing centre, fewer are being processed each year and the wait times are getting longer. In 2006, 195,385 applications came in and 270,851 were processed. By contrast, 290,854 came in last year and 153,825 were processed ... This summer, there were 270,848 applications on file, which will take an estimated 19 months to put through."[10]

CIC had just admitted that, in 2010, over 137,000 Canadians were ignored by their own government while they waited patiently for proof that they really do belong here in Canada. In the meantime, their lives, and often their families' lives, are turned upside down.

Two years earlier, in testimony before the House Citizenship Committee, I had forewarned of the backlogs. I also warned the media. In June, I had coffee with Patrick Brethour, the *Globe and Mail*'s western editor and reporter in Vancouver. I explained the problem to him. But somewhere along the way (maybe it was the newspaper's bureaucracy, maybe it was its editors, or maybe it was Patrick), that newspaper too decided to ignore the problem, thus leaving its readers mostly unaware of it. That's when I decided to email CBC's Peter Mansbridge, asking him whether, as an Order of Canada recipient, he thought the treatment of Alice McKay was the proper way for our government to treat Canadians.

He responded, saying that CBC had been instrumental in getting the Lost Canadian story out. I wrote back, telling him I was the guy behind the CBC stories. I continued: "While *The National* has been better than any other national broadcaster in telling our story, your coverage has still been poor. You've told several individual stories, but never has CBC really delved into the root cause. The bottom line is, the Canadian Citizenship Act is seriously flawed. The very thing that unites us together as Canadians is not even Charter compliant, which allows the government to blatantly discriminate against their own people."

I then asked him if I could be a guest on his program *Mansbridge One on One*. He said he'd consider it in the future.

My point was, instead of focusing on a few individual stories, why not look at the bigger picture? Why are Canadians by the hundreds of thousands being denied basic rights? Why are other countries like Australia able to defend their people's constitutional liberties—sometimes within weeks—whereas, in Canada, it can take years? Isn't the government supposed to work for its people and not the other way around? In the US, Leland Davidson is taken care of, whereas in Canada, more than a quarter of a million Canadians (not foreigners) wait in CIC's citizenship queue.* What an amazing statement it is about the complacency of Canadians, being willing to accept such mediocrity from their own government. Can you imagine 2.5 million American citizens being denied their rights and the media not reporting it? The Americans wouldn't stand for it.

I don't think Mr. Mansbridge really understood the issue because not until the summer of 2014 did he get back in touch, and then it was only because of my constant prodding. I reiterated my desire to be on his show. His reply was to the effect that CBC, including *The National*, has covered the issue numerous times over the past few years and no doubt will again when and if it continues to make news. Going forward, CBC didn't do much with Lost Canadians, so my guess is that Mr. Mansbridge and his network deemed the repatriation of hundreds of thousands of Canadians as not being newsworthy. Or could it be that CBC is in bed with the government? What other explanations are there?

Back to Alice McKay. Thanks to the power of the press, the day after CBC broadcast her story, CIC capitulated, saying it would recognize her citizenship. Who says that the media doesn't matter?

In October, I called the office of Rick Dykstra, Jason Kenney's parliamentary secretary in Ottawa, and asked if he'd talk with me. We were just

---

* On the positive side, Canada doesn't easily issue ninety-five-year-olds driver's licences. Moral of the Leland Davidson story: be careful while on the roads in Washington State. Leland got his licence.

about to file for a judicial review regarding Jackie Scott and several others who were being denied citizenship wrongly, just because they had been born out of wedlock. Like his boss, Rick refused. As I had with his predecessor, Ed Komarnicki, I suggested that a court case was not the proper way to proceed. I reminded Dykstra's legislative assistant that the government was gambling "tens of billions."

It's like a professional pilot trying to forewarn the next crew about a severe safety problem and the captain taking over refusing to listen. ("Sir, we have a fire in the engine." Captain Kenney and co-pilot Dykstra: "Don't talk to me. I don't want to know.") Witnessing such self-inflicted ignorance from our elected representatives was always difficult. But that was this government's way. The conversation ended when the legislative assistant said that I'd get further by keeping away from the press.

With Dykstra's brush-off, I began soliciting several groups which, by now, had agreed to speak out against the injustice, and possibly become interveners in a court challenge. Among them were Pierre Allard of the Royal Canadian Legion; Marc Gionet of the Atlantic Human Rights Centre; David Eby of the BC Civil Liberties Association; and, most important, the Chinese community of Vancouver.

I had so appreciated the Chinese World War II vets showing up for Joe Taylor's citizenship ceremony. Instinctively, they understood the issue. After the war, their reward was receiving full rights of citizenship. They were finally allowed to vote; the catch, of course, is that they had to have survived the war. Die fighting for Canada and no dice.

I'm privileged to be a member of the Arizona chapter of the Tuskegee Airmen, the black American pilots of World War II. During the summer, I proudly joined the Chinese Canadian Military Museum Society in Vancouver, as well as ANAVETS (Army, Navy and Air Force Veterans in Canada) Pacific Unit 280, made up in part of Chinese World War II vets. I have a friend whose father wanted to be a pilot in World War II but was denied the opportunity because he was Jewish. What I've noticed is that when groups have been discriminated against and not afforded equal rights, they try harder than those that haven't suffered discrimination. In war, when governments tend to recruit any warm body willing to fight and die for them, minorities typically respond, risking it all in order to prove their worth, to show they can do their job even better than others, and to substantiate that it's their country too. Each person then sacrifices him- or herself for the betterment of the group, wanting only to return with honour, paving a path for others to follow.

In August, I was a guest speaker for the Chinese veterans. My talk reminded them of the days when they too had been denied equal rights of citizenship. Unlike most of my speaking engagements, where the members of the audience learn from me, on this occasion I became the student. Gim F. Wong explained how he'd been a top gunner for Canada, yet the government tried to deny his entry into the Air Force. The real reason was ethnicity, but the recruitment officer attempted to make it about religion. Gim was Buddhist, which at that time wasn't acceptable. In the end, the recruiter wrote down that he was Anglican, thereby allowing him to enlist—but not as an officer, because he hadn't attended school as a child, like other Canadian kids. Being Chinese, he wasn't allowed to attend the public school system until 1929. His story, fraught with discrimination, was typical. Gim went on to be a top gunner, risking his life every time he stepped on board his plane and, in the end, he did it as a flight officer.

Here's how Chinese-Canadian veteran Howe Lee described his life growing up in Armstrong, BC:

We were the only Chinese family. I grew up in a pretty good environment: There was some discrimination but not as bad as what my parents and family friends went through. Name calling was still common when I was growing up, and there were a few, when going home, that wanted to pick a fight. One of the challenging things in my life was how, because of discrimination against our pioneers and my parents, to survive in this environment. We learned that whatever we do, we had to do better.

What these men had lived through before, during, and after the war was incredible. They were teaching me. As I shook the hand of one elderly gentleman he said, "You're the only white man to ever understand what we've been through."

No, I didn't fully understand—no one could possibly grasp their stories unless they had lived them. But I did understand their citizenship problems, and they knew mine. Our insight into each other's problems and corresponding mutual respect deepened our bond.

After the war, Canada's infamous Chinese Exclusion Act was repealed, allowing Chinese people the right to vote. Yet, despite the vets' many awards and distinctions of service, the Canadian Legion refused to accept them into their membership. Not so with ANAVETS Pacific Unit 280—it put out the welcome mat. To this day, the Chinese are associated with the Canadian Navy, despite many being vets of the Air Force.

And what about the Chinese who gave their all, dying for Canada? According to Jason Kenney, they were not Canadian citizens, and he refuses to recognize them as such. How ironic that, during the summer of 2012, the Canadian War Museum featured an exhibit titled *One War, Two Victories*. Here's how it's explained:

> *One War, Two Victories* explores the experiences of Chinese Canadians who served in the Canadian Military and Volunteer Services and in Allied war efforts during the Second World War.
>
> Though denied rights and subjected to widespread discrimination before the war, many Chinese Canadians volunteered for military service and related duties, helping to secure victory abroad and greater equality at home. The exhibition presents fascinating wartime stories of unforgettable men and women, and their remarkable contributions to Canada and to the Chinese Canadian community in war and in peace.[11]

Yet, with Canada still refusing to recognize the citizenship of those who perished prior to 1947, the discrimination and denial continues.

More than 200 Chinese volunteered and fought for Canada in World War I. In return, they received nothing by way of citizenship recognition, and still couldn't vote. Bloc MP Meili Faille (who is half Chinese) once said, "There is no limit to virtue."[12] Could we not, as a country, be more accepting? Why can't we posthumously recognize these hero Canadians with citizenship?

On January 24, 2012, the Chinese-Canadian veteran exhibit Loyalty to Country opened to coincide with Chinese New Year. It was sponsored by none other than CIC and Jason Kenney, who, apparently, was still out there campaigning and wooing potential voters. The flyer noted "made possible by generous funding from Citizenship and Immigration Canada" in bold print, to make sure potential voters would notice.

There's another notable point in our history, captured in a report titled *Canada, 1941–1949: The Deportation and Internment of Canadians of Japanese Origin*:

> In February 1942, the prime minister Mackenzie King issued a series of decrees with the object of removing all those of Japanese origin to "protection zones" in the interior of the country. All Canadians of Japanese origin were sent to ghost towns in the Rockies, to camps, or to sugar beet plantations in other provinces such as Alberta or Manitoba. They lost all

their civil rights, as well as their property, which in 1943 was confiscated and disposed of by decree. Money arising from sales was used to cover the expenses of the internment of the former owners. It was a huge displacement: more than 20,000 men, women and children of Japanese origin, despite the fact that 13,000 of them had been born in Canada, were uprooted and taken from their homes . . .

The conclusion of the war did not put an end to the sufferings of the Nippo-Canadian minority. On 2 December 1945 a Canadian Supreme Court ruling, that the federal government had the power to deport Japanese Canadians and to withdraw their citizenship, was confirmed. They were given the choice between expulsion to a Japan devastated by war, or dispersion in the east of the country. Most decided to stay in Canada, but several groups did in fact leave for a country where they were considered foreigners. In 1947, under pressure from the church, from labour groups and from Asian countries, this expulsion programme was abandoned, but only after an attempt in 1946 to arrange a huge deportation of 10,000 people to Japan. It was not until 1 April 1949 that Japanese Canadians got back their liberty, and obtained the right to vote.[13]

Of the 196 Japanese-Canadian vets of World War I, fifty-four were killed, ninety-three were wounded, and only forty-nine returned home safely.* It took thirteen years after the war concluded for the surviving veterans to finally be granted by the BC legislature the right to vote. Today, in all kinds of government documents and books chronicling our history, and especially in Veterans Affairs publications, these vets are referred to as Canadian citizens, in direct conflict with the current stance by Citizenship and Immigration Canada.[14]

In December, the Liberals came out with their plans for a January 2012 convention in Ottawa. On the Liberal Party's website, Bob Rae wrote, "Canadians are counting on us to fight for Liberal values and to champion the cause of growth and prosperity. And they are calling on us to put forward a vision for our country that offers all Canadians hope for a prosperous future, and a sense of pride in what we can offer the world." Liberal Party president Alfred Apps added, "Liberals have always embraced the future with commitment, determination and optimism. We believe in the future of

---

* Almost 28 percent of the Japanese volunteers died for their country. Another 47 percent were wounded. Combined, that's 75 percent of the men either killed or injured. These men fought to prove their worth—as Canadian citizens.

Canada, because we know that the Liberal Party of Canada will once again be called upon to shape it."[15]

Of the five leading resolutions put forward at the convention, not one mentioned citizenship or Lost Canadians. Legalizing marijuana came in at number four.

In December 2011, gracing the cover of the Canadian edition of *Reader's Digest* was the question "Are You a Lost Canadian?" It took about ten years for that publication to do the story, but now that it had, it had done an excellent job. The article, in print and in the magazine racks, carried the subtitle, "How Unjust Legal Quirks Rob Canadians of Their Rightful Citizenship."[16] It explained the aftermath of Bill C-37 and the remaining deficiencies. The article was personalized with real-life examples, including Guy Valliere's story. Also mentioned were the pre-'47 issues, and how the government had insisted the problem was rather small, affecting about 450 people in total. The article then quoted CBC's numbers, which stated that at minimum there were 200,000 Lost Canadians. In subsequent months, *Reader's Digest* published a follow-up story saying that our issue was far from over.[17] Finally, we had the attention of a nationwide magazine.

I wish our issue was over, but it's not. It could be (with the stroke of a pen), but taking good care of its people doesn't seem to be a priority for Canada. Nor is it a priority of any of our major political parties. I've picked a lot on Harper in these pages. But then, he's the current captain, and our county's direction has a lot to do with his helmsmanship.

There have been recent uprisings all around the world because political leaders have put themselves above their people—those in Syria, Egypt, and Libya being just a few. Do we really want Canada on that same list of offenders? Our cherished country should be leading by example, for all its people. From Natives to the newly arrived, everyone should have equal rights and equal opportunity. It really is that simple.

On Christmas Day 2011, the *Globe and Mail* published an article titled "Harper Sees Trade Deals as Key to His Political Success."[18] That may be. But as Canada heads toward its 150th birthday, I believe the successful politicians will be the ones who put their people first. History is littered with those who didn't. And with those who refused to admit wrongdoings.

Such is the case in the not-so-true-North's Harperland. But history was about to change.

CHAPTER 19

TEACHING OLD DOGS NEW TRICKS

Democracy must be rooted in a rational philosophy that first and foremost recognizes the right of an individual. Democracy is not a synonym for justice or for freedom. Democracy is not a sacred right sanctifying mob rule. Democracy is a principle that is subordinate to the inalienable rights of the individual.
TERRY GOODKIND, *NAKED EMPIRE*

Never doubt that a small group of thoughtful, committed people can change the world. Indeed, it is the only thing that ever has.
MARGARET MEAD

IN A *Saturday Night Live* show from the 1970s, one with the original cast, there was a sketch titled "The Thing That Wouldn't Leave." It was about a houseguest who basically moved in. No matter how hard the host tried, no matter what the host did, the guest would not go away.

It's like that with the Lost Canadians. Our issue continues, all because of a lack of political will. Like dogs chasing their tails in an endless circle, the bureaucrats continue their discriminatory ways, to the detriment of the individual, of course; the politicians remain worse than indifferent (at times actually becoming obstructionists); and the media hold no one accountable. In a strong democracy, all three—bureaucrats, politicians, and the media— are integral, each being a watchdog of the other. And they ultimately answer to the people, the most important part of the equation. Democracy's downfall depends on uneducated and complacent electors, who fuel the flames of its destruction.

So why did the Lost Canadians become The Issue That Wouldn't End? Because Prime Minister Harper wasn't about to correct the problems, let alone admit or apologize for them; being equally resolute, I refused to capitulate. My determination has come from years of being a loud-mouth for human rights and equality. The lessons I've learned have come from my heroes, folks who also never backed down—people such as my parents, Dr. Malcolm Yasny, Jack and Shirley Rose, the Red Tails of World War II, Dr. Martin Luther King Jr., Dr. Vernon Johns, Rosa Parks, the Tuskegee Airmen, and the Chinese-Canadian vets. Chris Matthews, anchor of MSNBC news program *Hardball*, said it best: "Over time, people who advance liberties tend to win the argument." [1]

Since I penned the final words of the previous chapter much of significance has transpired. To recap, Jackie Scott was turned down twice by CIC for a 5.4 citizenship grant. It took almost four years for the bureaucracy to make its decision. Hence, it was back to the courts for us. The judge assigned to her case was the same one who'd ruled in Joe Taylor's case—and handed the government its head. The tens-of-billions-of-dollars gamble was indeed back on the table. [2]

From the sidelines we were thinking, *Way to go, Mr. Harper.*

Admittedly, to date, it's been the Conservatives who have tabled every piece of legislation to correct the Lost Canadian mischief. In that department, the Liberals, Bloc, and NDP have absolutely no bragging rights. But as time marched forward, Harper's covert methods of conducting his business meant it always took place behind closed doors—or, better stated, behind a sealed fortress. In the six years following royal assent of Bill C-37, the Conservatives had virtually no interaction with key stakeholders. For all intents and purposes, we'd been shut out. If not for our unrelenting behind-the-scenes pressure through the courts and one really close media ally, the *Vancouver Observer*, the government would have won this battle through attrition. All our remaining Lost Canadians would be dead.

In March 2012, Jenny Uechi, managing editor of the *Observer*, accompanied Jackie to a gathering in Surrey. To borrow verbiage from the movie *The Sting*, their mark was none other than Jason Kenney, who on this day was once again prowling for votes and goodwill for his party. The media, as in all events involving the minister, were there in abundance. But their questions dealt with matters pertaining to family reunification and immigration, something Mr. Kenney loved to talk about. Little did he know that his next step would be on a land mine.

As uncomfortable as it was for Jackie—she's a petite woman who doesn't much like the limelight—she wormed her way through the crowd, past the many media types, and, Jenny behind her with camera in tow, asked one simple question: "Was my father a Canadian citizen when he fought in World War II?"

Caught off guard, the normally boisterous Mr. Kenney remained where he was (probably with great trepidation), since rolling cameras would have documented a hasty retreat. This was a roadshow at a posh golf club, not exactly within the confines of Parliament, where his assistant will step in before there's a chance to respond, saving the minister's day. Trapped, he had no alternative but to reply. Mr. Kenney hadn't expected questions about citizenship, a subject for which he was ill-prepared.

Kenney: "Certainly not... obviously not... We didn't have citizenship."

His answer, unscripted, was crystal clear. Kenney's customary cool-headed, self-confident demeanour was shaken. Jackie continued her challenge, asking about all of Canada's pre-'47 war dead. The foot trap had been carefully placed.

Wanting to sidestep the issue and save face, Mr. Kenney stated that they are "heroes, but at the time, they were British subjects... We didn't have citizenship till 1947." Probably realizing that he was way out of his league, he ended the conversation with, "I'll take a look at your file."[3]

KA-BOOM. The trap's steel jaws snapped shut; the minister was caught. Ah, the power of a just-over-100-pound senior "citizen," with her wisdom of the ages, as she squared off against one of Harper's own burly Conservative Party thugs. No wonder politicians, and particularly those who don't know what the hell they're talking about, rarely come out alone into the open. Instead, like wolves in a den, they find comfort living in packs and hiding in lairs. Without knowledge they don't stand a chance, because actually confronting the truth can be uncomfortable. In question period, or anywhere in Ottawa for that matter, politicians delight in transferring blame to others—something that's impossible to do to a civilian. Jackie wasn't the Little Old Lady from Pasadena but, rather, the Little Old Lady from Canada. With immense passion, both she and her California counterpart were capable of putting the pedal to the metal.

Caught in the open and without backup, Kenney turned and walked away from Jackie, making his way toward the surrounding journalists, hoping the subject would revert to immigration and family reunification. How quickly they obliged, and how fascinating to watch. Like Jenny Uechi's, their cameras had caught Jackie and Jason's exchange, but unlike Jenny, they remained unaware of the significance of the moment they'd just witnessed.[4]

In a brief instance, in a not-so-chance encounter between two very unlikely foes, one delivered a knockout punch. For Lost Canadians, it was a game-changer. It also changed Canadian history.

How? Because by now our little gang of activists included more than average, everyday folks. I'd amassed a team of incredibly brainy scholars, researchers, writers, lawyers, academics, past and present politicians, bureaucrats, and people with a conscience. Many of them were products of the '60s, so they knew how to facilitate changes in government. We were like crash investigators combing piece by piece the wreckage of a downed aircraft. We left no stone unturned. Every tidbit of information, down to the tiniest detail, was examined. Our backgrounds were as diverse as a box of crayons. We nonetheless shared one common goal: to arrive at the truth in Canadian citizenship law and to correct the remaining deficiencies. Parliamentarians weren't about to do it—they had no interest. Besides, doing something because it was the right thing to do wasn't their shtick. Getting into power, holding onto power, keeping their jobs, that's what motivated them. If they'd been interested in helping Lost Canadians for moral reasons, they would have done it years before.

On D-Day—June 6, 2013—I was with Jim Karygiannis and a woman named Sarah Currie in the Charles-Lynch Press Conference Room. We were holding a press conference as Stephen Harper and Jason Kenney stood one floor above.

The Conservatives like to boast about how Bill C-37 restored citizenship to 95 percent of the Lost Canadians. And, yes, they do have those bragging rights. But I looked at it differently, through the lens of a pilot. My focus was on the 5 percent they willingly left behind.

Think about Sully Sullenberger, captain of US Airways Flight 1549 that ditched on the Hudson River. Everyone was rescued. He and his crew were heroes, obviously, but would they have been if they'd intentionally left passengers behind? No way. And in that regard, citizenship-wise, neither was Stephen Harper.

He must have cringed, watching the press conference remotely, as I said, "The whole issue we're talking about is discrimination, right here in Canada. In World War II, in Germany, only 6 percent were Jewish. The lesson to be learned is that in human rights, you don't leave out 5 percent of your people."* I then called on the prime minister and the citizenship minister to

---

* I stand corrected; 6 million Jews were murdered during World War II, but Jews made up only between 0.2 and 0.3 percent of Germany's population. Nevertheless, my point remains.

sit down with me and fix the issue, for good: "All the political parties want this, so the hang-up is right there at the top. Canada is a country that should have acceptance, being a beacon of light in human rights, and it starts with people like Sarah and her husband."[5]

Sarah and her spouse, Mike, were two of the many "left behind" folks from C-37. By complete coincidence, they were both born in Lahr, Germany, both babies of parents serving in the Canadian military. The families returned to Canada, and they grew up as typical Canadian kids in typical Canadian surroundings. It wasn't until they were adults that they met, fell in love, and married. Following family tradition, Mike enlisted. Now, after having completed three full tours of duty in Afghanistan as a Canadian soldier, CIC was telling Mike that he had not demonstrated a "substantial connection" to Canada, and hence his and Sarah's adopted baby from Haiti would not be recognized with citizenship.[6] Can you imagine telling a decorated Canadian warrior that he isn't Canadian enough? It all went back to the Conservatives attaching their ill-conceived second-generation born-abroad clause in Bill C-37. Quite seriously, had Sarah been Canadian through the immigration process, the couple would have no problem with their baby's adoption and his subsequent citizenship. The Conservatives had actually given more rights to immigrant Canadians than to Canadian-born Canadians, and the Curries were living proof.

As I do so often when coming face to face with Lost Canadians caught in CIC's legal limboland, I apologized. I didn't have anything to do with Sarah's quandary except that I was trying to fix it, but it was embarrassing that the leaders of my country were telling a military family they haven't demonstrated a "substantial connection." I also knew there were problems for others, more potential land mines that today's innocent children could grow up to face, like the Curries' son.

In the here and now, much of our issue was dealing with senior citizens who were brought to Canada as babies and infants, adopted with no formal paperwork. Documents accepted for decades were now being rejected. So what happens in fifty or sixty years when the Curries' son retires? Will CIC reject him, saying that his paperwork from half a century earlier isn't in order? Without legislative change and bureaucratic understanding, the possibility was very real for him, as is such a possibility for who knows how many future orphans who have no "official" record of exactly who they are or where they were born. Their CIC problems will certainly one day surface, creating a whole new breed of Lost Canadians. While our battle was about them, it was also about getting CIC to correctly implement current law.

That alone proved quite the challenge as Lost Canadians continued showing up at my email doorstep with regularity, many having been told by CIC that they weren't citizens when in fact they were. Like this one:

Hello Don,
I am a Canadian mother of two adult children born in the US (1966 & 1968) to myself and an American GI father. Both daughters lived in Canada since Dec 1968, have worked here, had their children here and have been productive Canadians. Both still only have their landed immigrant cards. We never heard about the Lost Canadians until just recently.
In Dec of 2011 the oldest daughter moved to the Bahamas... [and now she's] trying desperately to get back to Canada, the only country she knows as home. She has to return to Canada before her 3-year limit to be out of Canada expires in December 2014 if we were given the correct information.
Can you please contact me as soon as possible to see if there is anything we can do to help get her back home.
Thank you in advance for any assistance you are able to provide.
Dee Sinker

The fact is, Dee's daughter, because she was born after 1946, was a Canadian citizen under C-37—legislation passed into law six years before she got rejected—and the retroactive effects had made her a Canadian citizen since birth. CIC's denial of her citizenship was based entirely on former discriminatory laws no longer on the books. It was like herding a bunch of cats: the bureaucrats were all over the place in their interpretation of the law. They just didn't seem to have a clue.
There were others:

Mr. Chapman:
I have been reading about the situation concerning the "Lost Canadians" and have noticed that you are at the forefront of addressing the wrongs done to them. My situation is very similar to many of those labelled "Lost Canadian." The Harper government has not only maintained the status quo with their policies on citizenship and discrimination but in their supposed attempt to address the "Lost Canadian" situation they created a new class of "Lost Canadians."
My father was born in 1966 to a Canadian father and American mother. His father tried to register him as a Canadian but was informed since he was not legally married and his son was born out of wedlock his

son was not eligible. My father had wanted to immigrate to Canada and watched closely throughout the years for a change in the laws. In 2004 he was able to apply for a grant of citizenship under the case of *Augier v. Canada* which addressed somewhat the concern of children born out-of-wedlock to Canadian fathers abroad. The court ruled that it was discriminatory because the same rule did not apply to Canadian mothers who had children out of wedlock. The issue was that my father, Karl, was only recognized as a citizen from 2005 onward and he had three children before that date. This made my siblings and me ineligible for citizenship. In 2009 people in my father's position were retroactively given citizenship from birth thereby eliminating that hurdle, however, the same bill limited citizenship for children born abroad to just the first generation, making it a bitter-sweet moment.

My family has very deep roots in Canada and were amongst the first settlers to settle in Canada. I have always identified as a Canadian (even though my government may not want to recognize this fact). What makes me most upset is that people who were not discriminated against, their children who are second generation born abroad born in the same year as me (1988) were given the benefit of Canadian citizenship. But because my father was born out of wedlock and was born to a parent of the wrong gender, not only is he a person of less worth than children born in wedlock to Canadian mothers, but his children bear the same second-class status. I have applied 2 times for a citizenship certificate and both times have been denied. I have tried immigration consultants and have gotten nowhere. I am not someone who just wants Canadian citizenship with no attachment to Canada, I am a person who has been excluded and has been trying to be a part of Canadian society. With the labour shortage that Canada has and the immigration quotas it must maintain, it makes no sense that Canada should exclude those who have ties with the nation historically and via family members. I am not asking the government for preferential treatment, but merely to be equal to other Canadians.

I am writing this to ensure you are aware of this and perhaps you can make people aware that these laws passed have consequences and that perhaps it is best to address this situation fully before it becomes a mess that involves another generation. Had Canada addressed my father's case earlier my case would not have been an issue. Let's stop perpetuating the discrimination.

I thank you for your time and applaud your great work.

Maverick J. Snowdon

And then, just when I thought I'd heard everything, this came in:

Hi Mr. Chapman,
I've just discovered your website and can't help but think of my father-in-law. He was born in 1942 as a "bread box baby" with no birth date.
  He has been denied citizenship because there is no record of him being born.
  Could you offer any insight on how he should proceed?
  Thanks for your time.
  Noreen

A bread-box baby? Hmm ... what's that? A Google search revealed the actual term is "butterbox baby," which led me to the website of the Canadian Children's Rights Council. And there it was, their story. Was it ever a shocker. Running under the banner "The Selling/Murdering of Canadian Children," the article told the gut-wrenching narrative of the Ideal Maternity Home, an illegal "for-profit" orphanage in East Chester, Nova Scotia, operated from about 1928 through the late 1940s.[7] Babies, hundreds and hundreds of them, were either immediately adopted—often by a US family—or murdered.[8] Today, there's a mass grave in which the infants were buried in small mitred pine boxes from a local dairy, just the right size for newborns.[9] The survivors call themselves "the lucky ones."[10] Indeed they are, in every way but citizenship.

Without a birth certificate, how does one prove who one is, or when and how one got to Canada? Several of the babies were born in Canada, but to who, where, when? For many of these children, coming into this world was an insurmountable misfortune. The "lucky ones," as seniors, now faced an entirely new enemy: Citizenship and Immigration Canada. For some, this obstacle *would* prove insurmountable. Their birth, their identity, their very existence had yet to be officially validated. Essentially, they too were buried, not in a "butterbox" but somewhere in the backroom filing cabinets of CIC. And they were far from being the only ones in citizenship limboland.

Enter Canada's home children, around 100,000 European orphans from World Wars I and II. For the most part they were British, though some were probably smuggled into Britain from Germany or surrounding countries. From the late 1930s to mid-1940s, many a Jewish family handed their babies over to gentiles willing to help. What parents wouldn't try to save their children? Some of the kids sent to England were probably children of

Holocaust victims. I say "probably" because who knows for sure? Identities have vanished.

As described on the British Home Children in Canada website, "Once in Canada, the children were not usually adopted into new families, but rather were taken into households, to be trained and to work as indentured agricultural labourers and domestic servants until about the age of 18... Canadians needed the cheap labour."[11]

At the beginning of *Anne of Green Gables*, L.M. Montgomery's fictional character. Anne (with an "e" on the end) epitomizes these orphaned kids, having endured the often harsh treatment many did.

Gilles Duceppe's father was a home child, as was former Conservative senator Brenda Robertson's father. Same thing for Marion Vermeersch and her brother, Peter Brammah.[12] In the half to a full century after their arrival, over 100,000 young immigrants produced countless first-generation Canadians, who multiplied and produced who knows how many further generations of descendants, meaning scads and scads of Canadians will trace their roots back to the home children: estimates are as high as 2 million people. Now throw into the mix CIC saying that citizenship didn't exist before 1947. So, if true, were all these people really Canadian? From Jackie Scott's court case, here are the exact words of the government: "While her father was a British Subject and had been born in Canada, he was not a citizen in 1945 when Mrs. Scott was born because the former *Canadian Citizenship Act* had not come into force yet."[13]

So now our battle included not just the born-out-of-wedlock war-bride children like Jackie but also Canada's World Wars I and II war dead. That's another 111,000 people, roughly the equivalent of wiping out the entire populations of Fredericton, Moncton, and Miramichi, New Brunswick, combined. On the west coast, you'd eradicate the entire city of Kelowna. Rather than wrapping up this jigsaw puzzle, new pieces were constantly being added as other historically maligned groups were thrown into the pre-'47 mix—like Indo-Canadians and other Asians, First Nations, and certain religious denominations.

Judith Wise wrote to me back in 2010, saying that her father had graduated in medicine from the University of Toronto in the 1940s: "My father was only in the states... because of discrimination in Canada. His faculty advisors at the University of Toronto had apparently suggested that as a top student he would want to do a fellowship abroad, because at the time Jewish doctors in Canada could only practice in Jewish hospitals. He was either first or second in his class and went to Chicago on a fellowship to study cardiology with Louis Katz, who pioneered research on blood cholesterol in heart disease." Judith's father never wanted to leave Canada, but to complete his residency, he had no other choice. Hospitals in Toronto wouldn't accept Jewish doctors. So what the US gained was Canada's loss, big time. In 2014, Judith and her family were being denied citizenship, all because of the effects of religious discrimination seven decades earlier, and CIC's insistence that citizenship didn't begin until 1947. Who knows how many thousands of others were out there like the Wise family?

In October 2012, my wonderful and supportive mother died. At least she passed with the comfort of knowing that her citizenship had been restored. Bill C-37 captured her, along with some three-quarters of a million others. With Mum gone, her now-vacant house in Gibsons was the perfect Lost Canadian think-tank headquarters for the summer of 2013. My extraordinary team now included the likes of Fred Colbourne, whose father died fighting for Canada in World War II. Fred had been captured by C-37—he lost his citizenship back in the late 1940s. Robert Addington's mother met her British beau when he was stationed in Canada during the war, training to be a pilot. They fell in love and married; he completed flight training, then got stationed back in the UK. In May 1943, Robert's mother followed, crossing the Atlantic in Convoy HX 239 from Halifax. Subsequently, they had three children, and in 1951 the family settled back in Canada. Ironically, had Robert and his siblings been born out of wedlock, they'd have been considered property of their mother and thus would have been citizens of Canada. Their CIC sin was being born in wedlock. For about three years, everything was fine, until his sister Frances caught the attention of the authorities. To use a really, really not-politically-correct phrase that was standard phraseology back then, she was "retarded." Hence, she fell under the last of the four specific categories on CIC's "disabled"-and-thus-not-acceptable list: "idiot."* Robert describes it best:

> My sister, born in 1947, also in the UK, was mentally handicapped. When my family settled in Canada in 1951, she had to come in, as did our younger brother and I, as a landed immigrant because under the law of the day we could not claim citizenship through our Canadian mother. (Had we been born out of wedlock, we would have been Canadian by birth.)

---

* Again, the four categories: married women, minors, lunatics, and idiots, each classified under the same "disability" for their national status.

In 1954, my parents made the difficult decision to place my sister in an institution because she had become unmanageable and my mother could no longer care for her at home. Shortly after that, her case came to the attention of the immigration authorities. My sister was found to be in the inadmissible class of "idiots, imbeciles, feeble-minded persons, epileptics, insane persons, and persons who have been insane at any time previously" (Immigration Act, R.S.C. 1952), and was ordered deported. Legally, my father, my brother and I could have been deported also, but the order did not include us, perhaps because my mother was Canadian and her father, R. C. Wallace, was well known in Ottawa, having served as president of two Canadian universities and as a member of the Canadian delegation to the founding conference of UNESCO in Paris in 1946.

Fortunately for our family, the deportation order was never carried out. My father made it clear to the government that he would not apply for Canadian citizenship as long as there was any possibility of my sister being deported. When the government changed in 1957 the new minister, Davie Fulton and his successor, Ellen Fairclough (Canada's first female cabinet minister), assured my father that they would never deport my sister, though of course they could not speak for any future government. This assurance apparently satisfied my father, who took Canadian citizenship, and I with him, in 1959. My sister remained in Canada under Minister's permits that had to be renewed annually.

In 1977, the revised Citizenship Act allowed persons born abroad, including those born before 1977, to claim citizenship through either parent. We got the deportation order quashed and my sister became a citizen at last, fortunately during the lifetime of both my parents.

For Robert, it was personal. Although he had become Canadian through the immigration process, he too wanted to do what was right for fellow Canadians—his sense of right and wrong was tethered to a strong moral compass.

Peg Bosdet was a member of the exclusive group called Intertel, meaning she's in the top 1 percent. Most people are aware of the brainy IQ crowd called Mensa. Intertel is above Mensa. She's at the top of the top. She's also Charles Bosdet's wife, so she was well familiar with CIC's unrelenting and dismissive ways.

Jackie Scott, who worked for a lawyer many moons ago, provided research, motherly love, and pampering while coordinating everyone's in- and outbox. She was like the team manager.

Melynda Jarratt, who stayed put in Fredericton, was a treasure trove of the history of the war brides and their era. In Ottawa, there was Jan Makins and Janet Laba, who made their way to the national archives whenever asked. It was a summer of abundant discovery, of renewed sense of purpose, and of extraordinary resolve.

And, unlike the prime minister, we weren't willing to leave anyone behind, including Theresa Kenney. Born in New Brunswick in 1916, Theresa at age thirteen moved with her mother to the Boston area after her father died. She spent most of her life there, as a teacher and Catholic nun. In 2004, longing to return to her home and native land, Canada, she moved back to Miramichi. In her words, "I love Canada. I wanted to be near my father." He was laid to rest at St. Michael's Cemetery. Keenly aware of her advanced age, Theresa knew that her priority was to be buried as a Canadian citizen. But CIC wasn't so accommodating—it was making her go through the immigration process, which took years—not something a ninety-four-year-old has in great measure. She'd filed applications with CIC long before but then discovered they'd been misplaced somewhere within the bureaucracy. In her words, "If I have to wait another three years, I may not be around to receive it. I may have gone to the other side."

In 2010, Benjamin Shingler of the *Telegraph-Journal* had called, asking me to comment about Theresa's situation. Here's what I said: "If we are truly going to be the compassionate and caring country we believe that we are, then this is the kind of situation that we need to address." Shingler then called Citizenship and Immigration Canada, but it refused to comment. At the end of the article he quotes Theresa: "If I had known this process would have taken as long as it has, I probably never would have started it."[14]

In November 2013, at age ninety-seven, Theresa indeed went to "the other side." At least one of the items on her bucket list had come to fruition: she was laid to rest near her father in Miramichi's St. Michael's Cemetery. For CIC, the attrition game was working. One less Lost Canadian in the queue.

After Bill C-37, it became obvious that the bureaucracy had not changed its spots. Once the bill passed, CIC had granted me one meeting with one of its top people, Kennedy Hong (as described in Chapter 16). I pleaded that CIC recognize folks like Theresa, but I don't know of anyone who got a 5.4. CIC's adversarial ways continued unrelentingly. Basically, all it did was rearm, taking aim against lone individuals, who, by themselves, didn't stand a Custer's chance.

In July 2010, as I mentioned earlier, I had talked with Nicole Girard, director of the Citizenship Legislation and Program Policy Division at Citizenship and Immigration Canada. With "stateless babies" beginning to turn up on CIC's radar, and with the government ignoring its own promise to give citizenship to any stateless baby, Harper's folks finally began to understand that, in the real world, actual problems were created by not recognizing the second-generation born-abroad folks. So back to the legislative drawing board they went, again trying to reinvent wheel. The result? A new new bill was introduced to correct the "unintended consequences" of C-37. While the fallout probably caught the Conservatives by surprise, for everyone else it was obvious from the get-go. We knew this was going to happen. It meant that, yet again, at significant cost to taxpayers, another bill, C-467, got introduced.[15] I sent Nicole a brief detailing the remaining problems and their solutions, which, if she had implemented them, would have eradicated the Lost Canadian issue permanently. It was so simple. But Harper's government did things the Harper way, and it wasn't about to listen. It was like choosing to keep smallpox extant.

The only substance coming out of Nicole's and my conversation was that, for the first time ever, someone in the know at CIC fessed up, admitting to there being at least three-quarters of a million Lost Canadians.* What a far cry from the 450 figure this same department admitted to before C-37. My brief was for naught. After C-467's demise, another new new new second-generation bill popped up, but that too never saw the light of day. It was like throwing taxpayers' dollars down a constantly flushing toilet, with absolutely no benefit to Canadians, all because the Conservatives refused to listen to us in the first place. Worse, stateless babies were being born to actual Canadian citizen parents. Harper wasn't just violating one but two UN conventions on human rights to which Canada was a signatory: the Rights of the Child and the Reduction of Statelessness.

In the meantime, more folks were emailing me with horror stories, like not being able to collect their hard-earned Old Age Security or to get a driver's licence. There was nowhere for them to turn except to me. The government held the vaccine but refused to administer it. And time and again, even after decades of fighting this battle, I would come across a whole new category of people being victimized by CIC. Imagine my surprise when I discovered that First Nations still had a dog in this fight.

---

* I still believe CIC is downplaying the numbers. Our estimates are around 1 million Lost Canadians.

Dear Don Chapman,

I was so relieved to find similar stories to mine published in the *Vancouver Observer*! I am also in this situation, as a "lost Canadian" but in a different way...

I am part of generations of Canadian aboriginals (or Indians) in Canada—my mother, grandmother and great-grandmother all belong to a reserve near London, Ontario. Unfortunately, I was born in the USA. (Indians have the right to live or work in either country—Canada or USA by way of treaty.) My family and heritage is of Canada.

My mother moved me to Canada when I was a child to be near the rest of our family. Our entry was legitimate, legal, and my mother was within her rights to move us here. I grew up and even went to school here, but after turning age 18 I was no longer allowed to be here. After years of seeking clarification, I found out I only had "protection" in Canada until age 18. In which, after becoming an adult I must apply for either Indian status or Immigration Status in order to remain living here. I do not qualify for Indian status because of ongoing discrimination in the Indian Registration Act and I cannot apply to remain here because there is no Permanent Resident application recognizing my form of entry in order to apply.

In other words, if you were brought to Canada as a child by a recognized Canadian Indian parent, there is no application you can apply under. I didn't fully realize this until this year.

In 2007 an immigration officer informed me I was "stuck in a grey area of the law" because "there is a lot of confusion with Indian status card holders." He told me to apply for "Proof of Citizenship," so I applied. 2008 I received my response, which said I needed to apply for Indian status myself first, then apply for citizenship. As I mentioned, I do not qualify for Indian status. From then on I've spent these years actively seeking a solution to my unfounded "status in Canada."

In 2010 I wrote CIC with a proposal to add an immigration category to recognize and include children of Canadian Indians to be able to apply to further their legit residency. In summary, their response was [that the] Humanitarian and Compassionate application is sufficient and my concerns were noted. The Humanitarian and Compassionate application is for refugees who would suffer severe hardship by returning to their home country; it has a 3% success rate, minimum 2 year wait and upon denial you face immediate action in deportation.

I have been continuing to research on my own and try to find an Act or Law that can give me proper recognition; so that I do not need to apply as something I am not, nor do I want to risk my family's life here, for an application that does not apply to me. I have had very little success. All the while my naive assumption was I was a Canadian still just needing some sort of paper stating so, until this year. In 2012, via telephone, I am told by an immigration officer I am an illegal immigrant with no rights, and can be deported at any time.

I have already established myself here in Canada, it is my home and where my family is. I am now a mother myself here! My son was born in Ontario, he is 4 years old. Because of my unfound status in Canada I have not seen one penny of Child Tax Benefits for him. I'm sure you are aware, ALL children receive these benefits in Canada—even ones not born here. Yet, my Canadian-born son is denied because I do not have status.

Is there anything you can do to further awareness to include this? Is there any advice you can give to help?

Heather Harnois

I immediately responded to her email, and got this reply:

Sir, you cannot begin to imagine the joy you just brought me, in even just an offer to call.

I have written and talked to many organizations seeking advice/help. I have a large binder containing all the copies of letters I've written for *years*. Most never replied and the ones who did, wished me "good luck." No one has ever admitted it's discrimination nor offered to follow up.

Thank you so much.

Heather Harnois

Straightaway, I knew that Heather and I were soulmates. I so related to her being rejected by Canadian organizations and by the government. Her situation was a no-brainer: acceptance—she had a Canadian-born child. Putting Heather's rights aside, her son's rights were spelled out in the Canadian-sponsored UN Convention for the Rights of the Child—like being raised by his mother in Canada; having the right to food, clothing, and education; the right of government help if poor or in need; and, most important, the right to legal help and fair treatment in a justice system that respects his individual rights. Of the fifty-four articles in the convention, for the Harnois clan, Canada was failing to respect eleven of them. It was outrageous. Could it get worse? Well, yes.

You are my last hope...

I truly hope this letter makes it to someone. My name is Donovan McGlaughlin. I am 59 years old. My mother was a Canadian and my father was American Indian. I am a lost Canadian.

My mother and father were victims of the Residential schools. In 1954 they knew the only way to keep me from being also being rounded up and taken away as a youngster, was not to register my birth. No forms were ever filed with the government, including a birth certificate for me. I never thought much of it and just existed through life. I tried many times over the years to get help and was told time after time by government officials there was nothing they could do to help me.

I spent my life just getting by, until I met my wife. She showed me that I was worth something. Our children were born in 2007 and 2008. I made sure they had birth certificates and were able to receive all the benefits of being a citizen.

On October 5, 2010, I had a massive heart attack that almost killed me. Only by the grace of God did I survive. On October 6th I was to have an interview with Canada Border Services to decide if I was to be removed from the country. This was postponed until February of 2011. I had a telephone interview with an officer from Vancouver. Originally I was going to be sent to the US, but I am not, nor have I ever claimed to be an American citizen. I am Canadian. Even my own country doesn't want me. During this interview I was informed I was not a citizen of any other country, ergo I must be Canadian. So no removal order was filed.

I have had no support since my heart attack, no medical coverage. Every person with whom I've talked to in government has turned their back on me and will not help in any way.

I have never had a real job before because I have no SIN, no driver's licence, no birth certificate, not one piece of "official" paper to prove who I am [or] that I am Canadian.

Border Services, according to the way I understand it, recognized my mother as a Canadian. But there is nothing for me.

I went to the RCMP and gave them everything I could, fingerprints, scars, tattoos, photographs of everything that could help prove who I am. They found nothing. I am not in their system or any other law enforcement computer in the world. I am not a criminal, but that is how I have been treated.

I do not want or need a passport, what I need is the right to be a person. I feel like less than a dog, because dogs have more rights than I do. I cannot even volunteer to help my children with their school activities, because I am not a citizen.

We live in Dawson City, Yukon. Population of about 1500. The nearest city is Whitehorse, 500 km away. I have found no one including a lawyer that can or will help us. I am terrified that the day will come when I am taken away from my family. Or worse yet my children will have their citizenship revoked because of me.

I desperately need help. I have nowhere to turn, and have tried everything I know how to solve this and I am at my last straw.

I have no one to offer advice on what to do. I have spent countless hours searching the internet for any clue, any piece of information, that can help me. But I have always come up empty.

I am tired of living like this. Uncertainty, fear, and tears are what my life is. I want to be able to enjoy my children's lives without fear of being taken away. They deserve to have their father.

Thank you for your time in reading this. I have so much more to say but I will leave it at this. I hope beyond all hope that there is someone out there that can help.

Donovan McGlaughlin
Dawson City, Yukon

I called the Aboriginal Peoples Television Network, and instantly they latched onto something CTV's *W5*, CBC's *Fifth Estate*, and Global News' *16×9* had rejected: an investigative news story on Lost Canadians. And did it ever do a great job of telling Heather and Donovan's stories.[16] Not that it motivated the government, because in January 2014, when the feds announced that a "new and improved" bill would soon be introduced in Parliament to correct the Lost Canadian deficiencies, Heather and Donovan would be left behind.

A few months earlier, in July 2013, the revolving door at CIC's head office in Ottawa again turned. In the position of citizenship minister, Jason Kenney went out and Chris Alexander came in. Given that he was a former diplomat, we figured he'd know the advantages of two-way conversations.* It wasn't till February 2014 that we actually came face to face. It was at Vancouver's Canadian Club, at a sponsored luncheon with the new minister as the keynote speaker. Anxious to make his acquaintance, I attended, along with Jenny Uechi of the *Vancouver Observer*. Alexander admitted on camera,

---

* As of March 26, 2015, he has not met with me, nor have we talked by phone. It's been total silence.

finally, that citizenship had indeed existed before 1947, but his caveat was that that citizenship was "not as we know it today."* Certainly he'd been well briefed, knowledgeable of the corner Mr. Kenney had painted him into. He agreed to meet with me if I made it to Ottawa.

A month earlier, Alexander had been interviewed by CBC regarding a bill he was about to introduce, which later became Bill C-24:

> Alexander said the reform will aim to give Canadian citizenship to "Lost Canadians" who had seen it denied from them for one reason or another over the years.
>
> "We want to make sure that those loopholes that have done great injustice to a few people for all of those decades are closed, and that Canadian citizenship embraces all of those it should have embraced from the beginning."
>
> "Some are children of war brides, some have other complicated circumstances which should never have barred them from citizenship, and we have to fix the legislation."[17]

Finally, an admission that what they were doing was wrong. The light at the end of Jackie Scott's tunnel wasn't just from an oncoming train. (Yet even with Minister Alexander's admission that what CIC was doing was patently wrong, the government's judicial case against recognizing Jackie's citizenship pressed forward.) Bill C-24 would capture the pre-'47 folks.† However, it still raised questions. Why was the government pressing forward in the courts, denying Jackie and others like her? What public good was being served? Bill C-37 was supposed to have corrected the mischief—in fact, the all-party unanimous recommendation, if followed by Mr. Kenney, would have done just that.[18] But it took constant pressure—five straight years of my being an unrelenting thorn in the government's side. But what probably swayed it most was Jackie's lawsuit, and knowing it'd be defeated legally and morally, lose face, and look foolish. CIC recognized Mr. and Mrs. Santa Claus as citizens, but not our war dead.[19]

As I read the legislative summary of C-24, it was clear to me that the bill left people behind. The fix was just enough to satisfy the courts. When

---

* It was a cop-out answer. I don't exist today the way I did in 1960, but I existed. Likewise, Canadian citizenship didn't exist in 1925 the way it does today, but nonetheless it existed.

† It would take at least seven decades for CIC to accept the Canadian out-of-wedlock war babies from World Wars I and II. People like Eric Clapton would finally be citizens, but under C-24 it would be at some unknown date in the future. The government wasn't telling.

White Star Lines, owner and operator of the *Titanic*, was asked how many life rafts were on the ill-fated ship, the reply was "As many as required by law." Whether survival equipment on board the *Titanic* or the government's new legislation for Lost Canadians, it was the bare-bones minimum. Not one of my suggestions to Nicole Girard from four years earlier had been embraced. Some unsuspecting citizenship minister in the future would be passed a torch of legislative deficiency. But at least some of our Lost Canadians would be rescued now.

Hearings on C-24 commenced in March 2014, the bill's short title, "Strengthening Canadian Citizenship Act," probably meant to make it sound appealing while diverting the media's attention. It worked. The Conservatives had put into it all kinds of bad things.[20] While it helped some of our folks, it also gave huge powers to the minister to strip others of their citizenship. It was the equivalent of putting into an anti-abortion bill a clause allowing executions. It was in incredibly bad taste. Adding to the stench, buried deep in the fine print, was a complete change to how a person would challenge the government judicially. It would be far more difficult in the future, because power was being taken from the courts—despite the Supreme Court having recently nixed Harper in some of his ambitions, like doing away with the Senate—and instead gave more control to the prime minister.

As I stated at the beginning of this book, pilots have a huge system of checks and balances. Any strong democracy must have the same. In C-24, this crucial element was being diminished. It reminded me of the abolitionists in Britain, their agenda nicely buried in a bill having to do with cargo ships flying flags of convenience. The key was to hide it in mundane legislation and hope that no one in opposition was paying attention to its intricacies. Same thing with Canada and citizenship. MPs were woefully ignorant of the subject, as were the media, and both had little interest in doing research. It was the perfect place for the Conservatives to insert backhanded legislation. And the hall monitors were gone—the NDP, Liberals, and Conservatives did not advocate for a Lost Canadian to testify at any of C-24's hearings.

Just over a year before, the US House of Representatives held hearings on birth control and female reproductive rights. The Republicans, holding a majority, did not allow one woman to testify. Likewise, at all the hearings regarding a bill having to do with Lost Canadians, not one Lost Canadian was allowed to testify—not in the House, nor in the Senate. It was a first for the Lost Canadians; in the past, they'd always been invited to testify. The

Conservative majority in particular knew that our words would not be to their liking. How shameful, really, because we were anxious to explain, on the record, that Canadian citizenship had existed legally since Confederation: there were numerous Supreme Court decisions supporting this, laws were passed, it had even been discussed in our House of Commons, as well as in the British House of Lords.[21] When our Canadian soldiers marched off to World War II, they were given a handbook that said they were fighting as Canadian "citizens."[22] In 2013, in our Supreme Court, the attorney general of Canada argued that the Metis had been full citizens of Canada in 1870 so therefore weren't entitled to land claims.[23] Yet, in Jackie Scott's ongoing court challenge, this same government claimed citizenship didn't exist before 1947. The Conservatives were arguing both sides, and no one in opposition challenged them, probably because they too didn't know.

Not so for our group: on our archaeological dig, we'd uncovered a whole different history, a more shameful one. Canada had a very dark past in the arena of discrimination.[24] We learned about the Canadian branch of the Ku Klux Klan, of Hitler's government contacting Canada in the 1930s, inquiring about Canadian racial discrimination.[25] Hard to believe, but Mackenzie King's government responded. Our country was one of the models for Apartheid in South Africa.[26] Canada wasn't anything close to the accepting country it is today—accepting, of course, except in citizenship law. In that regard we cling to our discriminatory past. We also cling to a blatant falsehood: that citizenship began in 1947.

It didn't.

We had our proof. We had uncovered a lie going back to at least the mid-1940s. It had to do with Chinese Canadians in small towns such as Barkerville and Likely, BC. In a true democracy, the Chinese Canadians in these towns, being the majority of the population, would be able to elect whomever they pleased to run them. That, of course, depended on their being able to vote. Realizing this, BC cancelled their municipal voting rights, and since the provincial voters lists were derived from the municipalities, and the federal lists came from the provinces, by excluding the Chinese locally, you disenfranchised them from the country. For a time it worked—that is, up until around 1945.

The Liberals were in power; Mackenzie King, an indisputable racist. With Canada being a charter member of the newly formed United Nations and knowing he'd have to give the returning Chinese-Canadian war vets the right to vote, Mackenzie King wanted their support.[27] Obviously, no one would willingly vote for a party that had persecuted them, but what if they didn't know? It was easy: just tout the new citizenship act, which came into force on January 1, 1947, as the first time ever that there was citizenship in Canada. Then blame past discrimination on the Brits. Instead of being the oppressors of the Chinese, the Liberals would be regarded as their liberators.

It worked. For decades, the Chinese voted Liberal. As Fred Colbourne, now one of the world's leading experts on Canadian citizenship, writes, "The claim by Citizenship and Immigration Canada that citizenship was created by the 1947 Citizenship Act is unhistorical, a fiction developed to promote the Bill before Parliament" (see Appendix 2). It was political grand-standing at its worst, and for the next seven decades, the falsehood became CIC's reality. Total revisionist history. And the powers that be weren't interested in the truth.

Such was the case when I went to testify on Bill C-24 before the House Citizenship Committee. Melynda Jarratt and I were scheduled (our appearance paid for by the Canadian taxpayers), and when it came our turn to speak, the Conservative MPs decided to go in camera, meaning they voted us out of the room.[28] Accompanying me was Heather Harnois, the First Nations woman whose story is told above. She too got the boot. It was appalling that of the five Conservative MPs on the committee who voted against allowing us to testify, Costas Menegakis's family had come from Greece; Ted Opitz's parents came from Poland; Joe Daniel hailed from Tanzania; Devinder Shory came from India; and Chungsen Leung came from Taiwan. What gall, immigrant MPs telling a First Nations woman that she had no right to a Canadian identity.* Before the meeting began, I walked up to Leung, asking if our war dead had been Canadian citizens. His answer was astounding: "I really don't know." It was his job to know. He was being paid to know. But he hadn't a clue. What if the warrior laid to rest in the Tomb of the Unknown Soldier, our national hero, was in fact a non-Canadian Chinese or First Nations person?

Two weeks later, I watched as other witnesses testified. The parliamentary secretary to the citizenship minister, Costas Menegakis, stated, "The Citizenship Act was first introduced in 1947." His point was that, prior to the act, we weren't Canadian citizens. Probably thirty times in the previous several months I'd called Mr. Menegakis's folks, asking for a meeting. They

---

* Even the name "Canada"' is derived from our indigenous peoples. The Huron-Iroquois word for village or settlement is "Kanata."

refused. His ignorance was self-induced: he wasn't interested in the truth. The Conservative MPs were like that, almost clones of the top guy himself.

Bill C-24 got passed straight down party lines—the objectionable sections all had to do with the minister's new-found ability to strip Canadians of their citizenship. Harper limited debate to just one day. Then it was off to the Senate, which too had become highly seasoned with partisanship. I was again shunned. In *Star Trek* terms, the bill went through both chambers at warp factor 10.

After royal assent we learned it would take at least a year for implementation of the bill, and possibly a year or two after that for those covered to get their proof of citizenship. Why were we not surprised? Seventy- to ninety-five-year-old senior citizens—people the government admitted to having suffered "great injustices"—were now required to wait even longer. I emailed Mr. Alexander's chief of staff, explaining how some folks may not live to see their citizenship. He sided with his bureaucrats. I sensed little sympathy. The minister, Chris Alexander, despite his promise to meet with me, had yet to do so. He remained aloof.

Déjà vu. It was back to business as usual, the citizen against the government. That's when I got this:

Dear Mr. Chapman,
I have been following your struggle with the Canadian citizenship problem for war brides and their children for some time.

I am in the same situation as Jackie Scott. My parents met and were married in England during the war. I was born in 1943 and came to Canada with my mother aboard a ship in 1945. I requested and was given a citizenship card three years ago. I have been denied OAS pension four times. I have never lived anywhere else but Canada. They insist I provide a Ship and date upon arrival in Halifax NS before approving my pension. I have requested a search through Archives Canada and still after some months have not heard anything. The last denial was received by mail on Thursday last, just in time for Canada Day. I am beginning to believe they are just being insulting and hurtful and don't really care. I have been struggling financially for some time now and applied for OAS before my 65th birthday. I am now 71 and am losing my hope that anything will happen. I can't believe these people can be so hurtful. I have lived and worked in Regina SK since 1970. Please respond and thank you.
Sincerely,
Janet Eileen Smith

Sonny and Cher could have been singing about Canada: "And the beat goes on, yes, the beat goes on."

Regrettably, in the years to come, there will be many more letters like Janet's. Simply put, our issue continues because the government refuses to correct it. Our supposed representatives have forgotten, or possibly intentionally ignored, the fact that they were elected to represent Canadian citizens, to protect their interests, to make their lives better, and to uphold Canadian values, such as fairness, compassion, human rights, inclusiveness, acceptance, diversity, peace, order, and good government. In every category, the Lost Canadians have been deprived. The Liberals, the NDP, and the Conservatives have failed.[29] The only party whose leader was speaking out on our behalf was the Green Party. Elizabeth May made citizenship and the rights of individual Canadians a priority issue of the party—a stark contrast to the Liberals' Justin Trudeau and the NDP's Thomas Mulcair. They were and remain great disappointments. Canada, it seems, isn't very good at taking care of its own.

But it *is* good (outstanding, actually) at spin-doctoring, making it appear to the world as though it embraces all that is good with equality and human rights. Below are quotations from five recent Canadians who came into our family as honorary citizens, four under Mr. Harper's watch and one under the Liberals'. Not missing a beat, in wonderfully staged photo-ops, top politicians from the party of the day proudly presented them with their newly minted certificates of Canadian citizenship. As Lost Canadians, watching from afar, being shunned, we thought, *What would these civil rights activists say about us? If only they knew.*

Government leaders are amazing. So often it seems they are the last to know what the people want.

This was the way I was brought up to think of politics, that politics was to do with ethics, it was to do with responsibility, it was to do with service.

Please use your liberty to promote ours.
—Aung San Suu Kyi, Burma (Harper)

Everybody makes mistakes. Never regret them, correct them.
—Aga Khan IV, Ismaili Imamat (Harper)

One child, one teacher, one book and one pen can change the world.
—Malala Yousafzai, Pakistan (Harper)

Dangerous consequences will follow when politicians and rulers forget moral principles.
—the Dalai Lama, Tibet (Harper)

A nation should not be judged by how it treats its highest citizens, but its lowest ones.
—Nelson Mandela, South Africa (Chrétien)[30]

Just maybe our own government should pay heed. And they will, but only if voters demand it at the polling stations.

To me, a veteran of seven parliamentary bills, three of which passed (two unanimously), after decades of fighting Ottawa's hundreds of bureaucrats and MPs alike, including three prime ministers, it has become painfully clear, and I say this without reservation, that the real, honest-to-goodness bona fide "lost" Canadian, in fact, the exceedingly "lost" Canadian, is none other than Stephen Harper. May his methods of non-representational government soon rest in peace.

PART 4

WRAP UP AND ANALYSIS

CHAPTER 20

THAT'S A WRAP

You feel as if everyone should write a book before they die, but their book is already written. The pages live within those they've touched.
COACH OWEN CLARK, IN THE FILM *GRACIE*

WHEN ONE PEELS away everything but the underlying elements, our issue is really about discrimination, with an emphasis against women—the result being the loss of one's citizenship. Deciphering the matter through my pilot lens, I often compare the issue to being in the cockpit of an airplane during an emergency with an engine fire. Let's say the fire warning bell is going off, the left-engine fire handle is illuminated, and I don't have a clue what to do next (although that's not the case—I'm well trained on the procedures). But to illustrate the point, I'll make myself out as the one who's both ignorant and incompetent. I turn to the other pilot and say, "I don't know what to do."

The pilot, who just happens to be female, responds, "I know exactly what to do."

To which I say, "Because you're a woman, I don't want to know."

In the next scene, the plane crashes and everyone dies. It's almost hard to imagine that a person could be so filled with discrimination that they willingly ignore knowledge and, in doing so, they too suffer the consequences of their ignorance.* But that's really what transpires whenever discrimination

---

* In a sense, there is good and bad discrimination. Clearly, it's acceptable to discriminate between good and bad people, like wanting your children to hang out with friends of good character. In using the word "discrimination" as I do here, I'm talking about illogical or irrational decision making, often associated with deep-rooted prejudice.

is allowed to fester, no matter what form it takes. And, regrettably, it happens all the time. It's not just the victim who suffers but also the perpetrator and society.

Our existence in this world is limited at best and yet, as humans, we expend enormous amounts of energy and time on stupid issues, like the Lost Canadians.* It would be far better for humanity if we used our time on really important causes, like finding cures for cancer or developing green energy. The nanosecond that discrimination is discovered, no matter what form it morphs into, it must be eradicated. Should women have equal rights with men? Yes, absolutely. How about blacks and whites and everyone in between? Of course.

Equal rights, equal opportunity, period and full stop.

In citizenship law, especially with Canada wanting to be known as an enlightened human-rights country, the Lost Canadian issue should have been resolved a long, long time ago. The amount of energy exerted in fighting both for and against us could have been put to much better use for humanity in other areas. Same thing with the enormous costs: there are much better ways to spend taxpayers' dollars.

Like so many other issues, ours should have been an open-and-shut case. My words before the Senate are as true today as they were when I first answered the good senator's question on how to correct the problem, by comparing it to the advice I'd give to my children when they make a mistake. *Admit it, apologize, correct it, then go on.* And those words are just as true for a country as for young kids—it's not rocket science. In fact, it's more important for a country because youngsters learn by example.

In that sense, how hypocritical is it for Canada to claim leadership in women's rights while fighting tooth and nail in its own courts to deny people citizenship because of gender? And then it goes to war in Afghanistan, in part, to help Afghan women achieve equal rights with men. It sort of defies imagination.

What Canada risks by not fixing the Lost Canadian debacle is a permanent loss of credibility with its people, and with the world. The obvious example is the Vietnam War and Richard Nixon.† Before the war, Americans were overall more than willing to volunteer for their country "when

---

* I call the Lost Canadian issue "stupid" in that it should never have been allowed to go on and on for decades and maybe even more than a century. Anyone can see the foolishness of keeping old discriminatory laws alive.

† In North America, the war is known as the "Vietnam War," whereas in Vietnam, it's referred to as the "American War."

duty called." With Watergate, the public discovered that "their" president had been less than honest, putting his own interests above the people. And life in the States (and, for that matter, the world) was never the same. Both events did lasting damage to America's self-perception.

My belief and my hope for Canada is that our country doesn't go down that path, but rather becomes a beacon of light for the world. And it all can begin by nurturing our own people with human rights and dignity. There is much to gain by doing it right, and far more to lose by doing it wrong.

CHAPTER 21

ANALYSIS AND RECOMMENDATIONS

*I have a dream that one day this nation will rise up and
live out the true meaning of its creed: "We hold these truths to
be self-evident: that all men are created equal."*
DR. MARTIN LUTHER KING JR., "I HAVE A DREAM"
SPEECH, AUGUST 28, 1963

Everybody is somebody.
LARRY JACKSON, PRESIDENT, ARCHER-RAGSDALE
CHAPTER OF THE TUSKEGEE AIRMEN

ALL PLANE ACCIDENTS and incidents are studied with the purpose of discovering what went wrong; then, recommendations are made to improve aviation safety. No one wants a repeat of an accident. Here, I use the same principle to analyze and suggest improvements to citizenship law and practice in Canada.

The sentiment embodied in the epigraph that opens this section is a great starting point. In 2011, two men, the Honourable Albert Ludwig and Robert Kulhawy, wrote what they call the "Canadian Creed," in which they tried to encompass all that Canada stands for. Highlighted are a couple of the major themes, such as the rule of law and "equal rights and benefits under the law—without any discrimination based on race, national or ethnic origin, colour, religion, gender, age, or mental or physical disability."[1]

Making it more official, CIC, under Jason Kenney's guidance, came out with a new publication, *Discover Canada: The Rights and Responsibilities of*

Citizenship. In it is talk about the rule of law and equality of rights. There's also a sidebar titled "The Equality of Women and Men." Here's the first sentence: "In Canada, men and women are equal under the law."[2]

Even Stephen Harper in his Throne Speeches regularly talks about the "rule of law." For example, in his very first Throne Speech in 2006, the governor general said, "More broadly, this Government is committed to supporting Canada's core values of freedom, democracy, the rule of law and human rights around the world."[3]

Without question, equality of rights and rule of law are principles our government leaders love to flaunt. The former is pretty much self-explanatory, but what exactly do they mean by "rule of law"? As defined by the United Nations' secretary-general, it's "a principle of governance in which all persons, institutions and entities, public and private, including the State itself, are accountable to laws that are publicly promulgated, equally enforced and independently adjudicated, and which are consistent with international human rights norms and standards."[4]

This was meant as a guideline for international observance. I have presented here numerous examples of violations of this principle by Canada. I haven't, nor has anyone I've worked with, ever been able to identify the fundamental motivations harboured by the federal government to account for these violations. That remains a puzzle, because it's hard to imagine anyone benefiting.

The UN pronouncement includes the words "laws that are publicly promulgated." Obviously, to expect citizens to be accountable, laws must be made known. This one principle has been routinely and persistently violated by the Canadian government. By failing to publicize important laws, it kept them secret while applying them against its people. Thus, the vast majority of Lost Canadians got trapped simply because they didn't know, and they were not alone. Our MPs and senators are also ignorant of the laws. This sort of secret and vindictive practice must stop.

The media are equally guilty of withholding vital information from the people. If the government were to openly announce important changes of law, and the media were to actively pursue all related issues, informed Canadians could easily observe these rules. But again, the government often does the opposite. In the past, it has not only kept the media in the dark but, at times, pressured them to squash stories potentially embarrassing to it. A potent weapon used to accomplish this is the cutting of funding or the changing of the tax structure against organizations that could pose a threat to the government's image. An internal affairs arm of the government should be established to police such activities, and to hand out severe punishments to violators, be they individual citizens or high government officials.

The other UN words of interest are "all persons, institutions and entities, public and private, including the State itself, are accountable to laws ... equally enforced and independently adjudicated." CIC has made a mockery of these words, picking out many innocent and harmless citizens for relentless persecution while favouring others, especially foreigners and the rich and famous, with a fast track to citizenship.

Just over six decades ago, as a beacon of light to the world, one of our fellow Canadians, John Peters Humphrey, was the principal author of the United Nations' 1948 Universal Declaration of Human Rights, to which Canada was an original signatory. The declaration stressed the importance of equal rights, particularly for men and women; of security of the person; and of the right of an individual to a nationality, and it provided that no one shall be arbitrarily deprived of his or her nationality.[5] Canada is also a signatory to several UN conventions on human rights: the Reduction of Statelessness, the Elimination of All Forms of Discrimination Against Women, and the Rights of the Child.

Clearly, Canada has obligations to uphold, and our country has not been living up to those commitments. One such example: despite strong pressure being exerted by the proponents of Bill C-37, there still remain six potentially discriminatory and arbitrary ways to be denied citizenship.

As with all plane crashes, a chain of events leads up to the accident. When digging into what I would call the "citizenship accident," one must define the contributing factors. All three branches of government—executive, legislative, and judicial—played a factor. The glue binding them together are the bureaucrats. All share some form of guilt. Outside of government, there are the supposed watchdogs of government: the media, independent film producers, bloggers, organizations, and, most important, individual Canadians. They too played a role.

Of everyone mentioned, let's begin with the obvious: the politicians. Supposedly representatives of the people, our legislators instead have often put their self-interests above the interests of their constituents. And they did it openly and with impunity. In aviation, we've noticed a definite pattern: that more accidents occurred when the captain—the leader of the entire operation—ran the cockpit with an iron fist. By the 1980s, pilots were being taught that, while there does need to be a captain in charge, the safest way to get an aircraft from point A to point B was through team effort, whereby everyone was to make their opinions known. From the operations and dispatch folks to maintenance personnel and gate agents, everyone associated with the flight was encouraged to contribute. Safety became a collaborative effort, all crewmembers mandated to provide their input, and all sharing in the responsibility. Once this policy of shared responsibility was implemented, the aviation accident and incident rate declined both significantly and immediately.

We also have a thorough system of checks and balances. Every pilot's responsibility is to speak out if something doesn't look right; nothing is taken for granted. In our system of government, and particularly in Canada, there exist relatively few checks and balances, particularly on the prime minister. It reminds me of the old-time supreme airline captain—and the corresponding higher accident rates.

So, just what are the prime minister's checks and balances? Inside the Conservative Party's caucus, politicians vie for coveted cabinet positions, so an MP is probably much more likely to advance into the prime minister's inner circle by going along with his every word than by questioning it. Here's an example of a Conservative voting against his own party. In 2007, Bill Casey of Nova Scotia said he couldn't support the Conservative budget because "it doesn't allow his province to fully benefit from offshore oil and gas revenues without losing equalization payments from the federal government."[6] Casey said, "I believe that the government of Canada signed a contract with my province of Nova Scotia and it's not being honoured." His punishment is best described by the next day's headline: "Tory MP Ejected from Caucus After Budget Vote." By voting as his constituents desired, putting his riding and province above his party, he gets thrown out of the caucus. The subliminal message sent to the other Conservative MPs is that obedience equals acceptance. Do as the prime minister says.

But what if the prime minister is wrong?

In aviation, we always have at least two pilots, just in case one of them makes a mistake. In Canadian politics, a lot rides on the judgment of just one person: the prime minister. Being human, individuals can and do make errors. Back to what if the prime minister is wrong? Answer: Canadians suffer.

One clear example of checks and balances is the government-imposed regulations on Canada's banking system, which basically saved our country from a complete financial meltdown in 2008. MP Andrew Telegdi told me how the Liberals at one point considered relaxing those rules but in the end did not. Fortunately, Mr. Harper kept the status quo. But what if he had instead done away with our banking regulations? A single individual could have decimated Canadians with one wrong decision.

The media too has few checks and balances. In the last few decades, the entire dynamics of the business has changed. Journalism now comes under the scrutiny of bean counters, who answer to their respective CFOs and CEOs, who in turn answer to their shareholders, whose only concern is to maximize profits. Britney Spears commands a much larger audience than old-women war brides, and the media coverage reflected that. Hence, the media shares huge blame for not holding the government accountable in citizenship law. Doing the right thing is not part of the media equation. Today, it's pretty much all about money.

Then there's the Canadian Radio and Television Commission (CRTC). Here's how it describes itself: "An administrative tribunal that regulates and supervises broadcasting and telecommunications in the public interest ... Our mandate is entrusted to us by the Parliament of Canada, and administered through the Minister of Canadian Heritage." Its mission? "We recognize the importance of communication services to Canadians. And we are dedicated to ensuring that the needs and interests of Canadians are at the centre of the system that provides those services."[7]

Given the huge deficiencies in the effectiveness of the Canadian media, where does an individual Canadian turn for help? You could write a letter of complaint to the CRTC, but then, as the Lost Canadians can tell you, your letter might never see the light of day. The CRTC doesn't get involved with print media, but anything using public airwaves, such as television and radio, must conform to its standards. Once again, look at the weak link in this chain: "The CRTC reports to Parliament through the Minister of Canadian Heritage," who, of course, reports to the virtually unchecked prime minister.[8]

Now let's look at independent film producers. Their production funding, called envelopes, may come from broadcasters. A second source is Telefilm Canada. With Lost Canadians, the broadcasters weren't interested, and Telefilm Canada gets federal funding and thus is accountable to the government (which means the prime minister). Hence, the hands of most independent film producers were tied.

How about human rights and non-profit organizations? Overall, they remained silent about our issue. Although only a few organizations openly admitted this to me, their concerns were legitimate, and specific to prohibitions against lobbying the government. The intent is sound, but they should be allowed to advocate in the arena of equality and human rights.[9]

It's interesting that almost every such organization uses the same buzz-words in their mission statements, claiming in their own unique ways to "stand on guard for thee." But translating those words into actions is quite another thing. Almost no one came forward to help. It was even worse in the public sector, where life support (money) came from the government. The Status of Women and Veterans Affairs are two examples and, worse, their top people were MPs, owing their jobs to the prime minister. Their response typically came in one of two ways: "It's not our department—contact the minister of citizenship" or "We will forward your concerns on to the minister of citizenship and immigration." The Canadian Human Rights Commission was absolutely useless. Its mandate excluded discrimination in citizenship law. Ironically, the government dictated the commission's mandate. Always, the path through the public sector had connections to the prime minister.

And everything always boiled down to money. I found everyone in Canada—in both the public and the private sectors—at all times desperate for funding, so much so that it often left the organization impotent to carry out its mandate.

The hallowed walls of Rideau Hall proved to be pretty much impenetrable. On occasion, I did converse with Rideau Hall's media representatives, and its public relations people too—the former were of no help, the latter sympathetic but, overall, no better. The governor general, no matter who it was, would make wonderful statements about Canada being accepting, abiding by the rule of law, and affording equal rights and equal opportunity, as well as about the importance of our vets and military. But with Lost Canadians and the obvious abuses in equal rights, the governors general were either unaware or by design couldn't speak out. In Canada, by design, everyone, including the governor general, must be allowed a voice for equal rights.

Of the governor general's many duties, one is presenting to outstanding Canadians awards—for student achievement; for notable accomplishments in the arts, science, women's rights; for meritorious and heroic service—right on up to the Order of Canada (OAC). Not a single person has ever been recognized for accomplishments regarding Lost Canadians. Many folks, like Nobel Prize recipient Willard Boyle, were recognized with the highest honour within the OAC, the Companion of the Order of Canada, the second Bill C-37 became effective and he was once again a Canadian citizen. But for those who sacrificed a huge part of their lives, who gave their all to right this wrong for a million or so other Canadians—folks like Magali Castro-Gyr, Charles and Peg Bosdet, Jeff Wan, Melynda Jarratt, Robert Addington,

Fred Colbourne, and Jackie Scott, among others—they've never even been given a high-five by the powers that be. Something is amiss.

Even CIC honours select individuals with citizenship awards. In its words, "This prestigious award pays tribute to Canadians who have made an important contribution in promoting the rights and responsibilities of Canadian citizenship."[10] Again, I know of no Lost Canadian who's been recognized.

The Court Challenges Program, which was envied by many countries around the world, was terminated by an executive decision by Stephen Harper.[11] That alone eliminates a huge check and balance on the prime minister: the judicial side of government. One hopes that, with the prime minister appointing Supreme Court judges, there's no inherent bias.

Whoever holds the purse strings exerts his or her influence over content. Today, CBC in particular is feeling the financial pinch, trying to make do with far less. Since I penned the first words of this book, the broadcaster's financial condition has only got worse, almost to the point of crisis. Being a targeted victim of huge government cutbacks, it, along with all the other media outlets, doesn't want to bite the hand that helps feed it. I find it no small coincidence that CBC's investigative journalism unit has been gutted.

Similar story with Canadian newspapers and magazines. Although supposedly more able to escape the financial pressures of government interference, they are often owned or controlled by media conglomerates with assets regulated by the government, and which, like the CRTC, come under the prime minister's scrutiny. Same with Shaw Media, which owns *Global National* and Corus Entertainment; Bell Media; and CTVglobemedia. The smaller independent media are going by the wayside, being replaced by a handful of huge, concentrated, often multinational, conglomerates. For a time, the Aspers owned and controlled the *Vancouver Sun, Vancouver Province, North Shore News, National Post*, and Vancouver's Global Television Network. Whenever there is government regulation or oversight, there exists the potential for these companies to have self-imposed censorship, not wanting to upset the apple cart. It also raises huge red flags about possible conflict of interest—are the huge corporations acting in their own best interests or in Canada's best interest? To get a licence to operate or to buy assets of another broadcaster, they must have government approval, which they obtain by convincing the government that it is they that will best serve the Canadian people. This alone is often at odds with the interests of their shareholders. The question is, do they exert too much control or influence? *Time* magazine publishes a Canadian version, but its editors in the States told me they do not have much interest in covering Canadian stories. They certainly attached no importance to the Lost Canadian story, telling me they didn't have a reporter in Canada. Often the only "Canadian" content in the magazine is the Canadian address on the masthead, and the Canadian price. "Canadian" should be about Canada.

Furthermore, the media's interests take into account their investors, not the public. Investigative journalism is extremely costly and, as Rupert Murdoch brought to light, the business model is all about profits. The media have gravitated toward the entertainment side, with real news vying for space next to the Hollywood stars.

Like the prime minister's enormous control, just a handful of corporate titans have a lot of influence over public opinion. But, as the Occupy Wall Street crowd point out, the interests of the 1 percent don't always run in tandem with the remaining 99 percent. Case in point: the Lost Canadian story would have produced no profits, and certainly wouldn't have scored points with the government. The media paid little interest.

The bureaucrats and politicians don't fully understand or appreciate citizenship. Immigration, however, is a means to securing votes, a lesson not lost on the political parties, which often use it as a means to an end: getting themselves elected. Immigration should benefit the country, not the party. Once again, the prime minister exerts great influence over immigration policy.

A huge deficiency in Canadian citizenship law is that, unlike in many other countries, citizenship is a legislative privilege rather than a constitutional right. In our system, politicians determine who is or is not Canadian. As any naturalized Canadian can attest, in citizenship ceremonies, the judges articulate that citizenship is a two-way street, the government having obligations to its people, and the people having obligations to their newly found country. Fair enough, but what if the political winds change? Let's take a worst-case scenario: Fifty years from now, the Nazi Party rises to take majority control in Canada, then immediately passes legislation saying that if you are not a Nazi, you aren't Canadian. This is pretty much what Hitler did when he came into power: the very first thing on his agenda was to cancel the citizenship of all Jewish Germans. In Canada, we must not allow ourselves to be vulnerable. Citizenship must be enshrined in our constitution.

There's also a deficiency in how bills go from implementation to law. It's best described through example:

About six years ago, Charles Bosdet made a presentation to four of the parties. After witnessing the writing, passage, and implementation of Bill s-2, it had become painfully obvious to me that Ottawa's modus operandi was inefficient, often ineffective, wasted colossal sums of money, and frequently didn't serve the people it was supposed to. Bill c-37 exemplifies this. Yes, the bill did some wonderful things to correct past injustices. But it was written in such a way as not to fully correct the problem, leaving 5 percent of the Lost Canadians behind for the worst of reasons. It remained ripe for legal challenges. In hindsight, there were many judicial proceedings, at great expense to individuals and Canadian taxpayers alike. Charles Bosdet and Jeff Wan (of *Benner v. Canada*) had come up with a much better way to take bills from conception to law. I accompanied them to a meeting room in Centre Block where Bill Siksay of the NDP, Meili Faille of the Bloc, Andrew Telegdi of the Liberals, and Ed Komarnicki of the Conservatives listened.

What Charles did was to come up with a better mousetrap. What if someone coordinated all the various departments and people and, along the way, recorded their thinking, so that the intent and meaning of each key contributor was preserved. In the event of future litigation (and there would undoubtedly be future litigation), the courts would be able to decipher exactly what the parliamentarians had intended. The Privy Council Orders in the 1940s clearly gave out-of-wedlock war-bride kids like Jackie Scott the right to citizenship, yet today, that's not how CIC interprets it. Their rationale, their rejection, is a product directly of the minds of later bureaucracies. Over the decades, denial became the norm and the standard response of CIC, prompting multi-billion-dollar court challenges.

Yet another deficiency lies with Canadian academic institutions. Universities should not serve only to educate students; they should also be a place of free dialogue and expression. Very few universities and professors gave the Lost Canadians the time of day. Considering that our issue dealt with politics, equal rights, women's rights, citizenship, journalism, law, history, sociology, you name it, it touched many areas of academia. I once met with a political science major from UBC. He contacted his professor, saying that he wanted to study our issue. The reply? He didn't feel that we were a subject worthy of the student's time. My daughter at SFU wrote a paper on the Lost Canadians; her political science professor dismissed the subject as fictitious. Our institutions of higher learning can and must do better than this. They should encourage dialogue and search for better ways to run the country.

The next problem is the legal profession. As court decisions were being ignored, where was it in challenging the bureaucracy? In 2011, our governor general, David Johnston, gave a speech to the Canadian Bar Association, saying that its members do not do enough pro bono work for the public good. Enough said.

Parliamentary procedures need to be scrutinized and changed where applicable. For example, a report released in July 2012 stated that arcane rules are keeping MPs in the dark about billions in government spending. One enormous problem is that spending plans (called estimates) for each fiscal year beginning April 1 don't take into account the federal budget, which is typically released about the same time, and which can significantly affect spending. It means that the spending blueprints are not getting proper oversight by the MPs, keeping them mostly "blind" to government spending.[12] Plain and simple, this should not be happening. Parliament must improve its ways.

Another deficiency lies squarely with the Canadian people themselves. Canadians have become incredibly complacent and rather ignorant of their history. Pilots are an amalgamation of all the pilots we've ever flown with, emulating the positive qualities while avoiding the bad. Countries too should learn from other nations. If Norway has a better mousetrap in health care, we should adopt it, or at least adapt it into our medical system. In general, Canadians are fully aware that huge problems exist in government, yet they don't demand better. In politics, you get what you deserve and, unlike in Australia, where citizens are required to vote, Canadians are allowed to ignore the ballot box, something done by far too many.

The Lost Canadian issue happened, really, because the Canadian people didn't demand their repatriation. For example, tens of thousands of Canadians are currently trapped in the citizenship queue, not being able to prove they truly are Canadian. Why do we allow this to happen? Governments are supposed to work "for" the people. During World War II, it was extraordinary how the Danish protected their Jewish population, smuggling them into Sweden. In their absence, their property, possessions, and animals were cared for and returned on their arrival home. The Danes were a shining example to the world. Seeing injustice, they rose up in unison because it was the right thing to do. Taking away one's citizenship, and all the rights associated with it, is appalling, and our government has gotten away with it because the voters didn't demand better. The media weren't moved to fully report the abuse because Canadians were much more infatuated with Britney Spears, so therefore our politicians weren't held accountable, which allowed the bureaucrats to systematically eliminate everyday Canadians from the rosters. The root cause of the problem boils down to the Canadian people not being sufficiently engaged. One of the themes of the newly opened Canadian Museum for Human Rights, a question the museum wants people to ponder, is: What would you do? Overall, Canadians are far too complacent.

In my pilots' union, we say, "You don't get what you deserve, you get what you negotiate." Let me add, "If you're unwilling to protect your rights and the rights of others, soon there will be no rights."

In the end, Canadians must be responsible for their country. As was so aptly stated in the 1940s Canadian schoolbook *Building the Canadian Nation*, "The 'civil liberties' they are called, and we can be sure that we shall enjoy them only so long as we value them enough to preserve them. They did not come easily. Therefore, the responsibility of protecting civil liberties rests where it must always rest in a democracy, on the people themselves."[13]

Recommendations
Canada and/or Canadians must:

- Create a separate portfolio for citizenship, not connected with immigration or multiculturalism. Otherwise, there exists a potential for a conflict of interest.

- Appoint a citizenship ombudsman so that Canadians have an advocate for their rights. The ombudsman must be accessible. Although individuals must provide whatever proof they have that they are citizens, the onus must be on the government to prove they are not citizens. Documents that were accepted as proof of citizenship decades ago must still be accepted today.

- Remove citizenship from the sphere of political determination.

- Make citizenship a Charter right. As a safeguard for all Canadians, we must enshrine citizenship as a constitutional right.[14]

- Judge people on a case-by-case basis as the exception, not the norm. Citizenship must be easy to understand, and people must be confident that, by operation of law, they are citizens.

- Provide for some form of amnesty that accepts people who have been in Canada most of their lives, growing up and believing themselves to be citizens. In June 2012, Barack Obama agreed to legitimize upward of 800,000 people who were illegal aliens, having been brought to the US as young children. President Obama stated, "They pledge allegiance to our flag. They are Americans in their hearts, in their minds, in every single way but one: on paper." Further, they "study in our schools, they play in our neighborhoods, they're friends with our kids . . . It makes no sense to expel talented young people who, for all intents and purposes, are Americans." Obama then said that acceptance was "the right thing to do," and that the US "is a better nation than one that expels innocent young kids."[15] Canada could learn a human rights lesson from its southern neighbour. Our government must become even more accepting and accommodating.

- Ensure government works to benefit the people. Having hundreds of thousands of people not being able to prove their status is deplorable. The government should hire more case processors. Australia can process citizenship applications in weeks to months, so why can't Canada?[16] Is our bureaucratic system that inferior to that of our southern-hemisphere cousin, or is our dedication to fellow citizens so lacking, or both?

- Require the media to tell Canadian stories, secure that the government won't pull their funding. CBC has strayed from its mandate. The US has PBS (Public Broadcasting Service) and NPR (National Public Radio). Having something similar in Canada would greatly benefit Canadians.

- Fund investigative journalism, even if that means with taxpayers' dollars. The payoff is the continued freedom of our country, which requires top-notch investigative journalism.

- Preserve and digitally archive knowledge and provide arms-length government funding.[17] Our libraries have seen recent cutbacks, yet Archives Canada provides a wealth of information crucial to our future, with librarians often being the essential link in gaining access to these historical records.

- Celebrate and nurture our culture. This takes funding. Cutting back in areas of culture affects future generations, making Canadians less understanding of who they are. Canadians must be proud, and knowledgeable. They must know their history.

- Recognize that education is paramount. The public and the MPs need to become a great deal more informed. How can MPs represent their portfolios when they don't understand them?

- Always strive for 100 percent when it comes to human rights; 95 percent is not good enough.

- Make cabinet ministers more accessible, not just to their supportive party members but to the public in general.

- Ensure that MPs are allowed a free vote.

- Develop a daily political news program that better exposes Canadian issues than does what is currently available. The US has several television shows about politics. (One network, MSNBC, airs each weekday *The Rachel Maddow Show*, *Hardball with Chris Matthews*, *PoliticsNation with Al Sharpton*, *The Last Word with Lawrence O'Donnell*, and *The Ed Show*. Other networks also produce their own shows.) In Canada, such a show must be open to viewer suggestions for content and topics, since no one knows the issues of daily life better than Canadian individuals who live it.

- Make all Canadian legislation Charter compliant. Canada must immediately begin work on a new citizenship act. It cannot be partisan, as citizenship belongs to all Canadians regardless of party affiliation. Academia, the Canadian people, bureaucrats, all political parties, everyone needs to be involved.

- Get back to basics: bureaucrats should work for the politicians, politicians for the people.

- Demand better from our government. Canadians deserve superlative representation. People must be assertive: your voice is your vote, and your vote is your voice.

- Study, and possibly adopt, various electoral systems, such as proportional representation.

- Engage primary and secondary school students in Canadian history, and what it means to be a good Canadian citizen, including our shared Canadian values.

- Accept all our World War II born-out-of-wedlock kids. Germany has done this; Canada must do the same.

- Ensure equal rights for all. Most immigrant Canadians are deemed to be born in Canada for the purpose of passing on citizenship. All first-generation born-abroad Canadians must have the same right as immigrant Canadians to prove their "connection" to Canada. If they prove a "substantial connection," they should be deemed to have been born in Canada for purposes of passing on citizenship.

- Grant the right to Canadian citizenship to all second-generation born-abroad children who were born prior to April 17, 2009, to Canadian mothers and foreign fathers.

- Do away with the age-twenty-eight reaffirmation rule, so that all those affected are immediately recognized as citizens.

- Grant the right to citizenship to all children born to a Canadian parent prior to April 17, 2009, regardless of being born in or out of wedlock.

- Immediately grant citizenship to children born stateless to a Canadian parent.

- Recognize citizenship as having been in existence back to Confederation.

- Immediately recognize as being Canadian citizens those approximately 200 people who remain disenfranchised.[18]

- Do not hold private individuals accountable for the mistakes of CIC. Citizenship and Immigration Canada has been inconsistent over the years in giving out accurate information.

- Phrase government-sponsored survey questions fairly so as not to obtain predetermined results.

- Adopt a more American-style way of conducting parliamentary hearings. The US Congress has congressional investigations. Similarly, our Canadian Parliament holds hearings, but the witnesses are generally allowed just minutes to explain their position. The MPs are also given an extremely limited amount of time for questions. The process needs to be updated so that issues can be discussed at length. As it is, parliamentarians are often so ignorant of the subject matter, they don't know what questions to ask, and the witnesses don't have enough time to explain the issues.

- Ensure, for balance, more independent oversight for parliamentarians, who are involved with the broad strokes, and for regulators and bureaucrats, who do the nitty-gritty work.

- Ensure some sort of continuity within government portfolios, rather than a rotating door when it comes to cabinet ministers and committee members. MPs must learn and understand the portfolios they represent.

- Make citizenship a priority in Canada. Immigration is important, but the objective is to turn immigrants into good Canadian citizens, not the other way around.

- Engage Canadians in their country. They, and they alone, determine its future direction via the power of the ballot box. Their judgment, or lack thereof, will affect their children, grandchildren, and all future generations. What our country becomes lies in the balance.

- Strive to achieve a passionate and well-informed public. Nothing is as important to a democracy.

- Put the collective good of the people first. No matter what party clamours to be elected, when casting their vote, Canadians should take into account our fine Canadian traditions and values. "Peace," "order," and "good government"; "fairness," "compassion," and "human rights" should not just be feel-good slogans but goals to which we aspire. Building a better country for our children is a worthy achievement.

- Learn from each other when determining our common values. English Canadians, French Canadians, and the First Nations people all have their unique and wonderful ways. Canadian identity should be an amalgamation of the best qualities of these cultures. We must be proud of being Canadian, and of the country's First Nations heritage.

- Believe that one person, one voice, can and does make a difference. As the late Steve Jobs said through one of Apple's ads, "The people who are crazy enough to think they can change the world, are the ones who do."[19]

APPENDIX 1

LOST CANADIANS ON CITIZENSHIP

Charles Bosdet on Citizenship and Nationality

CANADIAN CITIZENSHIP lives or dies on the interpretation of laws—and not just Canada's. Citizenship and Immigration Canada asserted Charles Bosdet was not Canadian, claiming his father—born to a Canadian engineer working in Mexico—was a Mexican citizen. Yet CIC's claim was impossible under Mexico's Constitution, as Charles, and later the Mexican government, informed CIC. Charles explained:

> Dad was a Mexican national—*not* citizen—at birth, as was everyone born in Mexico. His mother says she registered him at the nearest Canadian outpost four months after he was born—as a Canadian.
>
> My Dad was 6 years old when the family moved to BC—far too young under Mexican law to be anything except a Canadian. Mexico's Constitution of 1917 stated that (1) everyone born in Mexico (foreigners included) was deemed a Mexican *national*, and (2) no one born in Mexico could become a *citizen* until [a] they reached the age of majority and then [b] swore in as a citizen with the local Mexican authorities. The age of majority was 21 for single people and 18 for married folks.
>
> This was a point of contention with CIC. According to [a supervisor in CIC's Sydney, Nova Scotia, citizenship processing centre], her office treated "national" and "citizen" as "the same thing"—but Mexican law didn't and the Mexican Embassy told CIC that during a series of faxes

with CIC Ottawa when it was reviewing my file independently. So CIC was insisting my Dad was Mexican when the Mexican government itself was telling the world—in its Constitution, which CIC refused to acknowledge, and in the faxes to Ottawa—that that was impossible.

Marion Vermeersch on Her Status (post—Bill C-24)

PEOPLE OFTEN fall within several classifications on CIC's long list of rejection categories. Such is the case for Marion Vermeersch, who was born out of wedlock in 1945, in England, to a Canadian-soldier father and British war-bride mother. Brought to Canada before 1947, she lived as a productive citizen, exercising all the rights of being a citizen, up until 2003. That's when her problems began. Her documents, those required for proof of status, birth, and landing in Canada, had been accepted by CIC for decades. In 2007, it changed the rules retroactively and dismissed the old forms as inadequate. Problem is, there are no other forms.

Acceptance, welcoming Marion as a proud Canadian citizen, should be a no-brainer. But when the government isn't compassionate, or knowledgeable of the country's laws, it's the individual who gets destroyed. The bureaucrats and politicians do not feel the consequences. Here's Marion's predicament, all beyond her control.

I do not want to apply for the 5.4 grant but I certainly understand and am supportive of those who feel they would like to submit an application for one. I personally do not believe that it is right for one person to have such powers as to be able to choose to grant or revoke citizenship, outside the court process. I was lectured (putting it very mildly) by CIC staff when I first discovered the loss of my citizenship in 2003, told that I "must have known I was not a citizen all those years and had no right to vote. You could be charged with federal offences for doing so."

I have always believed they were wrong and I am indeed a citizen— have been since 1945 by law.

I did apply for a permanent resident card when this happened and received it in December 2005, but it expired in 2010. When I tried to renew that, I was told my documents from 1946 were no longer honoured as proof of legal entry, and I was unsuccessful.

I am not sure if I will qualify under this legislation, anyway, as they say my father was not a citizen and could not have qualified—he arrived in Canada as a home child in 1926. As I was born in England during World

War II (he enlisted with the Royal Canadian Artillery in 1939), that would make me a "second generation born abroad," would it not?

Wonder what they will do with any of us who don't qualify when this legislation actually comes into practice?

Paul Diekelmann on His Status (post–Bill C-24)

PAUL WAS born in the US in 1932, in wedlock, to an American father and a Canadian mother. The marriage lasted a short time, and Paul and his mother returned to Canada in 1935. In time, she married a Canadian man. For being born in wedlock, Paul's been denied citizenship for eighty-two years. Although Bill C-24 captures him, the government, by delaying its implementation, keeps folks like Paul from being recognized. Age, gender, and family status discrimination continues, despite new legislation. The politicians and bureaucrats just don't seem able to get it right.

I will wait for the bill [C-24] to become law—Britain/Canada owes me that! From 1934 to 1954 in Sydney, NS: At grade school I swore allegiance to the monarch of Canada/Britain every day; was indoctrinated with British/Canada history; member of Canadian/British Boy Scouts for six-plus years; attended the first Canadian Boy Scouts Jamboree July 16 to July 24, 1949, at Connaught Camo, Ottawa; was a member of RCAF cadets in high school; denied enrolment in RCAF and RCMP in 1952 because I was not born in Canada; saluted the Union Jack and sang "God Save the King" at various events and stood up with others at the playing of "God Save the King/Queen" at the start of every movie in theatres. I lived as a Brit/Canadian during my formative years when psychological/sociological foundations were imbedded into my young psyche. I left Canada in December 1954 as a de facto "Canadian." I married a Canadian girl in 1955. My wife and children are Canadian citizens. I am an alien immigrant in my childhood home!!

Archaic British law still prevails. God Save the Queen!!!!

Fred Colbourne on Citizenship:
What Parliamentarians Need to Know

FRED COLBOURNE is probably the world's preeminent expert on Canadian citizenship, despite his never being formally trained in law. Although many Lost Canadians were lawyers, Fred had two traits that clearly set him apart. First, he had a lifetime experience in legislation. Second, like me, he had a burning desire to right an historic wrong.

Fred was born in Toronto in 1931 of a father who was born in Newfoundland. In the 1920s, his father's family relocated to Ontario. Only one of his eight great-grandparents was born outside what is now Canada, and he was born in the UK. In 1945, Fred's father was killed in Germany during active service with the Canadian Army.

In 1963, Fred received a Canada Council scholarship to study at the London School of Economics. In 1974, he registered in the UK and thereby automatically lost his Canadian citizenship. Three years later, the new citizenship act allowed dual citizenship, but the provision was not retroactive until the current act was amended in 2008. In 2009, his Canadian citizenship was restored back to 1974. He was then seventy-three years old and had already spent thirty-five years as a non-Canadian citizen.

In Fred's words: "My situation arose because those who draft legislation continue to apply the injunction against retroactivity to both benefits and penalties. While it is not fair to apply penalties retroactively, denying benefits on the same basis creates unequal treatment of persons in similar situations. Denying benefits in this way has no place in modern Parliamentary practice."

Here are his thoughts on current citizenship legislation:

Canada needs an entirely new nationality act to replace the Citizenship Act.

1. A person acquires Canadian nationality and certain civil duties, rights, and protections at birth and acquires citizenship and further civil duties and rights at the age of majority. Canadian nationality is a fundamental civil status recognized internationally. "Canadian Citizenship" refers to the rights and duties of Canadian nationals within Canada.

2. Canadian nationality and citizenship are inherent in the Constitution Act of 1867. The proclamation for the 1901 census defined the classes of persons who had both Canadian nationality and the rights and duties of citizens. Statutory definitions of "Canadian national" and "Canadian citizen" have not established the existence of these civil states but merely defined who possesses the rights and duties of these civil states. "Canadian citizenship" and "Canadian nationality" have been confounded ever since the 1901 census.

3. The Immigration Act of 1910 defines which classes of persons were not subject to border control by reason of their rights as citizens.

4. The Naturalization Act of 1868 was purely local legislation that conferred Canadian nationality and Canadian citizenship on aliens, defined as persons who were not British subjects.

5. The Canadian Naturalization Act of 1914 was an act respecting British nationality and aliens that empowered the governments of British territories to confer British nationality on aliens that was recognized throughout the Empire.

6. "British subject" status and "Commonwealth citizen" status became synonymous in 1948 with retroactive effect. Canada adopted this part of the British Nationality Act by an amendment to the Citizenship Act.

7. "British subject" was never a status in lieu of "Canadian national" or "Canadian citizen" but a supranational status that included Canadians. In Canada, "British subject" has been replaced by "Commonwealth citizen," not by "Canadian citizen" or "Canadian national," as CIC and its ministers have claimed.

8. The Canadian Nationality Act of 1921 was incorporated into the Citizenship Act of 1947 along with the Naturalization Act. The definition of "Canadian national" was based on the definition of "Canadian citizen" in the Immigration Act. This is exactly the reverse of the same definitions in the British Nationality Act.

9. Until 1921, the only legal basis for defining who were "Canadian nationals" and "Canadian citizens" was the census and its proclamations. The first statute to define who has Canadian nationality and citizenship was the 1921 Canadian Nationals Act. As Minister of Justice Charles Doherty explained in committee, the definition of "Canadian citizen" by reference in the 1921 act has the same legal force as if the words were written right into the 1921 act.

10. Until 1921, the census alone defined the classes of persons who held Canadian nationality and Canadian citizenship. The Federal Court took judicial notice of the existence of Canadian citizen status.

From the coming into force of the Canadian Nationals Act of 1921, a statutory definition of "Canadian citizen" and "Canadian national" replaced both the census definition and the common law definition applied by the Federal Court to resolve cases under the Alien Labour Act of 1906.

11. After 1921, Parliament used the terms "Canadian citizen" and "Citizen of Canada" in the Copyright Act and the 1923 amendment to the Trade Mark and Design Act, and in various wartime orders, such as Order-in-Council 4068.5 (1939) Constituting Special Committee of Cabinet on Demobilization.

12. The claim by Citizenship and Immigration Canada that citizenship was created by the 1947 Citizenship Act is unhistorical, a fiction developed to promote the bill before Parliament.

Esther Harris on Her 5.4 Status

ESTHER HARRIS is a Lost Canadian not covered under C-37. Five years ago she applied for a 5.4 grant. In March 2015 she got this reply from CIC:

1. *We received your application for Canadian citizenship (grant of citizenship) in 2010. We followed that with a letter acknowledging receipt of your application(s), and a study book called Discover Canada. Please consider delays in mail delivery before contacting us. We started processing your application in 2013.*

How ironic that Esther becomes eligible for citizenship as a landed immigrant in just five months. CIC took her money, then left her hanging for half a decade. It proves a genuine lack of sincerity and the inadequacy of the government. Australia processes folks like Esther in weeks. For Canada it takes years, unless, of course, the government wants you. Then it's as simple as the "stroke of a pen."

THE REVISED HISTORY
OF CANADIAN CITIZENSHIP

LET'S DISCOVER WHERE Canada's been...

For the most part, the country's northern European settlers were of British and French descent. As a direct result of the English defeating the French in the pivotal battle on the Plains of Abraham, our country evolved with a distinctly British bent. Embraced was the parliamentary system, which included English law and English customs. Accordingly, the Brits wrote our working model for identity back in the mid-1800s, classifying "married women, minors, lunatics, idiots" under the same disability for their national status.[1] What that meant was that married women were property, or chattel, of their husbands, with children being property of their fathers if born in wedlock, and property of their mothers if born out of wedlock. The stigma of the scarlet *A* was tightly woven into the fabric of the Canadian consciousness, and its victims weren't just women but also very much their children.

That's the crux of the Lost Canadian issue, which when taken down to its basic element, is blatant discrimination aimed at gender. The Lost Canadian story, in many ways, is intertwined with women and equal rights. It could be said that we are the children of the Famous Five.[2]

Who are they?

Five Alberta women challenged the federal government in the 1920s on issues of gender and equality. It began with Emily Murphy, the first woman police magistrate, not only in Canada but throughout the British Empire. On her first day in court, a lawyer demanded her replacement, claiming that, under the British North America Act, Murphy was not really a "person." Although Alberta recognized her status, the rest of Canada did not. Forthcoming were several challenges, and in 1928 the Supreme Court of Canada ruled that women, under the BNA, were not entitled to vote, run for office, or serve as elected officials. They were chattel. By 1929, the case wound up before the British Privy Council, which decided to recognize Canadian women as real "persons." From that moment forward, women in Canada could be judges and senators. What they did not gain—not until 2009 for many women—was the right to pass citizenship to their own children, as a child's "citizenship" was basically derived through the man—unless the child had been born out of wedlock. It's hard to imagine that in 2015 this archaic law remains in force, but it does, and it's mostly aimed at people born before 1947. Further muddying the pre-'47 waters is that women who married non-British-subject men before 1947 lost their Canadian status when they married. Thousands of women were rendered stateless.

It was only through the implementation of Lost Canadian Bill C-37 in 2009 that many Canadian women actually gained equality with men to pass citizenship onto their children—but going forward only.[3] Problems and discrimination, while much less than before C-37, remain in law retroactively.

What a difference a century makes, not just for women but for a country. Canada has indeed climbed a mountain, but is not yet all the way to the summit.

Just some 150 years ago did Canada officially become a country, and what a history it's had. In the late 1850s, hundreds of Chinese miners joined with tens of thousands of gold seekers during the BC and Yukon gold rushes. In just a few years, thousands of Chinese were residing in BC communities such as Barkerville and Likely. In the 1870s, it was agreed that BC would join Canada, but only on condition that a railroad be built to connect our country's two coasts. The Canadian Pacific Railway wanted cheap labour, as did the prime minister of Canada. That fuelled further Chinese migration. During World War I, another wave of Chinese came to Canada, but this time it was for the war effort, and in a sense they were just passing through. Around 140,000 Chinese were recruited for war-related work in Europe; 84,000 arrived from China in Vancouver, where they travelled by rail to Halifax, then boarded ships bound for Europe. Government fear was that some might jump the train while in Canada, so the men were locked in the railcars and put under armed guard until they reached Nova Scotia.

Although they never engaged in actual combat, estimates are that between 10,000 and 20,000 succumbed nonetheless. Canadians didn't know anything about the mission, as it was top secret. Today, it's still not well known. During World War I, approximately 300 Chinese Canadians volunteered for military service, as did many Japanese Canadians. They wanted to fight for *their* country. Today, there's a monument in Vancouver's Stanley Park honouring the Japanese, and the Department of National Defence has published a book, *Fighting for Canada*, about the Asian soldiers of World Wars I and II. All are described as outstanding "Canadian citizens." Around 800 Chinese Canadians served in our military forces during World War II, many directly in harm's way.

Consider this: Could it be that a Chinese-born Canadian is buried in our Tomb of the Unknown Soldier? Well, yes, it's possible. If so, then this same unknown Canadian hero was never really Canadian, at least according to today's government. This reeks.

It also keeps the discriminatory ways of the past ongoing into the present. Ethically, we as a country can do better. We must do better.

Let's look deeper into Canada's racist past, beyond the Chinese.

In 1885, the Chinese head tax was implemented. Back then, Canada considered the Chinese to be "heathens," as most weren't Christians. Same thing with First Nations people. The idea of the head tax was to discourage immigration. Besides, the railroads were mostly complete (built on the backs of the Chinese), and Canada didn't want more Chinese. To be blunt, Canada was a white country and the government wanted to keep it that way. In 1914, the Japanese ship *Komagata Maru* was chartered to take its mostly Sikh passengers from Hong Kong to Vancouver. British subjects were supposed to have free rein moving from one Commonwealth country to another, so Canada, in order to prevent an invasion of "brown people," imposed a condition for entry that has come to be called "continuous journey," meaning for a person to be admitted to Canada, he or she must arrive directly from their country of birth or nationality.[4] That was basically impossible, because a non-stop trip from India to Vancouver didn't exist. Yes, but Hong Kong to Vancouver was feasible—and it also went from one British colony to another non-stop. In May 1914, the boat arrived in Vancouver's Burrard Inlet. Immediately, government officials denied its entry, which forced all 376 passengers to be ship-bound for the next couple of months. Essentials like food and water were denied them. Children were on the boat. In the end, only twenty-four people were admitted into Canada. The boat was forcibly turned around in July and escorted by the

HMCS *Rainbow* into open ocean. On arrival in Calcutta, a British gunboat stopped the ship. A riot ensued on board, the result being that nineteen passengers were killed, some escaped, and most of the remaining passengers were arrested, then sent back to their villages and kept under village arrest for several years. The denial of entry into Canada had everything to do with discrimination based on race *and* religion.

Regarding Japanese Canadians, between 1945 and 1947, Canada stripped many of them of their citizenship, deporting 4,000 to Japan, a war-torn country with little food and shelter for its own people, let alone foreigners from Canada who knew little to nothing of the culture and language.[5] Some 2,000 were Canadian-born, and of those, almost 700 were children under the age of sixteen. By 1949, with a new prime minister (Mackenzie King was out) and Canada's entry into the United Nations, the restrictions were lifted and the people were offered an opportunity to return.

In 1910, Canada passed the Immigration Act, which wasn't so much about immigration as it was about determining who belonged and who didn't. It defined what a Canadian citizen was. There were three distinct levels, as upheld by the Supreme Court in 1946:

"Canadian citizen" in turn is defined by clause (*f*) of the section as "(1) a person born in Canada who has not become an alien," "(2) a British subject who has Canadian domicile," or "(3) a person naturalized under the laws of Canada who has not subsequently become an alien or lost Canadian domicile."[6]

Take note that there is no reference to race. The court did not say that a person was a citizen if born in Canada but only if white, green, or blue, has red hair, or wears tennis shoes. The only condition was that he or she was born in Canada. And the enumerator instructions in the 1921 Canadian census were clear: the words "national," "Canadian," and "citizen" all meant the same thing.[7]

This highlights an interesting dichotomy. Take the situation of Douglas Jung, Canada's first Chinese MP, the first Chinese-Canadian delegate to the UN, and a Canadian soldier in World War II. He was born in Canada in 1924. His registration papers from the Department of Immigration and Colonization, Chinese Immigration Service state: "This certificate does not establish legal status in Canada." In so many words, the Chinese were told by officials that they were nothing more than "registered aliens." By now, many Chinese were second- and third-generation born in Canada who didn't have Chinese citizenship, which meant that if they weren't Canadian, they were stateless.

Was this true, or were government officials simply doling out false information? For sure, the government wasn't their friend. Canada was an incredibly racist country, with many racist politicians. Of the many ethnic groups, the Chinese and First Nations bore the brunt of that.

In 1896, BC passed legislation stripping the Chinese of voting rights in municipal elections. It was a Catch-22. The electors list for federal elections came from the provincial electors list, and the provincial list came from the municipal list. Hence, no voting rights. The Chinese were completely disenfranchised, with no possible way to facilitate change.

Here's the exact wording from BC's 1895 Provincial Elections Act: "No Chinaman, Japanese, or Indian shall have his name placed on the Register of Voters for any Electoral District, or be entitled to vote at any election."[8]

In 1886 and 1907, riots broke out in Vancouver, and it wasn't the Chinese committing the mayhem but members of the white population who felt threatened by the cheaper Chinese labour. The 1907 riot began in Bellingham, Washington, then moved north into Vancouver's Chinatown and Japantown, with white supremacist groups demanding a "white Canada." In 1925, Glen Brae, now known as Canuck Place, became Canada's official headquarters of the Ku Klux Klan. It was a product of the time, which fortunately is now a thing of the past. Not until 1929 could Chinese children like Gim Wong attend public school in Vancouver.[9] In the early 1930s, Frank Wong, born in BC, went swimming in a public pool. Authorities had the pool drained and cleaned when he got out.

The year 1938 was a bit of a milestone for citizenship and the Chinese. In the Supreme Court decision of *Shin Shim v. The King*, a case in which the government attempted to deny a woman born in Canada the right to stay, the court ruling stated: "Notwithstanding the contrary opinion of the Chinese Immigration Controller, the applicant was in fact born in Canada and as a Canadian citizen was entitled to her discharge from that officer's custody."[10] In other words, the Chinese Exclusion Act did not apply to Canadian citizens.

There it was, directly from the Supreme Court: a person born in Canada was a Canadian citizen, regardless of race, with all the rights and responsibilities of Canadian citizenship. Yet, despite the *Shin Shim* decision, the government continued issuing certificates of identity to the Chinese that stated they were nothing more than "registered aliens" and lacking legal status. Hmm, something seems amiss.

It was, and it gets worse.

In the 1930s, Hitler's government contacted the Canadian government, wanting to learn how Canada could get away with being so discriminating based on race. Unbelievable as it sounds, Canada responded, helping the Nazis. And Germany wasn't the only country to take notice; our country—more specifically, Canada's treatment of the First Nations people—became one of South Africa's role models for Apartheid.

By the 1940s, Canada was entrenched in its exclusionary ways. Earlier I mentioned two small BC towns. Barkerville at one point had a population of 11,000, 7,000 of whom were Chinese. The town of Likely was almost all Chinese. The province, knowing the power of the ballot box, knowing that, in a democracy, the majority rules, wanted no part of a community governed by the Chinese. The answer? Keep denying voting rights. And that's voter suppression, an infringement of basic rights.

Mackenzie King was Canada's prime minister from 1935 to 1948. He was undoubtedly one of the most racist leaders Canada has ever seen. His administration's policy regarding anyone who was Jewish and wanting to immigrate to Canada was short and to the point: "None is too many." This policy was reflected in King's actions. During the war, he deliberately denied entry to the Jewish ship MS *St. Louis*, Canada being the last hope for the more than 900 passengers on board.[11] It's estimated that, as a result of Mackenzie King not allowing any of them refugee status, a quarter of them were murdered in concentration camps after their return to Hitler's Third Reich.

Canada indeed has a past, and my discussion completely leaves out other minorities, like the African Canadians. They too have their stories.

In 1945, the United Nations officially got its start, and three years later, on December 10, 1948, it formally adopted the Universal Declaration of Human Rights. Canada as a charter member of the UN had a problem. Enter a man named John Peters Humphrey from New Brunswick, the principal author of the Declaration of Human Rights. Canada was proud of Humphrey's contribution, so much so that it wanted to be known in the future as a human rights country. The problem? With such a high profile regarding human rights, how could Canada go unnoticed in the world theatre as a country that enthusiastically embraced the declaration yet blatantly discriminated against the Chinese and First Nations? It would be discovered as a country of hypocrites. It was indeed a quandary, but there was a way out. Why not use the upcoming citizenship legislation in Parliament as a stepping stone to a new, inclusive Canada? Yes, but how? Easy: make up a story that killed two birds with one stone.

Back to voter suppression. Before 1947, the Supreme Court determined that the Chinese were in fact Canadian citizens, but that wasn't well known, then or now. After a century of drinking our own bathwater, we've accepted a lie as truth. Back then, the Chinese were being told by the government that they had no legal status—and their official documents supported this. The Chinese believed it, and so too did the public. And, as non-citizens, they didn't have the right to vote, and no one questioned it.

It is well known that before 1947, Canadians were British subjects; not so well known is that British subject status existed in Canada until 1977. Before '47, we were British subjects, British nationals, Canadian nationals, *and* Canadian citizens—all four. Canadians have never been well versed in their identity, but as anyone from yesteryear will recall, when asked their nationality, the answer "Canadian" wasn't accepted. It had to be Scottish, Irish, British, French, and so forth. We were hyphenated Canadians.[12] In 1947, the lack of any sort of public understanding of Canadian citizenship was a perfect way to disguise the truth and to win over the Chinese vote.

Politicians, being politicians, care a great deal about votes. Their objective isn't always about the people they represent; rather, they want to keep their jobs, promote their party, and belong to the party in power. At times they actually go against their own constituents. Mackenzie King was a Liberal and his party was in power in 1946. Although they were the main obstacle regarding Chinese voting rights, King knew the laws were about to change and very much wanted the Chinese vote. It was a prime concern. But think about it: Who in their right mind would vote for a party actively discriminating against them, especially when it resulted in a decades-long denial of their benefits and rights? No one. Take for example a non-white person. They'd never want a white supremacist representing them—not even a reformed one. Likewise, if the Chinese had known the truth, they'd never have wanted Mackenzie King or the Liberals acting on their behalf.

King's answer was the 1947 Canadian Citizenship Act, which recognized the term "Canadian citizen." Make up a story implying that British rule allowed the discrimination but that, with a new Canadian citizenship act, this would not be the case. The Chinese would have full citizenship, with all the rights and responsibilities that came with it, including the vote. After great political spin-doctoring, the Chinese were led to believe that the

Liberals were their liberators rather than their suppressors. To be fair, after 100 years, *all* parties in Canada share blame, but back then, the Liberals held the reins. Consequently, that mythical 1947 supernova of Canadian citizenship began with their leadership. Would the Chinese vote en masse for the Liberals, seen now as emancipators? Yes indeed. For decades, the Liberal Party was their top choice at polling stations across Canada.

Our work as Lost Canadians, passionately researching citizenship and Canadian history while striving for truth, is how we uncovered the evidence supporting everything I say above. It's been an incredible journey, with all sorts, from historians and other academics to everyday people, adding their bits of knowledge. Regrettably, most people and politicians in Canada remain blissfully unaware. Hopefully, this will change. Education and enlightenment is always the answer.

Canadian citizenship began with Confederation in 1867, as evidenced by the first governor general's statement in his first Throne Speech.[13] He talks of a new Canadian nationality.

Further evidence came to light in an icing-on-the-cake moment in 2013 when Canada's attorney general argued successfully in the Supreme Court in a case revolving around the question of whether Canadian citizenship existed before 1947. The attorney general said that it did, and the Supreme Court agreed. The Metis in Manitoba were declared as having been "full Canadian citizens" in 1870, thus slamming shut the door on the pre-'47 citizenship discussion.[14]

The idea that citizenship began in 1947 is flat out wrong. This blatant fabrication began because of political grandstanding, plain and simple. We must now set the record straight. Make no mistake, our Chinese and Japanese, or anyone "born in Canada," *were Canadian citizens*. That includes Douglas Jung. It also includes Fred Ho and Quan Louie, two Canadian-born men from Vancouver who fought and died in Canadian uniforms during World War II. It's not fair nor justified that they be remembered as nothing more than "stateless registered aliens." They were ours, rightful and proud Canadian citizens, just like everyone else. They earned and certainly deserve their place in Canadian history.

Finally, if citizenship didn't exist before 1947, then none of Canada's war dead—all 111,000 of them—were ever citizens. Thus, the fate of the Chinese affects our war dead. Their collective identity now lies in the hands of our citizenship minister and prime minister and, of course, of the people of Canada. Acceptance, not exclusion, is the answer.

ACKNOWLEDGEMENTS

AS IT SHOULD, thanks first and foremost goes to my family—my wife, daughters, and parents. Next, thanks goes to all my friends, many of whom I met on this long crusade. Thanks too to the old-time journalists, who work tirelessly for our independence and civil liberties. Life would not be the same without their investigative expertise. And to our veterans, many who have fallen while guarding our freedoms. I wish to acknowledge also the courage and dedication of some really unlikely heroes—the pilots and flight attendants post-9/11. Everyone thinks about the New York firemen when they think about 9/11. No question, they deserve great accolades. But in the days following the attacks, although many would be faced with health issues, their job was over. Not so for the flight crews manning our skies. It's easy to forget that they were the first to die on that horrific day. Even now they remain a first line of defence. They're professional, extremely well trained, with their priority number one being the safety of their passengers, and not leaving anyone behind. If only governments were as dedicated to the people they serve.

In the book of heroes, there's always room for another name. Dr. Vernon Johns, Howard Zinn, Nicolas Winton, Viola Desmond, and Frederick Bissett are rather unknown. But through their actions and deeds—and because of others like them—the world changes for the better, one life at a time.

The list of people needing to be thanked would more than double the size of this book. There are folks I know and don't know who got involved. They, and everyone who ever advocated, spoke out, or maybe just listened with a sympathetic ear, did make a difference. I'd like to, in time, thank each of you personally. For now, please accept my gratitude here.

NOTES

Introduction: Raining Ashes

1   The figures are from Veterans Affairs Canada, "Second World War (1939–1945)," http://www.veterans.gc.ca/eng/remembrance/history/second-world-war (45,000 war dead) and Veterans Affairs Canada, "First World War (1914–1918)," http://www.veterans.gc.ca/eng/remembrance/history/first-world-war (66,000 war dead) and include figures for Newfoundland.

Prologue: Against All Odds: The Story of Flight 811

1   Byron Acohido, "Terror in the Sky—Flight 811 Lost a Cargo Door and Nine Lives—Boeing Is Still Wrestling with Solutions and Settlements," *Seattle Times*, January 4, 1992, http://community.seattletimes.nwsource.com/archive/?date=19920105&slug=1468634.

2   Ibid.

3   Judith Valente, "Roots of Tragedy—Parents Seek Reasons for Death of Son," *Wall Street Journal*, February 26, 1990, retrieved from http://community.seattletimes.nwsource.com/archive/?date=19900227&slug=1058277.

4   National Transportation Safety Board, Aircraft Accident Report PB90-910401, NTSB/AAR-90/01, United Airlines Flight 811, Boeing 747-122, N47 13U, Honolulu, Hawaii, February 24, 1989, http://www.airdisaster.com/reports/ntsb/AAR90-01.pdf.

Chapter 1: The Long and Winding Road

1   Chapman Learning Commons, UBC, "Benefactors: The Chapmans," http://learningcommons.ubc.ca/about-us/.

2   Dominion of Canada, Citizenship Act, 1947, 20th Parl., 2nd Sess., c. 15, part 3, ss. 18(2). (Subsection 1 included minor-aged children who lost their citizenship when their "responsible" parent took out citizenship in another country.)

3   I also have a deep loyalty to the US, which accepted me as one of its own, treating me far better than Canada ever has. An analogy, for me, is marriage: you have your parents and your in-laws. Ideally, you love and embrace both. That's how I feel about the two countries. Canada is my natural parents, the US, my in-laws.

4   While I'm not keen on former US president Woodrow Wilson, particularly because of his disgraceful actions against Alice Paul, an early women's rights suffragist, he did say something quite apropos to my battling the Canadian government. From his 1916 address to the World's Salesmanship Congress in Detroit: "If you want to make enemies, try to change something."

Chapter 2: I'm Not Alone in This Universe

1   As stated in the advertisement "Pathfinders International, Canadian Immigration attend free seminars by Maj. Gen. Atma Singh AVSM, VrC & Brig. K.S. Sodhi," *The Hindu,* April 21, 2001, 1.

2   Mata Press Service, *Asian Pacific Post,* January 19–February 8, 2006, 24.

Chapter 3: Is There Political or Bureaucratic Intelligence in the Universe?

1   House of Commons, *Debates,* vol. 137 (138), 37th Parl., 1st Sess., February 4, 2002, http://www.parl.gc.ca/HousePublications/Publication. aspx?Language=E&Mode=1&Parl=37&Ses=1&DocId=1384905#SOB-118932.

2   This is my recollection of his words. It was an incredible moment, one that has stuck in my memory.

3   Again, this is my recollection of what was said.

4   This and the preceding quotation cited in Michael Den Tandt, "Relatives Visited Montreal So Hardliner's Grandchild Would Be Born Canadian Citizen," *Globe and Mail,* June 24, 2005.

5   Bill C-18: An Act Respecting Canadian Citizenship, 37th Parl., 2nd Sess. (second reading and committee referral version, November 8, 2002), http://www.parl.gc.ca/LegisInfo/BillDetails. aspx?Language=E&Mode=1&billId=534202.

6   This bizarre oversight almost certainly happened because just a handful of MPs in the House were aware of the Lost Canadian issue. Amazing that the very gatekeepers of Canadian identity and citizenship had no clue. Hence, there was virtually no bureaucratic oversight.

Chapter 4: The Politics of Politics

1   House of Commons, Standing Committee on Citizenship and Immigration, *Evidence,* no. 014, 37th Parl., 2nd Sess., January 28, 2003, http://www.parl.gc.ca/HousePublications/Publication. aspx?DocId=659537&Language=E&Mode=1&Parl=37&Ses=2#Int-389179.

2   Ibid.

3   House of Commons, Standing Committee on Citizenship and Immigration, *Evidence,* no. 019, 37th Parl., 2nd Sess., February 10, 2003, http://www.parl.gc.ca/HousePublications/ Publication.aspx?Language=E&Mode=1&Parl=37&Ses=2&DocId=688319&File=0.

4   Ibid.

5   Ibid.

6   Dominion of Canada, Citizenship Act, 1947, 20th Parl., 2nd Sess., c. 15, part 3, ss. 18(2). Subsection 1 included minor-aged children who lost their citizenship when their "responsible parent" took out citizenship in another country.

7   *Sieradzki v. Canada (The Minister of Citizenship and Immigration),* 2003 FCT 225, http:// decisions.fct-cf.gc.ca/en/2003/2003fct225/2003fct225.html.

8   House of Commons, Standing Committee on Citizenship and Immigration, *Evidence,* no. 043, 37th Parl., 2nd Sess., February 18, 2003, http://www.parl.gc.ca/HousePublications/ Publication.aspx?DocId=723265&Language=E&Mode=1&Parl=37&Ses=2#Int-435677.

9   Ibid.

10 Ibid.

11 House of Commons, *Debates,* vol. 138 (085), 37th Parl., 2nd Sess., April 7, 2003, http://www. parl.gc.ca/HousePublications/Publication.aspx?Pub=Hansard&Doc=85&Parl=37&Ses= 2&Language=E&Mode=1#Int-495838.

12 This and the following quotation are from the *Canadian Museum for Human Rights* video, produced by Paperny Films.

13 As told to me by Magali.

14 House of Commons, *Debates,* vol. 138 (116), 37th Parl., 2nd Sess., June 11, 2003, http://www. parl.gc.ca/HousePublications/Publication.aspx?Pub=Hansard&Doc=116&Parl=37&Ses= 2&Language=E&Mode=1#Int-605174.

15 Many Canadians today believe their government imposes long delays on old people who need medical treatment, something all Canadians are legally entitled to. Could this be a pattern, the government simply waiting for them to die, thereby saving valuable dollars?

Chapter 5: In This Corner, the Prime Minister; in That Corner, the Lost Canadians

1 Bill C-503, *An Act to Amend the Citizenship Act* (John Reynolds), 37th Parl., 3rd Sess. (introduction and first reading version, March 25, 2004), http://www.parl.gc.ca/LegisInfo/BillDetails.aspx?Language=E&Mode=1&Bill=C503&Parl=37&Ses=3.

2 Senate, Bill S-17, *An Act to Amend the Citizenship Act* (Sen. Kinsella), 37th Parl., 3rd Sess. (first reading version, March 25, 2004), http://www.parl.gc.ca/LegisInfo/BillDetails. aspx?Language=E&Mode=1&billId=1359028.

3 House of Commons, Standing Senate Committee on Social Affairs, Science, and Technology, *Minutes of Proceedings, Evidence,* Issue 6, April 22, 2004, http://parl.gc.ca/Content/SEN/Committee/373/soci/06evc-e.htm?Language=E&Parl=37&Ses=3&comm_id=47.

4 This and the following quotation are from ibid.

5 Charles's and my quotations in this passage are from House of Commons, Proceedings of the Standing Senate Committee on Social Affairs, Science, and Technology, *Evidence,* Issue 7, April 29, 2004, http://parl.gc.ca/Content/SEN/Committee/373/soci/07evb-e. htm?Language=E&Parl=37&Ses=3&comm_id=47.

6 Citizenship and Immigration Canada, *Submission in Response to Testimony before Senate Standing Committee on Social Affairs, Science and Technology on Bill S-17, Thursday, April 29, 2004,* April 30, 2004, 2. A copy is in the author's possession.

7 House of Commons, *Debates,* vol. 139 (050), 37th Parl., 3rd Sess., May 7, 2004, http://www. parl.gc.ca/HousePublications/Publication. aspx?Pub=Hansard&Doc=50&Parl=37&Ses=3&Language=E&Mode=1#SOB-929566.

8 C-503 was the House Lost Canadian bill, where S-17 was the same bill in the Senate. C-18 was the government-sponsored bill for a new citizenship act. There was unanimous party support for a new act: Bill C-18—The Citizenship Act of Canada—November 1, 2002, http://www.parl. gc.ca/About/Parliament/LegislativeSummaries/bills_ls.asp?ls=c18&Parl=37&Ses=2.

9 *Augier v. Canada (Minister of Citizenship and Immigration)* (F.C.), 2004 FC 613, [2004] 4 F.C.R. 150, May 17, 2004, http://reports.fja.gc.ca/eng/2004/2004fc613.html.

10 "5. (2) The Minister shall grant citizenship to any person who (b) was born outside Canada, before February 15, 1977, of a mother or a father who was a citizen at the time of his birth, and was not entitled, immediately before February 15, 1977, to become a citizen under subparagraph 5(1)(b)(i) of the former Act, if, before February 15, 1979, or within such extended period as the Minister may authorize, an application for citizenship is made to the Minister by a person authorized by regulation to make the application."

11 Such is the case when the MPs are completely ignorant of the very laws they are supposed to know.

12 In the 100-plus days since Birkett's announcement to the Senate admitting that CIC would ignore a Supreme Court decision, not one Canadian broadcaster deemed the story newsworthy—at least not until just hours before the drop-dead date, when only CBC reported it. The Canadian Bar Association continued to keep its silence as well.

13 Federal Court Index and Docket, *Wayne Karl Babcock v. The Minister of Citizenship and Immigration,* Court #T-1170-06, http://cas-ncr-nter03.cas-satj.gc.ca/IndexingQueries/infp_RE_info_e.php?court_no=T-1170-06.

14 Senate, *Debates,* vol. 142 (3), 38th Parl., 1st Sess., October 6, 2004, http://www.parl.gc.ca/Content/Sen/Chamber/381/Debates/003db_2004-10-06-e.htm#24.

15 Senate, Bill S-2: *An Act to Amend the Citizenship Act* (Sen. Kinsella), 38th Parl., 1st Sess. (third reading version, May 5, 2005), http://www.parl.gc.ca/LegisInfo/BillDetails.aspx?Language=E&Mode=1&billId=1447503.

16 This and the following quotation are from Senate, *Debates*, vol. 142 (6), 38th Parl., 1st Sess., October 20, 2004, http://www.parl.gc.ca/Content/Sen/Chamber/381/Debates/006db_2004-10-20-e.htm.

17 Senate, *Debates*, vol. 140 (024), 38th Parl., 1st Sess., November 15, 2004, http://www.parl.gc.ca/HousePublications/Publication.aspx?Pub=Hansard&Doc=24&Parl=38&Ses=1&Language=E&Mode=1#SOB-1006768.

18 "A military brat is someone, who, as a child, grows up in a family where one or more parents are 'career' military, and where the child moves from base to base, experiencing life in several different places." *Military Brat Life,* http://www.militarybratlife.com/articles/what-is-a-military-brat.html. That's the technical definition. For the purposes of this book, I define it as a person born outside Canada to a Canadian parent who is employed by the Canadian military.

19 Citizenship and Immigration Canada, "Celebrating Freedom, Respect, and Belonging," CIC *News,* October 18, 2004, http://www.cicnews.com/2004/10/citizenship-week-celebrating-freedom-respect-belonging-10205.html.

20 CBC News, *World Report* with Judy Maddren, November 16, 2004, aired at 8:09 a.m.

21 "Canadian Protest against Bush Visit," *Scotsman,* December 1, 2004, http://www.scotsman.com/news/international/canadians_protest_against_bush_visit_1_1049331.

22 "PM Refuses to Accept Resignation over 'Moron' Remark," CBC News, November 26, 2002, http://www.cbc.ca/news/world/story/2002/11/22/bush_ducros021122.html.

23 House of Commons, *Debates,* vol. 140 (035), 38th Parl., 1st Sess., November 30, 2004, http://www.parl.gc.ca/HousePublications/Publication.aspx?Pub=Hansard&Mee=35&Language=E&Parl=38&Ses=1#Int-1042658.

24 Terry Pedwell, "Minister Threatened over 'Stripper Law,'" Canadian Press, April 23, 2008, http://www.thestar.com/news/canada/2008/04/23/minister_threatened_over_stripper_law.html.

25 Office of the Ethics Commissioner, *The Sgro Inquiry: Many Shades of Grey,* June 2005, p. 14, http://ciec-ccie.parl.gc.ca/Documents/English/Previous%20offices/Archives%20from%20the%20former%20Ethics%20commissioner/Inquiry%20Reports/Public%20office%20Holders/The%20Sgro%20Inquiry.pdf.

26 House of Commons, *Debates,* vol. 140 (035), 38th Parl., 1st Sess., November 30, 2004, http://www.parl.gc.ca/HousePublications/Publication.aspx?Pub=Hansard&Mee=35&Language=E&Parl=38&Ses=1#Int-1042678.

27 Republic of Trinidad and Tobago, *Act No. 63 of 2000,* 5th Parl., 5th Sess., October 13, 2000, http://www.ttparliament.org/legislations/a2000-63.pdf.

28 House of Commons, *Debates,* vol. 140 (058), 38th Parl., 1st Sess., February 16, 2005, http://parl.gc.ca/HousePublications/Publication.aspx?Pub=Hansard&Doc=58&Parl=38&Ses=1&Language=E&Mode=1#Int-1132343.

Chapter 6: Ottawa's Nitty-Gritty, Down-and-Dirty Shenanigans

1 As told to me by Volpe's chief of staff, Stephen Heckbert.

2 House of Commons, *Debates,* vol. 140 (054), 38th Parl., 3rd Sess., February 10, 2005, http://parl.gc.ca/HousePublications/Publication.aspx?Pub=Hansard&Doc=54&Parl=38&Ses=1&Language=E&Mode=1#Int-1122945.

3 Bill C-302: *Italian-Canadian Recognition and Restitution Act* (MP Pacetti), 40th Parl., 3rd Sess., http://parl.gc.ca/LegisInfo/BillDetails.aspx?Language=E&Mode=1&billId=4327874.

4 This and the following quotation are from House of Commons, *Debates,* vol. 140 (058), 38th Parl., 1st Sess., February 16, 2005, http://parl.gc.ca/HousePublications/Publication.aspx?Pub=Hansard&Doc=58&Parl=38&Ses=1&Language=E&Mode=1#SOB-1131947.

5 *Manitoba Metis Federation Inc. et al. v. Attorney General of Canada et al.,* 2007 MBQB 293 (CanLII), December 7, 2007, http://www.canlii.org/en/mb/mbqb/doc/2007/2007mbqb293/2007mbqb293.html.

6 Canada Immigration Act, 1910: "Canadian citizen means: 1) a person born in Canada who

has not become an alien; 2) a British subject who has a Canadian domicile; or 3) a person naturalized under the laws of Canada who has not been subsequently become an alien or lost Canadian domicile."

7 Department of National Defence, *Dock to Destination*, "Interviews" (no page), http://www.canadianwarbrides.com/joetaylor/dock-to-destination-back.jpg (back); http://www.canadianwarbrides.com/joetaylor/dock-to-destination-front.jpg (front). The MacKenzie King quotation is from http://canadianwarbrides.com/cwb-national-archives.asp. August 31, 1946 press release from the Queen Mary. The morning of August 30, 1946, Prime Minister William Lyon Mackenzie King gave a welcoming speech to the war brides on board the ship. He congratulated the brides as well as congratulating Canada for "the splendid addition being made to its citizenship." http://www.pier21.ca/stories/dutch-war-bride-annette-archer

8 This and the following quote are from House of Commons, Standing Committee on Citizenship and Immigration, *Evidence*, no. 023, 38th Parl., 1st Sess., February 24, 2005, http://www.parl.gc.ca/HousePublications/Publication.aspx?Language=E&Mode=1&Parl=38&Ses=1&DocId=1662430&File=0. Ablonczy's footnoted comment regarding capital punishment is from House of Commons, Standing Committee on Citizenship and Immigration, *Evidence*, no. 018, 38th Parl., 1st Sess., February 8, 2005, http://www.parl.gc.ca/HousePublications/Publication.aspx?DocId=1611459&Language=E&Mode=1#Int-1111559.

9 House of Commons, Standing Committee on Citizenship and Immigration, *Fifth Report*, 38th Parl., 1st Sess., February 24, 2005, http://www.parl.gc.ca/HousePublications/Publication.aspx?DocId=1656492&Language=E&Mode=1&Parl=38&Ses=1.

10 House of Commons, *Debates*, vol. 140 (091), 38th Parl., 1st Sess., May 4, 2005, http://parl.gc.ca/HousePublications/Publication.aspx?Pub=Hansard&Doc=91&Parl=38&Ses=1&Language=E&Mode=1#Int-1260101.

11 John Ibbitson, "Caught Between a Blink and an Election," *Globe and Mail*, March 29, 2005.

12 I called Mr. Ibbitson, requesting he inform his readers about the shenanigans the Liberals were doing with Bill s-2, exactly as he had done regarding the budget bill. He ignored my request.

13 House of Commons, *Debates*, vol. 140 (091), 38th Parl., 1st Sess., May 4, 2005, http://parl.gc.ca/HousePublications/Publication.aspx?Pub=Hansard&Doc=91&Parl=38&Ses=1&Language=E&Mode=1#Int-1260101.

14 This and the following quotation are from House of Commons, *Debates*, vol. 140 (092), 38th Parl., 1st Sess., May 5, 2005, http://parl.gc.ca/HousePublications/Publication.aspx?Language=E&Mode=1&Parl=38&Ses=1&DocId=1823086#SOBQ-.

15 Irwin Cotler, "An Act of Remembrance, a Remembrance to Act," *Jerusalem Post*, February 1, 2011, http://www.jpost.com/Opinion/Op-Ed-Contributors/An-act-of-remembrance-a-remembrance-to-act.

16 This is my recollection of her words.

17 "B.C. Man Wins Citizenship Crusade," CBC News BC, February 6, 2005, http://www.cbc.ca/news/canada/british-columbia/story/2005/05/06/bc_lost-canadians20050506.html.

18 Jim Bronskill, "Parliament's Move to Assist 'Lost Canadians' Out of Step with Opinion: Poll," Canadian Press, June 5, 2005.

19 Geoff Nixon and Maria Babbage, "Canadian Boy, Iranian Parents Back in Toronto," Canadian Press, March 21, 2007, http://www.thestar.com/article/194533.

20 United Nations Human Rights Commission, Convention on the Rights of the Child, September 2, 1990, http://www.ohchr.org/en/professionalinterest/pages/crc.aspx.

21 Jim Green was born in the US. He moved to Canada as a Vietnam draft dodger. He's been a professor at UBC and was a leading advocate of the Downtown Vancouver Eastside. He also never offered to help me with the Lost Canadians, despite my repeated requests.

22 Only one council member agreed to meet with me: Tim Louis.

23 Senator Donald Oliver frequently makes wonderful statements on December 10, Human Rights Day. For Lost Canadians, his words were much more powerful than his actions.

24   Citizenship and Immigration Canada, "Canada, We All Belong!" news release, October 14, 2005, retrieved from http://www.how2immigrate.net/canadanews/canada-citizenship2005. html.

25   Citizenship and Immigration Canada, "Successful Citizenship Week Concludes," news release, October 24, 2005, retrieved from http://www.redshiftmedia.ca/wds/Upload/dir/jv/2005%20 CIC/Successful%20Citizenship%20week%20concludes.pdf.

26   Janice Harris, "Proclamation, Canada's Citizenship Week (October 17 to 23, 2005)," October 17, 2005, http://www.dnv.org/upload/documents/Council_Proclamations/ 051017canadascitizenshipweek.pdf.

27   Winston Churchill, *The End of the Beginning* (London: Cassell, 1943), 264, retrieved from http://www.winstonchurchill.org/learn/speeches/speeches-of-winston-churchill/ 1941-1945-war-leader/987-the-end-of-the-beginning.

Chapter 7: "Thee" Is You and Me

1   The French, both in France and Quebec, have what is termed the *Livret de famille*, or Book of the Family. At birth, one's name is recorded in this civil registry as being a part of the *famille*, and how dare any government employee or politician remove anyone's name from it. Not all Canadians know this, but Quebec—not Ottawa—was at one time in charge of its own immigration. Also, identity was at the heart of the separatist issue. For all of Canada—not just one group of us—a fundamental question remains: our identity, our uniqueness of being Canadian, who are we?

2   The morning of the second, my wife called, telling me that on New Year's Day I'd been quoted on CBC radio, along with Joe Volpe. Rob Miller, a Lost Canadian friend living up in Yukon, heard the story on the news. Volpe had said that the Lost Canadians wanted to unfairly jump Canada's immigration queue. I countered, saying no, our desire wasn't to jump the *immigration* queue because we should be in the *citizenship* queue. We were citizens, *not* immigrants. Bill S-2's intent was to restore our rights as Canadian citizens, not to make us immigrants.

3   Debra Black, "Immigration Experts Say Bill C-24 Discriminatory and Weakens Citizenship," *Toronto Star*, June 27, 2014, http://www.thestar.com/news/immigration/2014/06/27/ immigration_experts_say_bill_c24_discriminatory_and_weakens_citizenship.html.

4   Leonard Cohen sings "Un Canadien errant" ("A Wandering Canadian"), written by Antoine Gérin-Lajoie in 1842, following the Lower Canada Rebellion (1837–38). The song was adopted by the Acadians to symbolize the expulsion, exile, and suffering of their people between 1755 and 1763.

5   Canadian Civil Liberties Association, "About CCLA," http://ccla.org/about-us/.

6   Rudolf L. Tökés, *Hungary's Negotiated Revolution: Economic Reform, Social Change and Political Succession* (Cambridge: Cambridge University Press, 1996).

7   Lewis Siegelbaum, "1929: Collectivization: Liquidation of the Kulaks as a Class," *Seventeen Moments in Soviet History*, http://www.soviethistory.org/index.php?page=subject&SubjectID= 1929collectivization&Year=1929&Theme=436f756e74727973696465&navi=byTheme.

8   "None is too many" was a high-ranking government official's answer when asked how many Jewish refugees should be allowed into Canada during the Holocaust. In shutting most Jews out of the country, this in effect became Mackenzie King's policy. Manitoba Education, "None Is Too Many," Grade 6 Social Studies, *Canada: A Country of Change (1867 to Present): A Foundation for Implementation*, 2006, 6.2.4 (f) BLM, http://www.edu.gov.mb.ca/k12/cur/ socstud/foundation_gr6/blms/6-2-4f.pdf.

9   László Borhi, "Containment, Rollback, Liberation or Inaction? The United States and Hungary in the 1950s," *Journal of Cold War Studies* 1 (3) (1999): 67–108, doi: 10.1162/ 152039799316976814. Retrieved from http://www.coldwar.hu/html/en/publications/ rollback.html.

10   Jennifer Rosenberg, "U.S. Policy during the Holocaust: The Tragedy of *S.S. St. Louis* (May 13– June 20, 1939)," Mining Company Guide, 1998, retrieved from Jewish Virtual Library, http:// www.jewishvirtuallibrary.org/jsource/Holocaust/stlouis.html.

11 Alexandra Zabjek, "How 'the 56ers' Changed Canada," *Ottawa Citizen*, October 15, 2006, Citizen's Weekly, B4, retrieved from Hungarian Presence in Canada, http://www. hungarianpresence.ca/history/56ers-citizen-article.cfm.

Chapter 8: Lest We Forget ... Lest We Ignore

1 *Voices of the Left Behind* chronicles the experience of almost fifty children of Canadian soldiers who, after World War II, did not follow their dads to Canada but, rather, stayed behind in Europe. http://www.voicesoftheleftbehind.com. Website based on Olga Rains, Lloyd Rains, and Melynda Jarratt, *Voices of the Left Behind: Project Roots and the Canadian War Children of World War II* (Toronto: Dundurn Press, 2006). Paul Cornes's *No More Damned Secrets: An Anglo-Canadian War Child's Quest for Roots and Identity* (Hove, UK: Book Guild Publishing, 2013), is the story about the author, who was born out of wedlock to a British woman and Canadian-soldier father during World War II. Paul grew up in England not knowing his father. He discovered his "Canadian family" in his sixties. Clearly, the Canadian government had erected major roadblocks to keep out our own war children.

2 Today, some women are coming forward saying that between 1945 and 1985 they were coerced or forced into putting their babies up for adoption—the women use the term "abducted." The "baby for adoption" program was allowed by the government of Canada. The numbers are staggering: 350,000 babies were reportedly adopted under these circumstances. See the Justice for Mother and Child website at www.justiceformotherandchild.com for more details. See also Kathryn Blaze Carlson, "Curtain Lifts on Decades of Forced Adoptions for Unwed Mothers in Canada," *National Post*, March 9, 2012, http://news.nationalpost.com/2012/03/09/curtain-lifts-on-decades-of-forced-adoptions-for-unwed-mothers-in-canada/.

3 Barbara Ann Roberts, *Whence They Came: Deportation from Canada, 1900–1935* (Ottawa: University of Ottawa Press, 1988).

4 Eric Clapton was born to a Canadian-soldier father and a British mother. Because of the stigma at the time of being born out of wedlock, he grew up thinking that his mother was his sister. For his biography, see www.ericclapton.com/eric-clapton-biography.

5 While it wasn't the biggest migration to Canada—there were more Empire loyalists—it still represented huge numbers of people. In 1945 and 1946, the war brides and their kids made up 71 percent of Canada's entire immigration numbers.

6 Gwen LeFort, "War Bride in WWI," *Cape Breton's Magazine*, December 1, 1983, 47–48, retrieved from http://capebretonsmagazine.com/modules/publisher/item.php?itemid=1625.

7 Brian Lee Massey, "World War I Statistics," Canadian Great War Homepage, 2007, http://www.rootsweb.ancestry.com/~ww1can/stat.htm; Veterans Affairs Canada, General Statistics, http://www.veterans.gc.ca/eng/news/general-statistics.

8 Annette Fulford, "Canadian War Brides of the First World War," 2011, http://ww1warbrides.blogspot.com/.

9 Melynda Jarratt (master's thesis, University of New Brunswick, 1995), *The War Brides of New Brunswick*, chap. 2, 14.

10 Order-in-council re-entry into Canada of dependents of members of the Canadian Armed Forces, P.C. 1945-858 (February 9, 1945), which was passed in 1945 and remained in force until May 15, 1947. Under that order-in-council, where a former member of the Canadian Armed Forces who served during World War II was a "Canadian citizen" or had "Canadian domicile" within the meaning of the 1910 Immigration Act, his dependents were automatically granted the same status upon landing in Canada.

11 "'A New Way of Life' for War Brides," CBC Digital Archives, http://www.cbc.ca/archives/categories/war-conflict/second-world-war/love-and-war-canadian-war-brides/a-way-to-a-new-life.html.

12 After World War II, the Canadian government made monthly payments of between $5 and $8 to parents with children under age sixteen to assist in the costs of childrearing. "1945: 'Baby Bonus' Unveiled," CBC Digital Archives, http://www.cbc.ca/archives/categories/politics/federal-politics/federal-politics-general/baby-bonus-unveiled.html.

13   Hong Kong surrendered on Christmas Day 1941. Of the 1,975 Canadian soldiers there, 290
      were killed and 493 wounded. Another 260 died from the awful conditions of prison camps
      in Hong Kong and Japan. Canadian War Museum, "Operations: Hong Kong, December
      1941," Democracy at War: Canadian Newspapers and the Second World War, http://www.
      warmuseum.ca/cwm/exhibitions/newspapers/operations/hongkong_e.shtml.
14   The following quotations are from William Allister, *Where Life and Death Hold Hands* (Toronto:
      Stoddart, 1989), 234, 235, 235-36, and 238-40 respectively.
15   Mackenzie King favoured renewed immigration but did not wish to see a "fundamental
      alteration in the character of our population," which basically meant only white Brits and
      Americans would be accepted. He was also known for his "none is too many" policy on Jewish
      immigration to Canada. Personally scrutinizing all Jewish immigration applicants to the
      country in 1938, he kept a diary in which he recorded any action permitting an appreciable
      number of Jews to settle in Canada, saying it would "undermine the unity of the nation."
      In 1938, he stated, "This is no time for Canada to act on humanitarian grounds." Under
      Mackenzie King, during the twelve years that coincided with Hitler's Nazi regime, Canada
      accepted just 5,000 Eastern European Jews. The next lowest countries were Bolivia and Chile,
      welcoming 14,000. http://www.jewishvirtuallibrary.org/jsource/vjw/canada.html#5.

Chapter 9: Changing of the Guard

1   John Reynolds, when he was the interim leader of the Conservatives, did invite me to spend an
     evening at Stornoway, the residence of the leader of the official opposition.
2   Being a "former Canadian citizen" meant very little. I was forced to substantiate my value to
     Canada with regard to my character, validate my monetary net worth, submit to background
     checks and medical examinations, pay huge fees, wait in the immigrant queue for years on end,
     and then, only after being accepted, endure years of residency requirements and knowledge
     tests. Many of the people we were forced to deal with were citizenship ministers, bureaucrats,
     and citizenship judges who had also been immigrant Canadians. The difference: they were
     born in other countries to foreign parents and hence had never before been Canadian citizens.
3   After Paul Martin took Canada Steamship Lines international in the 1980s, the Canadian
     flags came down from three of its ships, replaced by the flag of the Bahamas—known as
     a "flag of convenience" country. CSL International (a division of the CSL Group) now owns
     eighteen ships that fly foreign flags. CSL ships have, over the years, flown the flags of Liberia,
     Cyprus, the Bahamas, and the tiny South Pacific nation of Vanuatu. CSL Group also owns
     eighteen ships that fly the Canadian flag, pay Canadian taxes, and employ Canadians. Martin
     handed the company over to his sons while he was prime minister, after years of holding it
     in a controversial blind management trust. But the practice of flying "flags of convenience"
     continued to attract attention. It was mentioned repeatedly in the campaign leading up to the
     January 23, 2006, election. "Paul Martin, Flags of Convenience," CBC News *In Depth*, March
     17, 2006, http://www.cbc.ca/news2/background/martin_paul/flagsofconvenience.html.
4   House of Commons, *Debates*, vol. 138 (115), 37th Parl., 2nd Sess., June 10, 2003, http://
     www.parl.gc.ca/HousePublications/Publication.aspx?Language=E&Mode=1&Parl=
     37&Ses=2&DocId=983252#Int-602218.
5   Prime Minister of Canada, Speech from the Throne, April 4, 2006, http://pm.gc.ca/eng/
     news/2006/04/04/speech-throne.
6   Imposing strict time limits on how long a person could be out of the country and changing
     the head-tax requirements, meaning a person might be forced to pay the tax twice or be
     denied entry, are two such examples. In *Shin Shim v. The Queen* (1938), the Supreme Court
     of Canada found the government wrong for not allowing a woman of Chinese descent into
     Canada. The court determined that since she'd been born in Canada, she was a legitimate
     Canadian citizen and hence was entitled to all rights and privileges of Canadian citizenship.
     Shin Shim v. The King, [1938] SCR 378, 1938 CanLII 20 (SCC), http://www.canlii.org/eliisa/

highlight.do?text=Canadian+citizen&language=en&searchTitle=Canada+%28Federal%29+-+Supreme+Court+of+Canada&path=/en/ca/scc/doc/1938/1938canlii20/1938canlii20.html.

7   It was similar to Mackenzie King's "none is too many" stance against immigrants who were Jewish.

8   *Augier v. Canada (Minister of Citizenship and Immigration)* (F.C.), 2004 FC 613, [2004] 4 F.C.R. 150, http://reports.fja.gc.ca/eng/2004/2004fc613.html; *Benner v. Canada (Secretary of State)*, [1997] 1 S.C.R. 358, http://scc.lexum.org/en/1997/1997scr1-358/1997scr1-358.html; House of Commons, Proceedings of the Standing Senate Committee on Social Affairs, Science and Technology, *Evidence*, Issue 6, April 22, 2004, http://www.parl.gc.ca/Content/SEN/Committee/373/soci/06evc-e.htm?Language=E&Parl=3&Ses=3&comm_id=47. From Patricia Birkett's testimony in the Senate, April 2004: "Witnesses mentioned a special provision of the current Act which gives access to citizenship to children born in wedlock outside Canada to Canadian mothers under the former Act (under the former Act, children born in wedlock could only derive citizenship through their father). This provision has been subject to Supreme Court rulings as it affects a provision that was seen to be discriminatory by virtue of the situation of a person's birth. This provision was included in the Act as a transitional clause and will expire on August 14, 2004." http://www.parl.gc.ca/Content/SEN/Committee/373/soci/06evc-e.htm?comm_id=47&Language=E&Parl=37&Ses=3?

9   The Citizenship Act of 1977 came into effect on February 15, 1977, doing away with the born-out-of-wedlock provisions, but only for those born after the act took force.

10   While this is only conjecture, I do believe the following was a huge factor in CIC's wanting to ignore the court decisions allowing in- or out-of-wedlock children their citizenship. It's the children born to Canadian soldiers and left behind in World War I, World War II, and the Korean War. Canada clearly didn't want them, erecting roadblock after roadblock over the ensuing years. Ignoring the *Benner* and *Augier* decisions was, I believe, CIC's way of slamming the door of acceptance shut, then bolting it tight, forever keeping the war babies out of Canada.

11   Magically, CIC produced all the needed forms almost overnight. Remember how Lost Canadians like me were forced to wait for more than a year after the passage of S-2 for CIC to issue the proper forms so that we could apply for citizenship? Amazing what CIC can do when it wants to.

Chapter 10: On the Scales of Justice

1   Voices-Voix, "About the Coalition," http://voices-voix.ca/en/about.

2   Voices-Voix, "Court Challenges Program," http://voices-voix.ca/en/facts/profile/court-challenges-program.

Chapter 11: Dog Poop, Farts, Toads, and Britney Spears

1   George Carlin: America Was Founded on a Double Standard, 1988, http://www.youtube.com/watch?v=vsJmYnHdvsc.

2   This and the following quotation are from Bill Bryson, *In a Sunburned Country* (Toronto: Doubleday Canada, 2000), 4.

3   David Bauder, "Young Get News from Comedy Central," AP, March 1, 2004, retrieved from CBS News, http://www.cbsnews.com/stories/2004/03/01/entertainment/main603270.shtml.

4   Pew Research Center, "Americans Spending More Time Following the News," *Ideological News Sources: Who Watches and Why*, Pew Research Center for the People and the Press, September 12, 2010, http://www.people-press.org/2010/09/12/americans-spending-more-time-following-the-news/.

5   "The CRTC is an administrative tribunal that regulates and supervises the Canadian broadcasting and telecommunications systems. Its mandate is to ensure that both of these systems serve the Canadian public." CRTC, http://www.crtc.gc.ca/eng/publications/reports/policymonitoring/2013/cmr1.htm.

6 "Canada's Walk of Fame Inductees Announced," CTV.ca, retrieved from http://www.
   pugetsoundradio.com/cgi-bin/forum/Blah.pl?m-1142186934/.

7 "Children of WWII Troops Still Fighting for Canadian Citizenship," CBC News, July 4, 2006,
   http://www.cbc.ca/m/touch/canada/story/1.610052.

8 Gerry Bellett, "Judge Asked to Rule on Status of War Brides, Kids," Vancouver Sun, May 31,
   2006, A3, retrieved from http://www.canadianwarbrides.com/wn_details.asp?id=185.

9 Joe Volpe letter to Bill Siksay, September 25, 2005, http://www.cbc.ca/news2/background/
   lostcanadians/pdf/warbrides-volpe.pdf.

10 Denying this person citizenship because she failed to notice an isolated ad in some faraway
   newspaper is, at best, a lame excuse. Even in legal actions, an individual has a right to be
   notified of some proceeding that affects them. It's required that all normal attempts at
   communication such as personal contact, certified mail to last-known address, and so on must
   be exhausted before employing the last resort of a newspaper ad.

11 This and the following three quotations are from a Curt Petrovich report, CBC News, World
   Report, July 4, 2006.

12 A common reproof to citizens of all democratic countries is "ignorance of the law is no
   excuse." But we all realize that this admonishment applies only to well-known common-sense
   infractions such as murder, theft, and kidnapping. To think that this reproof should apply to
   some remote and unpublicized rule of citizenship is absurd. To perpetrate injustice on the
   authority of such a rule is the ultimate of bureaucratic arrogance and irresponsibility.

13 "War Brides 60th Anniversary, 1946-2006," Canadian War Brides, http://www.
   canadianwarbrides.com/anniversary.asp; to view its sixtieth anniversary logo, see http://www.
   canadianwarbrides.com/anniversary-logo.asp.

14 Gerry Bellett, "Child of Canadian Soldier Wins Right to Citizenship: 65,000 Brides and
   Children Affected, Advocate Claims," Vancouver Sun, September 2, 2006, A3, retrieved from
   http://www.canadianwarbrides.com/wn_details.asp?id=213.

15 Search the Canadian Press news archive, http://www.thecanadianpress.com/news_and_
   information.aspx?id=1600. I found it interesting that Stephen Thorne works for the Canadian
   Press in its Ottawa press corps. He was also credited as a writer of the Lost Canadian
   documentary, which talked about the ongoing injustices against the Lost Canadians in
   citizenship law. I called and spoke to Stephen several times in 2006 regarding the war brides
   and Joe Taylor's legal challenge. Despite being a senior reporter for the Canadian Press, not
   one Lost Canadian story appeared in the Canadian Press in 2006. You'll find its self-described
   role and editorial value statements in their entirety on its website at Canadian Press, "Our
   People & Editorial Values," http://www.thecanadianpress.com/about_cp.aspx?id=104. Here it
   is, in part: "Every day, The Canadian Press tells people the story of their country, in all forms
   and from all corners ... It's the goal of all our reporters and editors to focus on real people—not
   just institutions—to show in human terms how events affect our lives."

Chapter 12: And the Winner in the Stupid Category Is ...

The media advisory that precedes this chapter was issued by Andrew Telegdi's office. Retrieved
from http://www.canadianwarbrides.com/documents/2006-10-04.doc. The epigraph
quotation is from a speech Harper made as leader of the Official Opposition in Victoria, BC,
to an audience of Royal Canadian Legion members on December 28, 2005, reported in CBC
News, "Conservatives Promise Bill of Rights for Veterans," December 28, 2005, http://www.
cbc.ca/news/canada/conservatives-promise-bill-of-rights-for-veterans-1.552446.

1 Youranter (Yahoo contributor), "Joe Taylor: Citizenship Wrongfully Denied," Yahoo Voices,
   October 28, 2006, http://web.archive.org/web/20140728215809/http://voices.yahoo.com/
   joe-taylor-104627.html.

2 This and the following two quotations are from billsiksay.ca, Issues, "Statement—Joe Taylor's—
   War Bride Children Press Conference," posted October 4, 2006.

3   House of Commons, *Debates*, vol. 141 (060), 39th Parl., 1st Sess., October 6, 2006, http://www.parl.gc.ca/HousePublications/Publication. aspx?Language=E&Mode=1&Parl=39&Ses=1&DocId=2388635#SOB-1687949.

4   News release, Andrew Telegdi, "Telegdi Calls Government Action in Joe Taylor Case a Step Back for Equality Rights of All Canadians," October 5, 2006. Copy in the author's possession. I want to reiterate that I was not a member of any political party in Canada. As a pilot, I must work with whoever is sitting next to me in the cockpit regardless of their views and affiliations. My beef was against anyone who stood against equal rights in citizenship law, regardless of their party affiliation. As a pilot, I look first at the captain and co-pilot, as they are the ones responsible. In politics, I looked first to the prime minister and then citizenship minister to solve this issue. If they didn't fix the problem, then I had no problem speaking out against their injustice.

5   Monte Solberg, speaking notes, Minister of Citizenship and Immigration to the Canada Day Citizenship Ceremony, "Canada: We All Belong," Gatineau, July 1, 2006, http://www.cic. gc.ca/english/department/media/speeches/2006/citizen-ceremony.asp.

6   Gerald Mayer, *Union Membership Trends in the US* (Washington, DC: Congressional Research Service), August 31, 2004; "10 Cities with the Most Union Members," *US News and World Report*, March 18, 2011, http://www.usnews.com/news/articles/2011/03/18/10-cities-with-the-most-union-members.

7   To reiterate, in 1997, the Canadian Supreme Court ruled CIC was discriminating based on gender, thus granting citizenship to all foreign-born children of a Canadian parent. Gender could no longer be a determining factor in denying status to people in this group. In 2004, CIC ignored the Supreme Court ruling; thus, Canada went back to blatantly discriminating against women. What I've just written reads as if I made it up. How could a government department get away with ignoring the Supreme Court? I don't have the answer. I just know it happened, and that it's wrong. Also, why do perfectly ordinary functionaries go to all that trouble to deprive perfectly ordinary people of their citizenship rights? And why is an individual's life totally altered, depending on where they happened to be on their twenty-fourth birthday? Or for that matter, what public good is being served by denying people citizenship simply because they were born in or out of wedlock, especially when many of their parents eventually married, legitimizing their birth?

8   "Good night, Mrs. Calabash, wherever you are," was Jimmy Durante's sign-off from his radio program.

9   Federal Court Index and Docket, *Joseph Taylor v. The Minister of Citizenship and Immigration*, Court # T-1024-05, http://cas-ncr-nter03.cas-satj.gc.ca/IndexingQueries/infp_RE_info_e. php?court_no=T-1024-05.

Chapter 13: Tora! Tora! Tora!

1   Barbara Porteous, interview with Gary Symons, CBC News, *World Report*, January 22, 2007. Recording in the author's possession.

2   "Lost Canadians: CBC Investigation," CBC News *In Depth*, March 2007, https://web.archive. org/web/20070329182808/http://www.cbc.ca/news/background/lostcanadians/.

3   This quotation and following statistics from "Lost Canadians: CBC Investigation," CBC News *In Depth*, March 2007, http://www.cbc.ca/news2/background/lostcanadians/index.html.

4   On January 1, 2008, Hubert Lacroix became president and CEO of CBC, appointed, in 2007, by Prime Minister Stephen Harper. He was appointed to a second term on October 5, 2012. It's a definite concern whether the very person in charge of CBC, the same person who owes his job to the prime minister, will remain impartial when news stories become critical of the government. It strikes me as analogous to the Syrian official deciding whether to allow the daughter of a Syrian general (accused of torturing a Canadian citizen) to have her baby in Canada: Would the official be impartial? The principle is the same whether we're discussing Syria or CBC. There are huge potential conflicts of interest.

5   Roy MacGregor was not speaking on behalf of the *Globe and Mail*, but rather as a private individual, who is a professional journalist making an observation.

6   The excerpts below are from the Hansard transcript, House of Commons, Standing Committee on Citizenship and Immigration, 39th Parl., 1st Sess., *Evidence*, no. 036, February 19, 2007, http://parl.gc.ca/HousePublications/Publication.aspx?DocId=2715536&Language=E&Mode= 1&Parl=39&Ses=1#Int-1912632.

Chapter 14: Mr. Smith Goes to Washington; Mr. Chapman Goes to Ottawa

1   As with so many Lost Canadians who spent their youth and formative years in Canada, it left a lasting impression. It reminds me of this quotation from a famous Canadian writer: "Tell your young Canadians that I wish for them one and all the best gift life can give them—a happy youth, in which is laid the foundation for a noble and useful maturity." Lucy Maud Montgomery, in a "Circle of Young Canada" column. *The L.M. Montgomery Reader*, vol. 1, *A Life in Print*, edited by Benjamin Lefebvre (Toronto: University of Toronto Press, 2013), 67.

2   Andrew Mayeda, "Harper Roasted After Friend Handed Plum Appointment," *Vancouver Sun*, January 30, 2007, http://www2.canada.com/vancouversun/news/story.html?id=bb2bd69b-da49-470a-b907-c7256cd51c80&k=28844.

3   House of Commons, Standing Committee on Citizenship and Immigration, *Reclaiming Citizenship for Canadians: A Report on the Loss of Canadian Citizenship*, 39th Parl., 2nd Sess., December 6, 2007, http://www.parl.gc.ca/HousePublications/Publication.aspx?DocId= 3159522&File=90.

4   This and the following two quotations are from House of Commons, Standing Committee on Citizenship and Immigration, 39th Parl., 1st Sess., *Evidence*, no. 038, February 26, 2007, http://www.parl.gc.ca/HousePublications/Publication.aspx?DocId=2740460&Mode= 1&Language=E.

5   This and the following quotation are from House of Commons, Standing Committee on Citizenship and Immigration, 39th Parl., 1st Sess., *Evidence*, no. 041, March 19, 2007, http://www.parl.gc.ca/HousePublications/Publication.aspx?Language=E&Mode=1&DocId= 2771730&File=0.

6   This and the following quotations in this passage are from House of Commons, Standing Committee on Citizenship and Immigration, 39th Parl., 1st Sess., *Evidence*, no. 038, February 26, 2007, http://www.parl.gc.ca/HousePublications/Publication.aspx?DocId= 2740460&Mode=1&Language=E.

7   In 1982 when the Charter came into force, all legislation in Canada was to be made Charter compliant within three years. In 2014, thirty-two years after implementation, the only legislation in non-conformity is the 1977 Citizenship Act.

8   This and the following quotation are from House of Commons, Standing Committee on Citizenship and Immigration, 39th Parl., 1st Sess., *Evidence*, no. 041, March 19, 2007, http://www.parl.gc.ca/HousePublications/Publication.aspx?DocId=2771730&Language= E&Mode=1.

9   This and the following quotations in this section are from House of Commons, Standing Committee on Citizenship and Immigration, 39th Parl., 1st Sess., *Evidence*, no. 044, March 26, 2007, http://www.parl.gc.ca/HousePublications/Publication.aspx?DocId=2796372&Language= E&Mode=1.

10   Ibid.

11   I did talk with Jack Layton while waiting to board a train from Ottawa to Toronto. He didn't come up to me; I initiated the conversation. In his best political-speak, he said he was aware of the Lost Canadians. From then on there was nothing but silence.

12   Fifty-plus British child care organizations sent some 100,000 home children between the ages of four and fifteen (alleged orphans) to Canada to work as indentured farm labourers and domestic servants. Perry Snow, "The British Home Children: The British Child

Emigration Scheme to Canada, 1870 to 1957," http://freepages.genealogy.rootsweb.ancestry.com/~britishhomechildren/. The home children situation in the aftermath of World Wars I and II is similar to the recent adoptions by Canadians of Haitian children. After the 2010 earthquake, the identity of many children was unknown, their parents having been lost during the earthquake. Could it be that, in fifty or sixty years from now, CIC demands to know these kids' real identities in order to allow them to retain their Canadian citizenship? CIC's not always recognizing the home children and war-bride documentation from half a century earlier—something its bureaucratic predecessors had accepted for decades—sets a horrible precedent.

13   *Taylor v. Canada (Minister of Citizenship and Immigration)* (F.C.A.), 2007 FCA 349, [2008] 3 F.C.R. 324, November 2, 2007, http://reports.fja.gc.ca/eng/2008/2007fca349.html.

14   "The Long Struggle and Sad Plight of Lost Canadians," *Vancouver Sun*, November 7, 2008, http://www.canada.com/vancouversun/news/editorial/story.html?id=ae5673d9-6ddd-4c3f-a468-3331aed760a5.

15   House of Commons, Standing Committee on Citizenship and Immigration, *Reclaiming Citizenship for Canadians: A Report on the Loss of Canadian Citizenship*, 39th Parl., 2nd Sess., December 6, 2007, http://www.parl.gc.ca/HousePublications/Publication.aspx?DocId=3159522&File=90.

Chapter 15: The Right Thing to Do for the Right Reasons

1   For photos of the Taylor citizenship ceremony, see Canadian War Brides, http://www.canadianwarbrides.com/taylor-joe-ceremony.asp.

2   In a March 23, 2009, letter to me, Roy wrote: "You have engaged in, continue to engage in, such a hard, long and heroic struggle to undo an injustice that has caused so much grief for so many innocent people. Your efforts have been a model of the best aspects of democracy in action. May the government's blatantly disgraceful policy soon disappear into the same dark history that set it in motion."

3   Eswyn Lyster's *Most Excellent Citizens: Canada's War Brides of World War II* (Bloomington, IN: Trafford, 2010), about the Canadian war-bride experience, is worth reading. Eswyn was such a wonderful person to work with, full of wisdom and British humour, plus a dash of motherly love. One time, in a moment of Lost Canadian darkness, she said, "Not to worry, Don, it took some time but in the end we beat Hitler. Surely we can beat Mr. Harper."

4   "Canada and Lebanon, a Special Tie," CBC News *In Depth*, August 1, 2006, http://www.cbc.ca/news2/background/middleeast-crisis/canada-lebanon.html.

5   "Canadian Evacuation from Lebanon Cost $85M," CTV, September 20, 2006, retrieved from https://web.archive.org/web/20120320094104/http://www.ctv.ca/CTVNews/World/20060919/evacuation_tab_060919/; "MPs Squabble over Cost of Saving Dual Citizens," *Ottawa Citizen*, July 19, 2006, retrieved from http://www.canada.com/topics/news/national/story.html?id=d0c57c7f-fc77-419e-86b3-aa42c02bd167.

6   "The Strange Hidden World of the Stateless," *Refugees*, September 2007, vol. 147 (3), http://www.unhcr.org/46d2e8dc2.pdf.

7   This and the following two quotations are from Senate, *Debates*, vol. 144 (38), 39th Parl., 2nd Sess., March 4, 2008, http://www.parl.gc.ca/Content/Sen/Chamber/392/Debates/038db_2008-03-04-e.htm.

8   House of Commons, *Debates*, vol. 144 (38), 39th Parl., 2nd Sess., March 4, 2008, http://www.parl.gc.ca/Content/Sen/Chamber/392/Debates/038db_2008-03-04-e.htm?Language=E#42.

9   Senate, Standing Senate Committee on Social Affairs, Science and Technology, Minutes of Proceedings, *Evidence*, Issue 5, April 10, 2008, http://www.parl.gc.ca/Content/SEN/Committee/392/soci/05eva-e.htm.

10   Charles Rusnell, "Internet Fraudster Lands in Edmonton Prison," CBC News, November 1, 2010, http://www.cbc.ca/news/canada/edmonton/internet-fraudster-lands-in-edmonton-prison-1.875527.

11   Bill Casey's website, letter, March 17, 2008, http://billcasey.ca/index.html.
12   Susan Delacourt, "Paul Martin Visits Jailed Canadian in Mexico," *Toronto Star*, March 13, 2008, http://www.thestar.com/news/canada/2008/03/13/paul_martin_visits_jailed_canadian_in_mexico.html.
13   "Brenda Martin Returns to Canada," CBC News, May 1, 2008, http://www.cbc.ca/news/canada/brenda-martin-returns-to-canada-1.728326.
14   CTV.ca News, "Brenda Martin Out of Prison, Goes Home to Mom," May 9, 2008, http://www.ctvnews.ca/brenda-martin-out-of-prison-goes-home-to-mom-1.294837.
15   Maureen Brosnahan, "Brenda Martin in and out of Prison Since Parole," CBC News, May 31, 2010, http://www.cbc.ca/news/canada/brenda-martin-in-and-out-of-prison-since-parole-1.875529.
16   "The Historica-Dominion Institute Calls for a National Day of Commemoration," February 19, 2010, https://www.historicacanada.ca/content/historica-dominion-institute-calls-national-day-commemoration. In later years I asked the Historica-Dominion Institute (now Historica Canada) to sponsor a petition for the remaining Lost Canadians, pleading on behalf of the war brides and their kids, and particularly for the World Wars I and II veterans of Canada, but they never showed any interest. In fact, more often than not, they wouldn't return my many phone calls and emails.
17   House of Commons, *Debates*, vol. 141 (083), 39th Parl., 1st Sess., November 21, 2006, http://www.parl.gc.ca/HousePublications/Publication.aspx?Doc=87&Language=E&Mode=1&Parl=39&Pub=Hansard&Ses=1&DocId=2523934&File=0.
18   Scott Deveau, "State Funeral for Last War Vet Wins Approval," *Globe and Mail*, November 21, 2006.
19   CTV News, "Canada's Oldest WWI Vet a Canadian Again," May 8, 2008.
20   House of Commons, *Debates*, vol. 142 (079), 39th Parl., 2nd Sess., April 15, 2008, http://www.parl.gc.ca/HousePublications/Publication.aspx?Language=E&Mode=1&Parl=39&Ses=2&DocId=3424172#Int-2422134.
21   Tonda MacCharles, "RCMP Raid a 'PR Stunt,' Tories Claim," *Toronto Star*, April 16, 2008, http://www.thestar.com/news/canada/2008/04/16/rcmp_raid_a_pr_stunt_tories_claim.html.

Chapter 16: Lucy in the Sky

1   Jane Seyd, "Source to Stay Secret in Blair Wilson Lawsuit," *North Shore News*, April 30, 2012, http://www.nsnews.com/news/source-to-stay-secret-in-blair-wilson-lawsuit-1.370268.
2   Expat (ex-patriot) definition: "A person who is voluntarily absent from home or country." Synonym: "Absentee—one that is absent or not in residence"; "exile, expatriate." www.thefreedictionary.com/expat.
3   Elizabeth Renzetti, "Jean Vanier, 2008," *Globe and Mail*, December 26, 2008, http://www.theglobeandmail.com/news/national/nation-builder/jean-vanier-2008/article729055/.
4   Many, many times I attempted to get Mr. Cherry involved. The closest I got to him was his agent. One thing was clear, either the agent, Mr. Cherry, or both ignored my pleas for help. I would have thought, especially with so many military folks being affected, and most likely his own children, that Don Cherry would have been more than willing to step forward and speak out. Nay, not so.
5   I joined the Gibsons Yacht Club, which for me was just a place to go have coffee on Tuesday mornings. I knew the members personally; they had front-row seats watching the Lost Canadians saga unfold for more than a decade, yet they still weren't willing to help. One of the members, an immigrant Canadian, looked at me and in front of others stated something to the effect of, "I couldn't care less about your citizenship." And everyone was okay with that. It was, sadly, typically Canadian. There was a total disconnect until, of course, they or a family member had citizenship problems.
6   Daphne Bramham, "War Bride, 87, Denied Passport," *Vancouver Sun*, September 4, 2010, retrieved from http://blog.lostcanadian.com/2010/09/vancouver-sun-war-bride-87-denied-new.html.

7   House of Commons, Standing Committee on Citizenship and Immigration, *Evidence*, no. 022, 40th Parl., 2nd Sess., June 11, 2009, http://www.parl.gc.ca/HousePublications/Publication. aspx?Docid=3979528&Language=E&Mode=1&Parl=41&Ses=1#int-2827201.

8   Tobi Cohen, "Government on the Hook for $1.5 Million in Legal Costs for Abandoning Woman in Kenya," *National Post*, November 8, 2012, http://news.nationalpost.com/2012/11/08/ government-on-the-hook-for-1-5-million-in-legal-costs-for-abandoning-woman-in-kenya/.

9   House of Commons, *Debates*, vol. 144 (097), 40th Parl., 2nd Sess., October 21, 2009, http://www.parl.gc.ca/HousePublications/Publication.aspx?Language=E&Mode=1&Parl= 40&Ses=2&Docid=4156818#int-2901645.

10 "You lie" YouTube video, http://www.youtube.com/watch?v=qgce06Yw2r0; Frank James, "Rep. Joe Wilson Sorry for Calling Obama Liar During Congress' Joint Session," September 9, 2009, http://www.npr.org/blogs/thetwo-way/2009/09/rep_joe_wilson_apologizes_for.html.

11 "Citizenship Act Creates a 'Stateless' Child," *Vancouver Sun*, September 25, 2009, http:// www.canada.com/vancouversun/news/editorial/story.html?id=c3a5560d-5170-4d4a- a318-a8675e759171.

12 "Ireland Saves Canadian's Daughter from Being Stateless," *Vancouver Sun*, October 9, 2010, http://www.canada.com/story.html?id=12fdf0eb-45b7-4ae5-a3be-6f3db6be3b4b. In 2015, more than five years after our march, Rachel still is not Canadian. Jason Kenney knowingly allowed her to be stateless.

13 CBC, *The National*, October 22, 2009, http://www.youtube.com/watch?v= smjrQPLeWkU&feature=results_main&playnext=1&list=PLCB2D57EC4F2D5EC2.

Chapter 17: The Gold Medal Olympic Gamble

1   "Amy Goodman Detained at Canadian Border, Questioned about Speech . . . and 2010 Olympics," transcript, *Democracy Now!* November 30, 2009, http://www.democracynow. org/2009/11/30/amy_goodman_detained_at_canadian_border.

2   Lalo Espejo, "Amy Goodman Gets Brilliant Story Idea from Canadian Border Guards," *Vancouver Observer*, November 27, 2009, http://www.vancouverobserver.com/politics/ 2009/11/27/amy-goodman-gets-brilliant-story-idea-canadian-border-guards.

3   By this time, Gary Symons and Susanne Reber had left CBC, both abandoning their twenty-year-plus CBC careers. Gary started his own business, and Susanne went to work in the US for National Public Radio.

4   Canada, Privy Council Order 858, February 9, 1945, http://blog.lostcanadian.com/2012/05/ order-in-council-pc-1945-858-and-lost.html.

5   *Taylor v. Canada (Minister of Citizenship and Immigration)*, 2006 FC 1053, http://decisions. fct-cf.gc.ca/en/2006/2006fc1053/2006fc1053.html; Federal Court of Appeal Decisions, *Taylor v. Canada (Minister of Citizenship and Immigration)* (F.C.A.), 2007 FCA 349, [2008] 3 F.C.R. 324, http://reports.fja.gc.ca/eng/2008/2007fca349.html.

6   Revised Statues of Ontario, 1927, Legitimation Act, c. 187, http://www.archive.org/stream/ v2revisedstat1927ontauoft#page/1918/mode/1up.

7   Links to Eswyn's letter to the Queen, complete with her reply, and the governor general's: Eswyn's letter, October 23, 2006, http://www.canadianwarbrides.com/joetaylor/lyster- e-qe-oct-23-06-01.jpg; Buckingham Palace, reply, November 9, 2006, http://www. canadianwarbrides.com/joetaylor/lyster-e-qe-nov-09-06.jpg; Canada's governor general, reply, March 5, 2007, http://www.canadianwarbrides.com/joetaylor/lyster-e-gg-mar-05-07. jpg.

8   According to the Canadian Museum for Human Rights' webpage, the museum's purpose is "to explore the subject of human rights, with special but not exclusive reference to Canada, in order to enhance the public's understanding of human rights, to promote respect for others and to encourage reflection and dialogue." https://humanrights.ca/about.

9   Canadian Museum for Human Rights, "A Canadian Conversation Part 2," Roundtable #1, transcript found at http://web.archive.org/web/20110408052616/http://humanrightsmuseum. ca/programs-and-events/programs-1.

10   Dan Robson, "Olympic Closing Ceremony Celebrates Canada," CBC News, March 1, 2010, http://www.cbc.ca/sports/2.722/olympic-closing-ceremony-celebrates-canada-1.886326.

11   "More Visible Minorities at Closing, VANOC Hints," CBC News, February 18, 2010, http://www.cbc.ca/news/canada/british-columbia/story/2010/02/18/bc-visible-minorities-olympic-ceremonies.html. Barbara Anne Scott had problems; Donald Sutherland's son Kiefer (not domiciled in Canada on his twenty-fourth birthday); the children of Bobby Orr, Wayne Gretzky, Neil Young, Michael J. Fox, and William Shatner.

12   "Ben Johnson: Canada's Shame," CBC News, September 26, 1988 (last updated February 14, 2012), http://www.cbc.ca/archives/categories/sports/athletics/running-off-track-the-ben-johnson-story/canadas-shame.html.

13   Andy Pasztor, "Doomed Pilots Talked of Inexperience," Wall Street Journal, May 13, 2009, http://online.wsj.com/article/SB124212789938210353.html; "Buffalo Crash Probe Focuses on Pilot Fatigue, Low Pay," CBC News, May 13, 2009, http://www.cbc.ca/news/world/buffalo-crash-probe-focuses-on-pilot-fatigue-low-pay-1.788169.

14   Bill C-3: Gender Equity in Indian Registration Act, 40th Parl., 3rd Sess. (introduction and first reading version, March 11, 2010), http://www.parl.gc.ca/LegisInfo/BillDetails.aspx?Language=E&Mode=1&billId=4336828.

15   British Columbia, McIvor v. The Registrar, Indian and Northern Affairs Canada, 2007 BCSC 827, http://www.courts.gov.bc.ca/jdb-txt/sc/07/08/2007bcsc0827.htm.

16   Colin McPhail, "Lost Canadians: The Biggest Story You've Never Heard," Brunswickan, November 3, 2010, http://thebruns.ca/lost-canadians-the-biggest-story-youve-never-heard/.

17   Jason Kenney, "Lost Canadians: Claims Don't Match the Facts," letter to the editor, Brunswickan, November 10, 2010, http://thebruns.ca/lost-canadians-claims-dont-match-the-facts/.

18   Don Chapman, "Lost Canadians: Let the Dialogue Begin," letter to the editor, Brunswickan, November 17, 2010, http://thebruns.ca/lost-canadians-let-the-dialogue-begin/.

19   "Don Chapman Is Reclaiming Citizenship for Lost Canadians," Globe and Mail, December 10, 2010, http://www.theglobeandmail.com/report-on-business/25/don-chapman-is-reclaiming-citizenship-for-lost-canadians/article1832924/.

20   Alex Dobrota, "'Lost' Canadians Get Citizenship," Globe and Mail, February 20, 2007, http://www.theglobeandmail.com/news/national/lost-canadians-get-citizenship/article80307/.

21   "Mr. Chapman at Open Mic Town Hall Meeting with Michael Ignatieff," video, http://vimeo.com/18815100.

22   Steven Chase, "The Harpers Go Bollywood in GTA Battleground," Globe and Mail, April 8, 2011, http://www.theglobeandmail.com/news/politics/ottawa-notebook/the-harpers-go-bollywood-in-gta-battleground/article1977247/.

23   "Akshay Holds 'Thank You' Screening for Canadian PM," Indian Express, April 12, 2011, http://www.indianexpress.com/news/akshay-holds-thank-you-screening-for-canadian-pm/775164/; Adrian Humphreys, "Riding Profiles: 'Battle of the Indo-Canadians' in Brampton," National Post, April 28, 2011, http://news.nationalpost.com/2011/04/28/riding-profiles-battle-of-the-indo-canadians-in-brampton/.

Chapter 18: Please, Put Me Out of Business

1   The first leader of a party to speak out was Elizabeth May of the Green Party; her party issued a media release back on March 2, 2007. "It's Time to Welcome 'Lost Canadians' Home, Says Green Party," http://www.greenparty.ca/en/releases/01.02.2007A.

2   House of Commons, Standing Committee on Citizenship and Immigration, Evidence, no. 006, 40th Parl., 2nd Sess., March 10, 2009, http://www.parl.gc.ca/HousePublications/Publication.aspx?DocId=3737340&Language=E&Mode=1&Parl=40&Ses=2#Int-2647465.

3   Audrey was referring to Bill C-3, giving Native women the same rights as men in passing on status to their children. If Audrey had been Native, she'd qualify under C-3. This is a real-life example of age, gender, family status, and racial discrimination happening in Canada in 2014.

4   Michelle Landsberg, "Plight of 'Incorrigible' Women Demands Justice," *Toronto Star*, May 6, 2001, retrieved from http://www.rapereliefshelter.bc.ca/learn/news/plight-incorrigible-women-demands-justice.

5   House of Commons, Standing Committee on Citizenship and Immigration, *Reclaiming Citizenship for Canadians: A Report on the Loss of Canadian Citizenship*, 39th Parl., 2nd Sess., December 6, 2007, http://www.parl.gc.ca/HousePublications/Publication.aspx?DocId=3159522&File=90. The unanimous, all-party committee Recommendation 4 stated that all first-generation children born to a Canadian parent, regardless if that parent was the mother or the father, no matter if the child had been born in or out of wedlock, inside or outside Canada, and *at any time*, should be Canadian citizens.

6   His Excellency the Right Honourable David Johnston Governor General of Canada speaking at the CBA Canadian Legal Conference, August 14, 2011, http://www.cba.org/cba/Halifax2011/main/default.aspx; Editorial, "David Johnston's Welcome Words to Lawyers," *Globe and Mail*, August 17, 2011, http://www.theglobeandmail.com/news/opinions/editorials/david-johnstons-welcome-words-to-lawyers/article2132725/.

7   Associated Press, "Centralia Man, 95, Has US Citizenship Confirmed," *Seattle Times*, April 5, 2011, http://seattletimes.nwsource.com/html/localnews/2014693062_apuscitizenship certificate2ndldwritethru.html.

8   April 9, 2011, edition.

9   Kathy Tomlinson, "Grandmother's Dream Trip at Risk over Government Red Tape," CBC News, December 5, 2011, http://www.cbc.ca/thenational/indepthanalysis/gopublic/story/2011/12/02/bc-citizenshipbacklog.html.

10 Ibid.

11 Canadian War Museum webpage, Exhibitions: One War, Two Victories, http://www.warmuseum.ca/event/one-war-two-victories.

12 House of Commons, *Debates*, vol. 140 (035), 38th Parl., 1st Sess., November 30, 2004, http://www.parl.gc.ca/HousePublications/Publication.aspx?DocId=1516241&Language=E&Mode=1#Int-1042735.

13 *Canada, 1941-1949: The Deportation and Internment of Canadians of Japanese Origin*, April 2, 2007, International Council on Archives, http://www.sansvoixsansvisage.net/rubrique9.html; on this subject see also *Reference to the Validity of Orders in Council in Relation to Persons of Japanese Race*, [1946] S.C.R. 248, 1946-02-20, http://scc.lexum.org/en/1946/1946scr0-248/1946scr0-248.html.

14 See Canadian Race Relations Foundation, *Fighting for Canada: Chinese and Japanese in Military Service* (Ottawa: Minister of National Defence, 2003).

15 Liberal Party, Liberal biennial convention, Ottawa, January 13–15 2012, http://convention.liberal.ca/, retrieved from http://www.johnmckayliberal.ca/site/?p=256.

16 "Are You a Lost Canadian?" *Reader's Digest* (Canada), December 2011.

17 February 2012 issue, 14.

18 John Ibbitson, "Harper Sees Trade Deals as Key to His Political Success," *Globe and Mail*, December 25, 2011, http://www.theglobeandmail.com/news/politics/john-ibbitson/harper-sees-trade-deals-as-key-to-his-political-success/article2283361/.

Chapter 19: Teaching Old Dogs New Tricks

1   *Newsweek* print ad, 2011.

2   Another group that never spoke out was the Canadian Taxpayers Federation. In fairness, while it sympathized, it said the issue was complicated and therefore difficult for it to explain in a manner the public could easily understand. I can understand the difficulty, from the federation's vantage, in quantifying the costs in terms of actual dollars squandered due to parliamentary ineptness.

3   Jenny Uechi, "Jason Kenney Tells War Veteran Daughter: Soldiers Were 'Heroes,' but Not Canadian Citizens," *Vancouver Observer*, July 2, 2014, http://www.vancouverobserver.com/politics/jason-kenney-tells-war-veteran-daughter-soldiers-were-heroes-not-canadian-citizens.

4   Ibid.

5   Recording in the author's possession.

6   Stefan Keyes, "Military Couple to Take Adopted Child's Citizenship Battle to Min. Kenney," CTV News, Ottawa, June 11, 2013, http://ottawa.ctvnews.ca/military-couple-to-take-adopted-child-s-citizenship-battle-to-min-kenney-1.1320892.

7   "ButterBox Babies," review of *Butterbox Survivors! Life After the Ideal Maternity Home* by Bob Hatlen (Halifax: Nimbus Press, 1992), www.canadiancrc.com/Butterbox_Babies_Book.aspx; Susan K. Livio, "Survivors of Dark Episode in Canada's History Trace Their Past," www.canadiancrc.com/Butterbox_Survivors.aspx.

8   For sale on the Antiquarius Antiques and Curiosities website is an original advertising booklet extolling the virtues of the Ideal Maternity Home, including a written testimonial by the son and daughter-in-law of the then lieutenant governor of Nova Scotia. They had adopted a child from the home. Here's what they said: "To ALL, into whose hands this book may come, let us say that our home has been made happy by this darling baby girl from the Ideal Maternity Home and we know the joy that can come to those who adopt a child, and we feel that the work being done by the Ideal Maternity Home is worthy of every aid that can be given it." http://www.antiquarius-antiques.ca/store/p57/Curiosity_-_Items_from_the_Butter_Box_Baby_Scandal%3A_Murder_of_Canadian_Babies.html.

9   Ideal Maternity Home Survivors website, www.idealmaternityhomesurvivors.com/the-story. Although most babies were buried in the butter boxes, some were actually burned in the home's furnace. http://www.angelizdsplace.com/child18.htm.

10   "The Story: Butterbox Babies," Ideal Maternity Home Survivors, www.idealmaternityhomesurvivors.com/the-story/.

11   "The British Home Children," compiled by Lori Oschefski, British Home Children in Canada, http://canadianbritishhomechildren.weebly.com; Library and Archives Canada, "Home Children," http://www.bac-lac.gc.ca/eng/news/podcasts/Pages/home-children.aspx.

12   Marion Vermeersch, born out of wedlock, came to Canada with her war-bride mother and Canadian-soldier father before 1947, along with her brother Peter Brammah. Peter was adopted by Marion's father. Marion worked for the government; Peter is retired from the Royal Canadian Navy and the Calgary Police Service. Both are still being denied citizenship.

13   Federal Court, Respondent's Memorandum of Fact and Law, court file no. T-418-12, p. 8.

14   Benjamin Shingler, "Miramichi-Born Senior Citizen Says She'll Continue to Push for Her Canadian Citizenship," *New Brunswick Telegraph-Journal*, October 8, 2010, retrieved from http://blog.lostcanadian.com/2010/10/telegraph-journal-miramichi-born-senior.html. Since Theresa was a nun, I called Catholic organizations across Canada, from the local church in Gibsons to the archdioceses of Vancouver, Toronto, and Montreal, asking them to advocate for her. None ever did.

15   Openparliament.ca, Bill C-467, December 13, 2010, http://www.parl.gc.ca/LegisInfo/BillDetails.aspx?Language=E&Mode=1&Bill=C467&Parl=40&Ses=3.

16   Francine Compton and Cullen Crozier, "Lost Canadians," APTN Investigates, April 21, 2014, http://aptn.ca/news/2014/04/21/lost-canadians/.

17   Susana Mas, "Canadian Citizenship Rules Face Broad Reform in 2014," CBC News, January 24, 2014, http://www.cbc.ca/news/politics/canadian-citizenship-rules-face-broad-reform-in-2014-1.2508758.

18   House of Commons, Standing Committee on Citizenship and Immigration, *Reclaiming Citizenship for Canadians: A Report on the Loss of Canadian Citizenship*, 39th Parl., 2nd Sess., December 6, 2007, http://www.parl.gc.ca/HousePublications/Publication.aspx?DocId=3159522&File=90.

19   There was always something so absurd about CIC that it bordered on the comedic. In December 2013, just in time for Santa's annual trek (Jason Kenney declared him a Canadian citizen in 2008), the new citizenship minister, Chris Alexander, actually issued Mr. and Mrs. Claus official Canadian passports. Then, as if that's not enough, he gets his picture taken with

them for publicity purposes. Seriously, how can they be Canadian citizens when our war dead weren't? You just can't make this stuff up. "All Santa Wants for Christmas Is . . . an ePassport," CIC government website, December 20, 2013, http://www.cic.gc.ca/english/department/media/photos/2013/2013-12-20/photo.asp. Although Santa was definitely around before 1947, there is no official record of his birth, where he was born, or if he was born in or out of wedlock.

20 Bill C-24, An Act to Amend the Citizenship Act and to Make Consequential Amendments to Other Acts, 41st Parl., 2nd Sess., http://www.parl.gc.ca/LegisInfo/BillDetails.aspx?Language=E&Mode=1&billId=6401990.

21 Wilfrid Laurier, prime minister of Canada, debates from the House of Commons, March 13, 1900: "At the opening of the century, the American people opened their vast territory to all the nations of the earth, and granted *citizenship* to all who came, giving them perfect and absolute equality with themselves. We in Canada for the last forty years have been doing the same thing. We have opened our country to the immigrants of the world, we have invited them to come, and as soon as they come, by conforming to the laws, they obtain *full citizenship*, and every right we ourselves enjoy we cheerfully give to them. Well, Sir, was it not fair and right, and is it not the rule of the civilization of the nineteenth century, that if a young nation opens its door to foreign immigration, an implied obligation rests upon that nation to give to the immigrants the same rights of *citizenship* which its own people enjoy?" (Emphasis added.) http://documenting-canadian-citizenship.com/Debates/House%20of%20Commons%20Debates%205th%20sess%208th%20Parl%20Vol%201%20March%2013%201900%20see%20page%201843.pdf.

22 Canada, Department of National Defence, *The Battle of Brains, Canadian Citizenship and the Issues of War* (Ottawa: King's Printer, 1943), 158: "We must, and will, win the war. Every citizen has, in wartime, a very special duty to his country, his community, and to himself as a citizen of that country. You may rest assured that the other citizens of Canada, who are still at their civilian posts, watch you with pride and in some cases envy."

23 *Manitoba Metis Federation Inc. v. Canada (Attorney General)*, [2013] 1 SCR 623, 2013 SCC 14, http://canlii.ca/t/fwfft; Documenting Canadian Citizenship, documenting-canadian-citizenship.com.

24 The Supreme Court heard a case regarding stripping Canadian citizenship away from Canadians of Japanese descent: 700 were children born in Canada. In what has become one of Canada's more shameful moments, the Supreme Court allowed the government to go forward. *Reference to the Validity of Orders in Council in Relation to Persons of Japanese Race*, [1946] S.C.R. 248, http://scc-csc.lexum.com/scc-csc/scc-csc/en/item/8297/index.do.

25 In James W. St. G. Walker, *"Race," Rights and the Law in the Supreme Court of Canada* (Waterloo, ON: Wilfrid Laurier University Press, 1997), 24, there is a discussion about the Canadian government's official response to a question posed in 1938 by the resident ambassador of Nazi Germany. On behalf of the German government, Dr. H.U. Granow asked the Canadian Ministry of External Affairs to outline any federal or provincial statutes which "make race (racial origin) of a person a factor of legal consequence." On behalf of the Canadian government, O.D. Skelton acknowledged that there were racial aspects to immigration law and to "certain provincial laws affecting Asiatics." There were no "special provisions" for "native Indians," but these statutes were said to be "protective [rather than] restrictive." http://blog.lostcanadian.com/2014/11/lost-canadians-revised-history-of.html.

26 Radio Canada International, "Canada and South Africa Share a Dark Past," http://www.rcinet.ca/english/archives/column/the-link-africa/TruthandReconciliationCanadaSouthAfricaResidentialSchoolsAbuses/; Maria-Carolina Cambre, "Terminologies of Control: Tracing the Canadian-South African Connection in a Word," *Politikon* 34 (1) (2007): 19–34, doi: 10.1080/02589340701336211.

27 In the 1920s, Canada was a member of the League of Nations. A requirement for membership was that a country must have its own citizens.

28 Matthew Millar, "Government Muzzles Expert Witnesses on Major Citizenship Bill," *Vancouver*

Observer, May 14, 2014, http://www.vancouverobserver.com/news/advocates-incensed-last-minute-muzzling-witnesses-major-citizenship-bill; House of Commons, Standing Committee on Citizenship and Immigration, *Evidence*, no. 027, 41st Parl., 2nd Sess., May 14, 2014, http://www.parl.gc.ca/HousePublications/Publication.aspx?DocId=6599330& Language=E&Mode=1&Parl=41&Ses=2.

29 Nowhere on the NDP website (July 25, 2014) does it say that a priority is citizenship. I am not aware of their leader, Thomas Mulcair, ever once speaking out on behalf of the Lost Canadians. In addition, despite my many, many requests to meet with him, he has refused. Justin Trudeau has also refused to meet with me personally. I have never heard him, as leader, publicly speak one word about our issue.

30 Aung San Suu Kyi, televised interview with reporter Barkha Dutt of NDTV, New Delhi, November 14, 2012; Aga Khan IV, March 10, 2014, 88th annual Stephen A. Ogden Jr. Memorial Lecture, Brown University; Malala Yousafzai, July 12, 2013, address to the UN General Assembly, New York; Dalai Lama, "A New Approach to Global Problems," *Mindful Politics: A Buddhist Guide to Making the World a Better Place*, ed. Melvin McLeod (Somerville, MA: Wisdom Publications, 2006); Nelson Mandela, *Long Walk to Freedom: The Autobiography of Nelson Mandela* (Boston: Little, Brown, 1995).

Chapter 20: That's a Wrap

There are no notes for Chapter 20.

Chapter 21: Analysis and Recommendations

1   The Canadian Creed, www.canadiancreed.ca.

2   Citizenship and Immigration Canada, *Discover Canada: The Rights and Responsibilities of Citizenship* (Ottawa: CIC, 2012), http://www.cic.gc.ca/english/pdf/pub/discover.pdf.

3   Steven Harper, Speech from the Throne, April 4, 2006, http://pm.gc.ca/eng/media.asp?id=1087.

4   UN Security Council, *The Rule of Law and Transitional Justice in Conflict and Post-Conflict Societies*, report of the Secretary-General, August 23, 2004, http://www.unrol.org/files/2004%20report.pdf.

5   United Nations, Universal Declaration of Human Rights, http://www.un.org/en/documents/udhr/.

6   This and the following quotation are from CBC News Nova Scotia, "Tory MP Ejected from Caucus After Budget Vote," June 5, 2007, http://www.cbc.ca/news/canada/nova-scotia/story/2007/06/05/budget-casey.html.

7   CRTC website, "About Us," http://www.crtc.gc.ca/eng/acrtc/acrtc.htm.

8   CRTC, "Frequently Asked Questions," http://www.crtc.gc.ca/eng/faqs.htm.

9   In the US, one such example is the Southern Poverty Law Center, which is "dedicated to fighting hate and bigotry and to seeking justice for the most vulnerable members of society. Using litigation, education, and other forms of advocacy, the Center works toward the day when the ideals of equal justice and equal opportunity will be a reality." SPLC, "What We Do," http://www.splcenter.org/what-we-do.

10 Citizenship and Immigration Canada, "Canada's Citizenship Award: Open for Nominations," news release, March 7, 2011, retrieved from http://news.gc.ca/web/article-en.do?nid=593979&wbdisable=true.

11 Voices-Voix, "Court Challenges Program," http://voices-voix.ca/en/facts/profile/court-challenges-program; *Law Times*, "Tories Chop Two Legal Programs," October 2, 2006, http://www.lawtimesnews.com/200610021298/headline-news/tories-chop-two-legal-programs.

12 Dean Beeby, "Wonky Parliamentary Rules Keep MPs Blind to Government Spending: Report," *National Post*, July 15, 2012, http://news.nationalpost.com/2012/07/15/wonky-parliamentary-rules-keep-mps-blind-to-government-spending-report/.

13 George W. Brown, *Building the Canadian Nation*, rev. ed. (London: J.M. Dent & Sons, 1950), 502.

14 Paragraph 20 of the government's response to Jackie Scott's court challenge says, "Canadian citizenship is a creation of federal statute and has no meaning apart from statute." *Scott v. Her Majesty the Queen in Right of Canada and Canada (Minister of Citizenship, Immigration and Multiculturalism)*, File T-418-12, retrieved from http://www2.lostcanadian.com/documents/Respondent-Memorandum-of-Fact-and-Law.pdf.

15 White House, Office of the Press Secretary, Remarks by the President on Immigration, June 15, 2012, http://www.whitehouse.gov/the-press-office/2012/06/15/remarks-president-immigration.

16 Actually, Canada can process applications "with the stroke of a pen" when the government desires. Former citizenship minister Elinor Caplan bragged that she could process anyone within twenty-four hours.

17 In anticipation of the Jackie Scott judicial review, one Lost Canadian spent several days at Canada Archives in Ottawa in the spring and summer of 2012. He discovered several letters from the 1940s written by the then Registrar of Canadian Citizenship, granting citizenship "by operation of law" to several children just like Jackie, suggesting that she too is, and has been, a Canadian citizen. This discovery would not have happened without libraries, records, librarians, and continued funding.

18 In 2009, a motion was put forward in Parliament with the names of several people who had been turned down for citizenship because of ongoing discrimination. Most of these people remain disenfranchised. Motion in Parliament, House of Commons, *Debates*, vol. 144 (097), 40th Parl., 2nd Session, October 21, 2009, http://www.parl.gc.ca/HousePublications/Publication.aspx?Language=E&Mode=1&Parl=40&Ses=2&Docid=4156818#Int-2901645.

19 "Think Different" advertising campaign.

Appendix 1: Lost Canadians on Citizenship

There are no notes for Appendix 1.

Appendix 2: The Revised History of Canadian Citizenship

1 *Law of Naturalization and Allegiance*, May 22, 1868, retrieved from Citizenship and Immigration Canada, *CP 14*, Appendix A, http://www.cbc.ca/news2/background/lostcanadians/pdf/ciccanadapolicy.pdf; CIC, *Forging Our Legacy*, http://www.cic.gc.ca/english/resources/publications/legacy/chap-5.asp.

2 The Famous Five Foundation, "The Famous 5 Women," http://www.famous5.ca/index.php/the-famous-5-women/the-famous-5-women.

3 Bill C-37: An Act to Amend the Citizenship Act, 37th Parl., 2nd Sess., January 9, 2008, http://www.parl.gc.ca/About/Parliament/LegislativeSummaries/bills_ls.asp?lang=E&ls=c37&Parl=39&Ses=2&source=library_prb.

4 Citizenship and Immigration Canada, "The 100th Anniversary of the Continuous Passage Act," http://www.cic.gc.ca/english/multiculturalism/asian/100years.asp; History of Metropolitan Vancouver, "*Komagata Maru*," http://www.vancouverhistory.ca/archives_komagatamaru.htm.

5 Canadian Race Relations Foundation, "From Racism to Redress: The Japanese Canadian Experience," http://www.crr.ca/divers-files/en/pub/faSh/ePubFaShRacRedJap.pdf.

6 *Reference to the Validity of Orders in Council in Relation to Persons of Japanese Race*, [1946] S.C.R 248, https://scc-csc.lexum.com/scc-csc/scc-csc/en/item/8297/index.do.

7 Sixth Census of Canada, *Instructions to Commissioners and Enumerators, 1921*, http://www.ccri.uottawa.ca/CCRI/Images/1921%20Enumerator%20Instructions%20-%20English.pdf.

8 Revised Statutes of British Columbia, 1897, http://bc.canadagenweb.org/vote1898/voteregs.htm.

9 Chinese Canadian Military Museum Society, "Gim Wong," http://www.ccmms.ca/veteran-stories/air-force/gim-wong/; Rod Mickleburgh, "Gim Foon Wong's Motorcycle Ride Turned the Tide on Chinese Head-Tax Redress," *Globe and Mail*, October 1, 2013,

http://www.theglobeandmail.com/news/british-columbia/gim-foon-wongs-motorcycle-ride-turned-the-tide-on-chinese-head-tax-redress/article14652999/?page=all.

10   *Shin Shim v. The King*, [1938] SCR 378, http://scc-csc.lexum.com/scc-csc/scc-csc/en/item/7144/index.do.

11   Eleventh annual Cégep Holocaust symposium, "Canada Was the Last Country to Reject the Plea of the St. Louis Ship," http://www.vaniercollege.qc.ca/events/holocausto4/st_louis.html.

12   Asia/Canada, "Hyphenated Canadians?" http://asia-canada.ca/asia-pacific-reality/asian-profile-canada/hyphenated-canadians.

13   Senate, *Debates*, November 7, 1887, http://www.parl.gc.ca/about/parliament/reconstituted debates/Senate/1/1/RecDeb_SEN_1867-11-07-e.pdf.

14   *Manitoba Metis Federation Inc. v. Canada (Attorney General)*, [2013] 1 SCR 623, 2013 SCC 14 (CanLII), http://canlii.ca/t/fwfft.

TEXT CREDITS

PERSONAL COMMUNICATION used with permission of the following people: Robert Addington, Charles Bosdet, Sandra Brown, Rod Burgess, Bruce Cadieux, Fred Colbourne, Velma Demerson, Paul Diekelmann, Dawn Erison, Heather Harnois, George Kyle, Howe Lee, James Lewis for Donna Lewis, Noreen MacDonald, Donovan McGlaughlin, Keith Menzie, Ron Nixon, Jenny Noble, Barbara Porteous, Bill Siksay, Dee Sinker, Maverick Snowdon, Marion Vermeersch, and Paul Vidler. Names and identifying details have been changed to protect the privacy of some individuals.

Chapter 8

Page 123-124 Gwen LeFort, "War Bride in WWI," *Cape Breton's Magazine*, December 1, 1983, p. 47-48. Used with permission; pp. 127-129 William Allister, *Where Life and Death Hold Hands* (Toronto: Stoddart, 1989), 234-240. Used with permission of Mrs. Mona Allister.

Chapter 11

Page 182 Gerry Bellett, "Judge Asked to Rule on Status of War Brides, Kids," *Vancouver Sun*, May 31, 2006, p. A3, retrieved from http://www.canadianwarbrides.com/wn_details.asp?id=185. Material reprinted with the express permission of: Vancouver Sun, a division of Postmedia Network Inc.; page 185 Curt Petrovich report, CBC News, *World Report*, July 4th, 2006. Used with permission of CBC Licensing.

Chapter 12

Page 190 Press Conference Media Advisory, October 4, 2006, retrieved from http://www.canadianwarbrides.com/taylor-joe-bio.asp.

Chapter 13

Page 205 Captain Bruce Richards, personal communication. Used with permission; page 205-206 Barbara Porteous, interview with Gary Symons, CBC News, *World Report*, January 22, 2007. Used with permission of CBC Licensing.

Chapter 15

Page 245 Excerpt from Disney's *Selma, Lord, Selma*, Buena Vista Home Entertainment, 2004.

Chapter 18

Page 311-312 Editorial, "David Johnston's Welcome Words to Lawyers," *Globe and Mail*, August 17, 2011. http://www.theglobeandmail.com/news/opinions/editorials/david-johnstons-welcome-words-to-lawyers/article2132725/ © The Globe and Mail Inc. All Rights Reserved; page 318 Text from *One War, Two Victories* exhibit webpage. Courtesy of the Canadian War Museum; page 318-319 *Canada, 1941 to 1949: The Deportation and Internment of Canadians of Japanese Origin*, April 2, 2007, International Council on Archives, http://www.sansvoixsansvisage.net/rubrique9.html. Used with permission.

ABOUT THE AUTHOR

DON CHAPMAN was born in Vancouver, B.C., but lost his Canadian citizenship as a six-year-old. He's been fighting the government ever since, becoming the face of the Canadian citizenship rights movement. He coined the phrase "Lost Canadians" that is now used widely to describe other Canadians in his position. He has testified several times before both the House and Senate, and has been interviewed by major media outlets around the world, including CBC television and radio, CTV, *Maclean's*, the *National Post*, the BBC, *Le Monde*, *The Economist*, *Reader's Digest*, the *Wall Street Journal*, and the Aboriginal Peoples Television Network. He's also spoken at various universities and organizations worldwide. Chapman is a United Airlines pilot, currently on leave. He blogs at www.lostcanadian.com.